OUTSIGHTS

Inequality from Inside and Out

Nicole Meredith

Lorne Tepperman

Rock's Mills Press

Oakville, Ontario

PUBLISHED BY

Rock's Mills Press

www.rocksmillspress.com

Copyright © 2017 by Nicole Meredith and Lorne Tepperman

ILLUSTRATION CREDITS: Figures 1.3 and 1.4 are based on information from the Statistics Canada Labour Force Survey and CANSIM Table 282–0004, and adapted from charts on the Nova Scotia Education and Training website. Table 2.1 is based on Government of Canada, "Sponsorship of Adopted Children and Other Relatives: The Sponsor's Guide" (2016; IMM 5196), retrieved from http://www.cic.gc.ca/english/information/applications/guides/5196ETOC.asp#table3. Table 2.2 is based on data from the *Financial Post*, March 1, 2016. Table 2.3 is based on data from Statistics Canada, Census of Population, 2006. Figure 2.1 is based on data in Statistics Canada, "Study: Changes in wealth across the income distribution, 1999 to 2012" (2015). Figure 2.2 is based on data in "It's More than Poverty: Employment Precarity and Household Well-being: (Toronto: United Way/PEPSO/McMaster University Social Sciences, 2013). Figure 3.1 is based on data in Statistics Canada, General Social Survey. Figure 3.2 is based on data in Julie Cool, "Wage Gap between Women and Men" (Library of Parliament Background Paper 2010-30-E, 2010). Figure 3.3 is based on data in Statistics Canada, "The Surge of Women in the Workforce" (accessed at http://www.statcan.gc.ca/pub/11-630-x/11-630-x2015009-eng.htm). Table 4.1 is based on data in R. Morisette and R. Sultan, "Twenty Years in the Careers of Immigrant and Native-born Workers" (retrieved from http://www.statcan.gc.ca/pub/11-626-x/11-626-x2013032-eng.htm). Figure 4.1 is based on data from the Public Health Agency of Canada, retrieved from http://www.phac-aspc.gc.ca/aids-sida/publication/ps-pd/youth-jeunes/chapter-chapitre-2-eng.php. Figure 5.1 is based on data from Statistics Canada (http://www.statcan.gc.ca/tables-tableaux/sum-som/l01/cst01/health26-eng.htm) and the World Health Organization. Figure 5.2 is based on data from Statistics Canada, CANSIM tables 051-0001 and 052-0005, accessed at www.statcan.gc.ca/pub/11-402-x/2010000/chap/pop/c-g/desc/desc04-eng.htm. Figure 6.1 is based on data from Freeman et al., *The Health of Canada's Young People: A Mental Health Focus* (Ottawa: Public Health Agency of Canada, 2011). Figure 6.2 is based on data from Statistics Canada, accessed at www.statcan.gc.ca/pub/91-209-x/2013001/article/11788/fig/desc/desc07-eng.htm. Figure 7.1 is based on the most recent data available from the CIA *World Fact Book* and World Health Organization. Figure 7.2 is based on data from the Public Health Association of Canada, accessed at www.phac-aspc.gc.ca/publicat/2009/0c/longdesc/figure-1-eng.php. Figure 8.1 is based on data from Statistics Canada, accessed at www.statcan.gc.ca/pub/85-002-x/2016001/article/14309/tbl/tbl09-eng.htm. Figure 8.2 is based on data from numerous sources, including the World Health Organization and the BBC. Figure 9.1 is based on data from the International Labour Organization, World Bank, accessed at http://data.worldbank.org/indicator/SL.UEM.1524.ZS?year_high_desc=true. Figure 9.2 is based on data in Global Affairs Canada, Statistical Report on International Assistance 2013–2014, accessed at http://international.gc.ca/development-developpement/dev-results-resultats/reports-rapports/sria-rsai-2013-14.aspx?lang=eng. Figure 10.1 is based on a chart in Hugh MacKenzie, *CEO Pay in Canada* (Canadian Centre for Policy Alternatives, 2016), and on calculations using the current minimum wage in Ontario. Photographs are as credited in the text and as follows: Page xiv: Kenny McDonald (www.flickr.com/photos/jellymc/9730228067). Page 33: Brave New Films (www.flickr.com/photos/walmartmovie/17191529) and Rick Collins/UFV (www.flickr.com/photos/ufv/14235844439). Page 64: Thunder Bay Museum; Ali Shaker/Voice of America. Page 102: Kenny McDonald (www.flickr.com/photos/jellymc/9325442836) and C. Presutti/Voice of America. Page 149: Chronicle Journal Times, New Thunder Bay, 1978/Girl Guides of Canada (www.flickr.com/photos/girlguidesofcan/8639456369) and Terry Ozon (www.flickr.com/photos/ozontw/7166457496). Page 173: Jason Paris (www.flickr.com/photos/jasonparis/4784973341) and Ryan (www.flickr.com/photos/ryanready/5914352128). Page 235: Andy Burgess (www.flickr.com/photos/asburgess/4200177889) and Patrick Feller (www.flickr.com/photos/nakrnsm/8272406879). Page 286: Rick Harris (www.flickr.com/photos/rickharris/6585996361) and uros1210/Shutterstock. Cover photo: Albina Tiplyashina/Shutterstock.

Library and Archives Canada Cataloguing in Publication is available from the publisher. Email Rock's Mills Press at customer.service@rocksmillspress.com.

ISBN-13: 978-1-77244-029-4

Contents

Each chapter begins with a list of learning objectives.

Introduction

There are many different types of inequality and many different opinions about them, even within the academy. But unlike scholarly subjects over which academics have a monopoly—quantum mechanics, for example, or ancient Greek—social inequality is also a "real life" problem familiar to ordinary people. It is not just a topic for the "ivory tower"; almost everyone, even the least academically inclined, holds views on one type of inequality or another. The purpose of this book is to better understand inequality by carefully considering some of these varied perspectives, to determine whether and how they converge.

This approach grew out of our acknowledgment that most readers of this book—undergraduate sociology students—are *not* white, middle-class, middle-aged, able-bodied men with secure, well-paying jobs. On the other hand, most sociology professors and textbook writers *are*. Consider, for example, that while growing numbers of women are employed by universities, the majority hold part-time or sessional positions, as opposed to the tenured positions that men continue to dominate.

Because they are often written by a certain "type" of person, many sociology textbooks are problematic in three ways: (1) they overemphasize the sociology of "life on the inside"; (2) they do not question life on the inside; and (3) they lack an understanding of "life on the outside."

The typical academic sociologist is what we will call an "insider," because he has a lot of insight into white, middle-class, North American society, and has enjoyed success in that society. He is able to carefully gather and analyze data that provides useful insights into the scale, causes, and consequences of social inequality, as well as some potential remedies for it. But he has almost no first-hand knowledge of that inequality to complement his intellectual understanding.

Contrast this insider with the kind of person we will call an "outsider." There are many kinds of outsiders; in fact, their shared defining feature is that they are *not* insiders. Not white, not male, not middle class, not middle-aged, not able-bodied, and not born in North America—such people are examples of outsiders. They usually have experiences with, and perspectives on, inequality that differ from those of the typical insider. Such perspectives offer valuable insights into these issues, ones we would overlook if we only considered an insider's perspective. What's more, outsiders are likely concerned with aspects of inequality that do not even cross the minds of insiders: where they will find their next meal, how to access Canada's supposedly universal health care system, and ways other than education to climb the social ladder.

That is because outsiders are vulnerable members of North American society: victims or potential victims of the way life is organized here. "Life on the outside" is characterized by uncertainty, dependency, prejudice, and unfairness: it is the exact opposite of the ivory-tower existence enjoyed by professors and textbook authors. As a result, outsiders are likely to be critical of people on the inside, and especially skeptical of insiders' views on everyday life on the outside. Outsiders are also highly knowledgeable about life on the outside: they have a deep, often personal understanding of things like sexual harassment, racial discrimination, unemployment, and so on.

This book attempts to bridge the gap between the views of insiders and outsiders by evaluating some of their different perspectives on social inequality. Our method for tackling such a broad subject follows from Canadian sociologist Dorothy Smith's "standpoint theory." Building on the work of Karl Marx and Karl Mannheim, Smith was concerned with what counts as knowledge, and who gets to define and produce it (Wood 2005).

The essence of her theory is that our position in the world fundamentally shapes our perception and understanding of any given issue. Smith first put her ideas forward in a critique of the discipline, where she pointed out that sociological theories and discourses are conventionally written from a male standpoint (DeVault 2006, Hekman 1997). Moreover, these male voices were located in the "relations of ruling," backed up by authoritative institutions like the academy, government, law, business, and so on (Grahame 1998).

Not only do these institutions organize and facilitate what goes on in the world; they also produce the authoritative explanation of *why* things happen as they do. They write the scientific, technological, and cultural narratives that rationalize the status quo. Smith (and Marx) would say that such "abstract knowledge" is produced and re-produced in the interest of preserving those relations of ruling.

For the most part, we believe these narratives because the institutions that back them are considered legitimate, authoritative producers of knowledge. We ignore, silence, or at the very least misrepresent the voices of people who actually *experience* issues like poverty, unemployment, racism, and sexism. Such an approach is often reasonable, since academics are highly knowledgeable in their fields. As we will see, however, unquestioning belief in any kind of knowledge claim can be problematic. First, a retrospective look at any academic discipline will reveal a long history of getting things wrong. Academics are aware of this, which is why they champion the scientific method: they know that only by constantly questioning knowledge claims and exploring alternate explanations and solutions for a given social problem can we hope to eventually obtain better, more rounded understandings of that problem. Second, privileging one type of knowledge claim necessarily means discounting another. Although we are often wise to prioritize the knowledge claims of academics, we must not do so at the expense of those put forward by the people living through the challenges we study. Silencing or ignoring outsiders' first-hand knowledge will mean we never develop policies that effectively reduce the consequences of inequality that they experience on a daily basis. Third, and perhaps most importantly, the academy is not the only institution that produces knowledge claims widely believed to be authoritative. Most often, wealth and power determine whose views are most widely heard. By carefully analyzing such views, rather than unquestioningly accepting them as objective facts, we may find that they are not objective at all, but subjective, biased, and shaped by a desire to preserve the status quo.

In the face of these challenges, Smith developed *institutional ethnography*, a method of sociological inquiry that studies people's everyday experiences and the ways in which they are affected by prevailing power structures. Her goal was to encourage people to question commonly accepted understandings of reality. To that end, she suggests that we foreground the perceptions of "ordinary" people that are often overlooked, both in the sociological literature and in society at large. Ordinary people are often the ones most knowledgeable of and affected by inequality. Building on Smith's foundation, *our* goal is to put the views of insiders and outsiders into dialogue: we want to encourage readers to take a fresh look at the truth claims put forward by insiders, and think critically about the ways they try to justify or legitimate those claims.

Consider a concrete example used by Smith. She noted that it was the domestic work of women that freed men from having to provide for their own bodily comfort and allowed them to pursue more abstract intellectual goals. Men work as they do because women are there to care for them. Men then benefit from the abstract knowledge they gain from higher education and the workplace—the same knowledge that forms the basis of social power structures. Written texts—including sociological and scientific theories—are often based on such abstract knowledge, and contribute to upholding the "ruling practices" that promote the perspective of socially dominant groups. Women's knowledge, on the other hand, is more "embodied," by which Smith meant "derived from experience." This form of knowledge is rarely privileged in the same way as men's: it is not widely disseminated through academic theory, nor is it framed as a type of "objective truth." In fact, precisely *because* it is derived from deeply personal, embodied experience, the type of knowledge most often obtained by women is dismissed as subjective and partial.

Smith's institutional ethnography attempts to question the prevailing power structures of institutional knowledge by exploring such embodied knowledge. Hearing the accounts of disadvantaged individuals, Smith proposes, will provide us with new perspectives on power, community, conformity, and inequality. By taking up a woman's point of view, for instance, we can learn to see our world in a different, perhaps enlightening way. By suggesting that the female perspective could open up new and useful means of producing knowledge, Smith made a valuable contribution to feminist theory. But her ideas were also important for other traditionally marginalized groups—racial and sexual minorities, the victims of class inequalities, and so on—whose voices have been similarly erased from dominant discourses.

Standpoint theory thus allows us to gain a deeper, perhaps more accurate understanding of our world by considering the perspectives of people who live through troubling experiences (Grahame 1998). Through a standpoint approach, we not only gain a more accurate understanding of the lives of the disadvantaged; we also gain fresh perspective on dominant, privileged groups and the institutions that allow for and preserve their privilege (Wood 2005).

That being said, we need to modify Smith's theory somewhat, to recognize some discrepancy between social position and social views. Not *every* white or able-bodied or male professor (for example) holds pro-establishment "insider" views. Nor does being an outsider guarantee impartiality: not every non-white or handicapped or female non-professor holds anti-ideological or even clear and realistic views of the world. Indeed, many working-class people hold conservative political views and, in effect, vote against their own class interests. Likewise, many women—even battered women—accept patriarchal rationales for their own subordination. And many LGBTQ people or ethnic or racial minorities criticize themselves for failing to "live up to" their society's normative expectations.

So, in this book, when we speak of "insider views" or "outsider views," we mean views that reflect the interests of the insider or outsider group respectively, and are sometimes shaped by an individual's social position. We want to avoid making essentialist claims that frame all women, for instance, as part of a unitary group with identical values, interests, goals, and points of view. Instead, we are more interested in exploring different perspectives on and explanations for some of the disadvantages many Canadian women face today.

Similarly, we want to avoid oversimplifying the ways in which various axes of inequality can intersect. Although each of the following chapters focuses on one type of inequality—namely, those grounded in class, gender, race, age, and sexuality—these categories are far from distinct. Someone who is an insider on one dimension may be an outsider on others, as would be the case with an impoverished white woman, or a wealthy queer black man. These features intersect to produce unique experiences of inequality, advantage, and disadvantage for every individual. Although each chapter is organized primarily around one type of inequality, that does not mean that each type of inequality is discrete.

The keen-eyed reader will find some correlation between our categories of "insider" and "outsider" views and the traditional textbook categories of functionalist, conflict, symbolic interactionist, feminist, and postmodern theory. Most sociology textbooks equate functionalist theories with pro-establishment ways of thinking—that is, with insider views—or, at least, with political complacency and indifference to issues of inequality. That is because these theories have focused on the supposedly beneficial or system-enhancing aspects of inequality. Conflict and feminist theory are often equated with anti-establishment ways of thinking—that is, with outsider views. On this insider-outsider spectrum, symbolic interactionism and postmodernism are harder to classify, since we can find examples of both insider and outsider views in both camps.

This schema, however, is very simple and may even be simplistic. The depiction of functionalism as a one-dimensional, pro-establishment approach fails badly if you consider the empirical work of mainstream sociologists throughout the twentieth century. Not every mainstream sociologist was a social critic, but one need only read functionalist Robert Merton's classic analysis of anomie to be persuaded that even functionalists can savage the establishment. And for their part, many "conflict theory" analyses are one-dimensional attacks on a particular kind of disadvantage—whether due to class, gender, race, or otherwise—and not an attack on inequality in general.

So, to reiterate, this book is organized around different points of view, not around specific subpopulations (i.e., white versus black, rich versus poor), nor around different sociological approaches or "paradigms" (i.e., functionalist versus conflict theory). Each chapter reviews different perspectives on inequality, beginning with a section entitled "Insider Views." Insiders are those who are advantaged on a particular dimension of inequality (such as class, gender, race, etc.). Their position of advantage means they produce knowledge claims that are typically backed up by those authoritative institutions mentioned above, and that are therefore more likely to be accepted as fact. Much of the time, those truth claims serve to justify and perpetuate the status quo, which is self-serving, since the existing social system favours insiders.

Next in each chapter comes a section called "Second Opinions," which includes critiques of insider views from academics. Here, researchers push back against the narratives insiders have used to rationalize inequality, providing empirical evidence that paints a different picture of reality or alternative theoretical explanations of that reality. For example, feminist scholars explain sexual deviance differently than functionalist scholars who, on this dimension, can be categorized as holding insider views. The Second Opinions sections serve two purposes. First, they encourage us to think critically about dominant perspectives put forward by insiders. Second, they provide data that can help us develop the best-informed opinions possible. Ideally, this means that fewer people will form opinions about inequality while lacking empirical information about its causes and consequences.

The last core element in each chapter is the "Outsights" section, which features outsiders describing and explaining their experiences. Examples include women analyzing housework, black people analyzing racial identity, and poor people analyzing unemployment. Such views are important, we propose, because they should inform the policies that aim to reduce inequality and its consequences. That is not to say that outsiders should be the only ones responsible for developing policy initiatives; but their input should be considered when shaping the policies that are supposed to be improving their lives. Insiders and academics cannot be the only ones involved in policy design, because their knowledge of inequality will always remain partial. Outsights are needed to round out the debate.

Because this is a textbook for use in sociology courses, it will rely a great deal on outsights gleaned from within the sociological literature. But we will also go outside that small community to find other evidence and illustrations of outsider experiences. Our sources here include newspaper and magazine articles that quote outsiders directly, and materials written by outsiders themselves. These accounts will trouble the idea that insiders and academics alone could possibly give the entire, true story of everyday life in Canada without consulting the people who suffer under inequality. It will also show our readers—many of whom are outsiders—that they can make valuable contributions to the debate, by bringing their own experiences and "outsights" to the discussion.

This book does not, however, propose that sociological knowledge is merely the documentation of unmediated, anecdotal first-hand experience. Nor do we propose that anyone's opinion, however ill-formed, is as legitimate as anyone else's. Instead, we will use research to come to the best-informed conclusions possible, showing, in the process, that some people's opinions on these subjects are merely opinions. We will also propose that rigorous research can, in many instances, help us understand inequality better than mere anecdotal experience. To accomplish that goal, each chapter closes by calling attention to areas of agreement and disagreement between insiders and outsiders, and by suggesting how we might resolve those disagreements through further research.

This book has three agendas. First, it aims to draw attention to the range of inequalities that persist in present-day Canadian society through an investigation of their causes and consequences. Second, it examines how people of different social standpoints experience those inequalities, and how they attempt to either justify and sustain or challenge and change them. Finally, it asks what position sociologists occupy in this discussion of inequality: can we provide insights that will help bring these debates (closer) to resolution?

In the end, we conclude that sociologists have an obligation to ensure that the voices of outsiders permeate public debates about inequality. While insiders possess the power needed to ensure their voices are heard, outsiders are silenced and marginalized by definition. Neither insiders nor outsiders hold the "right" view on every issue related to inequality, but to assess which views are most accurate, we must ensure everyone is heard. We therefore present both sides of the debate throughout this book, complemented by the research of academics who offer alternative ways of thinking about these issues. Putting these three standpoints into dialogue will offer us a clearer view of social inequality than any one standpoint on its own. In this way, sociologists can play an important role in making good social policies that take into account the needs of the people they purport to benefit.

Living in the Shadows. Kenny McDonald, 2013

CHAPTER ONE

The Problem of Inequality: Real or Imaginary?

LEARNING OBJECTIVES

In this chapter, you will:
1. Distinguish natural differences from social inequalities
2. Learn how inequality is constructed as a social problem
3. Explore intersecting inequalities and interlocking oppressions
4. Investigate social stratification and social mobility in Canadian society today
5. Understand the belief systems Canadians use to justify and perpetuate inequality

---

INTRODUCTION

Americans love to imagine re-inventing themselves as tycoons, like F. Scott Fitzgerald's Jay ("the Great") Gatsby. These perennially popular "rags-to-riches" stories, in which wholly "self-made" men (and occasionally women) pull themselves out of poverty through their own initiative, reflect the widespread belief that everyone can succeed if they work hard enough.

This idea of the **American Dream** encourages many disadvantaged people with the hope they may enjoy a better tomorrow if they continue to slave away today (Hedgehog Review 2013). Even in Canada, which developed historically as a cultural contrast to the populist United States, many people—especially immigrants—embrace similar hopes and expectations. But evidence suggests that the American Dream is unattainable for most people in Canada and the U.S. alike: it is little more than a fairy tale we continue to tell ourselves and instill in our children.

Beginning with Max Weber, sociologists have long known that people have unequal **life chances**: that is, unequal opportunities to gain wealth, power and esteem. In our society, the class into which you are born largely determines the class you will occupy for the rest of your life (Wright 2005). In turn, economic inequality persists from one generation to the next, perpetuating a gap between the rich and the poor, and restricting mobility across that gap.

Not surprisingly, low-income children are usually aware of their limited opportunities for success. Compared to other children, they expect less career

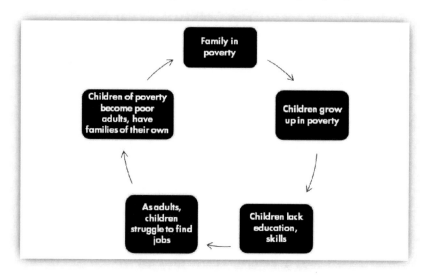

Figure 1.1: The Cycle of Poverty

success and may even come to think there is little point in trying hard (Rodriquez 2006). Bleak circumstances undermine their motivation. To secure the educational and occupational opportunities needed to improve their lot, the poor need money. To obtain money, they first need opportunities: affordable housing, education, a job. The oft-used phrase **cycle of poverty** is thus an apt one.

Political conservatives often argue that people born into low-income families can turn their lives around if only they work hard and persevere. By this logic, people who remain poor are lazy and unmotivated. Throughout this book, we will return to this **victim blaming** narrative, which holds disadvantaged people responsible for their condition, despite the odds against them.

Of course, economic circumstances alone do not determine people's life chances. Other variables, including inequalities related to race, gender, age, and sex, also play a part. For example, in many countries, black people are less likely than white people to get a loan, secure a stable job, or be treated fairly in courts of justice. Some have proposed that education, rather than race, is responsible for these differences in life chances. More will be said about the confusing intersection of race and class in a later chapter.

Whether we are examining Canada or another country, we can see that poverty in one generation breeds poverty in the next (Wagmiller et al. 2006). By contrast, children born into families that have never been poor have less than a 5% chance of slipping into poverty. On this score alone, the American Dream seems out of touch with reality, given how reliably we can predict people's life chances simply by knowing what economic class they were born into.

WHAT IS INEQUALITY?

Social inequality refers to the organization of a society around a set of human differences that have been stacked hierarchically, with certain groups privileged over others (Deslauriers 2004, Harris 2006). Social inequality not only distinguishes people, it also places them in competition with one another: rich versus poor, powerful versus powerless, respected versus disrespected, socially included versus excluded, safe versus endangered, and so on, through a huge catalogue of different statuses. In turn, these different groups are allocated unequal opportunities and rewards.

Many natural differences distinguish people from one another: some people are tall, others short; some beautiful, others plain-looking; some smart, others less so. As sociologists, we are interested in how these natural differences are made into social inequalities—how they are "socially constructed"—and in the consequences of this inequality-producing process (Deslauriers 2004). Why, for instance, is it so fundamentally important that men are biologically different from women? Or that young and old people exhibit different abilities than middle-aged people? Human societies organize themselves around sex and age; but why these attributes, when we might just as well group people by hair colour or shoe size?

Many believe that the categories of sex and age (among others) have emerged as socially important because they mark the most fundamental differences between people in terms of their natural skills and abilities. For example, women are fundamentally different from men in that they have the physiological ability to give birth. Old people are fundamentally different from middle-aged people because, on average, they are physically weaker, often causing them to depend on younger people for care and support. However, these **natural differences** are not problematic in and of themselves; they are _made_ problematic when we assign meanings and values to them—for example, when we claim that a person's sex or age necessarily determines the type of life they can live, the type of work they are capable of doing, or the roles they should fill.

This happens when we say, for instance, that women are naturally inclined towards caregiving and domesticity because they are capable of giving birth, or when we decide that old people are no longer capable of doing valuable work. None of these claims is inherently true. Rather, we have produced these narratives—these ways of making sense of the natural differences among people—over centuries of social learning and reinforcement.

Sociologists call the results of this long process **social constructions**. Many would argue that the entire world in which we live—our "reality"—is socially constructed (Harris 2006). The objects, people, animals, and ideas we interact with all have social meanings assigned to them. Because of these social meanings, we treat certain people differently than others. According to sociologists, nothing is bad, deviant, abnormal, or problematic until we say it is (Woolgar and Pawluch 1985, Croucher 1997).

That is true of social inequality as well: it is not natural, normal or inevitable, nor is it intrinsically bad or good. It is also true for anything we consider to be a "problem" in society, such as crime, violence, drugs, and so on: these activities are socially constructed as **social problems** (Croucher 1997). There are many other situations and events that *could* be conceived as social problems, but which are largely ignored (Woolgar and Pawluch 1985). Countless groups vie for attention, desperate to attract notice for what they see as a worthy, underrepresented cause. But because we can only focus our attention on and contribute resources towards a few social problems at a time, a great many issues that could potentially be considered significant "problems" remain on the periphery of public consciousness (Hilgartner and Bosk 1988).

That's why we know that social problems are socially constructed: they follow a standard trajectory, gaining massive public support and then gradually losing it (Hilgartner and Bosk 1988, Haines 1979). During the first part of this process, a group or organization—call it the "protest group"—draws attention to a condition they claim to be undesirable or damaging. Second, a broader official institution or organization recognizes and declares the original group's complaints as "legitimate." Third, the protest group voices its dissatisfaction with the procedures set in place to deal with the issue, eventually rejects those procedures, and sets up alternative or counter procedures of their own.

The first part of this process has a lot to do with narrative-building, or **claims-making** (Woolgar and Pawluch 1985). Certain types of claims—ways of talking about and understanding a given social problem—are more widely believed than others. For example, a claim is more likely to gain popularity if it is supported by prominent, prestigious, and wealthy figures able to access the mass media to marshal public attention (Croucher 1997, Haines 1979).

Social problems are also more likely to gain traction if they align with popular, deeply entrenched values and beliefs. For example, people are much

4

more likely to feel concerned about poor children than poor under-employed men. That is because children are widely believed to be weak and blameless, while full-grown, employable men are not. Dominant norms, values, beliefs, and political procedures thus work to ensure that certain conditions do not come to be defined as social problems (Croucher 1997). Often, such "problem non-definition" requires people to mobilize those traditional, widely held values and beliefs to ensure things stay as they are.

People also tend to endorse social problems whose solution does not require fundamental redistributions of wealth or power. Thus, they are more likely to support legislation that bans job discrimination against LGBT people—an inexpensive expression of solidarity—than to support legislation that provides subsidized, regulated daycare, free university tuition, or a higher minimum wage, which are all very expensive initiatives.

For these reasons, inequality often fails to attract the attention and funding that other social problems do. Because inequality tends to favour the very same prominent public figures whose support would be needed to challenge it, and because remedying inequality may require a costly redistributive effort, people tend to tolerate inequality rather than examine, oppose, or try to change it.

In large measure, social inequality has been deemed a "closed" or "enclosed" social problem. Enclosure happens when the range of legitimate definitions of a social problem, and actions deemed appropriate to manage it, become limited to those of a single group or movement (Haines 1979). That single movement comes to monopolize acceptable ways of thinking about the given condition. Enclosure often involves restricting the number and type of people "qualified" to offer their perspectives on the topic and propose potential solutions. A social problem has been successfully enclosed when "professionals" and "experts" come to dominate discussion of it to the exclusion of alternative approaches.

Through enclosure, the dominant perception of the "problem" becomes institutionalized: so widely endorsed that essentially all (powerful) groups see it as a universal truth. Any person or group proposing an alternative understanding will struggle to be heard. Up against what is seen as concrete "fact"—that is, the dominant perspective—these alternative viewpoints are dismissed as silly, outlandish, or even dangerous, threatening of traditional institutions. From this perspective, we can see the "American Dream" as precisely that kind of enclosure: it declares that social inequality is not a problem because people can overcome their disadvantages if they work hard enough.

Similarly, the notion that human differences naturally produce inequality makes inequality appear inevitable (Williams-Myers 1983). The dominant groups we call insiders draw on this popular idea to justify the way society is organized and to legitimate their privilege. When such narratives become so widely believed, people resist attempts to question them. Nonetheless, in this book we will encourage readers to engage in such questioning. For example, we will propose that natural differences do *not* cause or explain inequalities: inequalities are socially constructed, arbitrary, collectively made up, and therefore *changeable* (Deslauriers 2004, Alexander 2007). It may be unsettling to think that our world, the meanings we attach to experiences, and the issues we see as "problems" are merely social constructions (Harris 2006). But this unsettling effect is helpful: it can undercut people's comfortable, sometimes smug and self-serving understandings of the world.

In saying that social inequality is a social construction, we do not mean that inequality is imaginary, does not exist, or that people are not subjected to its real, traumatizing consequences. Social inequality is real. Social constructionism is simply an approach that helps us identify and explain these consequences and the factors that produce them.

Because inequality is socially constructed, people understand it in different ways across different cultures (Alexander 2007). But there are also variations within cultures. Some Canadians talk about, and therefore construct, inequality as a troubling social problem that needs to be fixed. Others construct inequality as normal, acceptable, and even necessary for a productive, efficient society. We construct some types of inequality as just and deserved, others as shockingly unfair. We also construct inequality by "performing" it: acting out the different behaviours expected of us, given our social positioning. For example, people use words, body language, and dress to signal social status. We thus perform differences in visible ways, and these performances help to reproduce inequalities.

Our task, then, is to study the social construction of inequality: to examine what "inequality" means to people, how they have come to hold those meanings, and what discourses they draw on to help explain, legitimize, and thereby perpetuate their individual understandings of inequality (Woolgar and Pawluch 1985). In doing so, we walk a fine line between analyzing the processes through which social problems are constructed, and participating in that construction. That is, when we claim with authority that a given issue *is* a problem, and that we *know* its extent, causes, and consequences, we are contributing to shaping that issue as a social problem.

Bearing this in mind, we have organized each of the following chapters around several competing perspectives or standpoints, each of which reflects one way in which inequalities are constructed in our society. By drawing attention to the ways these standpoints overlap and diverge, we will show that some constructions of inequality are less informative or productive than others. Only by considering this wide variety of perspectives can we hope to gain a well-rounded view of inequality—one that will help us develop policies to effectively reduce it.

INTERSECTIONALITY

Every human can be "sorted" and categorized on many levels, given their various natural and cultural characteristics. Each of these features "intersects" to produce experiences of inequality that are unique to each individual.

The theory of **intersectionality** recognizes that one person may face several different types of inequality that interact in distinct ways, depending on the situation at hand (Choo and Ferree 2010). People often fall into more than one marginalized social category and experience multiple kinds of social inequality as a result (Wood 2005).

The theory of intersectionality emerged in the late 1980s from Kimberlé Crenshaw's examination of the implications of being both black *and* female (Carbado 2013). Crenshaw argued that black women often become the victims of two "interlocking systems of oppression"—racism and sexism—and thus confront an irreducibly unique experience of social inequality (Lindsay 2009). Innovatively, she proposed that it is impossible to disentangle one type of oppression from the other (Choo and Ferree 2010, Lindsay 2009). This means that intersectionality does not function additively. Multiple standpoints (to use Dorothy Smith's term) cannot be added up, creating an experience of oppression or privilege two or three (or however many) times over (Geerts and Van Der Tuin 2013).

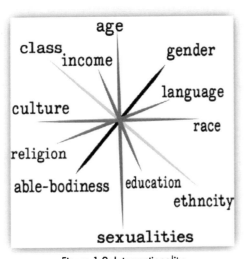

Figure 1.2: Intersectionality

There are theories that take such an approach. For instance, the **double jeopardy** model proposes that the more marginal categories a person belongs to, the more disadvantages that person will experience (Carbado 2013). By contrast, the intersectional approach interprets a person's experience of discrimination not as the sum of different kinds of discrimination, but rather, in individual terms, given each person's unique intersections of different social categories (Lindsay 2009, Choo and Ferree 2010). From this standpoint, race, class, gender and other kinds of social subordination must be examined as parts of a holistically tangled, deeply personal experience of social inequality.

Although originally developed in relation to black women's specific experiences, intersectionality has come to be applied much more broadly (Carbado 2013, Hancock 2007). Many scholars now recognize that identity is shaped by the intersection of multiple dimensions: people do not fit perfectly into any single identity group, and, conversely, no single dimension of identity eclipses all others (Crenshaw 1991, Lindsay 2009). Just because you are a man, for example, does not mean that you experience the world in the same way as all other men.

Or, to take a classic example from social theory, just because you are a working-class person, with a particular relationship to the means of production, does not mean you will experience or view the world in the same way as all other working class persons (despite what Karl Marx claimed). This fact helps to explain why, historically, the working class has had such difficulty developing **class consciousness**, and why other disadvantaged groups, including women, have been challenged in adopting a shared feminist agenda.

Intersectionality helps us avoid oversimplified generalizations (Nash 2008). It would be impossible to conduct an experiment on racism, for example, where that one variable can be isolated and its effects measured independently from any other, potentially confounding ones. We will never know what it is like to be *only* a white person or a black person, because we can never disentangle race from all the other "parts" that compose people. However, we *can* hope to gain a better understanding of what it may be like to be a white, middle-class teenager, or a black, wealthy grandfather.

Differences intersect in many ways, and because of all these unique combinations, Crenshaw argued that identity politics are less than fruitful. When only a single, one-dimensional category is considered, the intersections between that category and an almost infinite number of others are neglected (Crenshaw 1991). That's why universalist (or white) feminism has been criticized for assuming that all women, worldwide, necessarily share the same values, perspectives, and experiences, and should accordingly band together to protest sexism (Robinson and Nelson 2010, Stoetzler and Yuval-Davis 2002). Such an approach fails to address how being black, for instance, may change one's experience of being a woman (Geerts and Van Der Tuin 2013). By lumping different "types" of people into overly broad categories, we come up against the problem of **essentialism**: the idea these groups embody characteristics that make them intrinsically different from one another (Wood 2005).

Despite the theory's intuitive appeal, we lack a clear, rigorous intersectional methodology. Indeed, given the theory's implication that each individual experiences the world in a wholly unique way, how can we even discuss topics like "class inequality" or "gender inequality"? It would be impossible to analyze every possible combination of social difference (Geerts and Van Der Tuin 2013, Davis 2008).

To talk about social inequality at all, we must limit and organize our thoughts in some way. That's why the following five chapters are centred on five different types of inequality: class, gender, racial, age, and sexual inequalities. We realize this schema does not do justice to all the intersections among inequalities, but advance these categories for the sake of convenience and coherence.

To incorporate the intersectional approach into these seemingly non-intersectional chapters, we will consider yet another intersectional dimension: *situation*. Not only do people's experiences and perspectives change based on their unique combination of race, sex, class, age, and so on; they also shift as people move through different circumstances into different social interactions unfolding in different spaces. It means one thing to be a wealthy white woman in a suburban shopping center (a friendly, familiar environment), and something entirely different to be a wealthy white woman in a "bad" neighborhood after dark (a hostile, unfamiliar environment).

Throughout this book, we will take an intersectional approach to a variety of *circumstances*. Although centred on broad categories of inequality, each chapter will draw upon certain moments that we will elucidate through an intersectional approach. Consider, as one example, nannies who immigrate to Canada from the Philippines and experience a variety of mistreatments related to gender, racial, class, and age inequalities. These nannies live with, and take orders from, other women—most often, wealthy white women. In this case, one "type" of woman is privileged over another, and may even abuse her position of power (Robinson and Nelson 2010).

The standpoint of a live-in nanny is thus especially useful, given her unique situation: outside of the dominant, privileged group, marginalized due to her race, low social class, and gender, but simultaneously living within a privileged household, privy to the private lives of her wealthy employers. This position is sometimes referred to as the "outsider within" (Wood 2005), and is one of the standpoints we will adopt in our discussions of social outsights.

It was Donna Haraway who called our attention to the importance of circumstance. Her theory of **situated knowledges** reinforces the need for this type of intersectional approach.

SITUATED KNOWLEDGES

In the late 1980s, Haraway suggested that our understanding of **objectivity** is deeply flawed (Haraway 1988, Hinton 2014, Stoetzler and Yuval-Davis 2002). In fact, what most people consider to be objective is highly *subjective*. Most of the time, Haraway proposed, viewpoints that seem neutral or detached are those of white, upper-middle-class, heterosexual men. When we look at an issue from a so-called "different" perspective, we almost always highlight the fact that we are talking about how a non-white, non-wealthy, non-heterosexual, non-male person may see things.

Dominant perspectives, narratives, and ways of knowing are invented by "invisible" groups whose perspective is framed as a "disembodied view from nowhere" (Hinton 2014). On the other hand, "different" perspectives are always explicitly "embodied." They are offered by distinct "types" of people: women, the elderly, gays, and so on. Haraway contends that we consider these second opinions in a problematic way, by tying them to the *bodies* of the people who propose them, so that they always appear subjective and biased.

For example, consider the short biographies of scholars that often appear in textbooks. White, male scholars with Western names are usually described in terms of their qualifications: where they attended school and received their degrees. Non-white, non-male, non-Western scholars are described in terms of what their "unique" experiences allow them to contribute to a discussion. We normalize the white male point of view as objective and universal, using other perspectives merely to round out the discussion.

Haraway argues that we should not take the white male perspective as "objective" or neutral, because it is anything but. Although framed in objective terms, the views of white men are just as embodied and subjective as those of women, racial minorities, and so on (Longino 1993). When we fail to recognize that a certain perspective is indeed subjective, we no longer "see well" (Stoetzler and Yuval-Davis 2002). Privileged people are invested in ignoring inequalities because these unjust structures perpetuate their power. To maintain their privileged position, the white men voicing supposedly objective views lay claim to the right to observe and comment on the world from an invisible, "unlocatable," and therefore "conquering" standpoint.

These "insider" perspectives are merely privileged; they are not necessarily correct. One type of privileged, authoritative position is that occupied by academics. Haraway encouraged people to think critically about the ways in which academics' assertions are typically accepted as facts. When a person claims to offer an "objective" view, he is aiming to legitimate an inherently subjective perspective (Stoetzler and Yuval-Davis 2002, Wood 2005). The public plays into this by privileging insider/objective/scientific views over all other ways of knowing.

Doing so may often be well-advised, because scientific research does yield useful insights we would do well to heed. But when we always privilege scientific claims, we risk delegitimizing other ways of seeing and understanding. Scientific, university-produced, government-backed, industry-funded, "official," "authoritative" knowledge may occasionally confirm less accepted types of knowledge; but, more often, it silences and marginalizes other knowledge producers by dismissing them as uninformed or biased (Brown Parlee 1996, Hinton 2014).

Haraway was not denouncing science, nor was she suggesting that scientific "knowledge" is merely a shell game. The speed of sound, the temperature at which water boils, the structure of the atom—these are not matters of idle conjecture about which one person's opinion is as good as another's. However, social science—and by extension, social policy-making—can never be as exact in its conclusions as experimental physical science. We must recognize that multiple insights into a given social problem are not only tolerable, but also absolutely necessary. We cannot start a discussion by excluding certain perspectives, effectively ending the debate before it has begun.

When it comes to social inequality, silencing or dismissing disagreement is risky, not to mention undemocratic. As Haraway and Smith suggested, one person may be incapable of truly understanding and accurately analyzing another's experiences (Hinton 2014). For example, we should not assume a man can better describe a woman's experiences than the woman herself.

This is not to say that *only* those people who live marginalized, subjugated lives can talk meaningfully about such experiences. True, a man will never know what it is like to inhabit a woman's body; but the theory of situated knowledges does *not* propose that only women can study gender (Stoetzler and Yuval-Davis 2002). Rather, it is meant to foreground the reality that all knowledge claims, no matter how objective they may seem, are *not* objective. They are generated by specific, embodied people in specific circumstances. The wider the variety of standpoints we consider, the better our understanding of the issue at hand will be.

Many of the same concerns raised about intersectionality have been raised about situated knowledges—especially the concern that listening to multiple perspectives on a given topic does not advance our understanding of that topic very far (Heckman 1997). Accordingly, Haraway asserts that we must continue searching for "a usable doctrine of objectivity." That is, we must come up with a better, more accurate way of seeing the world. Most importantly, this new "objective" perspective must recognize power differences and the ways certain positions and perspectives exercise power over others. Haraway claims that we do not need a notion of objectivity that "transcends" real, lived experience: while we should *not* strive for **omniscience**, we *should* strive for more "enforceable, reliable accounts" of the world that are not just a matter of rhetoric or assertions of dominance. Ultimately, Haraway argues that our

11

notion of "objectivity" needs to change from transcending and universal to embodied, specific, and situated.

To accomplish that goal, Harway proposes that we draw the perspectives of marginalized, oppressed, or subjugated people into discussions of inequality. Such views are less clouded by a desire to assert and maintain power and more likely to reflect actual experiences, rather than dominant ideologies. Moreover, these subjugated people are more likely to challenge traditionally privileged, "objective" perspectives (Heckman 1997).

The problem is learning *how* to see from such subjugated perspectives. Haraway explicitly warns of the dangers in trying to see the world through others' eyes. First, we may romanticize or otherwise distort those different perspectives. Second, we risk appropriating subjugated perspectives, using them for purposes that the subjugated individual may not approve of or have intended (Walby 2007). Finally, we must bear in mind that subjugated perspectives are not wholly "innocent" (Wood 2005). Outsiders have their own interests, histories, and experiences that shape their views. No one, however "subjugated," can offer an entirely objective truth claim.

So, in analyzing the social experiences of different groups, we must avoid the past errors of Western scholarship, including oversimplifying and stereotyping the people we are studying. Consider what Haraway calls the figure of the **essentialized Third World woman**. For many North Americans, the phrase conjures up an image of a poor mother burdened with many children, oppressed by her patriarchal society, living somewhere far away. This way of thinking about non-Western life perpetuates stereotypes and an opposition between "us" and "them."

In this book, we will work hard to avoid painting such pictures. Haraway's theory of situated knowledges will help us distinguish between narratives that have been constructed by others situated at a safe remove from difficult living conditions, and explanations for those conditions produced by those who endure them. At the same time, we will be careful not to discard dominant, widely believed perspectives altogether (Stoetzler and Yuval-Davis 2002). We still need to understand **hegemonic narratives**, and the experience of life "on the inside." At the very least, our understanding of "insider" views will provide a point of comparison against which we can weigh the experiences of "outsiders" and the "second opinions" provided by academics.

One critique of Haraway's theory is that it seems to rule out the possibility that one perspective is more accurate than another. According to Haraway, there is no particular social position from which people can offer an objective truth (Wood 2005). This is known as **relativism**: the idea that all perspectives are equally valid, and no one view more "true" than another.

In one sense, relativism is refreshing and enlightening. But it is also paralyzing in the same way as a thoroughly intersectional approach. You can never hope to solve a social problem if you begin with the assumption that there is no essential or reliable knowledge of the problem. This premise, for the present two authors, is unacceptable. We will juggle between two opposed ideas—essentialism and relativism—in search of a convincing middle ground.

One response to this dilemma is to suggest that, although no perspective is absolutely "correct," some perspectives are better than others. For example (and in keeping with what Haraway herself would propose), a poor person probably has a more accurate understanding of what it's like to use a food bank than does a wealthy person. That does not mean that impoverished outsiders should always get the last word on inequality, or that the input of insiders should be ignored. It simply means that if we are to study food banks, we should consult the people who actually use them.

While recognizing that all knowledge is situated, we must also strive to find those situations that produce the most "objective" knowledge. The notion of objectivity needs to be reformulated. We should seek out knowledge claims that are likely "less false—less partial and distorted" (Wood 2005). Reworking our understanding of objectivity in this way would allow us to position ourselves somewhere between essentialism and relativism, using multiple perspectives to get at something resembling "truth."

The point of this book is not to "speak for" women, racial minorities, poor people, the homeless, or other outsiders—it would be impossible to get their stories exactly right anyway. Our goal is to call attention to certain views of certain types of inequality that are often edited out of dominant narratives. We must let the marginalized and the silenced to be heard; they must be allowed to participate in examining, exploring, and explaining the world they live in.

THAT'S NOT FAIR!

On some abstract level, everyone wants to be treated equally. When privileges, rewards, opportunities, and resources are distributed unequally, our knee-jerk reaction is to declare how "unfair" that is. In that sense, people mean "fairness" when they say "equality" and "unfairness" when they say "inequality" (Almas 2010).

Yet, in stark contrast, there is also a widespread belief that certain types of inequality are natural, inevitable, and justifiable, and that society cannot function without them. However, the kinds and degrees of inequality people are willing to accept vary widely from one society to another (Melamed 2012).

In North America, people often debate how best to structure society: whether we should strive to level the playing field, or accept our currently unequal, unfair society (Osberg 2006). One approach to achieving greater equality is **strict egalitarianism**. From this perspective, any degree of social

Nicole Meredith and Lorne Tepperman

inequality is unfair and undesirable. Strict egalitarians contend that everyone should always get an equal share of society's resources (Melamed 2012). Interestingly, most young children endorse this view. As they grow up, however, children come to hold **meritocratic** views on income inequality, eventually trying to justify wage differences by arguing that more productive workers should be paid more (Almas 2010). Those who endorse this view argue that unequal rewards (like differences in income) create an incentive for hard work (Trump 2013) and help to maximize effort, efficiency, and productivity, benefiting society as a whole. By this logic, those who provide others with the most valuable services should be rewarded the most (Williams 2013).

This rationale is frequently used to justify high incomes for wealthy insiders. For example, the founders of Google, Sergey Brin and Larry Page, have (some would say) made our lives easier and more productive. Thus they *deserve* to enjoy a very large share of society's wealth (Williams 2013). Confiscating their just rewards in the name of equality or income redistribution would be "unfair."

On the other side of the equation lies the massive population of poor outsiders. By the same logic, the poor should be held responsible for their circumstances. However, as we will see throughout this book, poverty is, at least in part, the result of structured, systemic inequality (Eells 1987), and as such beyond the control of the individual, however ambitious or motivated (Cozzarelli 2001).

Many people—in fact most—would disagree with that assertion. In the United States, only 30% of voters endorse the view that poverty is due to bad luck (Zilinsky 2014). Similarly, a report issued by the Salvation Army indicated that 43% of Canadians believe that "a good work ethic is all you need to escape poverty," while 23% claim the poor are poor because they are lazy (Proudfoot 2011). From this perspective, economic inequality is far from unfair; rather, it is a product of indolence and a lack of the so-called **Protestant work ethic** (Cozzarelli 2001). The opportunity to get ahead (it is argued) is open to all, and those people who have prospered are simply those who have seized that opportunity. The poor deserve to remain poor because they have not chosen to change their situation.

Sometimes, even the poor themselves believe in notions like the American Dream. They accept other people's indictments of their own laziness, irresponsibility, and general inferiority (Fave 1980, Melamed 2012).

What people consider "fair" reflects the norms of their society. People with authority and influence work hard to legitimate the status quo and the inequality it supports (Melamed 2012). Even your peer group—friends, family members, teachers, and other personal acquaintances—influences your perception of inequality. Their endorsements of inequality, and the narratives

14

they use to justify it, can be powerful enough to override your personal, intuitive beliefs about what is "fair" and what is not.

Narratives that frame inequality as logical, inevitable, or socially useful, whatever their intended purpose, perpetuate the current, unfair state of affairs. On some level, we all know this. Why, then, do we cooperate in elaborate victim-blaming narratives that *justify* an objectively unfair reality, where the privileged few flourish at the expense of the majority? Part of the answer lies in our resistance to change and comfort with the **status quo.**

STRATIFICATION

Perhaps the most popular way of explaining inequality is in terms of functionality. Social inequality is universal: there is no known society that distributes money, power, and prestige equally among all of its members. Is that because inequality actually benefits society as a whole? In an attempt to answer these questions, sociologists Kingsley Davis and Wilbert Moore (1945) developed the **functional theory of stratification.**

This theory holds that certain jobs are more valuable than others. Without doctors, for example, a society's level of health and well-being would rapidly decline. By contrast, we wouldn't care as much if, tomorrow, every nail salon disappeared, because we wouldn't be harmed as much. Not every job is equally valuable to society, and doctors are generally viewed as more valuable than manicurists (Tumin 1953, Cullen and Novick 1979).

But (the functionalist argument runs) there is a scarcity of people suitable for important, demanding positions and willing to take them on. First, only a select few individuals have the necessary skills to perform these jobs successfully (Tumin 1953). Doctors, for instance, need to be smart and driven enough to make it through medical school, and then to maintain adequate standards of practice in a complex, rapidly changing field. Second, from this already small pool of suitable candidates, only a few are willing to become doctors. Long, irregular hours, emotionally draining patients, and huge responsibilities make the profession unappealing to many.

Third, to become a doctor, candidates have to make sacrifices: they receive little if any income while they are in school and training, yet need to find a way to pay for their education (Tumin 1953). Many would-be doctors also put off marriage and a family until they have graduated because of the high demands that medical school places on their time and energy.

To compensate for these deterrents, the functional theory of stratification suggests that society must offer people enticing rewards—a high income and elevated social status—to take on these difficult but important jobs. Davis and Moore argue that the functional importance of a social role will be defined by the dominant values in a society; but whatever those dominant values, incentives of wealth and prestige will be needed to attract the best candidates.

The same reasoning applies to jobs considered undesirable. For example, professional escorts often face social ostracism and stigmatization. To entice people to perform this type of work, they must be offered significant financial rewards. (As we will explore in a later chapter, Kingsley Davis also proposed that prostitution, like medicine, is functionally necessary to society, thus explaining its universality and longevity.)

The Davis-Moore theory of stratification tries to explain *why* people willingly accept greater sacrifices and responsibility but leaves many questions unanswered. First, there are practical problems in testing this theory. For example, how do we go about quantifying things like "hard work," "effort," or "ambition" (Roemer 2003)? Can we be sure that Zoe worked harder than Tim, making her "deserving" of a higher salary? Should we base our comparison of these two workers on the hours they put in? Their enthusiasm? Their efficiency or productivity? What if they work in completely different fields? Although the jobs that require the most education and earn the highest salaries enjoy the greatest prestige, that does not necessarily mean the people holding these positions are the hardest working.

A second flaw in the Davis-Moore theory is that certain jobs are highly rewarded because they have been deemed socially valuable, not because they are necessary to society's survival (Cullen and Novick 1979). Certain highly rewarded positions, such as elite athletes, movie stars, and celebrities, are hardly "essential." On the other hand, sanitation workers *are* highly necessary for our survival, but earn little compared to doctors, athletes, and movie stars. Clearly income and prestige are not allocated *only* according to the functional importance of a given job. Rather, they are allocated according to how valuable people *think* a position is, and the mass media, politicians, and professional associations manipulate our perceptions of value. As a result, the functional theory of social stratification does not account for our (sometimes irrational) privileging of certain positions over others.

Take the example of doctors, once again. There is a significant body of literature that suggests the most significant gains in life expectancy and well-being in the 20th century are due not to doctors or modern medicine but to proper sanitation, waste disposal, advanced methods of food handling, and so on. The same factors are responsible for enormous reductions in infant mortality. So, in fairness, we should be paying engineers and public health planners far more than we pay doctors. Functionalists should be arguing that it is garbage collectors and sewage system workers who deserve the high pay, not doctors.

The reason doctors and other highly paid professionals are paid so well is not because they're uniquely or supremely essential to society but because they're part of the elite that controls society and sets its own wages (on this, read about the historic professionalization of medicine as a strategy for ensuring the upward mobility of doctors; Larson 1977, Starr 1983). That is not to disparage medical doctors, but rather to put them in a proper social context.

In fact, few jobs are inherently and universally more valuable than others. Our opinions on what constitutes valuable work change over time and depend on social context (Cullen and Novick 1979). As a result, the demand for those positions changes too. When countries go to war, we value the military more, and people who work for or in the armed forces come to enjoy greater rewards under such circumstances (Abrahamson 1973). Conversely, as Western society has secularized, the demand for ministers of religion has sharply declined, leading to lower pay and job prestige, and fewer job candidates.

Then there are the people who lack any appreciable skills and make no important contribution to society, yet still enjoy high rewards. When people inherit their wealth, they have no incentive to fill one of the socially important positions we have described, yet are well-off nonetheless (Lasswell 1969). To be sure, some children born into wealthy families do become doctors, lawyers, bankers, and the like, but they need not make the same personal sacrifices to attain these positions as do children from poorer families. Functionalist theory would suggest that, not having made those sacrifices, these well-off individuals do not "deserve" to be rewarded highly when they complete their training.

This, however, is not how the world works. Nor do professionals hailing from lower-class origins earn more in order to compensate them for the extraordinary sacrifices they may have made to get through school while scrimping, saving, and working part-time jobs to make ends meet (Roemer 2003).

A fourth problem with the functionalist theory of social stratification is that the people at the top usually exert a great deal of influence over the allocation of rewards. Once people secure highly demanded, highly rewarded positions, the prestige, respect, and power they gain help them maintain or even increase these benefits. The fact that people in power monopolize wealth and authority undermines the notion that society operates as a free market in talent.

On the contrary, rigid class hierarchies bolster and reinforce the (generally untested) notion that there is only a limited amount of talent in a given society suitable for highly skilled occupations. If children from poor families are discouraged from seeking higher education, there is little chance we will uncover and cultivate their talents. For example, if a waiter can never save up enough money to go to university, we will never discover that he has the intelligence and dedication needed to become an engineer.

Systems of stratification that are stable and functioning smoothly—like our own—have built-in barriers that prevent certain members from exploring and discovering their own talents. Even now, when post-secondary education is much more accessible than it was fifty years ago, young people's likelihood of attending college or university still largely depends on their parents' income or the availability of well-paying part-time jobs. Thus, well-to-do children indirectly "inherit" their social class: wealthy parents provide them with the education and social connections they need for academic and (in turn) occupational success. That's why already-rich people are more likely than anyone else to wind up in the most highly rewarded positions.

This so-called **inheritance effect** negatively affects society as a whole: it excludes a huge fraction of the population from competing for the most important, challenging positions. As a result, the people who end up filling them are not necessarily the most suitable candidates (Joseph 1980). If barriers to equal opportunity are substantial enough, we may even wind up with a shortage of qualified, capable candidates to fill these important jobs, and our societal efficiency and productivity suffers.

Even in cases for which the Davis-Moore model seems to hold true (such as doctors) the enticing rewards we offer these professionals are likely excessive. Social stratification has produced a huge pay gap between the most and least rewarded members of society. True, we may need to pay brain surgeons more than manicurists to persuade them to complete the lengthy and difficult training involved, but perhaps we have overdone it. Why do lawyers, for example, make *so much* more money than their assistants? Given the respect and prestige that lawyers enjoy, wouldn't people still be eager to become lawyers even if they were paid only somewhat more than average?

More broadly speaking, the Davis-Moore model holds that highly educated professionals are paid more so as to compensate them for the time and money invested in their education and training. But since they are paid so much more, they quickly make up for what they lost—say, within five years of entering the workforce. This would suggest such people should be paid more—but only moderately more—than those who don't make similar investments in education and training.

The reason for the discrepancy lies, at least in part, in the fact that our expectations are based on our prior experiences. Because we have never known anything different—we have all grown up expecting to make a certain amount of money if we hold one job, another amount if we hold another—most people think that our system of stratification is logical and fair. However, our current system of rewards is only one way of organizing people into different social positions. It has not been proven to be the *only* or even the most effective way to organize society. We go along with it because it seems "normal" and logical to us, but other motivational systems are possible.

For example, consider that some people take genuine pleasure in their work, regardless of what it pays (Arneson 2013). Others feel they have an obligation to be "useful" by providing help—regardless of what they are paid—to other members of their community. Otherwise they do not feel challenged or fulfilled.

This is especially true of many jobs that are well-paid and in high demand by society. Many doctors, lawyers, university professors, and veterinarians (to name but a few) do what they do because they enjoy challenging themselves and feeling that they are making a valuable contribution. Others accept jobs that pay less than seems warranted by their importance to society or the amount of training required. Teachers, for instance, have accepted the burden of educating the next generation. Their relatively low wages hardly reflect their years of education or hefty responsibilities; many are, instead, motivated by their genuine love of teaching.

Ultimately then, high pay and prestige are not the only variables that entice people to perform valuable work. Contrary to the functional theory of stratification, there is a poor fit between what people are paid, the personal sacrifices they have made, and the value of their contributions to society.

EQUALITY OF OPPORTUNITY

The debate surrounding equality is not simply about whether inequality should exist or not. Rather, it hinges on *which types* of inequalities are just or unjust; *what degree* of inequality is necessary or desirable; and *how much* equality we can reasonably hope to attain.

Equality of opportunity is one of the types of equality that many people have in mind when they talk about a "fair society." People who think that some degree of social inequality is necessary and inevitable are unlikely to propose complete equality as a social goal. Instead, they are more likely to propose that we reduce the gap between the richest and poorest members of society, and that we pursue equality of opportunity rather than **equality of condition** (that is, completely equal rewards for everyone). Equality of opportunity means that your original place in the social hierarchy—your starting point at birth—should not prevent you from attaining a different, better social status in adulthood. In other words, equality of opportunity is meant to reduce the unfair advantage that often accompanies being born into a wealthy family (Moellendorf 2006).

More broadly, equality of opportunity is also taken to mean that people should be able to attain rewards that reflect their natural abilities and personal achievements (Richards 1997). Rewards, in this kind of system, will not be based on other, arbitrary variables, like race, sex, religion, sexual orientation, or social class at birth (Roemer 2002, 2003). Everyone striving for a given goal should have a chance of attaining it that is commensurate with their talents and abilities (Sachs 2012).

In a hypothetical or imaginary society with equality of opportunity, people move easily and quickly through social-class positions according to their ability and effort. They will have access to a similar set of resources, including educational opportunities, health care, housing, and so on.

Obviously, we are far from such a situation in our own society. In Canada today, people tend to stay in the same class for their entire lives. Often, they remain in the same class as their parents, and their parents before them. This has led researchers to coin the term **occupational inheritance**. "Inheritance" is an especially apt word to describe the process by which wealth, property, class position, and social status are transferred by the wealthiest members of society to their children (Sachs 2012). But it also describes the way poor parents often pass poverty, hardship, and lack of opportunity onto the next generation. Occupational inheritance reduces social mobility, whose extent varies over time and from one society to another.

Typically, people in the lowest and highest classes are the least mobile and most likely to inherit their parent's class. By contrast, people in the middle class are the most mobile, more or less equally upward and downward.

Whatever the society, most upward mobility is **structural**: it occurs because the higher (i.e., non-manual, white-collar) classes increase in size. Economic growth generates more high-paying jobs, providing more people with the opportunity to move up the income ladder. In contrast, little social mobility in any society occurs because of **exchange mobility**, or the displacement of the wealthy. To some degree, societies vary in their amount of intergenerational mobility depending on the degree to which wealth is redistributed through progressive taxation and social programs. But the main determinant of social mobility is the creation (and destruction) of good jobs.

That said, even structural expansion disproportionately benefits the highest income groups, offering only moderately more upward mobility for middle-income people, and very slightly increased opportunities for those with low incomes. Conversely, structural shrinkage results in more downward mobility for middle- and low-income people, and a less significant decline in opportunities for already prosperous people with high incomes.

Ultimately, the poor inherit poverty under all conditions, but especially when the economy is shedding well-paying, "good" jobs. Increased upward social mobility through structural expansion does *not* ensure social fairness or equality—only more fluidity in the middle. Under all conditions, we see class "stickiness" at either end of the income distribution—both top and bottom— with rich people and poor people following in their parents' footsteps.

Indeed, some have speculated there is *less* opportunity for upward mobility in contemporary Canada and the United States than was once the case. To find out, Chetty et al. (2014) carried out an analysis of U.S. administrative earnings records. They found that percentile-rank-based measures of intergenerational mobility remained extremely stable for the 1971–1993 birth cohorts. Said another way, children entering the labor market today have the same chances of moving up in the income distribution (relative to their parents) as children born in the 1970s.

However, the study also found that income classes are further apart than they once were. In other words, income inequality has increased since the 1970s, meaning that people have to work harder to move upward from one class to the next. Chetty et al. invite us to envision income distribution as a

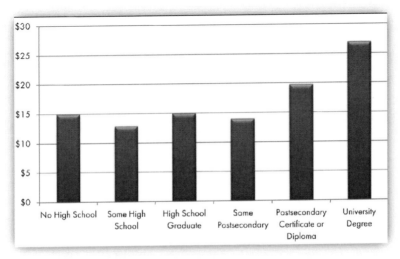

Figure 1.3: Median Hourly Wage by Educational Attainment, Nova Scotia, 2014

ladder. Though children's chances of climbing from a lower to a higher rung have not changed in the past thirty years, the rungs of the ladder have grown further apart. As a result, it is even harder for poor children to scale the ladder today than it was thirty years ago.

As we have seen, many think people should be held responsible for what happens to them. In order to maintain personal accountability yet mitigate the harsh effects of inequality, some researchers have suggested that we strive to make failure tolerable. If people fail to move up the class hierarchy—or even if they slide down it—the consequences should not be psychologically, socially, or financially devastating. We could accomplish this by reducing the distance between the poorest and wealthiest members of society, so that even the least successful people can still enjoy a decent standard of living (Wrong 1959).

This suggestion remains unpopular, especially in Western democracies where people are more willing to address equality of opportunity than equality of condition (Richards 1997). And even certain aspects of equality of opportunity have been left open for debate. The least controversial aspect involves the job application process (Arneson 2013). Most people would agree that everyone should be allowed to apply for good jobs and that positions should go to the most qualified applicant (Sachs 2012). This is called **formal equality of opportunity** (Joseph 1980).

A less widely agreed-on principle is **compensatory equality of opportunity** (Joseph 1980). It holds that everyone should be given an equal

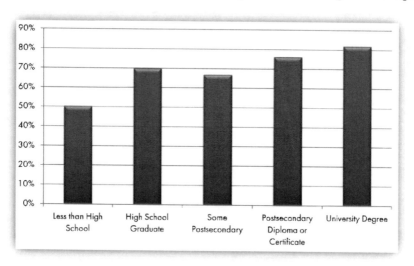

Figure 1.4: Employment Rate by Education Level, Nova Scotia, 2014 (ages 25 to 64)

opportunity to acquire the qualifications and skills that make for a successful application (Arneson 2013, Sachs 2012). In that case, the differences in people's performances will reflect true variations in talent, intelligence, and ambition.

The problem with compensatory equality of opportunity is implementing it effectively. How, exactly, do we compensate people for the disadvantage of being born into a poor family? How do we give everyone a truly "fair," "equal" chance to cultivate their natural skills and talents? And how do we genuinely level the playing field for the job application process, so that class-related factors don't intrude?

Instituting some form of equal opportunity would be a long, complicated process, fraught with confusion and accusations. Because opportunities have been unequal for so long, most marginalized groups remain at a disadvantage. Employment equity has helped to level the playing field, but employers are sometimes forced to decide between hiring a less qualified, less experienced person, or being accused of discrimination. Even a genuine attempt to equalize opportunities may perpetuate the status quo, since if candidates are selected on the basis of their superior performance, traditionally dominant groups will continue to prevail. They will have achieved preference through their unfair advantage, and then passed those same advantages on to their offspring (Arneson 2013).

Given equal opportunity, your family cannot *guarantee* you admission to a better university or employment at a prestigious company. However, advantaged families are better at identifying children's personal strengths, teaching them how to put those strengths to good use, and socializing them to become attractive job candidates.

Thus children raised in different families will enjoy different prospects for success. The efforts of a naturally intelligent, highly motivated young person may be obstructed by lower family income, while a less gifted, less motivated youth from a wealthy family slides effortlessly through a succession of private schools and educational enrichment opportunities (Richards 1997). Without abolishing the nuclear family and implementing some kind of collective, state-regulated institution for raising children, it is impossible to ensure that every child gets the same start in life. As a society, we can try to encourage healthy, productive parenting strategies, but we cannot impose a universal standard of parenting that would guarantee equal life chances for all youth.

For these reasons, absolute equality of opportunity, whether formal or compensatory, is impossible. We cannot even identify and measure, let alone control, all of the variables that advantage one individual while disadvantaging another. However, neither type of equal opportunity needs to be rigidly implemented. Rather, equal opportunity is a moral principle that should guide social planning in a progressive, egalitarian society. Despite impediments, we should work to reduce the *degree* of unnecessary or excess inequality, even if we cannot eliminate inequality altogether.

THE JUST WORLD HYPOTHESIS

Unfortunately, widely held, popular ways of thinking about inequality are likely to get in the way of this goal. Consider the problem of "just world beliefs," first discussed in ground-breaking research by Melvin J. Lerner in the 1960s. In one experiment, a student was selected at random to win a cash prize. After the award was announced, participants in the experiment were asked to explain why that particular person had won. A majority said the winner must have been an especially hard worker. That's what we are taught to say about winners in our society, even if it is really untrue (Rubin and Peplau 1975). We are also taught to blame people for their losses.

For example, when a student brought her experience of sexual assault to the attention of one university's dean of student affairs, she was told: "You are in part responsible for what happened to you because you put yourself in a compromising situation. . . . Actions have consequences" (Niemi and Young 2014). Blaming the victim is part of our learned cultural repertoire.

Though unrelated, both of these cases illustrate the **just world hypothesis**, which holds that people causally link virtue and reward, sin and punishment. In short, people get what they deserve—or so we like to think (Rubin and Peplau 1975, Niemi and Young 2014). As a consequence, people are likely to characterize the disadvantaged as "losers," and deservedly so. Such perceptions translate into social policies that justify continued oppression of these groups, or, at best, indifference to their plight (Bénabou and Tirole 2006).

In research that tested the just world hypothesis between the 1960s and 1980s, Lerner and others concluded that people *need* to believe the world is just. This belief helps them view the world as benign, or at least orderly and controllable.

Consider your own situation. You have decided to invest your time, effort, and money in a university education, in the hopes of eventually securing a stable, well-paying job. Your conviction that you will land that job follows from your belief that the world is a just, fair place, where investment and effort will pay off (Hafer and Bègue 2005).

Investment in a university education or other long-term goals is what Lerner referred to as a **personal contract**. You agree to give up certain short-term rewards and instead work towards maximizing your rewards in the longer term. Sacrificing immediate gratification makes you feel entitled to future rewards. As a result, Lerner writes, "people develop a commitment to deserving their outcomes and to organizing their lives around principles of deservingness" (cited in Hafer and Bègue, 2005).

But what if the world is not as just as we hope? In that case, there is no point investing time, effort, and money for longer-term payoffs. With no guarantee hard work will pay off, the personal contract breaks down—alongside our hopes and goals—and that is a scary situation to be in. So, people *want* to maintain their personal contract and believe in a rewarding future. They want to believe in what Lerner calls an **"illusion of control"**: the belief they can control their outcomes by staying motivated and sticking by their personal contract. To maintain confidence in a just world, we twist our perceptions of reality to bear out what we need to believe. And so we blame victims, ignore the structural factors that affect inequality, and imagine causal links between good behaviour and reward (Bénabou and Tirole 2006, Trump 2013).

In turn, these perceptions influence how we behave toward others. People perceived to be blameless victims evoke sympathy and a desire to help. By contrast, people perceived to be responsible for their circumstances are likely to be dismissed, ignored, or criticized (Wilkins and Wenger 2014). Interestingly, people who generally believe the world is just are quick to move from feeling sympathy to casting blame on the victim. Because so many people think the poor are to blame for their own poverty, we see enormous resistance to redistributive taxation, social welfare programs, unemployment payments, and other policies designed to aid disadvantaged groups.

Belief in a just world readily translates into lack of support for victims of inequality. Nowhere in the economically developed world is this belief stronger, and resistance to taxes more marked, than in the United States. According to the World Value Survey, only 29% of Americans think the poor are trapped in poverty, despite their own best efforts to escape it, as compared with the 60% of Europeans who hold such a view. Americans are twice as likely as Europeans to believe rewards will naturally flow to hard-working people who deserve them (Bénabou and Tirole 2006).

Because the belief in a just world is stronger in the U.S. than elsewhere, and because wealth and poverty are thought to reflect individual merit, not structured opportunity (Cozzarelli 2001), the United States is more **laissez-faire** than most European societies. Many Americans oppose redistributive policies and government intervention in general; in turn, the U.S. has one of the most dramatic gaps between the extraordinarily rich and the devastatingly poor of any economically developed country. Other developed societies, lacking this intense belief in a just world, impose higher tax rates and enact more generous social policies, and therefore take better care of the poor (Bénabou and Tirole, 2006).

Besides influencing social policy, the just world belief also shapes our perceptions of authority. In a world where people get exactly what they deserve, there is no reason to question the ruling class. Believers in a just world tend to respect the powerful insiders who dominate society through the institutions they lead, and sometimes even venerate them as inspirational do-gooders. Power and prestige are signs of merit, markers of hard work and perseverance.

People who believe in a just world are unlikely to support social activism as a means of bringing about societal change. They tolerate the status quo, and sometimes even praise it, because they think it is just, fair, and deserved. Societies dominated by such views tend to perpetuate social inequality (Rubin and Peplau 1975).

FINAL THOUGHTS

We have spent a good deal of time discussing people's thoughts and beliefs in this chapter because people are motivated by those thoughts and beliefs—by what they see and how they interpret (or ignore) it. Before delving into the particularities of any one type of social inequality, it is important to clarify how we think about "fairness," "justice," and "deservingness," and why we think that way. Particularly important is the fact that so many people resist thinking about social inequality at all, ignoring, distorting, or misunderstanding evidence that may contradict their beliefs. As Haraway reminds us, our values, beliefs, and psychological needs often cloud our vision, leading us to ignore inconvenient facts about inequality, protect an unfair status quo, and blame its victims. In the coming chapters, we will aim to arrive at a more accurate and reliable understanding of inequality by evaluating the competing viewpoints of those who endorse, question, and challenge it.

DISCUSSION QUESTIONS

1. Think of a time you used just world beliefs to rationalize something unfair that happened to you or a friend. Is there a different way you can account for what happened?
2. Have you, or someone you know, occupied the "outsider within" position? In what ways?
3. Do you think the functional theory of stratification adequately explains how our society is organized? Is there a better way we could motivate people to perform necessary, valuable work?
4. Think of three places where you could meet people who attempt to justify inequality. Where would these people be, how would they discuss inequality, and why might they talk about it in that way?
5. Can you think of a society, anywhere in the world, where meritocratic values are not the norm? What values do people in that society prioritize instead?
6. How might we break the cycle of poverty, other than by encouraging poor people to obtain a higher education?
7. Do you think you have an objective perspective on some social issues or aspects of your life? What topics do you think you're more likely to have a subjective perspective on?

FURTHER READING

Thomas Piketty. *Capital in the Twenty-First Century*. Harvard University Press, 2013.
F. Scott Fitzgerald. *The Great Gatsby*. Scribner, 1925.
Philippe Bourgois. *In Search of Respect: Selling Crack in El Barrio*. Cambridge University Press, 2010.

KEY TERMS

Affirmative action. Government policies that seek to increase the number of disadvantaged minorities in work positions through preference in hiring.

American Dream. The belief that as long as people work hard, they will succeed. Also known as a MERITOCRATIC VIEW.

Class consciousness. Awareness of one's social or economic class in society.

Double jeopardy theory. The more inequalities a person is subject to, the more disadvantages they will experience. Related to INTERSECTIONALITY.

Essentialism. Belief that groups have characteristics making them fundamentally different from one another.

Equality of condition. Condition under which everyone receives equal rewards.

Equality of opportunity. Condition under which the class you are born into does not prevent you from attaining a better social status.

Equality of opportunity (compensatory). Condition under which everyone has opportunity to acquire the necessary qualifications for a successful job application.

Equality of opportunity (formal). Condition under which everyone is allowed to apply for a job, and the position will go to the most qualified candidate.

Functional theory of stratification. A theory that some jobs are more valuable than others, because they take more time and sacrifice. As such, these jobs deserve their high levels of pay and prestige.

Hegemonic (as in hegemonic narratives). Socially dominant (narratives).

Illusion of control. Belief that if you stick to your goals, you will eventually achieve your desired outcome.

Inheritance effect. Tendency for adults to remain in the social class into which they were born as children.

Intersectionality. Overlap of different types of inequality.

Insider perspective. Tendency to favour and justify the status quo, usually held by people who benefit most from the status quo.

Just world hypothesis. Belief that virtuous and worthy people are rewarded, while less virtuous and worthy people are not.

Laissez-faire. Belief that the economy works best without government intervention.

Life chances. A person's probability of attaining desired rewards in life (including wealth, prestige, and authority).

Natural differences. Fundamental, biological differences between people, such as women's ability to bear children and men's inability to do so.

Objectivity. A process of reasoning that analyzes something without bias.

Omniscience. To have complete or unlimited knowledge.

Meritocratic view. The belief that if you work hard enough, you will succeed; equally, that people who get ahead deserve to get ahead. See AMERICAN DREAM.

Personal contract. Agreement with oneself to sacrifice short-term pleasures in order to work harder towards long-term goals.

Protestant work ethic. A religious commitment to leading a sober, thrifty, and hard-working life.

Relativism. Proposition that all points of view are valid, and none is better than any other.

Situated knowledge(s). Knowledge that grows out of first-hand experience in a certain social situation.

Social construction. The view that people make up or construct our understanding of reality. For example, the view that women are naturally better caregivers than men is a social construction.

Social inequality. The hierarchical organization of a society, with certain groups privileged over others.

Status quo. The current organization of society, with particular respect to the organization of power and privilege.

Strict egalitarianism. Belief that any social inequality is unfair and undesirable.

Subjectivity. To observe and analyze something in a biased, non-objective way.

Third World woman. An example of an oversimplified stereotype. Third World women are often seen as poor women with many children, who live in patriarchal societies far away from North America.

Victim blaming. The tendency to see a person as the cause of their own misfortunes, without considering how social circumstances might cause these problems.

CHAPTER TWO

Class Inequalities

LEARNING OBJECTIVES

In this chapter, you will:
1. Learn how to define and measure class inequalities
2. Consider the causes and consequences of victim-blaming
3. Examine risk factors for and responses to homelessness
4. Explore the link between higher education and upward social mobility
5. Weigh the pros and cons of outsourcing and precarious labour
6. Understand class status as a performance

INTRODUCTION

Vietnamese biology student Anh Cao made front-page news when he graduated from the University of Toronto in June 2015 at the top of his class. He had just been awarded the prestigious John Black Aird prize as top student, in addition to a silver medal from the Governor-General recognizing his exceptional academic performance (Campbell 2015). But newspapers like the *Toronto Star* were featuring Cao because he had slipped in and out of homelessness throughout his time in university.

Although he won several generous scholarships from both the Vietnamese government and the university, amounting to over $120,000 in total, and also worked while in school, Cao couldn't even come close to paying for tuition and living expenses. Having come from a family which earned only $500 a month, Cao found international student fees of $33,000 a year simply unaffordable. So, after arriving in Canada, he had slept in homeless shelters or at friends' houses, relying on his friends and their parents for food.

According to *Toronto Star* reporter Louise Brown (2015), Cao's ability to "overcome economic odds . . . speaks to his grit" and "to Canadian kindness." She continues:

Some of Anh Cao's hurdles were his own fault. If he hadn't grown so keen in first year to become a researcher in [a professor's] lab, he wouldn't have decided to take two summer courses to speed up his qualifications, and wouldn't have raided the fall installment of his scholarship to pay for them. So he most certainly would not have had to Google "homeless shelter for students in Scarborough" at the start of second year.

In this chapter, we will consider some of the flaws with victim-blaming narratives like Brown's. We will also examine our tendency to praise people like Cao for their "grit," rather than criticizing the circumstances that force people to exhibit such determination in the first place.

INSIDER VIEWS

People on the "inside"—middle- and upper-class people with secure incomes—often underestimate the significance and complexity of class inequality. They suggest that we can easily organize people into lower, middle, and upper classes based on income (Hardaway and McLoyd 2009). Popular magazines like *Maclean's* assert that "All of us equate certain earning levels with being rich, middle-class or just scraping by" (Hodges and Brown 2015). In practice, however, measuring class inequalities is a challenging task made all the more complicated by the fact that poverty, wealth, and income are each distinct (although related) concepts.

Table 2.1: Low Income Cutoff (LICO) Levels, 2016

Size of Family Unit	Minimum Necessary Income
One person (the sponsor)	$24,328
Two persons	$30,286
Three persons	$37,234
Four persons	$45,206
Five persons	$51,272
Six persons	$57,826
Seven persons	$64,381
If more than seven persons, for each additional person add:	$6,555 per person

In Canada, poverty is most often measured using the **low-income cutoff (LICO)** (Kazemipur 2002). This metric identifies people in substantially worse-than-average financial circumstances, showing which segment of the population falls below an income threshold based on the average percentage of pre-tax income that Canadian families spend on daily necessities, such as food, clothing, and housing. Using the LICO, we can determine the income at which a family will struggle financially because it is devoting a disproportionate fraction of its income to those essentials (Forouzin 2010). LICO cutoff points vary, depending on a family's size and where it resides. In general, however, a family is considered poor if it spends more than 64 percent of its household income on basic necessities (Kaida 2014). As you can see from Table 2.1, in 2016, the LICO in Canada was $24,328 for a single individual, and rose according to the number of individuals in a family.

In societies with extreme class inequality, many people fall near or below the LICO, while a privileged few enjoy extreme wealth. This is true of Western liberal democracies today, where the rich have become richer and the poor much poorer (Himelfarb 2014). Often, this top "1 percent" enjoys such a high standard of living because they control a sizeable share of the entire nation's wealth. For example, the American Walton family, which controls Walmart, is worth as much as the poorest 42 percent of all Americans combined (Bittman 2014).

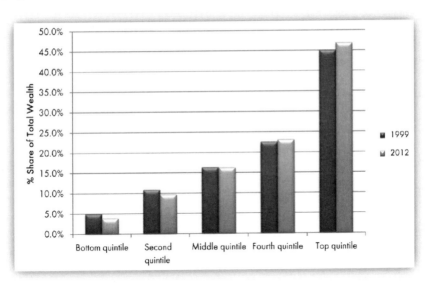

Figure 2.1: Percentage of Total Canadian Household Wealth Held by Each Income Group in 1999 and 2012

The situation in Canada is similar, though less extreme. In 2012, the wealthiest 86 Canadians had the same net worth as the poorest 11.4 million (Macdonald 2014). What's more, the wealth gap between the rich and poor continues to widen in Canada (Fong 2000). Between 2005 and 2012, the net worth of the top 10% of Canadians grew by 42%, while that of our bottom 10% declined by 150% (Flavelle 2014). As we will see, these trends are due, in large part, to a widespread adoption of neo-liberal capitalist values, including deregulation, low tax rates, and anti-unionism (Bittman 2014).

In recent years, scholars have debated the relative merits of discussing income inequality versus wealth inequality. While space does not permit a detailed treatment of this discussion, we at least need to distinguish between the two. Poverty, discussed above, is the condition of an insufficient income. People drift in and out of poverty, as their income rises above and falls below the LICO amount. People who are not in poverty also tend to evaluate their economic well-being in terms of their income. They view a high income as the key to comfort and prosperity—also, as an indication of social worth. However, a high income is often insecure, so income alone cannot be the basis of power or class position.

Rather, at the basis of power and class position we find wealth. The most powerful people in a society tend to be the wealthiest people, not necessarily the people with the highest income in a given year. By wealth, we mean all the accumulated property and financial assets that belong to a family or individual. This will include the ownership of homes, real estate, stocks and bonds, savings, and physical property such as cars, jewelry, furniture, and the like. If we look at the range of wealth in our society, we will find that it is even more extreme than the range of incomes.

Obviously, the two—income and wealth—are related. Wealth comes from income: income that is produced, earned, accumulated, invested, and protected. Anyone who has ever played the game of Monopoly knows that money invested (in property or otherwise) tends to grow through "rents," and, as a result, inequalities between players tend to widen. Our economy produces wealth, and our state protects investments and private property. The redistribution of wealth through taxation on incomes, investments, and inheritances is slight, with the result that, in Canada, poor people continue being poor, middle class people continue earning middle class incomes, and wealthy people get wealthier.

Indeed, economic historian Thomas Piketty in his book *Capital in the Twenty-First Century* (2013) emphasizes the fact that in the Western world today, wealth inequality is greater than at any time in the last hundred years. Two world wars, a Great Depression, and the rise of welfare states throughout the industrial world interrupted roughly two centuries' worth of extreme and growing wealth inequality. In the last 40 years, since roughly 1975, with globalization and market deregulation throughout the world, wealth has reasserted itself and inequalities of wealth have regained their historically high levels.

Above: Walmart, the world's largest retailer, has in recent years become the target of protests (like this one led by "Reverend Billy" Talens in Valejo, California) because of its low wages and the effects its stores have had on local stores and communities. (Brave New Films)

Below: Convocation at the University of the Fraser Valley, Abbotsford, B.C. The massification of higher education has led to social congestion. (Rick Collins/UFV)

It is important to understand that inequalities in wealth are different from those based on income. Though the Waltons are the richest family in North America, they do not earn an income, salary, or wages for hours of labour worked. Rather, their high standard of living is made possible by the wealth they inherit from a majority stake in Walmart. Other, more modestly wealthy Canadians enjoy similar advantages through property ownership or the stock market, both of which allow the already well-off to capitalize on different types of investments. By contrast, even the highest-earning professionals (such as lawyers or architects) will need to work for years to pay off their student debts, mortgage, and cover other expenses if they were not born into families that possessed some amount of wealth.

Despite their high incomes, these individuals will not be able to sustain as high a standard of living, and their children will not "inherit" their middle- or high-income status without pursuing financially lucrative careers of their own. Thus, wealth inequalities preserve the class structure by ensuring that wealthy families maintain control over sizeable sums of wealth and power. By contrast, income inequalities merely segment the working population into status groups with different earning levels and lifestyles, based on different types of work.

Table 2.2: Canada's Wealthiest Individuals

Name and Business Type	Net Worth	World Rank
David Thomson and family, media	$23.9 billion	25
Galen Weston, food processing and retail	$9.3 billion	116
Garrett Camp, online services (Uber)	$6.2 billion	188
James Irving, conglomerate	$5.4 billion	240
Bernard (Barry) Sherman, pharmaceuticals	$4.9 billion	286
Arthur Irving, Irving Oil, gasoline	$4.7 billion	308
Jim Pattison, conglomerate	$4.5 billion	324
Emanuele (Lino) Saputo, dairy products	$4.4 billion	338
Joseph Tsai, e-commerce	$4.2 billion	358
Mark Scheinberg, online gambling	$4.1 billion	369

So, contrary to the belief of many insiders, class inequality has to do with more than just the amount of money a person earns or even inherits (Hardaway and McLoyd 2009). It also involves the social status, reputation, and power that accompany wealth, and, conversely, the disadvantages, stereotypes, and lack of influence that often accompany poverty (Jereb and Ferjan

2008). Social classes are hierarchically ranked groups of persons who share a similar income and standard of living, as well as certain values, expectations, and behaviours.

Marx put forward the classic conception of social class in the mid-1800s (Jereb and Ferjan 2008). The highest ranking "capitalist class" consists of the owners of the means of production. They enjoy a substantially higher-than-average standard of living, as well as great power and authority. Making up most of the population is the "working class," who sell their labour power to the owners of the means of production in exchange for a wage. They enjoy a much lower standard of living, as well as less—indeed, little—power and authority. In between is a small "middle class" that Marx called the "petit bourgeoisie," but which today goes by different names and has grown dramatically. Managers, professionals, and small business owners comprise this middle class.

Since Marx's time, and largely because of modifications introduced by Max Weber, sociologists have segmented each of these three broad classes into subcategories, drawing such distinctions as manual vs. non-manual labour, qualified vs. unqualified workers, higher- vs. lower-grade professions, and skilled vs. unskilled labour (Jereb and Ferjan 2008). Today, some definitions of class also take education into account. Middle-class people, for example, are often assumed to hold university or college degrees (Hardaway and McLoyd 2009). The *type* of job a person holds, apart from its salary, is also important, with some occupations conveying higher socio-economic status than others.

The Face of Poverty

Poverty and inequality are different concepts, but in societies with the most class inequality, poor people are more common and their circumstances are often dire. In recent decades, poverty has become more prevalent and concentrated, hitting certain segments of the population much harder than others (Kazemipur 2002). In Canada and around the world, poverty is racialized and gendered: women, racial minorities, and immigrants are especially likely to be poor and disadvantaged (Fong 2003, Dooley 1994).

In particular, Canada's Aboriginal population runs a much higher risk of poverty than any other group (MacKinnon 2013). Unemployment rates for Aboriginals have averaged around 25 percent (Kendall 2001), more than three times as high as the overall population (Rexe 2007). Aboriginals are thus highly vulnerable to all the harmful consequences of urban poverty, including inadequate housing and poor physical and mental health (Brown 2005). Natives living in rural and remote areas are even worse off. Many Aboriginals move off reserves in the hope greater opportunities exist in the city. They are often sorely disappointed.

Poverty rates vary by region and from city to city, but even within the same city, the gap between the rich and poor can be immense (Kazemipur 2002). Prosperous people tend to segregate themselves from the poor, creating concentrated pockets of urban poverty (Fong 2000). The spatial separation of the poor is even more pronounced in Canada than in the U.S.

Table 2.3: Employment, Income and Aboriginality in Canada
AGE 15 AND UP

Employment Indicator	All Aboriginals	First Nations	Métis	Inuit	Status Indians	Non-Aboriginals
Participation Rate (Women and Men)	63.0%	58.8%	70.1%	61.3%	57.8%	66.9%
Participation Rate (Women)	59.1%	55.0%	66.2%	58.9%	53.9%	61.7%
Participation Rate (Men)	67.3%	63.2%	74.1%	63.9%	62.2%	72.5%
Employment Rate (Women and Men)	53.7%	48.2%	63.1%	48.9%	46.8%	62.7%
Employment Rate (Women)	51.1%	46.1%	60.0%	49.1%	44.8%	57.7%
Employment Rate (Men)	56.5%	50.7%	66.3%	48.6%	49.2%	68.0%
Unemployment Rate (Women and Men)	14.8%	18.0%	10.0%	20.3%	19.0%	6.3%
Unemployment Rate (Women)	13.5%	16.2%	9.5%	16.7%	17.0%	6.4%
Unemployment Rate (Men)	16.1%	19.8%	10.5%	23.8%	21.0%	6.2%
Median Income	All Aboriginals	First Nations	Métis	Inuit	Status Indians	Non-Aboriginals
Median Income (Men and Women)	$16,752	$14,477	$20,935	$16,969	$14,095	$25,955
Median Income (Women)	$15,564	$14,490	$17,520	$16,599	$14,337	$20,640
Median Income (Men)	$18,714	$14,458	$26,464	$17,245	$13,802	$32,639

Because racial minorities are overrepresented among the poor, racial segregation often correlates with class segregation (Hajnal 1995). The poorer the neighborhood, the higher the fraction of its population composed of visible minorities (Kazemipur 2000). Black Canadians experience the worst residential segregation, and they, along with other visible minorities, are much more likely to fall on the lower end of the Canadian socioeconomic ladder (Fong

2000). Poverty rates among black Canadians can exceed 40% in major Canadian cities like Montreal and Ottawa. More than two-fifths of black people in Halifax and Asians and blacks in Montreal live in areas with poverty rates topping 30%.

Insiders and outsiders agree that racial minorities are overrepresented among the poor. Where they disagree is in how they explain this fact. Many outsiders believe the system has denied them opportunities to get ahead. By contrast, insiders claim that all Canadians have equal opportunities to succeed, making impoverishment an indicator of an individual's poor choices or failure to work hard.

What these insider narratives fail to recognize are the broader social patterns that structure poverty. To suggest that racial minorities are intrinsically less motivated and hard-working than the white majority is both prejudicial and statistically dubious. There must be something about our society's structure that renders such people less capable of upward mobility.

Of these two explanations for the racialization of poverty—individual choice and structural barriers—insiders are most likely to endorse the first. But given that they also recognize the disproportionate burden of poverty borne by racial minorities, their victim-blaming narratives seem like strategies designed to help perpetuate the status quo. Only by legitimating racialized poverty can insiders justify their unwillingness to address it.

Insiders often attempt to minimize the damaging effects of poverty, too, perhaps to downplay their own role in contributing to this social problem. Lengthy spells of unemployment are often demoralizing, undercutting a person's belief that he will ever find work again. But unemployment is also costly for society as a whole; unemployed people pay little or nothing in taxes and over the longer term, high unemployment leads to higher crime rates. While outsiders persistently emphasize these society-wide consequences of unemployment, insiders frame it as a personal problem to be resolved by the individual alone.

Affordable Housing and Homelessness

One of the most extreme consequences of class inequality is homelessness. In Canada, any "individual or family without stable, permanent, appropriate housing or the immediate prospect, means and ability of acquiring it" is considered homeless (Gaetz et al. 2013). The risk of becoming homeless is not limited to a certain population; homelessness is periodic, widespread, and transitional for many Canadians.

First, at the extreme end of the spectrum, is what we might call **absolute homelessness**—those people reduced to living on the street (Gaetz et al. 2013). Second, some homeless people are able to secure occasional shelter in facilities designed to accommodate them. However, due to overcrowding, they are never able to settle in but must move from one shelter to the next, sleeping wherever they can find space. A third group of homeless people is **provisionally accommodated**, staying as long as they can with friends or relatives, or living in institutions such as hospitals or prisons, but lacking a permanent home of their own. A fourth group consists of people at risk of becoming members of the absolute homeless. Also known as the **relatively homeless**, these people experience unstable housing conditions and, as a result, health and safety concerns.

Many people slip in and out of these different states of homelessness, so we lack an accurate count of the total number of homeless people in Canada (Burns et al. 2011). Most homeless counts are based on the number of people in shelters on a given night, and do not take into account the absolute, provisionally accommodated, or relatively homeless (Richter et al. 2011). This means a large fraction of our homeless population remains "hidden" and uncounted.

Bearing such complications in mind, researchers estimate that at least 200,000 Canadians are either unsheltered or use emergency shelters over the course of a given year (Gaetz et al. 2013). On any single night, there may be 30,000 Canadians who are homeless but as many as 50,000 more who remain uncounted.

The homelessness crisis in Canada is largely due to cuts to affordable and social housing projects beginning in the 1990s. Few new subsidized housing units were built, and many existing ones were sold to private owners. In many cases, previously affordable rental units were converted into more expensive condominiums (Jones et al. 2012, Richter et al. 2011). At the same time, federal income support programs lost some or all of their funding (Leo and August 2006). One-third of homeless people report they became homeless because they could no longer afford their rent (Aubry et al. 2012).

Because social (as opposed to individual) factors have driven up homeless rates, the homeless population is far from demographically homogenous (Richter et al. 2011). Single males between the ages of 25 and 55 are the most numerous, making up 47.5% of the identified homeless population. Young people account for an increasing fraction of the homeless, at 20%. First Nations, Métis, and Inuit people are heavily overrepresented among the homeless (Gaetz et al. 2013). Newly arrived immigrants also make up a large fraction, at 23%. The most vulnerable of the homeless—those who suffer the most—include the young, women, the mentally ill, families, single parents, minorities, and seniors.

The mainstream media fail to capture this population's diversity, portraying the homeless as a homogeneous group composed only of drug and alcohol addicts and the mentally ill. This is not surprising, given that the media are controlled by insiders, who are most likely to endorse this stereotypical image of homeless people. In turn, a majority of Canadians have also adopted such negative views. A survey conducted by the Salvation Army (2011) revealed that over 60% of Canadians believe that homeless people who are given money use it to buy drugs or alcohol. A further 40% of Canadians believe that the homeless are usually mentally ill.

True, some homeless people suffer from diagnoses that range from schizophrenia to more manageable affective or mood disorders, just like the rest of the population (Roos et al. 2013); and some do indeed have addiction problems. Mental illness and addiction do not, however, necessarily cause homelessness, nor do they necessarily prevent a person from escaping it. The main cause of homelessness is poverty (Aubry et al. 2012) and poverty, not mental illness or addiction, is also the main obstacle to exiting homelessness.

New immigrants and those with precarious citizen status are especially vulnerable to homelessness because they are often ineligible for social assistance. Many insiders assume that immigrants struggle to find suitable housing only upon arrival in Canada, but research shows that affordable housing still poses a problem for 40% of immigrants who have lived in Canada for four years or longer. About 8% of immigrants make ends meet by combining multiple families under one roof; but this practice requires larger, more expensive housing, or causes dangerous overcrowding. In the end, most homelessness is caused by broad social structures rather than the personal variables of addiction and mental illness that insiders typically use to explain it.

Youth are among the fastest growing subgroups of the homeless (Coates and McKenzie-Mohr 2010). On average, homeless youth have already experienced seven stressful events in their short lives, including abuse, assault, neglect, bullying, or trouble with the law, the combination of which drive them to flee home. However, after becoming homeless, youth experience an average of 6.4 additional stressful events. Such sustained trauma makes them more likely to experience long-term homelessness (Roos et al. 2013).

One common misconception about homeless youth (and homeless people in general) is that they are too lazy to attend school or get a job. Another Salvation Army study (2012) revealed that almost half of all Canadians believe that "if poor people really want to work, they can always find a job." One-quarter said they thought poor people are poor because they are lazy.

Research confirms that most homeless young people—as many as 70% in some areas of Canada—do not currently attend school (Klodawsky et al. 2006). However, this is usually a consequence rather than a cause of homelessness. Many homeless youth *want* to return to school, and are eager to put their work experience in the food, retail, or service industries to use. However, due to lack of funding, most shelters and programs can only provide a fraction of homeless youth with temporary food and shelter. Most homeless young people report they are forced to set aside academic and career aspirations because they are preoccupied with more pressing concerns, such as where they will find their next meal. For the most part, they are unemployed school dropouts because they are homeless, not because they are lazy or without aspirations. Structural inequalities provide a more convincing explanation of homelessness than individual choice.

Efforts to alleviate homelessness are well intentioned but usually underfunded. Consider the National Homeless Initiative (NHI), introduced in 1999, and renamed the Homelessness Partnering Initiative (HPI) in 2007. Local governments and community organizations were allocated $135 million annually to address "the homelessness problem." Different cities used their funding in different ways, with varying success. In Vancouver, government officials and community actors worked together to set goals and allocate funding. Their Community Advisory Board (CAB)—a panel of experts on homelessness in the city—came to be widely recognized as fair, inclusive, and transparent (Doberstein 2012). Perhaps as a result, Vancouver has seen a 68% reduction in absolute homelessness since the program's implementation (Gaetz et al. 2013).

In Toronto, by contrast, although a CAB was also established, funding decisions were made by a small group of municipal employees. Community and advocacy groups were consulted in the early stages of planning, but excluded from the later decision-making processes. As a result, homelessness remains a confusing and mysterious issue to the general public throughout the Greater Toronto Area (Doberstein 2012). Our inability to gather accurate information about homelessness and share it with comfortably housed Torontonians has likely contributed to the ongoing popularity of the flawed insider perceptions of homelessness noted earlier.

In addition, the federal government has not given local authorities the flexibility to use HPI funding to address location-specific issues (Leo and August 2006). Consider the differences between Vancouver and Winnipeg. In Vancouver, available housing is too expensive and lower-income Canadians are unable to afford it. By implementing affordable housing projects, Vancouver has been able to start addressing high rates of absolute homelessness.

By contrast, housing in Winnipeg is affordable, but many families that own houses cannot afford to maintain them. As a result, many Winnipeg residents live in substandard housing, and are at risk of becoming homeless. Different solutions are required in Winnipeg than in Vancouver, but Winnipeg was not permitted to allocate funding appropriately, since the formal HPI definition of homelessness was too narrow: only programs and initiatives designed to alleviate absolute homelessness were funded (Leo and August 2006).

This narrow definition of homelessness led many communities to allocate their funding towards programs that provide temporary shelter, food, and social services. However, none of these ameliorative programs help homeless people achieve long-term housing stability and security. In a sense, such programs institutionalize homelessness, which comes to be understood as an inevitable, permanent condition. Unlike affordable housing projects, which provide a lasting solution, ameliorative programs do not protect lower-income people from falling into poverty and homelessness: they only help the already homeless to cope.

Victim Blaming and the Culture of Poverty

Although programs like the HPI have enjoyed some success, we have a long way to go before all Canadians have access to safe, affordable housing. In large part, this is because there are no concrete plans to alleviate poverty or address income inequality, the primary causes of homelessness. We have yet to develop such plans because many do not view class inequality as an injustice or as a social problem in need of correction (Robertson 2012).

To repeat, homeless people are often said to deserve their fate (Belcher and Deforge 2012), while the insiders who make such pronouncements rationalize their own privilege by claiming their hard work justifies their wealth (Robertson 2012). Millionaire Steve Siebold endorses this perspective, writing: "While the masses are waiting to pick the right numbers and praying for prosperity, the great ones are solving problems." Such reasoning allows the well-off to view class inequality as acceptable or even just, rendering political action to reduce inequality unnecessary and wasteful (Hollis 2004, Wachocki 2014).

Even people who provide assistance to the homeless are trained to help homeless people address their (seemingly) individual, self-inflicted problems. They develop programs, action plans, and treatments to help individual *people*, without fully considering the systemic causes of homelessness (Tracy and Stoecker 1993). Similarly, some academic researchers fault the homeless for their own personal shortcomings by analyzing individual narratives of substance use and mental illness (Wright 2005). Consider the work of anthropologist Oscar Lewis. His **culture of poverty** theory suggests that the urban poor develop a distinct set of norms and behavioural tendencies, including impulsiveness, short-sightedness, and resigned acceptance of their marginalized status in society. Through **socialization**, they pass these dysfunctional values on to future generations.

The conservative American political scientist Edward Banfield argues that a culture of poverty develops out of a heightened concern with the present moment. By contrast, the middle-class accumulation of wealth requires foresight, planning, and sacrifice—what's often called **deferred gratification** (Kane 1987). For this reason, Banfield opposed the use of federal funding to alleviate poverty. He, like other academic insiders, thinks that economic rewards should and do come to people who behave in meritorious ways. Since some people will always "choose" to be lazy and focus on the present, poverty and inequality are inevitable.

Victim-blaming allows the middle and upper classes to feel their privilege is deserved, but it also produces the very same dysfunctional behaviours that Oscar Lewis observed. According to Gerald and Patricia Gurin (1970), who developed **expectancy theory**, victim-blaming reduces expectations among the disadvantaged. When we blame the poor for their condition, they internalize that blame, lose hope, and begin to think that their condition is inescapable.

Ultimately, victim-blaming is dangerous because it diverts attention from systemic inequalities (Wright 2005). By focusing on individual behaviours, we fixate on symptoms of the illness, rather than its root cause (Hollis 2004). It is necessary to view the world in terms of public issues rather than personal troubles, but such a perspective is not encouraged in highly competitive societies like our own (Carr and MacLachlan 1998, Robertson 2012). The insiders who have done well financially in our contemporary world are unlikely to endorse overall changes in policy that could potentially address systemic disadvantages but also threaten their own privileges.

Social Mobility

Insiders are similarly likely to view upward mobility as the just reward for particularly talented individuals, and as proof of society's fairness, openness, or even equality (Brown 2013). In a society with high rates of intergenerational mobility, every new generation appears to compete on a level playing field (Kearney 2006). In such a society, people supposedly succeed according to their talent and effort. Initiatives designed to facilitate social mobility thus often rank as high political priorities in developed liberal democracies.

And yet, over the past several decades, social mobility in North America has diminished, with the result that, increasingly, class origins in childhood predict class destinations in adulthood (Chan and Boliver 2013). In fact, many risk *downward* mobility: with the so-called "hollowing out" of the middle class and increased economic inequality, many people born into the middle class have had to struggle just to stay there. Some families have accomplished this through the addition of a second income. More women work outside the home today, and all work longer hours than they once did. Only through these efforts have many households been able to sustain a stable or comfortable income (Himelfarb 2014). However, if people must work harder and longer to preserve their original class status, how are they to improve it?

Many believe the solution is higher education. However, lower income children are unable to access higher education as easily as middle- and upper-income children. In many cases, low-income parents hold lower aspirations for their children, provide less encouragement, and involve themselves less in their children's education.

In all social classes, parental involvement contributes to students' academic performance and influences their chances of attending college (Hardaway and McLoyd 2009). In turn, the degree and quality of parental involvement depends on class and economic status. Highly educated, insider parents are likely to be heavily involved in their children's educations. They see their children's teachers as equals, and view the relationship with them as a partnership committed to the betterment of their children. On the other hand, working class, outsider parents are less likely to initiate contact with their children's teachers. These parents rationalize that teachers know what's best for children, and that learning happens at school, not home. Other working-class parents distrust teachers, often because of hurtful or frustrating experiences with schools in the past. With less parental support, working-class children perform poorly in high school, and become uninterested in continuing on to post-secondary education.

To perform well academically, students also need what sociologist Pierre Bourdieu termed **cultural capital**, the knowledge, skills, and values transmitted to children through the kind of informal education that occurs within the family (Remennick 2012, Scherger and Savage 2010). Middle- and upper-class insider families are better able to teach their children such skills, and often make a deliberate effort to cultivate cultural capital among their children by arranging additional tutoring, encouraging them to read for pleasure, and enrolling them in after-school activities (on this, see Lareau 2010). Often these adult-supervised activities, such as ballet classes, teach well-off young people "good taste" and provide an "enriching" experience. Children who do not receive such cultural socialization perform comparatively poorly in school, and are less likely to gain educational credentials as adults.

SECOND OPINIONS

Academics (especially sociologists) have long recognized that insiders and outsiders alike view education as the key to upward social mobility. That is why many disadvantaged people accumulate even more debt in their pursuit of a degree: they hope education will improve their life chances (Breen and Karlson 2013). But scholars offering second opinions highlight the problem posed by the growing numbers of highly educated young people unable to secure jobs that reflect their educational qualifications.

The Hypothesis of Merit Selection

Functionalist sociologists argue that the education system is meant to teach young people the skills most needed in our society, helping to produce workers to meet the demands of the labour market. To do so, schools must recruit the most talented members of society, whatever their race, sex, or class (Iannelli 2011). The related **hypothesis of merit-selection** holds that as our educational system becomes more meritocratic, class of birth will have less effect on academic performance (Brown 2013, Breen 2010). The same hypothesis predicts that employers will come to adopt a meritocratic mindset, hiring on the basis of expertise for the sake of efficiency and productivity. In other words, economic and social rewards will be allocated on the basis of merit, rather than class origins.

Sociological research has repeatedly disproven this optimistic hypothesis (Brown 2013, Breen and Karlson 2013). Academics studying class inequality note that the most meritorious students are *not* always the ones who obtain a post-secondary education or, later, a high-paying job. Rather, class origins, sex, and race continue to influence educational attainment and upward social mobility (Iannelli 2011). Attaining a university degree is rarely the guaranteed ticket to a better life students are encouraged to think it is. Many professions continue to be dominated by people from higher-class backgrounds, and may even have become *less* socially diverse in recent years (Byrom and Lightfoot 2013).

The Neoliberal Fallacy of Fairness

The recently renewed interest in social mobility reflects a distinctly neoliberal mindset that many sociologists dispute (Brown 2013). From a neoliberal perspective, upward social mobility will result if we motivate disadvantaged people to seize the employment opportunities right in front of them. Neoliberal thinkers contend that people from disadvantaged backgrounds simply need the chance to compete with their privileged counterparts in order to establish a fairer society. Many current political programs reflect such a mindset, by seeming to offer disadvantaged people opportunities to meet the high demand for skilled workers.

To a degree, this perspective is valid. Most social mobility *is* a result of structural expansion—the creation of new jobs—and today, the best new jobs require higher education. In the past, high rates of upward social mobility occurred in response to a rising demand for managerial and professional workers that was not being met by the number of middle-class youth entering the labour market. Under those circumstances, working class people gained job opportunities usually reserved for the middle class.

There is, however, another type of mobility: **relative mobility**, sometimes referred to as **exchange mobility**. This kind of mobility is made possible by the retirement, death, or replacement of people in existing jobs. Historically, advantaged people had the first shot at these positions. When upward mobility happens equally across different social classes, it is because the life chances of people in those different classes are becoming more similar. But this rarely—if ever—happens (Iannelli 2011).

High rates of economic and employment growth in the latter part of the nineteenth century and the decades immediately after World War II corresponded with high rates of upward social mobility. This mobility, however, was caused by the "absolute" shifts in occupational structure we noted earlier—more good jobs were created, opening some of them up to the lower classes—and not because people of all classes enjoyed more equal life chances. High rates of absolute social mobility do *not* confirm the hypothesis of merit-selection. Even when we observe lots of absolute mobility—many people moving through different class statuses—class-based differences in opportunity persist (Iannelli 2011). Being born into a middle-class family is still much more advantageous than being born into a lower-income family.

These findings have been neglected by neoliberal scholars and politicians. The "solution" to limited upward mobility, they say, is simply to motivate the poor to obtain an education, which prepares them for better jobs. But because members of different classes remain differentially treated, we live under a **fallacy of fairness**—the *illusion* that something is being done to address a rigid, immobile class structure (Brown 2013).

Part of the problem is that neoliberalism focuses on the individual as the unit of analysis, suggesting, for example, that if one lower-income person has been able to overcome the structural barriers to upward mobility, everyone else should be able to do the same. This approach ignores the reality that not everyone can achieve what one exceptional individual can. Even in a utopian fantasy of absolute equality of opportunity, not everyone can *be* the best, no matter how hard he tries. There are only so many spots at the top.

In fact, there is no society in which people are judged solely on their own merits; we are all judged in comparison with competitors. As a result, mobility is based on a competition that determines your standing in hierarchical *relation* to your peers. To succeed, you must stay ahead of the crowd; and when everyone moves ahead on an equal footing, we get a flood of people jostling for the same positions at the top.

What this means is that, as more people have obtained more education, education has lost its capacity to guarantee upward social mobility. Since the 1950s, formal education has exerted a declining influence on upward social mobility (Scherger and Savage 2010). Yet neoliberal policy continues to champion education as the ticket to upward mobility even though it cannot equalize the life chances of people from different class backgrounds unless there is also robust economic growth.

The Massification of Higher Education

Today, most working- and middle-class families do not experience significant intergenerational mobility. The few who move upward at all move a shorter distance upward than their counterparts of a generation ago. This is because the Canadian labour market has become "socially congested"—"crowded" by similarly-skilled people competing for a limited number of similar jobs. **Social congestion** is especially severe and noticeable in developed nations with large urban middle classes, where higher education is a norm and working-class jobs have either been moved offshore to lower-wage countries or eliminated by technological advances such as the use of robotics in manufacturing.

Social congestion creates an "opportunity trap." When everyone seeks the "advantage" of a higher education, this means of getting ahead constitutes a "trap," in that it *causes* the very social congestion it seeks to alleviate.

Over the past fifty years, as the demand for specialized knowledge and skills has risen, people have acquired skills and credentials to meet the demand. The number of people enrolled globally in higher education has more than doubled over the last two decades: there were 76 million post-secondary students in the mid-1990s, but 179 million by 2009 (Brown 2013). Yet as more people have gained these qualifications, the traditional middle- and upper-income jobs have become less widely available. Not only is there less room for upward mobility from the working to the middle class, but we are starting to see some *downward* mobility out of the middle class (Byrom and Lightfoot 2013).

Nevertheless, hopes of financial success through education persist. Attending college or university is such a standard choice for today's youth that those who choose alternative routes often become alienated from their peers, viewed as having made the "wrong choice" (Byrom and Lightfoot 2013). Young North Americans are encouraged to feel personally responsible for their future and entitled to certain rewards if they have paid the price. But many are set up for disappointment: in the labour market, only some will succeed, leaving the "failures" to be blamed for their own misfortune. The insider belief in the power of individual decision-making permeates the entire class structure: even many of those disadvantaged by such beliefs endorse this way of thinking.

The expansion of education opportunities has not eliminated occupational or income inequality. Instead, it has led to the "massification" of education, increasing the average level of educational attainment (Iannelli 2011). More people are getting an education, and that is a good thing; but the proportions of students from working-, middle-, and upper-class backgrounds remain skewed. Educational expansion has benefited people from all social classes but it did not and cannot create social equality. Working-class students are not supplanting middle- and upper-income students, nor (generally) are they filling jobs previously held by people of middle- and upper-income origins.

Academics offering second opinions have refuted insiders' view of education as a solution to our increasingly rigid social hierarchy (Scherger and Savage 2010). When every candidate for a job has a post-secondary degree, employers take other variables into account when deciding who to hire. Besides the "hard currencies" of credentials, scholarships, and work experience, employers consider the "soft currencies" of professional demeanour, punctuality, dependability, persistence, and networking skills. They interpret these and other "soft skills" as indicators of a candidate's ability to "perform" at work; and, as we have seen, white, middle- and upper-class parents are usually better able to impart these soft skills.

Insiders are correct in noting that higher education remains a young person's best investment in eventual job success; however flawed, higher education provides better opportunities than dropping out of school. But scholars offering second opinions have demonstrated that it is more challenging for lower-income youth to complete a college or university degree, let alone excel in their studies. Many students, especially those from low-income backgrounds, must work while in school, cutting into the time available to study. They are thus placed at a disadvantage relative to more privileged youth, whose parents pay for their tuition. Many working-class students also struggle because they fail to use the resources available to them. They do not feel as though they "belong" within the institution, whereas middle and upper income students are accustomed—and even feel entitled—to requesting and receiving guidance from authority figures, including teachers, librarians, administrative staff, and counsellors.

Moreover, to succeed academically, a student must share the values, practices, and expectations of the educational institution. For example, as a largely traditional, conservative institution, the university demands the erasure of indicators of working-class origins. Students from lower socioeconomic backgrounds are pressured to adopt the values of the upper middle class. In this context, poor grades increase their feelings of alienation, making them question their decision to pursue a higher education in the first place.

Many insiders attribute the lower academic performance of working-class students to their supposed lack of motivation and poor work ethic. But research shows that many universities are a poor social and academic fit for these young adults. These students *want* to succeed academically but often fail to find a place for themselves in environments that devalue their class-based customs, values, and identities. Given the unpleasant experiences they often face, many working-class students show great resilience and commitment.

Where insider views and second opinions diverge on the matter of education is on how just they perceive the existing system to be. Insiders hold that the system is fair: children from more affluent families typically succeed academically, and therefore deserve to obtain stable, well-paying jobs. But academics offering second opinions argue this pattern is far from just. Even when lower-income youth attempt to level the playing field by obtaining the same academic credentials as their wealthier counterparts, they still suffer a competitive disadvantage. The massification of education allows employers to select job candidates from more affluent backgrounds, whose cultural capital sets them apart. Class background and childhood socialization, not education, remain the key factors determining career and class destinations (Scherger and Savage 2010).

So education is a good thing, but it does not erase class differences. Hard-to-remove class effects not only affect people's personal lives but may cause political unrest. As long as people think that they can improve their standard of living through hard work and determination, they are unlikely to protest the status quo. But young people in developed countries are now highly educated but also frustrated and disillusioned. They were promised a better standard of living in return for their hard-earned education, but not all receive a return on their investment. Limited career opportunities, combined with mounting student debt, create a potentially explosive situation. Youth unemployment and underemployment may lead to a resurgence of class politics in Canada, as it has in other countries, and in rising rates of crime, addiction, and mental illness. Not only does class immobility suggest that Canada is failing to live up to its reputation as an egalitarian society that provides equal opportunities to all; the outsiders who are kept at a disadvantage by this class structure have become increasingly likely to voice their discontent with it.

OUTSIGHTS

People on the "outside"—in this case, people born into families with insecure and insufficient incomes—have different concerns than people who lead secure, prosperous lives. For this reason, they are likely to think and talk about matters that don't often pass through the minds of rich, comfortable people. Moreover, they will think differently about any given issue. Consider **outsourcing**: wealthy people don't think about it very much, and when they do, they typically envision all the ways it has benefited them and their society. By contrast, outsourcing almost always has a negative impact on outsiders, leading them to focus on its detrimental consequences.

Globalization and Outsourcing

After free trade between Canada, the U.S., and Mexico was introduced in 1994, the working classes in all three nations suffered. American production workers faced a 6.2% drop in average hourly wages. Mexican workers were already earning much less than their counterparts in the U.S. and Canada; in 1975, hourly compensation for workers in Mexico was a mere 23% that of American workers. By 1994, that figure had fallen to 14.5% and by 1997, three years after the free trade deal was signed, it was down to 9.6% (Cormier and Targ 2001). In other words, for every dollar earned by an American worker, his or her Mexican counterpart was paid a dime. Canada fared best in terms of wages, which merely stagnated, but experienced a widening trade deficit that led to job losses nationwide.

Today, Canada seeks freer access to markets in Asia, Latin America and the Caribbean (Zhang 2010). Increased foreign investment and access to foreign markets have resulted in greater economic interaction, integration, and even interdependence (Cormier and Targ 2001). This is all part of a phenomenon known as **globalization** (Anner 2001). Unskilled, semi-skilled, and sometimes even highly skilled workers in developed countries risk losing their jobs as a result. This is because globalization can promote a "race to the bottom," where investors move or "outsource" jobs until they find the cheapest possible labour (Smith and Zhang 2012). When production sites are relocated to low-wage countries, domestic plants are closed and local workers left unemployed.

Consider the challenges faced by Gerry Lenaghan of Brampton, Ontario, who lost her job at pulp-and-paper company Georgia-Pacific in 2009. Gerry says she "became very passionate about outsourcing" once she had experienced its negative consequences first-hand:

> The corporation said it was nothing personal; I told them I beg to differ. When you're on the receiving end of it, it's very personal. They got to continue on with business as usual, my life, however, was turned upside down. It was a stressful time for me. . . . Having to start all over again and pound the pavement for interviews was brutal because I hadn't done that in seven years. (Readers' Letters, *Toronto Star*, 2013).

In the last few decades, many North American and European jobs have been moved to China, India and other developing countries, which often lack strong unions and labour laws. Corporations like Nike, to use a widely known example, benefit from a labour force that works extremely long hours for very low wages (Mosco 2006).

In turn, outsourcing increases income and class inequalities. Unemployed workers suffer an immediate income loss and are often forced to accept lower-paying work, setting them further behind the owners of the means of production, who now enjoy reduced expenses and higher profits. Outsourcing tends to make the rich exponentially richer, while making life even more difficult for the already poor. As Lenaghan explains, "I am just one of many millions who have lost out to corporate greed" (Readers' Letters, *Toronto Star*, 2013).

Outsourcing especially affects workers with low skills, such as those employed in call centres. Call-centre positions are easy to computerize, and the necessary skills are easy to teach (or script). Because customer service is provided over the phone rather than in person, call centres can be located anywhere in the world, placing domestic call-centre workers at a high risk of losing their jobs. To cite just one example, 800 employees of Sears Canada were laid off when one of the corporation's call centres in St. Laurent, Quebec was closed down at the end of 2014. A former employee, Kadeem Steril, reports being shocked by the news that he would no longer have a job, confiding, "I thought it was going to be stable, I had a stable job." Steril's co-worker, Jean Leon, was rightly concerned about the future: "Some of us have been here for a long time and it's hard to find new jobs nowadays" (CTV Montreal 2014).

Jobs that require specialized skills and face-to-face interaction with customers—as when doctors interact with their patients, for example—cannot be outsourced as easily (Mosco 2006). Highly skilled workers, who often enjoy greater job security and higher pay in any case, are usually less affected by outsourcing than less skilled workers.

Outsourcing also decreases the bargaining power of employees, creating a more unequal relationship between workers and employers (Cormier and Targ 2001). Fearing they may lose their jobs at any time, workers feel they lack the power to challenge the terms of their employment—wages, hours, or working conditions. There has thus been a general decline in union membership under free-trade regimes, putting workers at greater risk of mistreatment (Chaykowski 2002, Brennan 2005). Specifically, the Canadian unionization rate – that is, the proportion of workers who are union members – dropped from 38% to 30% between 1981 and 2012 (Galarneau and Sohn 2015).

While blue-collar workers are hurt most easily and obviously, the challenges posed by free trade are no longer limited to the working classes. The type of work that can be outsourced has now grown to include knowledge-processing jobs. Credit, equity, and investment research as well as intellectual property and asset management are all being outsourced to an increasing degree (Mosco 2006). For instance, the Royal Bank of Canada replaced hundreds of Canadian employees with temporary workers from iGATE, an Indian outsourcing firm. One former employee said that the bank had made a habit of laying off Canadian IT workers "in favour of foreign counterparts." Employees were offered "a meagre severance package and no assistance . . . for getting internal placements" (CBC News 2013). Thus, jobs traditionally in the middle of the income distribution are starting to shift downwards (Zhang 2010).

Yet the domestic working class tends to blame its plight on foreign workers, not the corporations who make the decision to outsource. Especially in the U.S., the working class most often directs its animosity towards Chinese and Indian workers, who are accused of "stealing" jobs that Americans "deserve" (Cormier and Targ 2001).

Despite harmful outcomes for workers, globalization and outsourcing continue because wealthy insiders have successfully convinced many that they are driving the economy through job and wealth creation. Capitalists and their supporters assert that free trade opens markets, allowing for the most efficient allocation of resources. Each nation can concentrate on making what it is best at producing, and import the rest. Trade flourishes and wealth increases (Mosco 2006).

Supporters of free trade also argue that the most productive plants are foreign-owned. These plants engage in more research and development, are more innovative, and employ a larger fraction of skilled workers than Canadian-owned plants. One study reports that firms acquired by foreign companies increased labour productivity by 13%, were correspondingly more profitable, and were thus able to increase their employees' wages, paying them 3.4% more than domestic producers (Smith and Zhang 2012, Zhang 2010).

However, even if all these assertions are valid, the benefits of globalization most often go to business owners, investors, and highly skilled employees—not working class outsiders. For example, the higher pay that (occasionally) accompanies higher productivity goes mainly to highly educated, highly skilled workers (e.g., engineers, managers, and computer programmers). More often, however, the owners of the means of production simply enjoy greater profit margins after such increases in productivity, rather than sharing that profit with their employees. No wonder the earnings gap between the rich and poor is widening as globalization gains momentum.

Precarious Labour

To prosper in the global economy, employers continually try to reduce the cost of labour (Caldbick et al. 2014, Kachi et al. 2014). A deregulated, "flexible" labour market benefits employers by allowing them to alter the size and composition of their workforce in response to economic changes (Cohen 2013, Gonick 2011). For example, employers may cut permanent positions, opting instead for less costly contract labour. In many cases, this arrangement disadvantages workers, who work fewer hours per week and therefore earn less overall than permanent employees (Cranford et al. 2003).

Contract work is only one form of **precarious labour**, a category that includes various kinds of unstable, part-time, temporary, short-term, and "flexible" work (Caldbick et al. 2014, Kachi et al. 2014). Before 1975, precarious labour accounted for only 12 percent of all employment in Canada (Gonick 2011). Today, more than one-third of all jobs in Canada are not classified as permanent positions.

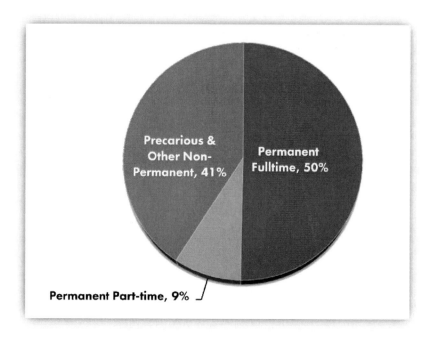

Figure 2.2: Forms of Employment in the Toronto-Hamilton Metropolitan Area, 2011

Precarious labour stands in contrast with traditional employment arrangements in most Western industrial nations (Cranford et al. 2003). Full employment used to mean a year-round, 9–to–5, stable position with benefits, and a steady (even if modest) salary (Caldbick et al. 2014). Typically, the jobs of white, able-bodied male breadwinners conformed to these standards. Today, however, even white, able-bodied men are unable to secure these traditional kinds of jobs (Vosko 2006). Growing numbers of employers are limiting their commitments to their employees, shifting the responsibility for training, health care, pensions, and other benefits and entitlements onto workers themselves (Cohen 2013, Kalleberg 2009). Some studies suggest that as few as 50% of working-aged adults in Toronto today hold the full-time, permanent positions that were once considered the norm.

The uncertainty of precarious labour undermines workers' health and well-being (Vosko 2006, Lewchuk et al. 2008). More traditional forms of employment provide financial stability, higher self-esteem, social inclusion, and other health-promoting advantages (Caldbick et al. 2014). By contrast, precarious workers are more likely to be psychologically distressed, fatigued, anxious, depressed, and even suicidal (Cohen 2013, Kachi et al. 2014). Temporary and contract workers are less likely to socialize with their colleagues, since they expect to leave the workplace once their contracts run out (Kalleberg 2009).

Some research suggests that the stress of ongoing job insecurity can be even more harmful to health than the stress associated with unemployment. In an effort to cope with this extreme stress, many turn to drugs, alcohol, tobacco, and unhealthy eating habits. Others, because of their lower incomes, are unable to afford nutritious food or adequate housing (Kachi et al. 2014). Still others work in hazardous conditions, risking serious injury. Yet contract workers are typically denied health and disability benefits (Forouzin 2010, Vosko 2006).

The financial uncertainty inherent in precarious work arrangements also deters many from marrying and beginning a family. Diana Mavunduse, now 41, reports spending most of the last decade juggling multiple contract and part-time positions to support herself (Mojtehedzadeh 2015). The Zimbabwe native notes, "Back home, I would be married already with children," but she has yet to consider the possibility of a family due to her hectic, stressful work life in Toronto. Referring to her stints as a telemarketer and cleaner, this highly educated international development specialist explains, "When you are working precarious jobs you don't have time to meet anybody." Having only recently secured a full-time, secure position at a social service agency, Mavunduse is now asking herself, "Is it too late for children?"

Note that these harmful effects apply mainly to people who would *prefer* more traditional work arrangements, but can't get them (Vosko 2006). There is a difference between people who are *unable* to secure a permanent position, and those who *choose* flexible arrangements, such as entrepreneurs and small-business owners (Caldbick et al. 2014, Gonick 2011). The latter are more likely to benefit from flexible work hours, the ability to pursue their own goals and interests, increased job satisfaction, and the ability to be independent, autonomous, and free from the stress of bosses and managers (Cohen 2013).

However, this type of self-selected flexible labour is largely restricted to people who have the capital to fund their own business ventures, or to support themselves while beginning their careers as freelancers (Cohen 2013). They are more likely to come from affluent backgrounds, or rely on a stably employed partner for financial support. Those who are successfully self-employed are technically considered precarious workers, but are less subject to the instability, stress, and health risks that plague the **precariat** as a whole.

That said, some people are forced into self-employment because of a lack of jobs in their area of expertise (Grant 2015). Anna Withrow of Toronto has worked as an independent communications and marketing consultant since 2001. With an unpredictable income ranging from $24,000 to $77,000 a year, including periods lasting several months when she earns nothing, Withrow says that "cash flow has been the biggest crippling thing. . . . If the right position came along, I would take it tomorrow."

Although it is now more common among traditionally privileged workers, including men of middle- and upper-income origins, precarious labour is hardly a new phenomenon. Women, racial minorities, immigrants with unstable citizenship status, people with disabilities, and young and old people have long been excluded from conventional employment arrangements (Cohen 2013, Hannif and Lamm 2005). That said, these marginalized people continue to be over-represented in precarious work (Gonick 2011, Vosko 2006).

Performing Social Class

Outsiders think differently about the essentiality of "class." Compared to insiders, they are more likely to view class as nothing more than a performance enabled by money. By their reckoning, people are born into a given class, but there is nothing innate that makes a person low-, middle-, or upper-class. In contrast with insiders, who define class in economic terms, outsiders often believe that differences in income, education, and occupation lack meaning in and of themselves; the implications of these differences for our everyday lives and for our interactions with others are socially defined (Yodanis 2006).

It's true that insiders also recognize that "class" is a performance art. For example, insiders acknowledge the importance of associating with certain people and avoiding others; humbling themselves to some people, and expecting others to be humble towards them; and diligently respecting some people, while demanding respect from others. Insiders even signal their social class to each other by decorating their homes in certain ways, reading highbrow books and magazines, and dining at costly restaurants in an effort to visibly associate themselves with a certain level of income, education, occupational attainment, and cultural taste (DiMaggio 1979, Yodanis 2006).

Insiders and outsiders alike thus recognize that class status is "performed." But insiders are more likely to over-simplify the types of class performances available to people, imagining that some would lack the ability to perform "upper class," even if they gained access to more money. This is tied up with the insider view that intrinsically "better" and more deserving people rise to the top. In response, outsiders are quick to point out that many at the top have inherited their money, making them less "deserving" of high social status than they like to imagine.

Considering the class performances of outsiders also highlights the "top-down" view of the class structure endorsed by the dominant majority. Insiders and even many scholarly accounts frame our class system as a rigid hierarchy, with the wealthy at the top, and everyone below striving to join those upper ranks. The wealthiest are imagined as demanding respect from all and humbling themselves to none, while the poorest perform their class by conferring respect upon everyone "above" them and expecting it from none.

From the outsider perspective, low-income people deserve just as much respect as those with higher incomes, but use methods other than costly displays of wealth to signal their class-based values. For example, outsiders often emphasize their strong work ethic, striving to prove that they work longer and harder than anyone else. Many make a point of discussing the precise number of hours they put in each week, the scant number of days they have off, and the amount of overtime they clock.

Working-class people also tend to juxtapose their unending labour with the supposed idleness of the rich, praising their own dedication while denouncing the laziness of the elite. In her study of social interactions in the local coffee shop of a small rural B.C. fishing community, sociologist Carrie Yodanis (2006) listened to low-income women voice their frustrations with their more privileged counterparts. One woman, Holly, offered particularly interesting insights because of her work cleaning the houses of those wealthy enough to visit the town just for their summer vacations. She says of these upper-class women: "They just have different ways about them because they have always had everything. I think they have never had to struggle."

Holly also took note of the different types of complaints her wealthy employers would make while socializing in the coffee shop themselves: she reports that one woman

> will sit there and complain about things like, her husband last night left a blanket on the sofa and didn't fold it – it's like, if that's all you have to worry about. . . . There was two women sitting there talking about it and one of them was saying, "Oh, you know what my husband did" and he didn't put his glass in the dishwasher, he will leave them in the sink. . . . It's just amazing the stuff they talk about... That's the last thing on most people's mind—it's kind of sickening really.

Rather than indicating a desire for a similar lifestyle, Holly distanced herself from her upper-class employers, seeking instead to make the concerns *she* had "to worry about" appear more legitimate.

Working-class people often broadcast their values as a means of differentiating themselves from the rich people they hate, fear, and envy. When members of the working class stray into middle- or upper-income territory—expressing a taste for highbrow art or entertainment, visiting areas of town monopolized by the wealthy, or taking (even inexpensive) vacations—others may be quick to remind them of their origins, criticizing them for becoming frivolous (Yodanis 2006). For example, when Holly suggested to her working-class friend Sharon that she would be avoiding a local county fair because it was "too dirty" for her liking, Sharon accused her of abandoning her roots in favour of the values espoused by her wealthy employers: "It is a fair, what do you want? . . . Just wear old clothes. Why don't you just go up to Mr. Rudolph's [a prominent summer-colony resident] and stay up there. You think you are all hoity-toity now that you are working up there."

For their part, middle- and upper-income people extol their own values and practices (Yodanis 2006). Upper-income women, for example, are more likely to volunteer, rather than work for pay. They often emphasize the philanthropic, community-building effects of their volunteer work, even explicitly contrasting this work with the dirty, poorly paying, unrewarding labour of lower-income women.

The experiences of outsiders demonstrate that social class can only be viewed as a rigid hierarchy from the standpoint of an insider. The wealthy assume that members of all other income brackets measure success in the same monetary terms that they do. However, working-class people appear interested not in performing the deference that the elite believe they deserve, but rather in asserting the value of the constant, dedicated labour they perform. From this perspective, class status is indeed performative, but members of each class imagine *themselves* as most deserving of a spot on top, and use their performances to demonstrate why their class-based values should be most highly regarded.

FINAL THOUGHTS

As we have seen, insiders and outsiders agree on some matters and disagree about others. Still other issues do not register on the radar of insiders at all. Both groups recognize that class inequality exists, but they disagree about its extent, who is to blame for it, and whether or not it is just and deserved.

It is in insiders' best interests to downplay the extent and negative consequences of class inequality, as they stand to benefit from that inequality. Unfortunately, insiders appear to have succeeded in obscuring the degree to which Canadian society is marked by economic inequality. Studies show that outsiders drastically underestimate the actual level of income inequality (Norton and Airely 2011, Norton and Kiatpongsan 2014). For example, the average American thinks that the richest 20% of the population controls 59% of the nation's wealth. In reality, however, that wealthiest one-fifth controls more than 84% of all American wealth. Similarly, Norton and Kiatpongsan (2014) asked 55,000 people from 40 different countries to guess how much the average corporate CEO earned, compared to the average unskilled worker. The average estimate was that the CEO earned thirty times what the worker did, when in reality, the ratio is 354 to 1. Most outsiders don't know how bad inequality really is.

Insiders also tend to blame outsiders for what little inequality they are willing to concede exists. They believe that, if only the poor had stayed in school longer, worked a little harder, and led more upstanding (e.g., sober, thrifty, and careful) lives, they might have avoided poverty. On this point, the insider perspective is incorrect; the evidence shows that many and perhaps even a majority of poor people are blameless victims of the way society is organized.

Indeed, in societies marked by extreme class inequality, everyone but the very rich—the so-called "one percent"—suffers to some degree. Vulnerable groups, including children, the elderly and the disabled, suffer the most (Jenkins et al. 2007, Brady 2004). It is also easiest to see why these groups are almost always blameless victims of poverty (National Advisory Council on Aging 2005). Children, for example, rely on their parents and the broader community for food, protection, and support (Forouzin 2010). Similarly, many seniors depend on others for financial support and care. When seniors do experience poverty, it is often due to a failure by the state to uphold its obligations to them, or the result of family members who have reneged on their filial responsibilities.

The notion of blameless poverty places the responsibility for poverty on society as a whole. This is generally a good thing, though it can deny poor people a sense of agency. For example, it contributes to the widely held perception of seniors as helpless dependents, undervaluing the contributions they do make to society (Barrientos et al. 2003). Similarly, positioning children as blameless victims of their parents' poverty merely shifts the blame on to low-income parents; it also devalues the resilience and independence many children develop in the face of such adversity (Lindsey and Martin 2003).

Amid the often conflicting views and interpretations of class inequality held by insiders and outsiders, sociologists have often acted as arbitrators. Sociological evidence can bring insiders and outsiders together around a common set of facts: namely, that there are too many large-scale patterns—including racialized, gendered, and aged poverty, as well as the advantages afforded to those with accumulated wealth—to plausibly suggest that inequality is the result of poor choices or a deficient work ethic. By adopting a new standpoint and examining our class structure from below, we can see there are greater forces at work than the individualistic motivations that insiders use to explain class inequality. Indeed, we have already observed that insiders born into wealthy families enjoy a variety of advantages that make them more likely to succeed in the educational and occupational labour markets than outsiders born into poor and even middle class families. In the coming chapters, we will see that these broader forces also include the systemic barriers posed by other inequalities related to race, gender, age, and sexuality.

DISCUSSION QUESTIONS

1. Do you think people need to be held accountable for their actions or inaction? How can we identify circumstances that are within (as opposed to beyond) someone's control and, in turn, avoid blaming people for matters they have no power over?

2. Is higher education the key to success today? If not, what steps should people take to improve their financial circumstances?

3. Have you ever held a precarious job? What are some of the drawbacks (if any)? If you think there are drawbacks, how do you justify keeping your precarious position?

4. How do you perform your social class, or construct the illusion that you are of a certain class? Consider the clothes you wear, books you read, movies and TV shows you watch, how (or if) you talk to your friends about your parents and their jobs, and so on. Do you take pains to emphasize or hide your class origins?

5. Do you think class inequality is unfair and troubling, or just and deserved? Should anything be done to shrink the growing gap between the rich and the poor? If so, what actions should be taken? How big of a gap is "justified"?

FURTHER READING

Danny Dorlin. *Injustice: Why Social Inequality Still Persists*. Policy Press, 2015.

Megan Erickson. *Class War: The Privatization of Childhood*. Verso, 2015.

Barbara Scheider. "Homelessness: Emotion Discourse and the Reproduction of Social Inequality." *Canadian Journal of Communication* 39:2 (2014): 235–248.

KEY TERMS

Cultural capital. Skills, values, and knowledge transmitted to children through informal education, usually by parents.

Culture of poverty. Theory put forth by Oscar Lewis claiming the poor develop norms and behaviours, such as resignation, dependency, idleness and shortsightedness, which they pass on to their offspring, rendering the next generation likely to remain impoverished.

Deferred gratification. Ideological principle that encourages individuals and groups to postpone immediate pleasure in order to work, train, educate themselves, or invest in some other way in the future.

Exchange mobility. Made possible by the retirement, death, or replacement of people in already-existing jobs.

Expectancy theory. Theory of motivation that seeks to identify the conditions necessary for worker motivation to occur.

Fallacy of fairness. The illusion that something is being done to address a rigid class structure when, in fact, policies and programs have been proven to be ineffective.

Hypothesis of merit-selection. Proposes that economic and social rewards will be allocated on the basis of merit, rather than class origins.

Neoliberalism. Body of ideas advocating minimal state intervention and economic freedom.

Precariat. The group or social class of people who are precariously employed.

Precarious labour. Category that includes unstable, part-time, temporary, short-term, and "flexible" work arrangements.

Relative mobility. Comparative chances of mobility for people born into different classes.

Social congestion. A labour market "crowded" by similarly skilled people competing for a limited number of similar jobs.

Social mobility. Movement of individuals between different positions within the system of social stratification in society.

Socialization. Process by which we learn to become members of society; the act of passing values, attitudes and behavioural norms on to future generations.

Soft currencies. Soft skills—professional demeanour, punctuality, dependability, persistence, and networking skills—considered to indicate a candidate's ability to perform at work.

Gender Inequalities

INTRODUCTION

In October 2014, the Canadian Association for Equality (CAFE) announced that it was the first men's issues group to be recognized as a registered charity in Canada (CBC 2014). Even before being granted charitable status, CAFE, along with other men's rights groups, excited controversy. When the group presented lectures at the University of Toronto, protesters set off fire alarms, barricaded entrances, and chanted "no hate speech on campus."

In this chapter, we explore why some people—mostly female outsiders and scholars offering second opinions—oppose the men's rights movement. We examine the (sometimes misguided) insider perspectives that sparked this movement, as well as those of outsiders, who say the movement's goal is not to protect men's rights but to challenge those of women (CBC 2014).

This chapter addresses questions on which insiders and outsiders remain divided: Is feminism a thing of the past? Are men and women treated equally in our society? Have women's rights been adequately addressed, freeing us to consider other, more pressing social problems?

INSIDER VIEWS

People on the "inside"—in this case, men—are largely blind to gender inequality. They hold that Canadian women have made impressive progress: they can now vote, attend university, work in any field they wish, marry when and whom they want, and have children if and when they choose (Digby 2003). True, women are more likely than men to be poor, malnourished, physically abused, and sexually assaulted. But insiders argue that such disadvantages and mistreatment are the products of poor choices. For instance, poor women may have had the chance to pursue an education and career, but "chose" to become stay-at-home mothers (Kullberg 2013).

Invoking the notion of "choice" or free will obscures the structural gender inequalities that continue to persist. We will examine strategies that insiders use to justify the status quo, making it seem fairer than it really is.

Men's Rights Movements

Insiders admit that women suffer some disadvantages, but often draw attention to the disadvantages associated with being a *man* in Canada. They correctly note that norms of masculinity impede men just as norms of femininity impede women. Some men, for example, feel they would be ridiculed for showing emotion or refraining from premarital sex, because such actions contradict traditional conceptions of "manliness" (Digby 2003).

During the late twentieth century, "men's rights" movements emerged that took some of these ideas to an extreme. Some men felt increasing levels of **female privilege** were leading to what they considered "male oppression" (Taylor 2008, Eriksson 2013). For example, *A Voice for Men*, the most widely visited "men's issues" website, features an article that claims: "It's official. Man is no longer ruler of planet Earth. Men lost that privilege way back in the Nineties. . . [H]uman males were tipped from their throne and replaced by their female counterparts."

It should be noted that the men's rights movement is neither the only nor the most significant response to feminism. Over the years, the backlash against greater rights for women has been spearheaded by a variety of religious, social and political organizations. Nor is the membership of the men's rights movement reflective of Canadian society at large: it is overwhelmingly white, politically and socially conservative, and for the most part drawn from society's lower economic echelons. It represents a narrow slice of society, and an extreme one. Most men's rights advocates are no more likely to view themselves as "insiders" than, say, the followers of populist political leaders like Donald Trump. Yet in espousing a traditional view of gender relations that favours men over women they are, if not insiders, at the very least reflective of an influential insider point of view.

The idea that men—historically privileged in almost every society—need to have their rights "defended" seems to most observers an affront to genuinely marginalized groups. Many men's rights advocates promote the traditional masculinities and male roles that feminists have worked to challenge (Fox 2004, Edley and Wetherell 2001). **Patriarchy** and male dominance, these activists suggest, are the most effective ways to organize society. By undermining patriarchy, they claim, feminists put society itself in danger (Taylor 2008).

At the same time, just as the men's rights movement is not the only backlash against feminism, it is not *only* a backlash against feminism. As Michael Kimmel (2014) observes, "'men's liberation' was born in a parallel critique of the male sex role. If women were imprisoned in the home, all housework and domestic drudgery, men were exiled *from* the home, turned into soulless robotic workers, in harness to a masculine mystique, so that their only capacity for nurturing was through their wallets." Men started to rebel against the straitjacket of gender conformity. Some became avid supporters of the women's movement, in hopes of a general liberation from gender restrictions. Others, following Robert Bly, sought mythic sources for male regeneration and male pride. Yet others, like the Promise Makers, a Christian men's organization, committed themselves to a better version of family-oriented masculinity. But some were simply angry and vented that anger against women, who were enjoying new protections under the law and making progress at school and work.

Some of the points made by men's rights advocates are valid, though often couched in problematic terms. They rightly note that women are not the only victims of domestic abuse and sexual assault (Taylor 2008, Digby 2003). Violence against men is a grave issue, but at the same time it would be unreasonable to suggest there is an epidemic of female brutality towards men: the most reliable estimates suggest that 80% of victims of intimate-partner violence are women, and of those who reported sexual offences to the police in 2009, 92% were women (Sinha 2013). Nor do feminists deny male suffering; they simply point out that men are the victims of such violence less often than women. That means there is likely a broader, researchable social pattern—systemic gender inequality—underlying this trend.

Men's rights advocates often contest what they believe to be "discriminatory" legal rulings related to child custody, child support, and alimony (Crowley 2009, Gartrell 2007). When couples divorce, women are much more likely than men to be granted custody of their children and, in turn, child support and alimony. Some men see these trends as indicators of female privilege: women, they say, enjoy the luxury of divorcing their husbands on favourable terms, because they know they will continue to be provided for financially and retain custody of their children.

Those who support "father's rights" say that women are free to work at any job they choose and to earn as much as men—so why should men pay alimony and child support (Edley and Wetherell 2001)? But women are usually granted child custody because of deeply patriarchal understandings of women as mothers with "natural" caring impulses (Crowley 2009). And, as we will see, when women receive alimony it is because of gender inequalities in the workplace that prevent them from earning as much as men do.

The men's movement does itself no favours when it presents its views in hostile ways. *A Voice for Men* features an article entitled "When Is It OK to Punch Your Wife?" in which a violent beating is described as "the least that they deserve." Some of this antagonism stems from a misunderstanding of feminism as blaming men for women's troubles and characterizing men as a homogenous group of violent, sexist, oppressive patriarchs (Datta 2004, Eriksson 2013). Such a perspective renders "women's rights" and "men's rights" mutually exclusive (Taylor 2008).

Denouncing feminism in this way is a scapegoating strategy: men who adopt this stance blame women for their own problems, which are primarily caused by other men (Digby 2003). Men are much more likely to be assaulted by other men than by their wives and girlfriends. It is men who traditionally insisted on "women and children first" in the face of disaster—something the men's rights movement frames as an example of female privilege, but which perpetuates stereotypes of women as helpless and weak.

Of course, not every man endorses these deeply **misogynist** beliefs: in fact, very few do (Edley and Wetherell 2001). A pro-feminist men's movement also emerged in the late 1960s and early 1970s (Fox 2004). It recognizes that men exercise disproportionate power and privilege, and that social problems like domestic violence, rape, and pornography are evidence of **sexism** and gender inequality. Most men, however, sit in the middle of the ideological spectrum, with more radical feminists at one extreme and men's rights advocates at the other. Inflammatory rhetoric, whether used by feminists or anti-feminists, undermines efforts to achieve gender equality and confuses the facts about sex-based inequality.

Domestic Violence

Insiders are likely to hold one of two equally harmful views about domestic violence and sexual assault. First, they may blame the victim for her suffering, minimize the abuse, and try to justify the actions of the perpetrator (Valor-Segura et al. 2011). People are more likely to hold these views when they also hold just world beliefs. When something terrible happens—like domestic abuse—belief in a just world is undermined. To re-establish it, people convince themselves that those who suffer deserve to suffer. If a woman is hit by her husband, she must have deserved it—perhaps she provoked him.

Above: Female office workers at Canadian Car & Foundry in Fort William, Ontario (now Thunder Bay) during World War II foreshadowed the immense increase in the number of women in paid employment in the second half of the twentieth century (Thunder Bay Museum).

Below: Hillary Clinton's campaigns for the U.S. presidency in 2008 and 2016 are perhaps the best-known recent attempts to challenge the so-called glass ceiling (Ali Shaker/Voice of America).

Second, insiders minimize the problem by declaring that today it is adequately managed through awareness and prevention initiatives (Dawson and Fairbairn 2013). For example, shelters allow victims of **intimate partner violence** (IPV) to leave home and live in a safe space with, and run by, other women (Hague 2013). Programs like the Ontario Women's Directorate's *Neighbours, Friends, and Families* educate the public about empowerment-based approaches to assisting women in violent relationships (Barrett and St. Pierre 2011).

Through such programs, Canada has set a global example in the treatment and prevention of violence against women. But many women continue to suffer domestic violence in silence, while single mothers live in poverty after fleeing abusive husbands.

The Gendered Division of Labour

Far more progress has been made in reducing the barriers to paid work for women in Canada, thus providing women with a greater degree of financial independence than ever before. Before the Second World War, Canadian families were usually headed by husbands who worked for pay, while wives stayed home to care for children and maintain the household. With the coming of war, women were called upon to fill jobs left open by the men who enlisted (Alves and Roberts 2012). Most of these women were laid off, or willingly left their jobs, when the war ended, since traditional views of men as breadwinners and women as housewives remained strong.

Then, in the 1960s, the expansion of higher education throughout Canada allowed more women to obtain university degrees and opened careers requiring such credentials to women (Wannell 1990). The gender revolution of the 1970s and '80s fanned this flame: between 1971 and 1986, the Canadian female labour participation rate increased by 85.2% (Connelly and MacDonald 1990). By 1987, two-thirds of Canadian couples were "dual earners," meaning that both husband and wife earned an income. A generation of children raised by working fathers *and* mothers came to think it was "normal" for women to work for pay, something that would transform those children's adult lives: married men who grew up in households with an employed mother spent more time on housework as adults than married men who did not. This trend has continued to the present day: by 2014, 69% of families with at least one child under 16 were dual-earner families, nearly double the rate (36%) in 1976. By contrast, the proportion of single-earner families with children had fallen by more than half.

Although women are much more heavily represented in the work force today, there is still evidence of a traditional gendered division of household labour (Milan et al. 2015). From an insider standpoint, allocating a greater share of housework to women is the most effective way to carry out domestic tasks, especially child rearing. According to these theorists, mothers are especially well suited to raise children, since they form the earliest attachments to children through pregnancy and breast-feeding. Since they are at home with children anyway, mothers can care for the household while their husbands are at work (Forste and Fox 2008).

Marxist theorists add that our capitalist society requires the low-cost social reproduction of a workforce from one generation to the next, and families are the best and cheapest way to raise these new workers. Unpaid mothers keep the family earners and earners-to-be healthy and well fed, housed, and cared for emotionally. They do so at no cost to the capitalist owners of the means of production who will benefit from the surplus value workers produce.

Childrearing thus continues to be a mainly female activity in Canadian society today. However, childbearing is no longer unavoidable, nor is procreation the sole purpose of sex. As the use of reliable contraceptives became increasingly common, women came to enjoy much more control over the timing of pregnancy (Littlejohn 2013, Perez et al. 2013). Now as then, of course, the most highly educated women, with the best career prospects, were the most likely to take advantage of these new contraceptives, leading to a later average age of first childbearing. Today, women can "schedule" childbearing around schooling and careers (Chiappori and Oreffice 2008), and many women view birth control as a decision they can and should make on their own, without negotiating with their partners (Fennell 2011).

Insiders claim that reliable birth control allows men and women to lead more similar lives than ever before. Even sexual stereotypes like the **double standard** (which rewards men who have sex with many women, but stigamatizes women who do the same) have changed because of the contraceptive revolution (Gordon 2012, Fennell 2011), though conservative politicians sometimes still argue for legislative restrictions on abortion, without success. Today, both men and women can be sexually "liberated," since women are able to avoid the potentially negative consequences (i.e., unwanted pregnancy) (Chiappori and Oreffice 2008).

Finally, insiders point to recent anti-discrimination policies as proof of gender equality. Canada's Employment Equity Act was designed to protect all workers in federal employment against discriminatory hiring procedures. Large companies and the federal government must have an equal number of male and female employees at all levels, at least in theory. As a result of such efforts, women and men can now pursue their educational and occupational goals in any field they choose. Insiders recognize that work remains to be done, but think we are on the right path.

SECOND OPINIONS

Some academics, however, question this sunny interpretation of gender relations. Because of their "outsider" status, women in the academy are more likely to recognize persistent patterns of gender inequality. Of course, not all female academics hold feminist views, but feminism is one obviously important theoretical approach to gender inequality. It assumes that women's experiences differ from men's in almost every walk of life. Social institutions, feminists suggest, are shaped by and contribute to perpetuating **male privilege**. Such privilege is largely normalized, rationalized by patriarchal value systems and institutions over the centuries.

Appearance Norms

Consider dominant norms of personal appearance. Researchers have repeatedly shown that women are more likely than men to be dissatisfied with their bodies (see, for example, Strahan et al. 2007, Strahan et al. 2008, Calado et al. 2011). In fact, *most* Canadian women are dissatisfied with some aspect of their physical appearance (Strahan et al. 2006).

Weight is a particular concern. Girls as young as 9 years old express the desire to lose weight (Ridolfi et al. 2011, Krcmar et al. 2008). Women often take extreme measures to alter their appearance (Pankratow et al. 2013, Jung and Lee 2006). For example, since 1992, the incidence of cosmetic surgery procedures has risen by 165% (Strahan et al. 2007). Other women follow extreme exercise regimes, intense diets, or even develop disordered eating practices such as anorexia nervosa or bulimia in pursuit of slenderness (Calado et al. 2011, Boroughs et al. 2010). Women are more likely than men to take such measures and especially to develop eating disorders (Stark-Wroblewski et al. 2005).

It would be difficult to exaggerate the extent of "fat talk" or "body talk," especially among adolescent girls (see, for example, Nichter 2000). Recent research shows that "fat talk" and the current obsession with a thin ideal have a domino effect, infiltrating and disturbing self-image at all ages. Ruffman et al. (2016) have shown how even toddlers adopt their mothers' prejudices against people perceived to be overweight.

In the mid-1980s, a sociocultural model of eating disorders was developed to explain the differing prevalence of such disorders among men and women (Strahan et al. 2007). This theory holds that the mass media constantly feature idealized representations of overly thin women that lead female viewers to become dissatisfied with their own bodies (Calado et al. 2011, Mischner et al. 2013). Magazines targeting women feature more material about weight and body size, and on television, people are twice as likely to comment on women's physical appearance as men's.

Women respond to these media representations in at least two different ways. First, some internalize standards of thinness, becoming dissatisfied with their own bodies (Pankratow et al. 2013, Fitzsimmons-Craft and Bardone-Cone 2012). According to **social comparison theory**, when people compare themselves to others and think that their own bodies fall short, they try to correct the mismatch, sometimes by developing disordered eating habits (Franzoi and Klaiber 2007, Sanderson et al. 2008).

Second, some women come to believe that everyone is deeply invested in the thinness ideal (Bergstrom and Neighbors 2006, Sanderson et al. 2008). Worrying they may be deemed unattractive, they strive to attain a slender fig-ure for the sake of conformity and acceptance (Jung and Lee 2006). These women start to view their own bodies from a third-person perspective, care-fully considering how others will see and judge their physical appearance, and internalizing others' reactions to their bodies (Ambwani and Strauss 2007, Fitzsimmons-Craft and Bardone-Cone 2012).

The vast majority of women will never be able to emulate the ideal of slen-derness promoted by the mainstream media (Boisvert and Harrell 2009, Darlow and Lobel 2010). Consider that the average American woman is 5'4" tall and weighs 140 pounds. The average American model, in contrast, is 5'11" tall and weighs 117 pounds. Models are thinner than 98% of the general female population, and a mere 5% to 10% of women are even physiologically capable of maintaining such a low body weight (Urquhart et al. 2011). Yet atypically slender models define our society's standard of slimness (Clay et al. 2005).

The Social Construction of Beauty

We know the current "standard" of beauty is socially constructed because the "ideal" female body changes over time. Centuries ago, being too thin was viewed negatively in Western societies. For both men and women, weight was a measure of wealth and high social status: your body testified to your ability to afford plenty of food, and, in particular, expensive meat. For women spe-cifically, fat indicated fertility, a characteristic respected and desired in a cul-ture that defined women as wives and mothers.

Over time, the meanings attached to women's bodies have changed dramatically. Obesity and being even slightly overweight are now seen as indicative of lack of self-control. Obese people—particularly obese women—are often stigmatized, while slim women are praised and viewed as sexually desirable, healthy, and fit (Urquhart et al. 2011, Mischner et al. 2013). There are economic, social, and psychological consequences of being fat, especially a fat woman.

Men are also evaluated based on physical appearance, but representations of men in the media are not as dramatically unrealistic as those of women

(Clay et al. 2005). For men, a broader range of physical characteristics are considered attractive. Perhaps as a result, men exposed to these images, even those who experience body dissatisfaction as a result, are less likely than women to internalize these ideals (Bergstrom and Neighbors 2006).

There are some variations in norms of female attractiveness. Melissa Milkie (1999) found that white high school girls typically read mainstream magazines such as *Seventeen* or *Teen*. Black girls, however, felt these magazines targeted whites, and usually opted to read *Ebony* or *Essence* instead. As a result, they were less affected by images that caused body dissatisfaction and low self-esteem among the white girls, correctly perceiving that black men are less fixated on women's body size and weight than white men. Studies continue to confirm that black women have fewer concerns about their weight and report higher body satisfaction, fewer negative thoughts, and a less intense desire to be thin than do white women (Schooler et al. 2004, Ristovski-Slijepcevic et al. 2010).

On the whole, though, North American women cannot escape intense social pressure to be thin (Strahan et al. 2008, Boisvert and Harrell 2009), even if some actively resist that norm (Stark-Wroblewski et al. 2005). Responding to the prevalence of body dissatisfaction and eating disorders among young North American women, many researchers advocate a "health-based" approach to body image. Women, they say, should focus on eating right, exercising, and living a healthy lifestyle, rather than obsessing over the number on the scale.

The general medical consensus is that a body that is fed well and exercised regularly will "naturally" shed "extra" pounds. This approach is definitely an improvement, but outsiders suggest it poses problems of its own, which we discuss below.

The Gendered Division of Labour

Insiders correctly note that growing numbers of men have taken on tasks like cooking that are traditionally seen as "women's work" (Szabo 2013). But scholars offering second opinions suggest that men, unlike women, are for the most part able to pick and choose their domestic chores.

When men cook, it is usually because they *want* to: they opt to prepare meals on weekends or special occasions, when they are not working. By contrast, women's cooking is more often care-oriented; they cater to the needs of their families, packing lunches and preparing dinners during the week, when other demands (like work) compete for attention (Szabo 2013). It is not that they have a special interest in or aptitude for cooking: they simply do not want to fight about the domestic division of labour every day (Beagan et al. 2008).

Women remain responsible for a disproportionate share of domestic tasks

(Kan et al. 2011). Even in societies where men are highly involved in childcare, women spend five times as much time with their children than do their partners (Durante et al. 2012). The more children a woman has, the more time she spends on housework and child care; the same relationship does not hold for men (Sayer et al. 2009, Creese and Beagan 2009).

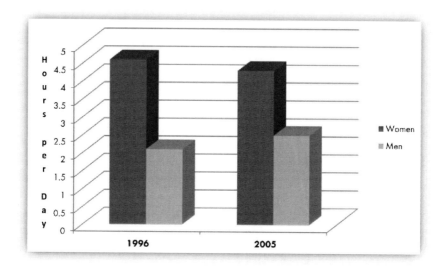

Figure 3.1: Time Spent on Unpaid Domestic Work by Canadians

Why does this unequal division of domestic labour persist? And, even if it is unequal, is it *unfair*?

While insiders hold that the unequal allocation of housework is a common-sense solution to constraints on male breadwinners' time and energy, scholars offering second opinions put forward other explanations (Forste and Fox 2008). **Bargaining theory** suggests the partner with the higher income has more say in decisions related to the distribution of household chores because he or she—usually he—sustains the family financially. Women often earn less than their husbands and therefore hold less bargaining power with which to contest the unequal division of labour (Luke et al. 2014). Over time, as more women entered the job market and rose to higher positions, their incomes increased and, with them, the ability to bargain their way out of some household chores.

However, this theory breaks down in cases where women are the sole breadwinner. These women still do more housework than their husbands, despite bearing complete responsibility for their family's income (Luke et al. 2014). To account for this gap, scholars advanced the concept of **gender dis-**

play. Salaries aside, women and men have been socialized to perform traditional gendered roles. The threat of social exclusion forces them to conform to socially constructed standards of "feminine" or "masculine" behavior. Throughout history, housework has been characterized as "women's work," so women continue to conform to gendered expectations by cooking, cleaning, and caring for children, regardless of income. In this way, they "display" their (socially constructed) gender identity.

The gendered division of labour holds negative long-term consequences for women. Many women leave paid employment during their childbearing years, and some fail to return. Men, in contrast, rarely do the same. The division of domestic labour is problematic because it forces women to choose between career and family—two often equally valued aspects of their lives and identities (Groves and Lui 2012). As well, a commitment to "intensive mothering" (Hays 1998) to the exclusion of all other economic and social activities has long-term financial as well as psychological and health consequences for many women.

To avoid forcing this choice upon women, some scholars and policymakers suggest we increase families' access to affordable, high-quality childcare. In theory, hired domestic help such as nannies, day-care providers, or cleaning services would free up women's time, allowing them to pursue their educational or occupational goals even after bearing children (Groves and Lui 2012). Problematically, however, only a few families can afford such costly services. Moreover, men usually view domestic help as a "substitute" for their own involvement in housework (Groves and Lui 2012). By contrast, women are more likely to end up "in charge" of maids, nannies, and housekeepers. Hired domestic help benefits men most, and perpetuates the belief that domestic work is "women's work" (Pinho and Silva 2010).

On the other hand, certain policy initiatives have made a difference (Forste and Fox 2008). The Swedish government offers subsidized day care and comparatively generous parental leave to encourage sharing of domestic labour between men and women (Thomas and Hildingsson 2009). To avoid men simply "transferring" their leave days to their wives, the government dictated that families would forfeit their days if fathers did not use them. This policy forced many fathers to play a bigger role in their children's early care. Partly as a result, sharing of childcare and household labour has become more equal in Sweden. In Canada there is the similar example of Quebec's provincial policy of universal daycare. In recent years, the Quebec program has been criticized as economically unsustainable, but this conclusion is, so far, unproven. Many (see, for example, Albanese 2014) believe it could ultimately serve as a model for a national program.

The Gender Pay Gap

A popular myth about gender inequality is that women are paid less than men for doing the "same work" (Kearney 2006, Barnet-Verzat and Wolff 2008). Economists used to explain this differential by pointing out that better-educated workers are paid more: if men are on average better educated than women, they will naturally earn more. However, this argument no longer holds, given women's high participation rates in higher education (Yap and Konrad 2009).

Women's lower wages are also sometimes attributed to their role as mothers. Employers argue that women will be less productive than men in the long term because they interrupt their careers to have and care for their children (Barnet-Verzat and Wolff 2008, Purcell et al. 2010). To compensate, employers offer women lower wages, or keep them in low-level positions that pay less (Isaac et al. 2012). Such an argument hinges on the patriarchal division of domestic labour discussed above: because the average woman assumes more childcare and housework duties than the average man, employers assume that this *should* be true for *all* women.

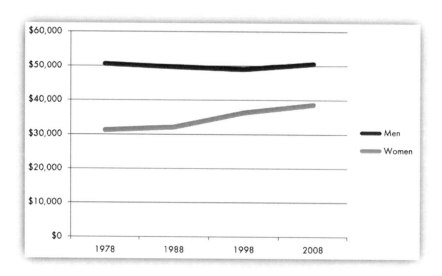

Figure 3.2: Median Earnings of Men and Women in Canada, 1978 to 2008
CONSTANT 2008 DOLLARS, FULL-YEAR, FULL-TIME EMPLOYEES

Indeed, some women *want* to prioritize their roles as wives, mothers, and homemakers, and opt out of paid labour altogether. There is nothing "wrong" with being a stay-at-home mother. But this role becomes problematic when it is imposed upon women who *want* to prioritize (or even just maintain) their careers. For example, some researchers, employers, politicians, and policy-makers wrongly assume that all women *want* and actively seek part-time work with flexible hours and the freedom to work from home, so they are better able to care for their children (Mastekaasa and Smeby 2008, Zeytinoglu et al. 2010).

These stereotypes disadvantage women in the labour market because they frame all women as falling short of the image of the "ideal worker": that is, one who is free from all non-work (i.e., family) demands and obligations (Budig 2002). Conversely, these stereotypes provide men with a general advantage in the labour market: employers routinely assume that men are the primary breadwinners, and thus more committed to their jobs out of a responsibility to provide for their dependent wives and children. In turn, fatherhood confers an advantage on male job applicants in the form of higher starting salaries, as employers want to ensure these men can support their families (Isaac et al. 2012).

Traditional beliefs about the "duties" and "responsibilities" of men and women persist, even though men are rarely the sole family breadwinners today. In 1890, a mere 2.5% of married white women worked outside the home. With each passing decade, the labour force participation rate for married women increased; by 2000, 66% of married women were working for pay, and 47% worked full-time (Kearney 2006). The assumption that men are the primary breadwinners, and that working women merely supplement their husbands' incomes, is unfounded in most instances.

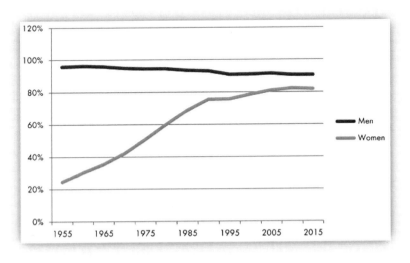

Figure 3.3: Labour Force Participation Rate in Canada
MEN AND WOMEN AGES 25 TO 54

By far the most common explanation of the **gender pay gap** is career choice: women and men choose to do different types of work, which correspond to different income brackets (Hultin 2003, Price-Glynn and Rakovski 2012). For example, more women than men perform clerical, retail, and service-sector work. These careers pay less than those men are more likely to enter, such as engineering or information technology (Kearney 2006). For this reason, it is wrong to say that women are paid less than men to do the "same" work: almost always, men and women are doing *different* types of work. The fundamental problem is that so-called "women's work" has been systematically devalued, compared to occupations traditionally dominated by men. But how and why do men and women choose different occupations (Fernandez 2006)?

As we have noted, "personal preference" is currently the most popular answer to this question. However, academics offering second opinions have long been suspicious of the rhetoric of "choice" (Hultin 2003, Stone 2007). In particular, they point to some flaws in **preference theory**: the insider belief that women make autonomous but disadvantageous "choices" (Broadbridge 2010). Preference theory holds that men continue to dominate the workplace because few women choose to prioritize their careers as men do. This is a subtle form of victim-blaming: it suggests women should be held responsible for their marginalized status in the labour market.

Instead, we should ask a different question: are women *able* to prioritize their careers in the same way as men? Probably not, for at least two reasons. First, men and women are funneled into different, differentially valued, and differentially rewarded types of work (Broadbridge 2010). Women are assumed to be "naturally" nurturing, caring, and empathetic, and are often hired into roles that emphasize these characteristics, such as nursing, social work, and teaching (Williams 2013, Smith 2012). Such work is highly skilled but low paying, at least compared to the types of jobs men are likely to hold (Price-Glynn and Rakovski 2012, Salami 2007). Men therefore opt out of such "women's work" in favour of more "manly" occupations that are higher paying and more prestigious (Cognard-Black 2004, Snyder and Green 2008). Second, given the privileging of "men's work" as deserving higher pay, most couples rationally decide to prioritize the husband's career as more important to the family's financial survival.

Contrary to what preference theory suggests, many sociologists hold that women's (and men's) choices are socially constrained from an early age. Consider the widely held belief that men excel at math and science, while women are naturally more caring and empathetic. Boys and girls internalize these assumptions (Mastekaasa and Smeby 2008); boys, for example, tend to overestimate their mathematical ability, and are more likely than girls to pursue a field of study leading to science- or engineering-related careers. Female science, technology, and engineering students remain a minority, and continue to be underrepresented in the workplace. Because men dominate these fields, they continue to be perceived as "men's work" (Fernandez 2006, Hedlin 2010).

Considerable evidence exists that shows that some men are more nurturing and emotionally expressive than some women, while some women are more assertive and mathematically capable than some men. Yet many people avoid a particular field because it clashes with their **gendered identity** (Hedlin 2010). For example, men expect their masculinity and heterosexuality to be questioned if they pursue "women's work," such as nursing. And because many women are deeply invested in protecting their "femininity," they view traditionally "masculine" labour, such as construction work, as inappropriate.

Family members and peers play an important role in this process (Salami 2007). Many parents are deeply involved in their children's career planning, providing advice, encouragement, and financial support. When parents disapprove of a child's career choice, they discourage them from pursuing that line of work. More subtly, the expectation of criticism, rejection, or marginalization for being "different" can drive people to make traditional gendered choices (Mastekaasa and Smeby 2008). Even though we tell children they are free to pursue any career they choose, they are also exposed to traditional beliefs about what type of work is suited to men or women (Fernandez 2006, Broadbridge 2010).

The rhetoric of choice is also used to explain why some women quit their jobs to become full-time mothers. In many cases, however, women are *forced* out of their jobs (Purcell et al. 2010). Many husbands support their wives' decisions to return to work after having children, but these same husbands choose not to take on a greater share of housework to allow their wives to devote adequate time to their paid work (Kullberg 2013, Sayer et al. 2009). Unable to balance family and career, women are forced to "choose"—but the "choice" is forced. Men rarely face the same dilemma.

The Glass Ceiling

Policies designed to curb gendered workplace discrimination have been in place for decades. Insiders champion these initiatives as evidence that we are well on our way to ending gender inequality. But discrimination plays out in subtle ways that fly under the radar of most official policies and procedures. Consider the **glass ceiling**: a form of workplace gender discrimination tricky to identify or measure, and therefore hard to mitigate.

In 1999, Carly Fiorina was named the new CEO of Hewlett-Packard, making her the first woman to head a company on *Fortune* magazine's list of the top 100 U.S. companies as ranked by annual revenues (Cotter et al. 2001). Fiorina's success was hailed as evidence the so-called "glass ceiling" had been shattered. Fiorina herself declared that women face "no limits whatsoever. There is not a glass ceiling."

Such statements are examples of the methodological individualism we discussed earlier: Fiorina's personal success has been used (mainly by men) to suggest that all women are able to climb the corporate ladder. But nearly two decades later, a mere 21 of the 500 biggest U.S. companies are headed by women (Cook and Glass 2014, Dang et al. 2014).

The concept of the "glass ceiling" was introduced in the late 1970s (Guo 2013) to describe an invisible barrier (or, more accurately, barriers) that prevents women from advancing in their careers, despite their qualifications, skills, and achievements (Isaac et al. 2012, Dang et al. 2014). The use of the ceiling metaphor implies that gendered workplace discrimination becomes more pronounced in the upper levels of the organizational hierarchy. However, there is also evidence of a **sticky floor**: barriers that keep women "stuck" on the lowest rungs of the career ladder (Yap and Konrad 2009, Russo and Hassink 2012).

We describe this barrier as "glass" because women can see through it to the higher management positions they desire (Guo 2013, Purcell et al. 2010). But in 1999 (the same year that Fiorina became H-P's CEO), evidence emerged of a **concrete ceiling** for women of colour (Cotter et al. 2001, Jackson and O'Callaghan 2009). These women experience the greatest disadvantage compared to white men, making it unrealistic for them to even *dream* of securing a corporate leadership role (Yap and Konrad 2009, Smith 2012).

As the very term "glass ceiling" suggests, barriers to women's advancement are largely invisible, consisting of subtle biases that most people fail to notice (Isaac et al. 2012), and are often attributed to physiological differences between men and women (Dimovski et al. 2010). Many employers assume that men are "natural leaders" who are innately assertive, ambitious, and competitive—all qualities commonly associated with achievement (Weyer 2007, Cech and Blair-Loy 2010).

Women, on the other hand, are often thought to be less competent, intelligent, and capable of leadership than men (Cook and Glass 2014, Yap and Konrad 2009, Jackson and O'Callaghan 2009). They are viewed as innately passive, overly emotional, and unprofessional—again, for physiological reasons (Cotter et al. 2001, Cech and Blair-Loy 2010). And despite growing academic success, women continue to be stereotyped as lacking educational credentials (Weyer 2007).

There has been much discussion in recent years about how leadership norms themselves are gendered in such a way as to exclude women. Yet there is increasing evidence that traits we tend to identify as "feminine"—collaboration, consultativeness, empathy—are as or more useful leadership tools than the traditionally "masculine" qualities of ambition, aggression, and so on. Both leadership styles are useful and a mix of them is ideal. But many people think that women cannot master both styles, simply because they are women.

Contrary to popular belief, however, gendered socialization, not physiology, is largely responsible for these supposedly "natural" differences. Women are rewarded for displaying their "femininity"—for being passive, pleasant, and deferential—throughout their schooling and at work. When they try to exercise authority, they are frequently criticized for being "bossy," "bitchy," and even "masculine." As a result of ongoing efforts to conform to socially prescribed **gender roles**, many women do not exhibit the qualities identified with successful leaders. Men, by contrast, are encouraged throughout their lives to take on leadership roles. Although there are indeed physiological differences between men and women, nothing suggests that women are incapable of exercising the confidence, assertiveness, and other qualities typical of leaders; rather, they are socially discouraged from doing so.

Women also face an uphill climb on the corporate ladder because most of the people making promotion decisions are white men. When filling jobs, people view candidates like themselves more favourably (Corsun and Costen 2001, Simpson and Altman 2000). This desire to work with people like ourselves is known as **homosocial reproduction**: it "reproduces" power structures (Purcell et al. 2010). In the "boys' club," corporate men bond over shared interests and network during "masculine" activities like golf. These networking opportunities have, in the past, tended to exclude women (Cech and Blair-Loy 2010, Wingfield 2009). As a result, women secure fewer mentors and sponsors, because powerful men do not identify with them (Jackson and O'Callaghan 2009).

Homosocial reproduction maintains white men in positions of power and women in subordinate positions. To advance in the face of these biases, women must outperform their male competitors by an almost impossible margin (Simpson and Altman 2000, Dimovski et al. 2010). Few people, men or women, are so extraordinarily talented, and therefore few women gain the opportunity to perform in top positions.

In the rare instances when women *do* make it to the top, they typically meet resistance (Robinson and Nelson 2010), endure intense scrutiny and performance pressure, and face hostile, defiant male colleagues (Cook and Glass 2014). No better example of this can be cited than that of Hillary Clinton. Female competence in a "man's job" violates social expectations for "feminine" behaviour, provoking anxiety and disapproval. By contrast, employees tend to accept orders and criticisms from male bosses quietly, believing that these harsh bosses are simply doing their jobs. Women have to advance by acting "like men," but then are censured for that very behavior (Jackson and O'Callaghan 2009).

At the same time, women in positions of authority are viewed negatively if they are "too" feminine (Dimovski et al. 2010). When female executives give directions or criticism, they are often seen as "bitchy," "controlling," or "moody," reflecting their supposed feminine emotionalism (Robinson and Nelson 2010). Similarly, mothers in executive positions are often criticized for being less committed to their work than to their home, family, and children (Kullberg 2013). To succeed, women leaders must strike a delicate balance between feminine and masculine behaviours—a challenging task not expected of men in positions of authority.

Despite the obstacles they have overcome, those few successful women leaders often believe the system is meritocratic and requires no change. To succeed, these women have had to work hard—harder than men in comparable circumstances—leading them to view success as a just reward for that hard work (Simpson and Altman 2000). Like Fiorina, these women come to see themselves as evidence of the system's fairness and legitimacy.

This point of view bodes ill for the many women who cannot overcome gendered barriers to success. Successful, powerful women will not use their influence to remove barriers for other women if, because of their own anomalous success, they think such barriers do not exist.

Many women possess the skills and credentials necessary to fill high-paying positions of power effectively. They also desire such positions: research shows that men and women in similar organizational structures value promotions equally (Cognard-Black 2004). While most women once privileged their families over paid employment, research shows that highly educated women now value their careers to a much greater degree (Kullberg 2013), and that women who pursue managerial careers are as committed and ambitious as their male counterparts. Both are equally willing to sacrifice time with their families and other non-work interests for the sake of occupational success. Yet women continue to be rewarded with high-status, high-paying positions much less often than white men.

The Glass Escalator

The same gender stereotypes that disadvantage women in the labour market often benefit men (Cognard-Black 2004). Because many people assume men are "natural" leaders, they garner higher wages and quicker promotions even in female-dominated areas of employment (Williams 2013, Kullberg 2013). As a result, where women come up against a glass ceiling, many men enjoy an easy ride up the so-called glass escalator.

Colleagues, superiors, and clients reinforce the glass escalator effect by thinking that male workers aren't "suited" for "women's work" (Williams 2013). For example, doctors and hospital staff are often surprised to see men working as nurses, and patients often mistake male nurses for doctors. Sometimes, colleagues and clients criticize such men for lacking ambition, or aspiring to fulfill their potential (Snyder and Green 2008). The sense that these men do not "belong" in women's work may push them out of "feminine" jobs and into managerial positions that are seen as more "appropriate" for men (Wingfield 2009).

Men also tend to be driven out of women's work because such work puts their masculinity and heterosexuality into question (Mastekaasa and Smeby 2008). Male nurses, for example, are often assumed to be gay, or at least effeminate. Male kindergarten and primary school teachers also tend to run into trouble because of gendered stereotypes: they are "supposed" to be caring and affectionate towards their students, and some people view their motives as pedophilic (Williams 2013). Such criticisms tend to push men into traditionally male-dominated roles, such as hospital administrator or school principal, and the higher pay and prestige associated with these positions tend to resolve any suspicions about their "manhood" (Kullberg 2013, Snyder and Green 2008).

The glass escalator tends to advantage white men (Smith 2012). Men of colour are less socially similar to their white bosses than white men, hindering their ability to network effectively. Second, racist stereotypes frame racial minorities—especially black men—as dangerous and prone to criminal behaviour. People thought to exhibit these traits are unlikely to succeed in "feminized" fields that emphasize caring and compassion. Third, racist stereotypes also frame racial minorities as less qualified, contributing to the perception that a job in caring professions such as nursing may be "too good" for them: they "should" be working in unskilled manual labour. Intersections of race and gender therefore dictate which men are permitted to ride the glass escalator (Price-Glynn and Rakovski 2012).

Most importantly, the glass escalator helps clarify the concept of the glass ceiling. It proves that the problems women face in seeking upward mobility are not due to **tokenism**: the restriction of opportunities for any person who was a rarity in his or her workplace, regardless of gender or race (Williams 1992). According to this theory, dominant groups exclude minorities to perpetuate their own advantage (McDonald et al. 2009). But men who succeed in "women's professions" are granted advantages because of their token status (Smith 2012).

Ultimately, women are doubly disadvantaged in the labour market. Women who work in female-dominated fields receive limited rewards because these types of work have been traditionally devalued. But women who work in male-dominated fields are likely to be excluded from social networks and other resources that facilitate success. Trying to reduce occupational sex segregation by encouraging women to do "men's work" and men to do "women's work" will not eliminate the gendered pay gap (Williams 1992). The labour market values and rewards "masculine" qualities, and assumes that only men embody such qualities. Until we challenge these assumptions, men and women will continue to experience different opportunities and rewards at work.

Sexual Harassment   — _Theories that help explain why women are more likely to face harassment_

One negative consequence of women's disadvantaged status in the labour market is workplace harassment. Workplace harassment can indeed happen to anyone, anywhere, but most physical and sexual assault victims are female (Charlesworth et al. 2011, Jablonska et al. 2007).

One theory aimed at explaining this fact, the vulnerable victim hypothesis, suggests that women, racial minorities, and those with the most precarious positions and least workplace authority are subject to the most harassment (Davidson et al. 2010, Hodson et al. 2009). A second theory, gender-role spillover, holds that men harass women because they are used to dealing with women in subordinate roles in other settings, including at home, and carry this patriarchal view over into the workplace. Finally, the paradoxical power-threat model suggests that women in positions of authority are most likely to face harassment, as they pose the greatest threat to men's dominance (Blackstone et al. 2012).

Harassment is also concentrated in certain occupations, such as sales (Lu-Ming 2013). Customers hold coercive power over salespeople, since ultimately they can choose whether or not to buy a product. Customers can also punish salespeople through negative word of mouth. These factors make some salespeople feel they must submit to their customers' desires, or at least tolerate harassment quietly.

Nurses are yet another vulnerable group (Hibino et al. 2009). Studies find that nurses are more likely to be stalked and harassed than workers in many other professions because some patients misinterpret care and attention as romantic interest (Maran et al. 2014). Because nurses interact closely and often physically with their clients, they may be exposed to inappropriate behaviours more often.

Of course, harassment occurs outside the workplace as well. Most women know their attackers personally: they are often current or past intimate partners. Such **intimate partner violence (IPV)** includes sexual, emotional, physical, psychological, and financial abuse, and affects up to 23% of all

Canadians each year (Barrett and St. Pierre 2011). Although some women commit IPV against their male partners, they are usually motivated by self-defense, acting out of fear their abusive partner is about to strike (DeKeseredy et al. 1997).

One type of IPV that may begin at a young age is **dating violence**. Between 25% and 55% of dating adolescents report experiencing physical or psychological abuse in their relationships. The specific types of abuse often reflect stereotypical gender roles: girls tend to be more psychologically abusive, while boys tend to be more sexually abusive (Sears 2007). In keeping with traditional patriarchal values, some boys think that being "manly" involves initiating and vigorously pursuing sexual activity with their partners. They are taught not to take 'no' for an answer, or else risk being seen as passive, submissive, and feminine. Such behavior while young is likely to persist into later adulthood (Dumas et al. 2013).

Several vulnerable populations are disproportionately victimized by physical and sexual assault, including elderly women (Herlitz and Steel 2005). Many offenders describe attacks on older women as expressions of anger and hostility, claiming they aim primarily to hurt their victims (Bainbridge et al. 2005). Older women are thus more likely to sustain injuries during a sexual assault. Many of these women also suffer from psychiatric and cognitive disabilities, rendering them less likely or able to defend themselves against their attackers.

In contrast, younger women are more likely to fight back. To compensate for the greater likelihood of resistance, attacks on younger women are often carried out by two or more assailants, and weapons are often used to force compliance (Bainbridge et al. 2005). Despite these differences, penetration and physical trauma are as likely in older as younger victims of sexual assault. Research, however, has focused on younger victims, likely due to a widely held belief that older women are no longer sexually desirable and therefore at less risk of sexual victimization. But that viewpoint is a form of discrimination in itself.

A similar stigma plagues women with disabilities: although they are widely viewed as asexual or sexually undesirable, they are, in fact, an especially vulnerable subset of sexual assault targets. Perpetrators may think that women with physical or mental impairments are powerless to resist, or easier to manipulate. In addition, women with disabilities may be hesitant to report the event for fear of being forced to leave their homes and relocate to a "safer" environment "for their own protection" (Dickens et al. 2006).

Aboriginal women run an elevated risk of IPV and post-separation violence (Brownridge et al. 2008). However, those who live on reserves and in other geographically isolated regions enjoy limited options as to where they may report abuse or seek support (LaRocque 2002). Their low incomes also pose barriers. Similarly, women of colour and immigrants report a lack of cultural sensitivity to their experiences of physical or sexual victimization, as well as a shortage of specialized services designed to address their unique needs. Others distrust service providers themselves, because of their different racial, ethnic, and class backgrounds.

Immigrant women usually face the added challenge of a language barrier, hindering them from reporting abuse or using support services. Others fear being ostracized for revealing "private" family issues to outsiders and challenging their husbands' authority (Atwal et al. 2013). Still others, especially illegal immigrants, fear that they will be deported if they make their problems known to the police and other authorities (Barrett and St. Pierre 2011).

Survivors of all ages, abilities, and races often feel ashamed, embarrassed, and even guilty following an attack, deterring them from reporting it. Some fear the perpetrators will retaliate and attack again. For their part, many men who have been abused by other men fear that people will assume they are gay if they report the abuse. Survivors of sexual assault—especially date rape— often do not want their friends and families to know what happened. Many are afraid they won't be believed, or that they will be judged or blamed for the attack (Danis et al. 2006). Their fears are, for the most point, valid: men— including police officers, most of whom are male—tend to attribute more responsibility for date rape to the victim (Vopni 2006).

Because of barriers to accurate reporting, sexual and physical assault data are limited and unreliable (Herlitz and Steel 2005). We likely underestimate the prevalence of sexual and physical abuse (Sears 2007). For example, the Ontario Women's Directorate estimates the number of date rapes formally reported to the police represent a mere 1% of those that occur (Vopni 2006).

OUTSIGHTS

People on the outside—here, disadvantaged or victimized women—feel the effects of gender inequality acutely. Insiders may claim that gender inequality has been adequately addressed, but many women still experience both subtle and explicit forms of sexism every day (Valor-Segura et al. 2011, Fernandez 2006). Most explicitly, **hostile sexism** refers to a general contempt for women, a belief that they should be "kept in their place" or confined to certain roles, and a belief that they must be dominated and forced into submission. People who endorse this type of sexism are more likely to try to justify rape by saying, for example, the victim was dressed revealingly and therefore "asked for it."

Benevolent sexism is less explicitly misogynist, and correspondingly harder to identify. It involves praising women who conform to gendered stereotypes while scorning those who do not (Valor-Segura et al. 2011). For example, women who fail to marry or have children, or who engage in extramarital sex, may be stigmatized.

Because there are at least these two types of sexism, gender inequality is more ambiguous than, say, economic inequality. Recall that there are various measures of class inequality, including income, social status and prestige. But how do we accurately measure the various forms of gender inequality?

One of the major failings of the insider perspective is its suggestion that gender inequality is uncomplicated—something that all women, everywhere, experience in the same way, and that can be easily addressed through anti-discrimination policies. This simplistic approach ignores the more complex and harmful types and consequences of gender inequality, which we address below.

Biology vs. Gender Performativity

The dominant view of gender in our society is dichotomous: femininity and masculinity are widely thought to be mutually exclusive categories. Traditional masculinity is associated with power and dominance, while traditional femininity is defined by its subordination to dominant masculinities (Winterich 2007, Hedlin 2010). Femininity thus implies passivity, modesty, and meekness—the opposite of masculine assertiveness and aggression.

People assume that these gendered qualities map neatly onto sexed bodies: men naturally and inevitably embody masculine traits, and women, feminine ones. When someone exhibits gendered characteristics that do not correspond with his or her body, people become uncomfortable and confused. For example, extremely muscular women challenge a commonly accepted gender dichotomy, blurring the line that is supposed to distinguish feminine females from masculine males.

For the most part, men and women are noticeably different physiologically. But these two discrete categories—masculine and feminine—cannot accommodate everyone tidily. For example, 18-year-old Emma Podolsky says that being a woman "always felt like an ill-fitting suit. Being non-binary is how I feel most authentic and most comfortable" (Hampson 2015). Sex differences are better described as a continuum than binary: some people conform closely to the broad definition of one sex or the other—they are clearly men or clearly women—while others do not (Deslauriers 2004).

There is also an important distinction to be made between "natural" differences and socially constructed ones. Men and women are physiologically different, and we assume that they are treated differently in our society for that reason. But men and women are not unequal, socially and politically, because they are biologically different. Instead, we come to see women as being different from men because they are treated differently, *made* to be socially and politically unequal to men.

Unfortunately, treating people differently may *make* them different. In past centuries, women were excluded from most forms of education and denied the opportunity to build a career outside the home. As a result, many women were less knowledgeable than men on most issues (Deslauriers 2004). In turn, they seemed perfect candidates to stay home and care for children. Because women did housework and cared for their siblings from a young age, people came to see their nurturing qualities as "natural," and to accept without question their ignorance of anything other than domestic tasks.

However, these qualities are not natural; they were *produced* by inequality. Denied the opportunity to do anything else, women knew little except how to be housewives and caregivers. When we try to explain inequality, we often confuse cause and effect. We use the damaging consequences of inequality—in this case, women's lack of education and forced conformity to the role of housewife—to prove that inequality itself is innate (Deslauriers 2004).

We know that gender is not intrinsically bound to sex because people have to be socialized and controlled into performing it—and because many people refuse to conform. If "manliness" or "masculinity" were a "natural" product of male physiology, society would not need to pressure men into conforming with masculine norms. Women too must be forced to adopt "feminine" traits and roles. Both men and women face social exclusion and marginalization if they fail to conform to gendered expectations.

Appearance Norms and Beauty Ideals

Processes of socialization and informal social control are particularly important in reinforcing traditional appearance norms. As we discussed earlier, scholars offering second opinions have shown that the mass media feed insecurities about physical appearance. The medical system may do the same, by affirming the thin ideal as the fit ideal. In particular, initiatives targeting obesity engage in a type of victim-blaming, framing weight as an individual health problem (Winterich 2007).

Most general practitioners use the body mass index (BMI) as a standard to evaluate a patient's weight (Darlow and Lobel 2010). Though every human body is unique, the BMI imposes a uniform standard of thinness on people whose physiology may bar them from attaining the shape, size and weight that have been medically designated as "right." Patients who fall outside of the weight range deemed appropriate for their height and age are instructed to exercise and diet to conform to these rigid expectations. If they fail to reach their "target weight," they are told they risk obesity-related ailments. Instead of focusing on general wellbeing, doctors encourage patients to focus on the number on the scale.

To obtain their "ideal," "healthy" weight, patients are told to lead an active lifestyle and follow a nutritious diet. Increasingly, doctors endorse popular games designed to promote physical activity, such as Nintendo's Wii Fit. Although seemingly harmless, outsiders have suggested that these efforts to "make fitness fun" may be a form of fat shaming. For example, 22-year-old Jessica says she "got sucked into" Wii Fit. Before starting, players must enter their weight and the game calculates their BMI. "According to the Wii Fit game," Jessica says, "I am obese [so] my character becomes obese as well. This is horrifying to look at. It makes me feel awful about myself" (cited in Greenhalgh 2015).

As Jessica suggests, constant exposure to the thin ideal inspires body dissatisfaction, guilt, and shame among women in particular. When doctors join the chorus, people feel even guiltier about failing to conform to appearance norms.

Advice prescribed by health-care practitioners is more often interpreted as fact than the tips and tricks in popular magazines or on TV. Thus, doctors are believed when they promise patients that proper eating and exercise habits will inevitably translate into a particular kind of body. But although some women easily maintain a slender figure, others will never achieve the thin ideal—or the toned, muscular one—no matter what they eat or how much they exercise. Consider the struggle 21-year-old Mai Ly faced in attempting to conform to these standards:

> According to the BMI chart, I am obese, standing at 5'6" and weighing about 235 pounds. My whole life, I was always a bit chubbier than the rest of the little girls. My best friends were always the smallest of the small, even though they ate enormous portions at least six times a day. I, however, was not that lucky. Everything I ate seemed to make me gain weight like crazy, even if it was healthy food in small portions. . . .
>
> I compare myself to my friends enough times to say that sometimes I wish I were them, which is sad, I know, but it's true in a sense. Every time I look at myself in the mirror, I feel like if I were as skinny as they are, I could take over the world (Greenhalgh 2015).

When diet and physical activity fail to produce the desired results, many women turn instead to disordered eating, cigarette smoking, "cleansing," and other habits intended to curb their appetite. Some of these women hit their appropriate BMI mark and look "healthy," even if they are far from it.

By endorsing the thin ideal promoted by the media, or the "fitness" ideal promoted by our health care system, women who diet, exercise, and otherwise discipline their bodies contribute to perpetuating dominant ideas about femininity and female beauty that focus on outward appearance (Winterich 2007). Body hair removal is another way through which the overwhelming majority of women participate in the policing of their own bodies. By painfully taming, removing, or reconfiguring the hair on every inch of their bodies, every Western woman rejects an aspect of her "natural" appearance—a characteristic she was born with—in an effort to conform to a culturally prescribed definition of "beauty" and "desirability."

In response, "girl power" campaigns, pop songs, and women's magazines try to empower women who are not pretty or slim by saying that "everyone is beautiful." This is plainly not true. Our culture's definition of beauty is predicated on exclusion: everyone who does not conform to a narrow set of culturally defined appearance norms is *not* beautiful. Today, "beauty" connotes delicate features, a slim figure, tallness, and youth, and not everyone possesses these features (Strahan et al. 2006). Individual preferences vary, in that we all find certain people more attractive than others; however, most people in our society would agree on which women are "beautiful" and which are not.

Parents and peers also influence young people's body image and self-esteem. Body satisfaction begins to drop in children as young as eight when their parents criticize their appearance, weight, and eating habits (Krcmar et al. 2008). Girls are especially vulnerable to such criticism, particularly if their mothers are dissatisfied with their own bodies and have disordered eating habits. For example, Mai Ly, who was quoted above, says that her family constantly advises her to lose weight: "The worst is my mother. . . . [S]he tells me that I will never find love because of my weight. It's funny because, even [though] I have a boyfriend now (not my first), she continues to tell me how it will never last" (Greenhalgh 2015).

Similarly, many young women become dissatisfied with their bodies when their friends and classmates criticize weight gain and praise weight loss (Sanderson et al. 2008, Urquhart et al. 2011). These all-too-common conversations are termed "fat talk" (Fitzsimmons-Craft and Bardone-Cone 2012). Some girls say that if they do not participate in such conversations, negatively evaluating their own weight, diet, and exercise habits, their friends will think they are "bragging" or overly confident. But the more girls and women engage in fat talk, the less satisfied they are with their bodies, and the greater is their risk of developing disordered eating habits. For example, college student Anahid writes:

> When there is so much talk about obesity, you feel bad about yourself
> as a person. Even if you are a kind person, you feel down because the

whole nation is saying that excessive weight is bad and that's it. It makes you look at yourself and think that there is something wrong with you. It makes you feel like a failure and, more importantly, it makes you feel as if you have failed others (King 2015).

Our culturally defined standard of beauty produces other negative consequences apart from eating disorders. Women seeking romantic partners are more likely than men to be evaluated on their physical appearance, with those who are thin drawing greater interest from potential partners (Ambwani and Strauss 2007). In contrast, outsiders like 22-year-old April observe that "[e]verything in my life has told me that power and happiness come from beauty, and now I feel as if I am conditioned to pursue it. Weight has become a ghost that doesn't leave me no matter what I do" (Greenhalgh 2015).

The Second Shift

Although insiders rightly note that women are now more able to obtain meaningful employment, they often ignore the fact that this transition has forced many women to work two full-time jobs: a "real," paying career, on top of a **second shift**, consisting of domestic labour. Indeed, women with children work an additional 73 8-hour-long shifts every year (Creese and Beagan 2009).

This is not to say that all women passively accept the responsibility for housekeeping and childcare. Many try to convince their husbands to participate equally in domestic work, but face resistance (Hochschild 1989, as cited in Perkins and DeMeis 1996). Some men (grudgingly) agree to take on more responsibilities, only to do them poorly or fail to finish them. So, in an attempt to maintain peaceful relationships with their partners, many women come to accept a disproportionate amount of domestic work.

Likely as a result, many overworked mothers report lower marital satisfaction, and poorer relationships with their children (Steven et al. 2001, Milkie et al. 2009). For example, Karen Larson, a merchandiser for Macy's, faced an extended second shift after her husband was made a partner at his law firm when their daughter was barely two years old: "I was running myself into the ground. . . . But what's worse, the stress of juggling everything was killing my relationship" (Casserly 2011).

For Stephanie Pollard, now a single mother of four who runs two businesses, the second shift meant the end of her marriage. She recalls preparing to head to the family cottage while pregnant with her fourth child: finding time to pack the clothes and food, mow the lawn, and fill the gas tank, all while working around her own work schedule so she could be prepared to leave when her husband returned from *his* job:

He would roll in and hop in the car and we would go, with me driving so he could sleep on the way because he was tired. . . . Toward the end, especially the last summer, I was really angry because I felt that I was doing everything and he was contributing nothing and then everything became a fight and everything was angry. . . . I didn't know how it had gotten to that point. . . . Looking back, I realize that I kind of enabled that behaviour. I never turned around and said: 'Fine, I'm not doing the laundry, either.' . . . I think his argument may be that he tried to contribute and I shut him down because it wasn't done right or when I wanted it to be (Kopun 2009).

The second shift can reduce the quality of women's paid labour and in turn, their chances of earning a promotion or raise (Kurtz 2012, Creese and Beagan 2009). The second shift also tends to negatively affect women's physical and mental health. The stress of such a heavy workload, combined with a lack of leisure time, can cause insomnia, exhaustion, anxiety, and depression (Krantz and Ostergren 2001, Tierney et al. 1990). Vicky Ioannou, a working mother of three from Waterloo, Ont., says, "I think women are generally more stressed. . . . My husband is involved, but it's mostly me making the arrangements. . . . And let's say I have an off day and just want to go out and have a bit of time to myself, I have to make the arrangements: 'Can you take care of the kids while I go out?'" (quoted in Thompson 2014). Mother Lidia Costi, who works both full- and part-time paid positions, notes, "I don't have a day to myself. At all. Sometimes I'm working 14 hours a day." Her long shifts mean she and other women like her are "always tired. . . . That's why we savour every moment to ourselves that we can get" (Thompson 2014).

Workplace Harassment

Ultimately, the second shift reproduces gender inequalities at home and in the workforce. Some aspects of work life blatantly reinforce the patriarchal gender relations that underlie the second shift. Recall, for example, the glass ceiling. When men are consistently in positions of power and women are always their subordinates, the structure of the workplace perpetuates the sense that women are inferior to men (Corsun and Costen 2001).

These power differentials are not only unfair and demoralizing: they are a prime cause of workplace harassment. By demeaning lower-status workers—who are disproportionately female—more powerful employees believe they can defend or elevate their own status (Hodson et al. 2009, Jackson et al. 2006). For example, former British Columbia volunteer firefighter Kirstin Rudolph reported her chief for sexual assault: "He would ask me to have sex with him in his office. . . . He would say if I want a promotion why don't I put on my knee pads and blow him under his desk" (Mayor 2015).

The more elusive **cyberbullying** is an even more prevalent form of workplace harassment (Piotrowski 2012, Borstorff et al. 2007). Cyberbullying consists of any inappropriate, unwanted social exchange via online or wireless communication technology. Many employees feel detached or "anonymous" when communicating electronically, and free to say things they would never say in person.

Another female firefighter says that a senior colleague offered to help her get her bearings when she started out, but eventually began engaging in cyberabuse: "He would send me very detailed . . . text messages about certain things that were sex-related. . . . And it continued and continued, and it just got worse and worse," until he finally attempted to assault her in their dorm (Mayor 2015).

Organizations adopt many strategies to prevent and manage workplace sexual harassment. Most have zero tolerance policies, under which any type of sexual behaviour, including sexualized jokes or banter, are grounds for discipline or dismissal (Jackson et al. 2006, Hodson et al. 2009). However, some question these policies, suggesting the broad definition of sexual harassment includes so many different behaviours (even supposedly "well-intentioned compliments") that workers' autonomy and freedom of speech are now threatened. These views normalize harassment so that many instances continue to go unreported, since victims fear they will be seen as "uptight," or that their attacker will not be disciplined in an overly lenient workplace and may even try to retaliate (Maran et al. 2014).

Kate Burnham, a former pastry chef at a Toronto restaurant, filed a complaint with Ontario's Human Rights Commission only after she was sexually harassed and abused for more than a year and a half. In her report, Burnham alleges that her sous chef would "leer" at her while "licking his lips," before "grab[bing] her breasts," once tearing at her jacket "until it popped open in front of co-workers." When she resisted, Burnham says her colleague called her an "angry dyke," and warned that her "attitude" put her job on "thin f— king ice" (Henry 2015).

Burnham also alleged that, on a second occasion, expecting to be handed an ingredient for a recipe, another chef asked for her hand, only to place it "over his penis." "It was horrible . . . a nightmare," she said. She finally decided to file a complaint when, in the restaurant's unisex staff change room, her superior "unclasped her bra from behind" and "laughed at her embarrassment. . . . That's when discomfort turned to fear for me and I just thought anything could happen to me. . . . I need closure," she says, "and I don't want this to happen to the next girl that's hired."

In response to Burnham's allegations, the restaurant issued a statement declaring that it had longstanding sexual harassment policies in place and was "committed to providing a safe work environment in which all individuals are treated with respect and dignity." Burnham's complaint was ultimately resolved through mediation, with terms of the settlement kept confidential (*Toronto Star*, September 15, 2015).

Rape Culture

The most widely shared experience among our present "outsiders" (i.e., women) is the fear of sexual assault. For some women, it is a constant source of terror, and it is a threat that has worried almost every woman at some point in her life. As Joan Tuchlinksy of the Sexual Assault Support Centre of Waterloo Region explains: "We plan our routes home, we lock the doors and walk in pairs. Men mostly don't ever think about that" (Thompson 2014).

The threat of rape makes many women feel unsafe in most supposedly "public" spaces. Many women also report feeling that they must self-monitor their behaviour while in these spaces, avoiding eye contact with others, for example.

Insiders, "women's rights" campaigns, and even researchers working in gender studies often frame gendered violence and mistreatment as a result of the victim's sex. For example, Plan Canada's "Because I Am a Girl" campaign declares that girls around the world "are more likely to live in poverty, more likely to be denied access to education, and more likely to be malnourished, *because* they are young and female."

When we say such things, we mean that women experience a range of unfair disadvantages because of structural gender discrimination. But there are more subtle implications. We are *not* making clear the fact that women endure these negative experiences "because of" other people, institutions, cultural values, or **social norms**. In this way, even those with the best intentions of helping women are subtly—and unintentionally—blaming women for their own victimization.

Women are not physically or sexually abused "because they are women." Women suffer these mistreatments "because" men—and, more rarely, other women—feel entitled to abuse them. True, men are generally larger and stronger than women, making it *possible* for them to overcome their resisting victims. But biology does not fully explain why physical and sexual abuse occurs. If men physically and sexually assaulted women simply because they are physically able to, then many if not most men would be violent rapists, and most women would be victims of physical and sexual abuse. Yet, even though they *could*, most men do not behave this way.

Alternatively, some explain sexual abuse through the notion of **rape culture**. In a patriarchal society, some men think they have the "right" to use women's bodies for their own gratification. For example, Lucia Lorenzi, a doctoral student at the University of British Columbia, alleged she was sexually assaulted by a fellow student who had taken a gender studies course with her: "That was sort of a wake-up call. This person could speak articulately about feminism, but still couldn't see that what he did was not OK" (*Toronto Star*, October 19, 2013). Even the way some insiders talk about women and sex may be interpreted as evidence of rape culture. For example, 24-year-old Anne-Marie Roy, a student union leader at the University of Ottawa, received an anonymous screenshot of a Facebook conversation in which five of her fellow student union leaders described sexual acts in which they would like to engage her. One wrote, "Someone punish her with their shaft," while another claimed, "I do believe that with my reputation I would destroy her" (Mehta 2013). Roy says she wanted to expose the incident as evidence of the rape culture she believes plagues campus: "They should be held accountable for those actions. . . . I think that it's very shameful to see that there are student leaders who are perpetuating [the rape culture] within their own circles."

Although the five men emailed Roy a letter of apology, she planned to discuss the matter at a meeting of the student federation's administration board. When the men learned this, four of the five sent her another letter claiming their Facebook conversation had been private, and that sharing it would violate their rights to privacy and freedom of speech. During the board meeting, Roy was issued a cease and desist letter that threatened legal action if she refused to "destroy" her copy of the Facebook exchange and stop distributing it to others. Roy said: "It was kind of like getting a double whammy, you get put in a very difficult situation and to have these men try to take all power away from me by telling me that I need to be censored and that I can't take action."

Eventually, the men withdrew their threats and resigned from their positions as student representatives, but Roy remains troubled: "I'm not surprised this is the reaction they're having because rape culture has been so normalized that it's very subtle, it's hard to point out because it's something that we see on a regular basis." She adds that she thinks "there needs to be a bigger conversation happening around our campus around rape culture" (Powless 2014).

Another powerful illustration of rape culture can be found in the 2016 trial of Stanford swimmer Brock Turner and his father's letter of support, which downplayed the effects of the rape and emphasized the potential harm to his son of incarceration. In response, the victim wrote an extraordinary 12-page letter reminding readers of why such behaviour is intolerable—that is, of the harm done to her and other victims like her. The letter touched a nerve, and led to calls that the judge who had overseen the case be removed.

The belief that men are entitled to women's bodies is deeply engrained within our society. Because such beliefs are so deep-seated, violence against women continues to be committed, tolerated, accepted as natural or inevitable, and even justified. People *can* be socialized to treat each other respectfully, but the process of changing values at the very roots of society has already taken generations and will no doubt require generations more.

FINAL THOUGHTS

Insiders and outsiders agree that men and women lead different lives. They disagree on whether the difference is inevitable, productive, and freely chosen. Men often suppose that women choose the different lives they lead—lives that limit them to household duties and "women's work for women's pay." But scholars offering second opinions have shown that many aspects of a "woman's life" are far from chosen, and also far from inevitable. And women outside the academy tell us that we are far from having considered all the issues we need to investigate.

In this chapter, we have discussed the hardships women face in the workplace. We noted that women are consistently disadvantaged in many occupations, while men are comparatively advantaged and rewarded. Nevertheless, liberal feminist scholarship urges women to "emancipate" themselves from patriarchy and gendered oppression by taking on paid work of any kind. Around the world, women are promised more dignity, respect, and fulfillment if they reject the role of the housewife and enter the labour market. Paid work, however, frequently produces a new set of challenges for women, including harassment, low wages, subordination, and the second shift.

Gender equality will never be achieved if most women remain financially dependent on men, nor if we continue to devalue the domestic and childcare responsibilities that are mainly allotted to women. But that doesn't make paid labour an easy solution to gender inequality. Capitalism exploits women's unpaid domestic work to reproduce the labour force, and women's *paid* labour to generate large profits. We cannot talk meaningfully about gender inequality without examining the fundamentally unequal capitalist economy. As we will see in the next chapter, the same can be said of racial inequalities.

DISCUSSION QUESTIONS

1. Do you support the men's rights movement, or at least some aspects of it? In what ways do gender norms and expectations negatively affect men? Would men benefit from a large-scale reconsideration of "what it means to be a man"?

2. Think of an advertisement designed to promote a healthy lifestyle, such as a gym promotion. In what ways does the advertisement engage subtly sexist rhetoric, endorse the thin ideal, shame fat people or reinforce the idea that health is tied to weight? What are some of the potential problems with campaigns suggesting that "everyone is beautiful"?

3. Is it a problem that household chores and childcare responsibilities are divided unevenly between men and women? What (if anything) do you think should be done to address the second shift? How else might we divide these tasks?

4. Do policies designed to reduce verbal harassment infringe upon our freedom of speech? Should people be allowed to say whatever they want, regardless of how offensive or prejudiced? If not, where do we draw the line between appropriate and inappropriate? Should conversations that were intended to be private be held to the same rules?

5. Do you think binge drinking should be taken into account in determining an accused's guilt in a rape case?

FURTHER READING

Cheryl Lynn Kelsey. "Gender Inequality: Empowering Women." *Journal of Legal Issues and Cases in Business* 3 (2015): 6–9.

Janell C. Fetteroff and Laurie A. Rudman. "Gender Inequality in the Home: The Role of Relative Income, Support for Traditional Gender Roles, and Perceived Entitlement." *Gender Issues* 31:3 (2014): 219–237.

KEY TERMS

Anorexia nervosa. An emotional/eating disorder in which one refuses to eat and has an obsession with weight loss.

Benevolent sexism. Non-hostile reinforcement of gender stereotypes.

Bulimia. Emotional/eating disorder in which one has an obsession with losing weight and undergoes periods of "bingeing"and "purging."

Bystander apathy. Social phenomenon in which witnesses of harassment distance themselves from it.

Concrete ceiling. Seemingly impenetrable barrier preventing women of colour from advancing up the corporate ladder.

Cyberbullying. Using an electronic form of communication for bullying.

Double standard. Principle that is applied unfairly and differently towards different groups. One common use involves praising men for having sex with many women, but criticizing women for the same behaviour.

Female privilege. Advantages granted to a person solely because they are female.

Feminism. Advocacy of women's equality with men.

Gender inequality. Unequal treatment based on one's gender.

Gender pay gap. The systematic difference between men and women's earnings.

Gender roles. Roles culturally taught to be appropriate for a certain gender.

Gendered identity. Identity tied to a specific gender.

Glass ceiling. An invisible barrier preventing women and racial minorities from advancing up the corporate ladder.

Glass escalator. The tendency for men in female-dominated fields to be perceived as "natural leaders," resulting in their being promoted more readily.

Homosocial reproduction. Tendency for people to want to work with those similar to them.

Hostile sexism. Contempt for women, belief they should hold a subordinate position.

Intimate partner violence (IPV). Sexual, emotional, physical, psychological, and financial abuse from an intimate partner.

Male privilege. Advantages granted to a person solely because they are male.

Misogynist. Prejudiced against women.

Patriarchy. System in which men are granted power.

Preference theory. Theory that women's choices are at the root cause of their workplace disadvantages.

Rape culture. Culture which normalizes the idea of men having the "right" to use women's bodies for gratification.

Rape. Forced sexual intercourse with a non-consensual partner.

Second shift. Women's assumption of a disproportionate share of domestic labour.

Sexism. Sex-based discrimination and prejudice.

Sexual harassment. Non-consensual sexual advances or conduct.

Social comparison theory. Theory that people determine their social and personal worth based on how they compare to others.

Social norms. Standards of what is and is not appropriate within a society.

Sticky floor. Workplace barriers keeping women in entry-level and junior positions.

Tokenism. Recruiting a small number of "token" minorities to create the appearance of diversity.

Victim blaming. Holding victims responsible for their misfortune.

CHAPTER FOUR

Racial and Ethnic Inequalities

LEARNING OBJECTIVES

In this chapter, you will:
1. Consider how immigrants are constructed as "threatening" to insiders
2. Evaluate whether racialized Canadians' experiences confirm our multicultural reputation
3. Distinguish between instances of chosen and imposed segregation among immigrants
4. Learn about the social forces that shape immigrants' and racial minorities' life chances
5. Define white privilege and assess its consequences

INTRODUCTION

On July 1, 1985, Toronto mayor Art Eggleton unveiled the "Monument to Multiculturalism" that stands in front of that city's Union Station (Merritt 2009). Designed by Italian-born painter and sculptor Francesco Perilli, the monument depicts a man about to join two meridians, surrounded by doves carrying the other six meridians towards the centre. As the first piece of public art you see upon exiting the train station, it welcomes new immigrants arriving in the city by rail.

The Monument to Multiculturalism reflects a widespread, insider perception of Canada as racially, ethnically, and culturally inclusive (Croucher 1997). Insiders—in this case, native-born white people—pride themselves on Canada's multiculturalism. Yet if we consider the lived experiences of many immigrants and racialized groups in Canada today—the outsiders of this chapter—it becomes evident Canada remains racially segregated and discriminatory to a surprising degree (Hardaway and McLoyd 2009).

In fact, the Monument to Multiculturalism itself speaks to some of the complications of creating a racially and ethnically "tolerant" society. According to sculptor Perilli, the monument depicts a single man "at the centre of the globe," arguably reinforcing notions of **ethnocentrism** in what is supposed to be a celebration of difference. Perilli also describes the doves surrounding

95

this everyman figure as "a peace symbol . . . meant to represent the cultural vitality of the people who, with the man, construct a new world, under the banner of dialogue and mutual respect" (Merritt 2009). White doves are not, perhaps, the best representatives of multicultural diversity, and their symbolic weight as "peace symbols" is part of a specifically Judeo-Christian tradition; other cultural and religious systems do not necessarily view these birds in the same way. A statue meant to celebrate diversity draws solely upon the white, Judeo-Christian values that constitute the dominant North American norm.

The point here is not to pick apart Perilli's work, but rather, to expose some of the pitfalls encountered in trying to create a multicultural society that welcomes and accepts people of all races, nationalities, and ethnicities. How did Canada's reputation for multiculturalism arise? To what extent is it a mere social construction—a way of congratulating ourselves for something we haven't fully accomplished (Croucher 1997)?

INSIDER VIEWS

People on the "inside"—in this case, Canadian-born white people espousing typically North American values like freedom, democracy, and equality of opportunity—likely underestimate the significance of racial and ethnic in-equality. They are also more likely to blame ethnic and racial minorities for their own circumstances, and especially for failing to "fit in" with prevailing Canadian norms and practices. For example, in addressing poverty, lack of education, and unemployment among Aboriginals, insiders might advise these outsiders to move to cities, where the best schools and jobs are found. Others have scapegoated Aboriginal peoples, using victim-blaming strategies to hold them responsible for their problems. In Winnipeg, First Nations mayoral can-didate Robert Falcon-Ouellette was told: "I know you. . . . You're that guy run-ning for mayor. You're an Indian. . . . I don't want to shake your hand. You Indians are the problem with the city. You're all lazy. You're drunks. The social problems we have in the city are all related to you" (Macdonald 2015).

Despite the persistence of such blatant racism, insiders are likely to suggest that contextual factors are the main source of problems for racial minorities, rather than prejudice and discrimination. A white native-born Canadian male might say it is not surprising immigrants struggle to find jobs in Canada: he would likely face the same problem if he moved to France or Pakistan. Others might argue that millions of immigrants have succeeded in Canada through hard work and education, and those now arriving will experience the same success in due course. But the economy is currently lagging—recent immi-grants just came at a bad time. While insiders are correct to highlight the range of variables, including economic conditions, that make experiences like immigration challenging for racial minorities, they may overemphasize the importance of these variables. In this chapter, we compare such insider views with those of outsiders to suggest that race, ethnicity, and discrimination also play a role, as Falcon-Ouellette can testify.

A Vertical Mosaic

Despite historically high immigration rates, Canada has not always been as welcoming of immigrants as we like to imagine. Throughout the nineteenth and early twentieth centuries, most white Anglo-Saxons shunned and devalued immigrants who were culturally or racially different, restricting their access to good jobs. Such ethnic exclusion led sociologist John Porter (1965) to describe Canadian society as a "vertical mosaic" in which English and French Canadians position themselves at the top of a racial hierarchy, with ethnic minorities below.

In his 1965 book, *The Vertical Mosaic: An Analysis of Social Class and Power in Canada*, Porter argued that ethnicity remained the most important determinant of social position for new immigrants. On arriving, immigrants tend to enter and remain in a particular occupational slot characteristic of their ethnic group. This "entrance status" hardens over time, so that people of certain ethnicities maintain the same occupational and social status for generations. In particular, groups brought to Canada to work in poorly paying, unskilled jobs remain largely restricted to that "niche" (Gosine 2000).

In contrast, Porter noted that British and French immigrants attained better social positions almost immediately upon arrival in Canada. Members of these two "charter groups" retain their previously established privileges, and (together with people of English and French descent already here) hold the power to ascribe a low entrance status to other immigrant groups of different ethnicities. But Aboriginals, already in Canada long before the British and French arrived, ironically find themselves relegated to the lowest social status of all in Porter's hierarchical mosaic.

Porter concluded that Canada's vertical class structure maps onto an unassimilated ethnic hierarchy, with racial and ethnic minorities disproportionately represented at the bottom of the hierarchy, and an elite, predominantly English and French ruling class at the top. Although it was widely accepted initially, Porter's theory is contested today (Lian and Matthews 1998, Herberg 1990). Many insiders assert that the concept of the vertical mosaic at the very least exaggerates the disadvantages immigrants face (Driedger 2008).

Dramatic changes in immigration policies and the ethnic composition of the Canadian population have occurred since 1965. Fifty years ago, ethno-racial-religious origin was indeed an important determinant of social status (Herberg 1990, Denis 1986). Since then, however, the immigration system has become more merit-based, leading insiders to propose that ethnic origins no longer pose a barrier to educational and occupational mobility in Canada. Insiders account for what vestiges of the vertical mosaic that remain by using the rhetoric of choice discussed in the previous chapter. If immigrants still face challenges, insiders say that is not because of the exclusionary practices of the dominant English-French majority but, rather, because of the way in which some immigrants choose to segregate and marginalize themselves after arrival.

The "Threat" of Immigration

A more conservative group of insiders consider immigrants to be an actual "threat" to native-born Canadians. Viewing immigrants as culturally different from "real" Canadians, they claim immigrants threaten to undermine Canadian values and institutions. For example, an anti-immigration group of Canadians called Immigration Watch Canada (IWC) suggests that Canada's immigration policies benefit people from other countries while disadvantaging native-born Canadians:

> [I]mmigration has to serve the interests of [a country's] own citizens. It cannot be turned into a social assistance/job-finding program for people from other countries. It should not be a method to suppress wages and provide employers with an unending supply of low-wage labour. It should never be a social engineering experiment that is conducted on Canada's mainstream population in order to make it a minority. But immigration has become those three things.

IWC seeks to inspire anxiety by creating a distorted sense of immigrants' numbers, describing immigration as an uncontrolled "flood" (Grove and Zwi 2006). Such a characterization is fairly common: illegal immigrants and refugees in particular have been described as "pouring" across borders, arriving in "waves," and threatening to "swamp" their host communities.

Asylum seekers in particular are suspected of having arrived illegally. Insiders may come to think we need protection *from* these "dangerous" refugees, rather than trying to protect them from their persecutors (Grove and Zwi 2006). The suggestion that migrants need to be housed in detention centres implies that they are untrustworthy and a potential threat.

As fear of immigrants and asylum seekers spreads, immigration laws and border security are tightened. Obtaining a visa becomes an ever more complex process, largely to ensure that people deemed "undesirable"—that is, uneducated, unskilled, impoverished, and often racialized—rarely gain legal entry. Such "undesirable" immigrants are accordingly framed as "uninvited," imposing demands upon their host communities rather than "contributing" to them (Grove and Zwi 2006). For example, IWC blames immigrants for problems ranging from high unemployment to lack of affordable housing:

> [O]ur high intake [of immigrants] has had major negative economic consequences for a minimum of 1.5 million Canadians who are looking for work. At the very least, it has forced many of them to compete . . . with immigrants for a limited number of jobs.
> Second, relentless high immigration has caused two results: (1) relentless demand for a basic human need such as housing and (2) relentless increases in house prices. The urban area which is the best example of this is Metro Vancouver where house prices are now the second highest in the world. . . . [M]any Canadians see that our governments seem to think that our urban areas can take infinite numbers of people. This attitude has turned many areas of the country into crowded, grid-locked, environmental disasters-in-progress— duplicates of the environmental catastrophes many recent immigrants come from ("Unjustified Immigration Levels against Public's Wishes" 2015).

Perhaps because of arguments like these, Canadians' attitudes towards newcomers have grown less favourable over time. One poll found that 46% of Canadians believe there are "too many immigrants coming to Canada," while 41% believe too many immigrants belong to visible minorities (Graves 2015).

Insiders sometimes succeed in efforts to characterize immigrants on their terms: to establish and reinforce boundaries, carefully screen potential entrants, deter the entry of "undesirable" groups, "quarantine" asylum seekers who do make their way into the country, and otherwise minimize unwanted contact (Grove and Zwi 2006). They encourage us not to consider individual lives and personal circumstances, but rather to fear a depersonalized mass "influx" of unwanted, potentially dangerous foreigners. Meanwhile, the tendency to view the entire immigration process as a form of charity creates an expectation that immigrants should be thankful for their admission into Canada, no matter how unfair or degrading the process was.

Multicultural Policies

Another group of white, native-born insiders insists that Canada is tolerant and unprejudiced, despite the negative view of immigrants discussed above. These insiders often cite long-established anti-discrimination policies. Canada's Charter of Rights and Freedoms (s. 15[1]), for instance, declares that "[e]very individual is equal before and under the law and has the right to the equal protection and equal benefit of the law without discrimination and, in particular, without discrimination based on race, national or ethnic origin, colour, religion, sex, age or mental or physical disability." Similarly, the Canadian Multiculturalism Act of 1988 requires all federal institutions and employers to act in accordance with the country's stated multicultural policy. And the Employment Equity Act, passed in 1986 and updated in 1995, is intended to ensure fair, non-discriminatory treatment for women, people with disabilities, Indigenous peoples and racial minorities (Government of Canada 2015).

The Employment Equity Act was indeed an important advance, in that it recognized the need for proactive steps to raise the socioeconomic status of historically disadvantaged groups. Rather than only trying to prohibit discrimination by employers—essential in itself—the Act is a form of what Americans call "affirmative action," or an advantage given to one group over another (Jain et al. 2010). Given that members of the mainstream automatically enjoy an advantage over visible minorities, such "special treatment" merely levels the playing field a little. Doing otherwise—treating members of all social groups exactly the same—would mean ignoring the historical disadvantages faced by certain social groups (Busby 2006).

Immediately after the introduction of the Employment Equity Act, there was a rise in labor force participation among disadvantaged groups (Jain et al. 2010). For many, this confirmed the efficacy of the Act, as well as demonstrating an ongoing decline in prejudicial hiring practices. However, disadvantaged groups, especially Aboriginals, remain underrepresented in the overall labour force, as well as in more "elite" sectors (such as law, politics, and business), and in the upper rungs of the corporate hierarchy (Backhouse 2005, Agocs 2002).

Moreover, the Employment Equity Act remains inconsistently and ineffectively enforced (Jain et al. 2010, Agocs 2002). The government representatives responsible for enforcing the Act often deem employers "barrier-free" without even inspecting them onsite (Deveau 2011). Employers who continue to maintain entry barriers for disadvantaged groups are rarely penalized. In the end, the Employment Equity Act shares some of the qualities of the Monument to Multiculturalism: both are referenced by insiders as "evidence" of Canada's "cultural mosaic," but neither paints a wholly accurate picture of reality.

SECOND OPINIONS

Critical Race Theory

Academics who focus on race, immigration, Aboriginal peoples, and related areas have resisted the insider views outlined above through the development of **critical race theory (CRT)**. The thrust of CRT is that race is a performance—a social construction—rather than an innate quality. There are no meanings intrinsically attached to the colour of one's skin; we collectively construct the assumptions so often tied to race (James 2009).

A related theoretical term is **racialization**, by which we mean the social processes and cultural contexts in which race is *made* important. Racialization describes the differentiation or categorization of people according to their perceived race or ethnicity. Racialization also means the imposition of a racial interpretation onto a situation that can be interpreted in other terms (for example, in terms of class).

CRT is also concerned with the ways in which race is actively ignored or erased. Certain liberal ideological concepts, including meritocracy, colour blindness, race neutrality, and multiculturalism, can serve to entrench racism more deeply. Despite antiracism legislation and the widespread adoption of a multicultural, liberal mindset, racial minorities in Canada continue to face discrimination in many areas, including employment, housing, education, the legal system, health care, and social services (James 2009, Hardaway and McLoyd 2009). In this sense, racism has become **institutionalized**: it is deeply embedded within the power structures that dominate our society, creating patterns of social disadvantage.

Many major institutions, however, declare themselves "colour blind" by *claiming* to ignore race in selecting applicants for jobs, mortgages, university admission, and scholarships, when race does, in fact, play a role. By doing so, these institutions merely normalize their structural racism (James 2009). The colour-blind policies meant to address the oppression of people of colour in fact perpetuate such oppression.

Race still matters in our society, no matter how many multicultural initiatives have been introduced (James 2009). Although explicit discrimination may be less prevalent, inequalities persist. That is because the past is hard to eradicate. Historically, the West used racist, exclusionary practices to gain advantage over people of colour throughout the world (Owen 2007, Moshman 2007). Relatively recent legislation does not come close to leveling the playing field: it is as though racism has been "locked in" by the past.

This so-called "lock-in model" does not, however, account for every instance of explicit racism that persists today (Hardaway and McLoyd 2009). Negative racial stereotypes continue to circulate. For example, despite research proving otherwise, many whites view largely black neighborhoods as chaotic and crime-ridden (Quillian and Pager 2001).

CRT seeks to challenge these prejudices. It has moved (at least academic) discussions on race and ethnicity from essentialism to **performativity**—that is, from a search for in-born racial "qualities" to a search for imposed racial labels and performances. While recognizing the important gains made during the civil rights movement, CRT proposes that institutionalized instruments of racial oppression continue to operate even as more overt forms of racism have been eliminated.

Above: Canada's Aboriginals, including this Vancouver woman, are dispropor-tionately affected by the consequences of social inequality (Kenny McDonald).

Below: Protests against police shootings of young black men, like this march in Chicago in November 2015, highlight the issue of discriminatory treatment under the law (C. Presutti/Voice of America).

Othering

North Americans learn to think in categories of two, or binaries: men and women, rich and poor, beautiful and ugly, and so on. Ambiguity and multiplicity make us feel uneasy. In defining ourselves, we often refer to what we are *not*. Canadians, for example, like to define themselves as "not-Americans." More broadly, people are usually sorted into two categories: "us" and "them" (Hicks 2007). We learn to view others who are "like us" as normal, and those who are (visibly) "unlike us" as abnormal, different, and "other."

In North America, white identities are constructed as the dominant norm, while all other racial identities are grouped together as the "other" (Perry 2001, Garner 2006). Through historical processes of racism and colonialism, "whiteness" has been constructed as superior, the standard against which all other races, ethnicities, and cultures are judged (Ahmed 2007). Insiders define racial others according to how they differ from the norm of whiteness. Whiteness allows people to occupy public spaces unnoticed, without suspicion or harassment. White supremacy and the structural disadvantaging of racial others is so deeply engrained in our society that it appears "normal" (Gillborn 2006, Owen 2007).

Some racialized people feel that, no matter how long they have lived in Canada, they continue to be seen as "foreigners" or "outsiders," because of physical appearance (Aujla 2000). As a result, racial minorities report being asked, throughout their lives, where they "came from." Many racialized immigrants—especially those of the second or third generation—self-identify as "Canadian," yet native-born white Canadians often insist they "must" be from somewhere else. Such probing of people's ancestry is most often a well-intentioned attempt at being inclusive, but it can serve to maintain **social distance**, persistently differentiating "foreigners" from "real" Canadians.

As a result of **othering**, racialized people are often denied the chance to flourish economically and socially in Canadian society (Moshman 2007). In turn, the other often feels marginalized and disempowered (Aujla 2000). Eventually, the distance and difference felt between "us" and "them" seem so pronounced that the relationship becomes one of "us" *against* "them."

Social Distance

Although othering creates the illusion of two wholly distinct categories—"us" and "them"—issues of racial and ethnic difference are more nuanced. Within each of the broad categories of white and non-white exist hierarchies of class and privilege. We know from familiar phrases like "white trash" that whiteness alone does not guarantee social acceptance. Likewise, some racial minorities are more disadvantaged than others (Garner 2006). And, as you might infer from the previous chapter, male and female members of different racialized groups are also likely to have different experiences of acceptance and exclusion.

In this sense, whiteness can be best understood as a kind of "resource" that people of varying backgrounds strive to access performatively. For instance, Irish, Italian, and other groups of European immigrants are obviously white in terms of the colour of their skin—at least, whiter than most people from the Caribbean or Africa. However, they remain culturally marked out from mainstream "Canadian" whiteness upon their arrival. "Whiteness" thus has to do with language, religious affiliation, and cultural norms, as well as the colour of one's skin (Fee and Russell 2007).

As a result, "white" immigrants are sorted into a hierarchy (Garner 2006). The American psychologist and sociologist Emory S. Bogardus (1959) made an important contribution in this area when he devised the concept of **social distance**.

Social distance describes the extent of intergroup segregation and, conversely, the willingness of group members to mix with other groups. To measure social distance, Bogardus devised a scale that ranks people's willingness to accept members of a certain race or ethnicity in a range of social relationships. These relationships include, from closest to most distant: 1) close relative by marriage, 2) close personal friend, 3) neighbour on the same street, 4) co-worker in the same occupation, 5) citizen in the same country, 6) temporary visitor in the same country, and 7) someone excluded from one's own country.

Social distance is like a ladder, and a group that is accepted at a certain level of closeness is also accepted at all the more distant levels. For example, a group deemed acceptable for close personal friendships would also be acceptable as neighbours or co-workers (Zhang and Van Hook 2009).

By asking respondents the same questions about their willingness to be close, we can calculate an average social distance measure for a series of "target groups": Jewish Canadians, black Canadians, Italian Canadians, and so on. In turn, we can uncover which "types" of minorities are most accepted and which are most rejected for the closest relations. As well, we can determine which "types" of people are most open to closeness with minorities, and which are most reluctant or hostile.

Not surprisingly, using Bogardus' scale, sociologists have learned that people who distance themselves from other groups often hold prejudices about those other groups (Wark and Galliher 2007). As well as influencing *social* distance, prejudicial attitudes also influence desired *physical* distance. For example, Americans who view Canadians negatively think that Canadian cities are further north than they really are (Kerkman et al. 2004).

Paradoxically, the most powerful way to reduce the prejudicial attitudes and stereotypes that underpin social distance is through close, personal inter-

increase in social media?

actions: by reducing geographic distance and increasing communication (Ata et al. 2009). This is because the desire to establish and maintain social distance usually stems from a fear of the unknown: a failure or unwillingness to socialize with or understand people supposedly unlike ourselves. For example, Americans who try to distance themselves from Canadians are found to have rarely interacted with Canadians. Similarly, the greatest hostility towards Muslims is voiced in those areas where few Muslims have settled.

The Racial Earnings Gap

Another way to measure prejudice is to consider the different wages earned by whites and non-whites. Immigrants and Canadian-born people of colour generally earn less than white Canadians (Morissette and Sultan 2015).

Table 4.1: Earnings of Native-Born and Immigrant Canadians, 1991 and 2010

	Men		Women	
	Immigrants	Native-born	Immigrants	Native-born
All workers				
1991	$35,290	$46,410	$23,740	$30,340
2010	$60,330	$70,210	$46,450	$49,870
Less-educated workers				
1991	$29,670	$42,480	$20,190	$24,850
2010	$46,600	$60,140	$38,610	$40,680
More-educated workers				
1991	$44,580	$53,900	$29,220	$37,370
2010	$83,060	$89,420	$58,560	$61,620

Some of this gap can be attributed to the different types of work that people of different races tend to do: racial minorities are less likely than white people to be employed in the higher echelons of management and finance. Even better-educated men who belong to a visible minority experience a "glass ceiling" effect: compared to white men of similar age and credentials, they are less likely to secure promotions (Guo 2013).

Unemployment and low education levels also account for some of the earnings gap. Recent immigrants to Canada are twice as likely as native-born Canadians to be unemployed (Oreopoulos 2011). Canadian-born whites are more likely to have postsecondary degrees, while racial minorities account for a disproportionate number of high school dropouts (Kearney 2006).

However, it would be wrong to say the earnings gap is "caused" by any of these factors. The poorer jobs available to racial minorities, racialized unemployment, and school dropout rates are *symptoms* of a long history of racial discrimination that continues today, albeit in more subtle fashion (Hardaway and McLoyd 2009). We confuse cause and effect because the idea that the labour market remains discriminatory is unpalatable, especially to insiders (Moore 2010). Instead, insiders reason that racial minorities would enjoy better employment opportunities and higher wages were they to acquire better credentials, skills, and experience. And to be sure, some research indicates that white and racialized people with the same level of education do earn the same amount. For example, a study of dentists graduating from the University of Alberta (Krahn and Smith 2008) showed that racialized (mainly Asian) dentists earned more than white graduates.

The situation is, however, complicated. After all, the chance that white, native-born Canadians and racial minorities will acquire the same qualifications is small, because of their very different upbringings. Racialized youth may be restricted to inferior schools, reducing their access to higher education and to occupations requiring it. Many other social variables, including poverty, abuse, neglect, and parental conflict, hinder young people from realizing their potential, and are more common among certain groups than others (Moore 2010).

Racial or ethnic discrimination is challenging to measure, given the number of other variables in play (Pager and Western 2012). The most explicit type of labour market discrimination arises only when equally productive workers—those who produce the same amount and quality of work in equal time, under equal circumstances—are treated differently in ways that systematically correspond to personal features, including race (Kearney 2006; Pager et al. 2009). To use a well-known example, a white employee may be singled out for a promotion or pay raise over an equally productive, equally qualified black employee. However, this happens relatively rarely, because it is so evidently one of the types of racial discrimination that is no longer legally or socially tolerated in Canada.

Many studies seek to identify prejudicial hiring practices by examining employers' responses to resumes that seem to signal applicants' race or ethnicity (Pager and Western 2012). In a typical study, identical fictional resumes are sent to employers in response to a job posting. The resumes differ in only one respect: the names of the fictional employees signal a given racial background. Black applicants might be named Latoya or DeShawn, while white applicants are named Emily or Mark. Typically, applicants with "white-sounding" names receive around 50% more callbacks than applicants with "black-sounding" names (Kearney 2006, Skaggs and Bridges 2013). Obviously, the same methodology can be used to compare fictional candidates with Pakistani, Arabic, Chinese, Italian, or other ethnic-sounding names.

In one such study, thousands of fabricated resumes were sent out by email in response to a variety of job openings in the Toronto area (Oreopoulis and Dechief 2011). Applicants with English-sounding names, Canadian educational credentials, and Canadian work experience were the most likely to get a response, with a callback rate of 16%. Resumes with Indian, Pakistani or Chinese names and Canadian experience had a lower callback rate of about 11%. And resumes with a foreign name, foreign educational credentials, and foreign work experience had the lowest callback rate of all, at 6%.

When the researchers tried to contact the employers who had received these fabricated resumes, only a few responded. Those who did spoke of in-house pressures to make "non-problematic" hires: employers said they didn't want to be blamed for opening their doors to trouble, and assumed that applicants with English-sounding names would be low risk. Other employers explained that they thought applicants with a foreign name or background might demand extra time off for religious holidays or international travel to see family members, and this would be inconvenient and costly to the company. — FAKE NEWS

Finally, the majority of employers said that foreign-sounding names, foreign education, and foreign experience implied that the applicant would lack sufficient English language skills or familiarity with local business practices (Oreopoulos and Dechief 2011). Effective communication skills are indeed becoming increasingly important, as we shift from a manufacturing to service economy. This transition caused employers to become more concerned about hiring workers with broken English, heavy accents, unfamiliar demeanors, and other characteristics that would not have been considered in hiring factory workers (Pager et al. 2009).

Yet, in the study by Oreopoulos and Dechief, all the fictional applicants indicated they were fluent in English. Perhaps, the authors reasoned, resumes with foreign-sounding names were not examined carefully, and were eliminated based on name alone. Or perhaps employers did not believe apparently foreign applicants' claims to fluency in English. One year later, Oreopoulos and Dechief released a follow-up study designed to determine whether these discriminatory callbacks were indeed motivated by legitimate concerns regarding potential hires' ability to work in English or French. This time, fictional resumes were distributed in Toronto, Vancouver, and Montreal. Some listed activities that were heavily language dependent. Others were sent in response to openings for jobs where strong language skills were less relevant. But the results remained consistent with the initial findings. Regardless of the position's language requirements, fictional applicants with English names were 35% more likely to receive callbacks than those with Indian, Chinese, or

Pakistani names (Decheif and Oreopoulos 2012). Most likely then, the discrimination uncovered by these studies is due in large part to racial or ethnic prejudice, rather than legitimate productivity concerns. Yet when employers were queried about these results, they continued to cite poor language and social skills as deterrents. These studies reveal how employers persist in discrimination at the hiring stages: many simply cite non-racial factors, such as foreign qualifications and experience, as driving their decisions (Moore 2010, Skaggs and Bridges 2013).

Such discrimination is difficult to prove because complete information on *all* the applicants for a given position would need to be collected and analyzed to draw an airtight conclusion. For this reason, victims of discrimination often struggle unsuccessfully to prove mistreatment (Pager and Western 2012). Unfair practices are often underreported, leading many to believe such practices are also uncommon.

It should be noted that a university education does not offer the same return for immigrants as native-born Canadians. Immigrants and native-borns with equal levels of education sometimes earn different wages, particularly if an employer has doubts about the quality of education or job experience an applicant received overseas. This same doubt is reflected in the requirement that foreign-trained doctors, dentists, lawyers, architects, and engineers must pass local licensing examinations, regardless of pre-immigration education and experience.

Research confirms that some forms of blatant prejudice persist despite anti-discrimination legislation (Moore 2010). But more subtle hiring practices stem from the flawed information to which employers have access (Kearney 2006). For example, an employer may assume that a potential hire has certain qualifications, experiences, and skills based on their supposed "knowledge" of other racially or ethnically similar people (Skaggs and Bridges 2013). If an employer has repeatedly been exposed to the stereotype of black males as uneducated, violent criminals, he is more likely to assume that the young black man applying for a job fits that description too. It's not so much that the employer has an irrational dislike of black people, but rather that he has been socialized to see a lack of employable features in black people. Statistics interact with people's prejudiced beliefs to create self-fulfilling prophecies.

The Aboriginal population arguably suffers under the greatest structural barriers, systematically denied access for centuries to the same opportunities as white, native-born Canadians (Kendall 2001). More than one-third of Aboriginals fail to complete high school (Pendakur and Pendakur 2011). The low socioeconomic status of many Aboriginals stems from their inability to succeed in mainstream educational and labour markets, an inability created by structural racism reaching back many generations.

In fact, the income gap between Aboriginals and Canadian-born non-Aboriginals is perhaps the most pronounced in Canada: between 10% and 20% for Aboriginal and non-Aboriginal women, and between 20% and 50% for Aboriginal and non-Aboriginal men (Pendakur and Pendakur 2011). After other variables are accounted for, Aboriginal and non-Aboriginal workers with the same level of education are still likely to earn different incomes. Aboriginals who do not self-identify as Aboriginal tend to be paid more than Aboriginals who do signal their Aboriginal identity (Lamb 2015). Those who advertise their "deep" Aboriginal identities fare worst of all in seeking employment.

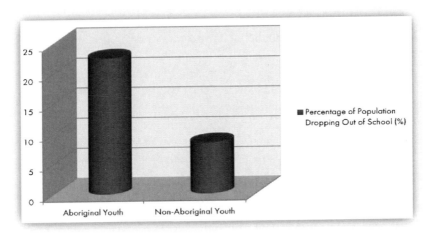

Figure 4.1: School Drop-Out Rates, Ages 20 to 24

Immigration Policy and Upward Social Mobility

Some immigrants come to Canada to escape war, poor living conditions, or infringements upon human rights—these are "push factors." But most immigrants—including those influenced by push factors—are also motivated by "pull factors": the hope of a better life for themselves and their families (Costigan et al. 2009). In particular, they hope to gain access to educational, social, and occupational opportunities they may not have enjoyed in their country of origin.

Many immigrants rightly believe that education remains the key to climbing the social ladder. This is especially true of visibly different racial minorities, who view education as a tool that helps overcome systemic racism. But many immigrants fail to obtain the rewards they expect, at least at first. Immigrants of European descent are more likely to enjoy success in Canada, while Caribbean immigrants are the least likely to gain social acceptance or upward social mobility. The experiences of Chinese immigrants are mixed. In a study of Chinese immigrants to Calgary and Edmonton, 70% of respondents confirmed that they had experienced "major" challenges in finding employment (Guo 2013). Although 43% said they had been able to achieve their educational or occupational goals, these same participants also reported that language difficulties, a lack of Canadian work experience and credentials, the failure of Canadian society to recognize their Chinese work experience, and the lack of a social network hindered their success.

Most respondents reported that they had downgraded occupationally since coming to Canada: their current job was not suitable for someone with their skills and credentials. Before their move to Canada, 77% had held jobs in the sciences, teaching, management, finance, or business. But after immigrating, only about 42% remained in these prestigious, high-paying occupations. There was a 17% increase in the number of immigrants working as manual labourers, while more than 11% found themselves unemployed following immigration.

Occupational downgrading undermined household income. More than 37% reported they now lived below the poverty line, compared to the figure of 16% for the Canadian population as a whole. Over the past 25 years, the earnings gap between immigrants and Canadian-born citizens has widened. In 1980, recently immigrated men earned 85 cents for every dollar earned by Canadian-born males. By 2005, recently immigrated men earned only 63 cents for every dollar earned by men born in Canada (Guo 2013).

At one time, sociologists argued that immigrants would experience higher incomes and greater financial stability after assimilating into the host culture. Difficulties finding employment were only short-term, mainly due to language barriers and unfamiliarity with Canadian customs. As immigrants learned English and gained an understanding of Western social norms—and after they secured a first job, providing them with Canadian employment experience—their earnings would begin to rise, eventually equaling those of native-born Canadians working in the same field.

Although this scenario proved true in the middle years of the twentieth century, from 1970 onward immigrants have found complete integration within the Canadian labour market to be out of reach (Wang and Lo 2005). Immigrants today experience greater income inequality for the first several years after their arrival than did earlier immigrants, despite the fact that three-quarters of them hold postsecondary qualifications, and more than 70% were admitted to Canada as "economic class" candidates—that is, skilled workers.

One factor to consider is that people from different parts of the world immigrated to Canada at different historical moments, in response to varying labour market demands. Fifty years ago, large numbers of southern European immigrants arrived to work in the construction and building trades; the economy was booming and well-paying jobs awaited them. Today, large numbers of immigrants are arriving from Asia, Africa and South America; fewer of them have the skills in greatest demand, the economy is growing more slowly than in the 1960s, and well-paying jobs are scarce for everyone, immigrants and native-borns alike.

During that same half-century, Canada became more culturally and racially diverse. Until the 1960s, a variety of measures served to restrict non-white immigration to Canada. The country's restrictive immigration policy was revised in 1967, allowing the entrance of people from many, varied cultures (Fuller and Martin 2012, Nadeau and Seckin 2010). But certain barriers remained. Immigrants are required to score 70 to 80 points out of a potential 100 in an evaluation of their education, job skills, occupational demands, age, and knowledge of French and English. Most immigrants are thus either educated professionals or students pursuing a university degree. Yet despite their credentials, many men of colour are only able to secure poorly paying positions in the service sector. African-Caribbean women appear particularly disadvantaged, largely restricted to work as caregivers, domestics, or unskilled service providers.

How and when people are permitted to enter a nation, and the ways in which they are expected to participate in that nation's economy, continue to shape their social and economic opportunities for decades. This is especially true for visibly different immigrants like the African-Caribbean population, since race serves as a constant indication of one's "foreignness" (Kazemipur 2000). For many immigrants, the appearance of difference leads to discrimination and poses an obstacle to their integration into the Canadian mainstream (Aujla 2000).

Besides a different physical appearance, immigrants' values, beliefs, and practices are sometimes also seen as threateningly foreign (Aujla 2000). As a result, insiders may strive to distinguish these values and practices from those viewed as "Canadian." Cultural and religious customs are another dimension by which immigrants may be segregated from mainstream society, precluding the full social, economic, and cultural integration that would facilitate upward social mobility.

The Devaluation of Foreign Credentials

Immigrants' employment-related struggles came as a surprise to many observers, since Canadian immigration policy explicitly favours educated and skilled applicants (Wang and Lo 2005). The Canadian points system prioritizes "employable" immigrants with credentials and work experience corresponding to current market demands. But all too often, immigrants' credentials and work experience gain them entry to Canada, but are then undervalued or ignored entirely (Fuller and Martin 2012).

Recent immigrants often find the job they held in their country of origin is difficult to obtain in Canada. For example, international medical graduates are required to pass federally administered exams before they are certified as able to practice. These exams are expensive and take considerable time to complete, and passing them is no guarantee of employment. In the meantime, skilled immigrants are forced to accept any job they can find—for example, as cab drivers or factory workers—to make ends meet (Teelucksingh and Galabuzi 2005, Remennick 2012).

Not all foreign credentials are disregarded. Rather, they are differentially rewarded according to the country in which they were obtained. Immigrants from Britain, the United States, Australia, and northern and Western Europe who arrive in Canada with foreign credentials tend to experience an advantage in the labour market (Guo 2013). All these nations are culturally similar to Canada, making Canadian employers more trusting of degrees and work experience obtained in these more familiar environments (Wang and Lo 2005). By contrast, immigrants with credentials from African, Latin American, or Asian countries experience an earnings penalty upon arrival. Almost 46% of Chinese immigrants with Chinese degrees report an annual household income below $20,000, compared to only 5% of Chinese immigrants with Canadian degrees.

Professional associations and prior learning assessment agencies contribute to this devaluation of certain foreign credentials. They have the authority to distinguish between acceptable and unacceptable forms of training, skill, and competency. In the end, the credentials and training experiences of some immigrants are dismissed as deficient simply because they are different and unfamiliar; some believe they are evaluated based on "arbitrary standards" that are "applied in a subjective case-by-case manner" (Basran 1998). In an effort to fully integrate immigrants into the Canadian labour market, Human Resources and Skills Development Canada launched the Foreign Credential Recognition Program in 2003. However, there are still no national standards for evaluating qualifications, and the provinces use varying and somewhat ambiguous procedures (Curtis, Elrick, and Reitz 2014).

In the end, professionals who immigrate to Canada confront three potential barriers to employment. First, assessment agencies function as gatekeepers, preventing many immigrants from retaining their professional status and credentials. However, attaining professional status is not in itself sufficient. A "glass door" or "glass wall" functions to keep immigrant workers on the professional "outside," excluding qualified immigrants from high-status, high-paying positions, which are reserved for white, native-born Canadians (Light, Roscigno and Kalev 2011). The glass ceiling is the third barrier facing immigrant professionals, to be dealt with only once the first two barriers have been overcome. For example, Chinese engineers who work for Canadian firms are underrepresented in management: the higher the level of management, the fewer Chinese employees (Guo 2013). The convergence of all three of these barriers—the gate, glass door, and glass ceiling—can ultimately cause underemployment, unemployment, and downward social mobility.

At the other end of the spectrum are immigrants who arrive in Canada qualified only to carry out manual labour. They search for, or are forced to accept, jobs in construction, agriculture, housekeeping, and the like. Already disadvantaged by their minimal education and skills, these immigrants often have a precarious legal status, with many in Canada only on short-term visas. Employers are reluctant to hire such people. For these immigrants, a so-called "sticky floor" poses the main problem: they remain "stuck" in low-level, low-paying jobs, which usually results in poverty and poor living conditions (Purcell et al. 2010, Kazemipur 2001).

Insiders often dismiss such concerns by noting that, with each generation that passes after arrival in Canada, upward mobility becomes easier (Nadeau and Seckin 2010). This is true, but only of a relatively small fraction of second-generation immigrant Canadians: namely, those from educated, affluent families who held high social status in their home country. These professionals are more likely to be viewed favorably upon arrival in the host society, and have an easier time assimilating. As well, skilled first-generation immigrants with stable, well-paying jobs are more likely to raise their families in safe neighbourhoods and send their children to better schools. Both at home and at school, these second-generation youth are more likely to build connections with native peers, gaining an opportunity to refine language skills and become more socially integrated within Canadian society.

Other second-generation immigrants, however, experience a *decline* in socio-economic status. Manual labourers are more likely to settle in the inner city, where their children may attend inferior schools in which immigrants are often isolated, and where tensions and hostilities break out between ethnic groups (Remennick 2012). These immigrants can often afford only small apartments in dangerous areas with less community engagement and few recreational activities for youth. Children without their own bedrooms often struggle to find quiet spaces to study and socialize with their peers. This struggle negatively influences both academic success and social integration.

Occupational downgrading among immigrants is especially troubling, as it affects subsequent generations (Remennick 2012). While first- and second-generation immigrants often demonstrate high aspirations and expectations for success, third and later generations may be less ambitious or hopeful (Portes and Rivas 2011). In particular, immigrant parents who lose occupational, financial, and social status upon arrival in Canada struggle to convey the importance of education, hard work, and commitment to their children. Having witnessed their own parents' inability to secure stable, well-paying jobs or a higher standard of living, second-generation immigrant children are skeptical of parents' claims that education is the key to upward mobility. Parents, in turn, grow distressed when their children are not motivated to succeed academically. Sometimes they interpret their children's skepticism and disappointment as proof that the decision to immigrate—one often made with their children's best interests in mind—was ill-advised.

It remains unclear how many immigrants struggle with such issues; much research in this area yields flawed, overly optimistic results because of methodological issues. For example, random samples of adult immigrants are rarely representative: immigrants who have been imprisoned, deported, or who have left the country for other reasons are never included in these samples. Yet such experiences indicate a failure to assimilate, and potentially, signal downward social mobility (Portes and Rivas 2011). Studies based on samples that do *not* include these people automatically report more positive findings on assimilation, painting a positive picture of the immigration experience that is not entirely accurate.

The Second Generation Advantage

It goes without saying that not all immigrants fully assimilate into their host societies. While some do come to self-identify as "Canadians" or "Americans," others combine these new nationalities with old ones, creating hyphenated identities. Still others maintain their original designation, refusing to incorporate their new "Canadian-ness" into their sense of self at all.

Immigrants adopt these labels according to specific patterns (Portes and Rivas 2011). Compared with children born abroad who immigrate to Canada at a young age, second-generation immigrants are more likely to self-identify as members of their host society. This is especially true of youths with parents of high social status. In fact, parents who are highly educated usually promote **selective acculturation,** actively encouraging their children to maintain aspects of their native culture *and* adopt some aspects of their new host culture, leading to the adoption of a hyphenated self-identity: for example, Chinese-Canadian rather than Chinese *or* Canadian.

But poorly educated parents who cling to their native culture can unwittingly drive their children to reject that culture and their ancestral identity (Portes and Rivas 2011). This process is called **dissonant acculturation.** Similarly, persistent discrimination by the host culture can reduce immigrants' self-esteem and drive them to adopt a "reactive identity." They become less likely to identify as members of the host culture, opting to maintain their nationality of origin. For example, they may identify themselves as Jamaicans rather than Jamaican-Canadians or Canadians. Less-educated visible minorities are more likely to adopt such a reactive identity, since they are more likely to experience discrimination.

The failure to assimilate can negatively affect immigrants' life chances. The age at which people arrive in Canada influences the degree to which they assimilate, and their corresponding chances for success. Those who arrive as young children can learn English and adjust to new cultural norms and expectations more easily. Second-generation immigrants enjoy an even greater advantage. They fare the best in terms of academic achievement, whereas those who immigrate as teens are less likely to perform well in school. Young people between 15 and 25 years of age are most susceptible to language barriers (Remennick 2012). They may not be able to read or write fluently in their native tongue, and that facility may decline even further as they struggle to learn a new language. The result is a kind of semi-literacy: they have only a partial grasp of two languages and are proficient in neither.

Children from lower-income immigrant families are especially likely to switch back and forth between their native and host languages, and to be embarrassed by the trouble they have expressing themselves. In turn, early language barriers may set off a kind of chain reaction: the resulting poor grades in secondary school bar these immigrants from post-secondary education, reducing their chances of upward social mobility. Middle-class immigrants, by contrast, often have the time and resources to ensure their children learn their ancestral tongue, as well as the language of their host culture, making them more likely to be bilingual (Costigan et al. 2009).

The "second-generation advantage" involves more than just proficiency in English. Middle- and upper-class immigrants encourage their children to learn the cultural customs of their host society, but also to maintain their native language, values, social traditions, and beliefs, making them "multicultural." These youth are also likely to have access to broad, multicultural social networks consisting of peers from both their native and adopted cultures. They can use their local connections and draw on their unique cultural background as a means of standing out from the crowd. Or, they can enhance their job search by using social services designed to help immigrants and racial minorities gain employment. This second-generation advantage can thus help some disadvantaged immigrant groups overcome the barriers to upward mobility posed by their host societies.

Although there are documented second-generation advantages, they are not available to all immigrants: some groups continue to struggle against barriers to upward mobility. There are different degrees of discrimination and acceptance, depending on the type of immigrant and the society in which they have settled, which reduce or intensify those barriers, regardless of how long immigrants have lived in Canada. For some groups, assimilation can even cause downward mobility—for instance, if they are assimilated into a culture that holds discriminatory policies and attitudes towards members of their racial or ethnic group.

Successful selective acculturation therefore requires a cohesive immigrant community and dedicated parents who employ unique strategies to help their children avoid assimilating into the disadvantaged segments of their host society. In particular, by retaining the values and customs of their home culture, immigrant children can better avoid street life and gang involvement.

The immigrant families who integrate most successfully are those who view their host countries as an opportunity for a new beginning, and who no longer look back with regret upon their home countries. These parents seek inclusion in their new societies and view their new culture and its people positively. In turn, their children often adopt a similar outlook, feeling a sense of gratitude to their new homes. These views transmit intergenerationally, with each generation instilling in its children the motivation to succeed in the host country.

Institutional Completeness

Because the benefits of selective acculturation are well documented, some insiders adopt a victim-blaming narrative to account for the disadvantages many immigrants experience upon arriving in Canada. They suggest that immigrants segregate themselves, refusing to assimilate and therefore limiting their educational and employment opportunities.

Indeed, many immigrants look for others like themselves when they arrive in Canada—specifically, for people who speak the same language and share similar cultural traditions. Gradually, immigrant groups build communities based on these linguistic and cultural similarities. As Raymond Breton (1964, 1978; Breton et al. 1980) has shown, many immigrant communities eventually develop **institutional completeness**: having built their own schools, churches, newspapers, lending societies, shops, and so on, these immigrants are able to carry out most of their daily activities independently. Their original cultures largely preserved, most members develop new social networks consisting largely of people from the same cultural backgrounds (Landry et al. 2007).

In part, institutional completeness is a response to real and imagined discrimination (Pasztor 2010, Zhou 2004). The "generations of exclusion" hypothesis contends that immigrants and their children are (or expect to be) excluded from the opportunities for mobility offered by the mainstream. This is not because they have failed to assimilate into that mainstream, but rather, because their host society is biased against people from their racial and/or ethnic background. Confronted with this real or imagined hostility, new immigrants congregate in order to survive financially.

An important distinction should be made between integration and cultural assimilation. **Integration**, also known as structural assimilation, refers to the inclusion of immigrants within the educational and occupational structures of the host society (Wsevolod 2003). It involves establishing connections within local communities, finding a job, and securing housing. Downward social mobility, poverty, incarceration, and teen pregnancy are all indicators of immigrants' failure to become integrated within the host society. **Assimilation**, however, refers to the degree to which immigrants adopt the cultural and linguistic norms of their host community. Although integration and assimilation are often related, success in one area does not guarantee success in the other. For example, an immigrant who has become fluent in his host society's language and assimilated well into his new culture may still struggle in the education and labour markets.

Integration is the end goal under Canada's multiculturalism policy. Newcomers are not asked to shed their ethnic identity, but are required to follow Canadian laws and contribute to Canadian society in ways that "we" deem fit (Adams 2007, Spinner-Halev 2001). Insiders, however, often view institutionally complete **ethnic enclaves** as signs that immigrants are resisting assimilation. Living, working, and socializing in communities composed almost exclusively of people from the same ethnic background, these immigrants have no apparent reason or desire to acculturate.

A good deal of research, however, suggests otherwise. Many, perhaps even most, immigrants do assimilate, adopting both cultural norms and the language of their host society. In fact, immigrants are unlikely to continue using their native language after the second generation, except perhaps with older family members who have failed to master English or French.

Institutional completeness often benefits recent newcomers, allowing them to ease into their new home. In such communities, immigrants are able to occupy a kind of "middle ground," rather than having to assimilate entirely or not at all (Pasztor 2010, Tully 2008). A community with a high degree of institutional completeness allows members to build social networks quickly and easily through already-established ethnic institutions (Zhou 2009), and those who establish these institutions—setting up their own restaurants or shops, for example—are able to avoid some of the difficulties associated with finding jobs in the broader society. The idea of hostile, threatening immigrants banding together in segregated communities remains popular among insiders only because it aligns well with the belief that immigration is bad for the host society and its native-born citizens. ✳

OUTSIGHTS

People on the "outside"—in this case, immigrants in general and racialized populations in particular—are likely to recognize the extent of racial and ethnic inequalities. Accordingly, they think and talk about matters that don't often occur to insiders. For example, consider the residential ghettos we mentioned in our earlier chapter on class inequalities: their very existence suggests that certain populations are indeed disadvantaged in Canadian society today.

Residential Segregation

Ghetto, in its modern usage, refers to a pocket of economic deprivation, usually in the inner city, and often inhabited by mainly racialized residents (Wagmiller 2007, Walks and Bourne 2006). But who creates and maintains these ghettos? As insiders point out, some instances of residential segregation are voluntary: certain ethnic groups want to live in institutionally complete neighbourhoods along with others like themselves (Fong and Wilkes 2003). At the same time, residential segregation can also be involuntary, imposed upon impoverished racial minorities by the dominant population.

Involuntary residential segregation is largely a product of economic inequality. As the income gap between white, native-born Canadians and racial outsiders widens, housing becomes unaffordable for minority groups who are disadvantaged in the labour market. Whites, who generally face fewer barriers to securing stable jobs, can usually afford to live in better neighbourhoods, while minorities are forced into less desirable ones (Iceland and Wilkes 2006).

That said, much residential segregation can be explained by social (as opposed to labour market) discrimination. At least some white Canadians tend to physically and socially distance themselves from racial minority groups they deem undesirable. They may even try to prevent members of such groups from moving into their neighbourhoods, fearing the value of their homes will decline as a result (Fong and Shibuya 2000). Real estate agents may be slow to serve members of minority groups, allowing others the opportunity to purchase a house or rent an apartment first. For example, a random survey of Aboriginal renters in Winnipeg by the Canadian Mortgage and Housing Corporation reported that one in three would arrive at a viewing for an available unit, only to be told it had "just been rented" (Macdonald 2015). Finally, unequal opportunities in the lending market pose a barrier for racial minorities seeking to buy: according to one recent study, Blacks and Hispanics are 56% more likely than whites to be denied a conventional mortgage loan (Charles 2013).

Uzma Shakir, who immigrated to Toronto from Karachi, Pakistan, explains the difference between "chosen" self-segregation and imposed isolation:

[C]ommunities are formed either by choice or by lack of choice. Rosedale is as much an ethnic enclave as Regent Park. In all multicultural societies ... people choose to live either with others who are like them (this can be class, culture or some other affinity) or that is all they can afford (*Toronto Star* 2011).

Developers and city planners also contribute to residential segregation. To maximize returns, investors buy "unproductive" land at a low cost, and then build luxury condominiums that will attract high-income residents (Fong and Shibuya 2000). Not only are the poor left behind in deteriorating neighborhoods, but developers seek to buy out and "gentrify" these "unproductive," "wasted" areas by erecting housing developments that target high-income residents. Increasingly unaffordable housing constitutes one of the main causes of residential segregation in Canada today.

A case in point: since moving to Canada from Bangladesh in 1998, Anthony Rosario has shared a two-bedroom apartment in Scarborough with his wife and their three adult children (Keung 2012). At $900 per month, rent absorbed half the family's entire monthly income. Two months before Rosario was able to move into a subsidized seniors' apartment at the age of 61, he was still sharing this two-bedroom apartment, now with his wife, son, daughter-in-law, and two grandchildren: "It's tough to live with so many people in so little space, but you are bound to live like this when you don't have money."

At the other end of the housing spectrum, gated communities are becoming increasingly popular (Vesselinov 2008). "Gating" began in the 1940s and 1950s as a means of limiting racial minorities' physical access to affluent white neighbourhoods. In the U.S., gated communities are often literally that— physically secure behind high walls that are sometimes topped with barbed wire (Walks 2014). In Canada, gated communities are more often surrounded by decorative wrought-iron fences or other boundaries that emphasize aesthetics over security. These "gates" are more symbolic than functional: they reinforce the social division between members of different races and classes. ✳

In her book *Walled States, Waning Sovereignty* (2010), political scientist Wendy Brown notes that the traditionally powerful white upper classes have turned to these gates, walls, and other barriers to visibly distinguish themselves from lower-income minorities. Ironically, the desire to establish and live within gated communities points to a heightened anxiety about personal safety, and thus "erodes" or "undoes" the authority and control dominant groups aim to assert. Wrought-iron fences can't keep people out; they are merely "performances" of self-defense and exaggerated expressions of power. Because they are costly and aesthetically appealing, these barriers are more effective signals of socioeconomic status than of unassailable security.

Ultimately, gated communities increase tensions between people of different races, ethnicities, and economic classes. Rather than questioning or trying to resolve the divisions between these groups, privileged whites choose to sequester themselves. Unsurprisingly, this formal segregation often reinforces an antagonistic opposition between "us" and "them."

The Myth of Multiculturalism

Canada's proudly self-proclaimed "multiculturalism" is regarded as a myth by many of the racialized "others" who are supposed to feel welcome and accepted in a multicultural society. You will recall the insider tendency to categorize people into broad, homogenous categories: "us"/"them," white/non-white, and so on. Outsiders are more likely to resist these rigid, dichotomous groupings, and to feel as though such labels do not do justice to their own subjective sense of self (Fee and Russell 2007). Indeed, these categories are largely constructed by the dominant white majority. Why would anyone outside that social group view or understand themselves in the same terms that are most often used to oppress and disadvantage them?

Consider the Aboriginal population as an example. The Indian Act, first passed in 1876, is federal legislation that determines who has "Indian" status, which in turn determines who can live on-reserve (Hanson 2009). Many non-Aboriginals think someone must live on a reserve and have official status in order to be a "real Indian." Under the Indian Act, however, certain people are classified as status Indians while others of similar ancestry and background are not (Fee and Russell 2007). Thus some people who identify as Aboriginal are excluded from an official designation and therefore from the right to live where they wish. At the same time, many status Indians live not on reserves but in urban areas, despite the common stereotype of Indigenous peoples as being confined to reserves.

The reserves themselves are in deplorable condition: small, geographically isolated, overcrowded, and deeply impoverished. Sara Mainville, chief of the Couchiching First Nation, says: "The status quo is so dangerous. I don't want my 10-year-old daughter to grow up feeling unsafe on city streets the way I did. This has to change" (Macdonald 2015). Yet the federal government seems unable or unwilling to improve the lot of Aboriginals either on-reserve or off.

Aboriginals are all too often stereotyped as lazy, uneducated, and alcohol-dependent, and therefore wholly to blame for their own poor circumstances. A self-identified "native," blogging under the pseudonym Lou James, describes being brought up in an Aboriginal community:

> My home was stereotypically native: abusive relationships dominated my younger years and permeate every aspect of my life today. My family, friends, and community have seen, and continue to see, disproportionate levels of murder, suicide, violence, sexual abuse, prostitution,

alcoholism, drug addiction, emotional abuse, homelessness, and poverty and the criminality that follows from all of this. . . .

. . . Every native person I know has, to varying degrees, lost his or her language, traditional knowledge, and sense of identity and belonging as native people.

I grew up in a town, province, and country that reinforced this as the dominant narrative about native people, except when we parade out a few traditional-looking natives to show off an integral part of the rich tapestry of the Canadian identity and imagination, and then congratulate ourselves for being so tolerant and multicultural (Huffington Post 2013).

In Canada, we like to think we embrace the ideal of multiculturalism. In the U.S., by contrast, it is easier to maintain more dichotomous understandings of race: there, whiteness is more rigidly opposed to blackness. The United States' history of slavery in particular continues to inform contemporary black-white race relations (Wortley 2009). The Canadian "other" is more varied: white, Canadian-born "insiders" oppose themselves to our Aboriginal population, immigrants, native-born people of colour, and, for some, even the Québécois. Presumably, we draw the idea of our "cultural mosaic" from the multiplicity of Canadian others. Yet those others continue to be defined primarily by insiders, not in ways that fit their own subjective identities.

In fact, attempts to depict Canadian race relations as "better" than those in the US may be misleading. The problem of race is at least on the agenda in the U.S., even for insiders. In Canada, politicians, historians, and other "authority" figures have convinced the general population that Canada is not, and never was, a white racist society. Many (white) Canadians are not only blind to their own racism, but deny it exists (Wortley 2009). Canadians are also likely to congratulate themselves for treating "their" Aboriginals, immigrants, and racial minorities better than in the U.S. From this perspective, racism is something endemic to *other* countries; if it happened here, that was in the distant past.

Outsiders persistently strive to bring the mistreatment of Aboriginal peoples to public attention. Hayden King from the Beausoleil First Nation in Huronia, Ontario, declares: "We have Native children being taken from families, kids dying of preventable causes in northern communities, and we haven't talked about any of it. You really have to ask: What will it take to compel Canadians to make these electoral issues?" Michelle Corfield of the Ucluelet First Nation expresses similar sentiments: "Canadians should be appalled. . . . Every citizen of Canada deserves to live in a country that recognizes them as equals. If we continue to do nothing, Indigenous people will fall from Third to Fourth World living conditions" (Macdonald 2015).

Others contest the idea that racism is a bigger problem in the U.S. than in Canada. Black human-rights lawyer Anthony Morgan writes:

> Being black in Canada can sometimes be suffocating.
>
> This feeling does not only come from being subject to anti-black racism in multiple domains of social, economic, cultural and civic life in Canada. It is overwhelmingly the result of carrying the exhausting burden of having to convince others of the truth of your lived experience. . . . "Maybe the store clerk is not following you but is only doing their job." "Maybe you didn't get hired because you're just not as qualified as the other applicants."
>
> Maybe. . . . But maybe not. . . .
>
> "But this is Canada!" our sense of Canadian racial exceptionalism pushes some of us proclaim. "It's Americans that have a race problem, not us!". . .
>
> Blacks in Canada are so often met with this kind of response . . . that just being black in Canada can feel deflating, paralyzing and oppressive (*Toronto Star* 2015)

Canada and the U.S. struggle with different racial tensions informed by different histories. Keeping that in mind, consider the fact that African-Americans, arguably the most disadvantaged racial "others" in the U.S., constitute about 12.2% of the total population. Aboriginals living in Canada constitute a mere 4.3% of our country's population (Employment and Social Development Canada 2015). As a result, Canadian Aboriginals have even less opportunity to influence the political system by voting than do American blacks. In fact, Indigenous peoples were denied the vote federally until 1960. Even with enfranchisement, the nature of our democratic system of "majority rule" makes it difficult for Aboriginals to advance their interests.

Indigenous peoples have nonetheless made huge strides in resisting oppression. They have successfully drawn public attention to infringements on their rights through well-publicized legal actions. Police brutality, sexual abuse in residential schools, forced relocation, and land-grabs have also drawn widespread attention.

We are slowly beginning to recognize just how poorly Canada's Indigenous peoples have been mistreated, but we have hardly begun to consider how we might establish equality between Aboriginals and the more privileged white population. Efforts to date consist of a series of official apologies issued by the Canadian government between 1988 and 2010. While these apologies at least recognize the wrongs of the past, they remain contentious, especially for outsiders. Few white Canadians are even aware the apologies were made, much less what they were about. Moreover, these apologies allow politicians and other non-Aboriginal Canadians to feel an unwarranted sense of closure and resolution.

"Go Back Where You Came From"

Multiculturalism is also perceived as a "myth" by certain groups of in who endure particularly negative experiences in Canada. While the) ⌐⌐⌐ ⌐⌐⌐⌐ to preserve some aspects of their home cultures, they report that others are viewed as unacceptable: immigrant outsiders are told that they can "go back to where they came from" if they want to continue engaging in certain practices deemed "un-Canadian." An especially controversial debate surrounds face and hair coverings such as the niqab, as well as the burka, a full body cloak worn by some Muslim women (Lépinard 2014). These garments, according to some insiders, directly infringe upon women's fundamental human rights, and perpetuate wearers' oppression by their patriarchal husbands. Epitomizing such views, former Prime Minister Stephen Harper declared that the niqab is "rooted in a culture that is anti-women." Fully 72% of respondents in a Global News/Ipsos Reid poll said they strongly or somewhat agreed with Harper's viewpoint (Logan 2015).

Protests, campaigns, and aid organizations have tried to "free" women who immigrate to Canada from these "sexist" practices. What these campaigns fail to acknowledge is that women are not a homogenous group of people with identical values, interests, or desires. Women who have lived in different places, who follow different religions, and who have spent considerable periods of their life immersed within different social contexts may want different things than white Canadian women (who are also far from homogenous). In particular, not every woman in the world believes that exposing a certain amount of skin constitutes "freedom." For example, one anonymous woman from Ottawa said: "The reason I am starting [to wear] the niqab is that I am seeing in society that there is an oversexualization of women and women's bodies. . . . Once I started [wearing the] niqab, I felt more comfortable, and it was a sort of barrier to stop the advances" (Payne 2015).

Humanitarian campaigns that aim to "free" women from face coverings thus fail to consider whether these women actually need or want "freeing." Instead, they assume that Western women—those who do not wear face coverings—live the lives that all women want (Lépinard 2014).When we try to impose our beliefs on others in this way, we are taking an "ethnocentric" stance: using our own culture as a standard of comparison against which to judge others. Although some immigrant women may indeed be pressured into wearing face coverings and feel oppressed by them, others do not: they have not been "brainwashed" into endorsing patriarchal values, they do not feel "oppressed" under them, and they do not wish to be "free" from them. They do not need white Westerners telling them what they "should" want, what they need, or what's "best" for them. By imposing our own understandings on these women, we are implying they lack the intelligence and autonomy to make informed decisions for themselves, or the strength and ability to assert their desires.

In fact, these attempts to "free" foreign women from (supposed) patriarchal oppression seem to *infringe* upon that very freedom. In principle, the majority of Canadians would agree that people should be able to freely choose to do whatever they want. Nada, a Muslim woman who immigrated to Canada from Syria in 2000, highlights the apparent contradiction here: "It's a way of wearing clothes. People are free to wear what they want to wear, the same as they pierce their noses, have tattoos" (Manole 2015). Similarly, Shomyla Hammad says that none of her other family members wear a niqab, and her husband initially opposed the idea: "I want every Canadian to know that [this] was the decision I [made] because I was in Canada. Anywhere else in the world, I wouldn't be able to [make] this decision. . . . Canada empowered me. Canada taught me how to be yourself and do whatever you want to do" (Logan 2015). Zunera Ishaq, who put off becoming a Canadian citizen as she waited for the courts to rule on the legality of a policy requiring her to remove her niqab during the citizenship ceremony, made a similar point: "It's precisely because I won't listen to how other people want me to live my life that I wear a niqab. Some of my own family members have asked me to remove it. I have told them that I prefer to think for myself. . . . To me, the most important Canadian value is the freedom to be the person of my own choosing." So, contrary to those campaigns that seek to free women from supposedly oppressive garments, only by letting women choose for themselves what they do and do not want to wear are we treating them fairly and equally.

Ultimately then, the debate surrounding face coverings seems not to be about face coverings at all: rather, some Canadians appear to interpret these garments as symbols of an entire culture and its values. That is, some Canadians (including the 72% of Global News/Ipsos Reid respondents who agreed with Harper (Logan 2015)) assume that face coverings are always and necessarily symptoms of sexism and female oppression. In turn, these Canadians feel compelled to argue that such symbols, and the values they supposedly represent, are unacceptable in Canada, where gender equality is valued. They make similar assumptions regarding the other values that immigrants from certain countries hold: just as they are assumed to be "anti-women," as Harper put it, they are also at times assumed to be religious extremists, homophobic, or racist.

Two points should be made in response to such assumptions. First, just as all white Canadians are not the same, every individual from a particular country, or of a particular religion, is not the same. Assuming, based solely on her appearance or the garments she chooses to wear, that an individual is a victim of sexism is prejudicial by definition. Assuming, based solely on his appearance or stated religion, that a man is a homophobic religious zealot is similarly prejudicial. As we will discuss in a later chapter, no individual can be treated as a representative of his or her entire culture, country, or religious group.

Second, however, acts of terrorism such as the 2016 Orlando nightclub massacre suggest that some acts of violence are indeed religiously motivated. Thus, a distinction must be drawn between "foreign" beliefs and behaviours that are tolerable in Canada—such as freely choosing to wear a burka or niqab—and those that are not – such as voicing or acting upon sexist, homophobic, or otherwise hateful beliefs. On this matter, we will have to prioritize equality and respect for all over multiculturalism. In Canada, we have determined that everyone, regardless of sex, race, religion, sexuality, and so on, should be treated equally, and that equality is not to be infringed upon in the interests of multicultural politeness. We do not demand that people live in Canada: only that they abide by Canadian principles of equality *if they choose to live here*. If this is ethnocentrism—as it appears to be—it is an ethnocentrism that took a thousand years to evolve and many lives to defend.

White Privilege

Throughout this chapter, we have noted that blatant racism is relatively rare in Canada today, but more subtle manifestations persist. White privilege is perhaps the most subtle way in which insiders perpetuate racial inequality – so subtle, in fact, that it often goes genuinely unnoticed, until outsiders call our attention to it.

The term was coined in the late 1980s, when American feminist and anti-racism activist Peggy McIntosh listed 50 privileges associated with being white. Number 46, for example, states: "I can chose blemish cover or bandages in 'flesh' color and have them more or less match my skin." With her list, McIntosh aimed to expose the ways in which white insiders take many aspects of their lives for granted.

Today, the phrase **white privilege** is widely used to describe those advantages that white people enjoy on a daily basis (Owen 2007). In McIntosh's (2008) words, it "is like an invisible weightless knapsack of special provisions, assurances, tools, maps, guides, codebooks, passports, visas, clothes, compass, emergency gear, and blank checks." Although often unnoticed by white insiders themselves, who prefer to think they have been rewarded for hard work, intelligence, or other individual qualities, these privileges are all too obvious to outsiders, who are acutely aware of the unfair benefits associated with being white.

Desmond Cole provides an outsider's perspective on white privilege, which he claims "is real" and affects everyone. White people, he argues, are not singled out or stereotyped for their perceived race or ethnicity. White privilege is the flip side of racism: if those of us deemed to be "visible minorities" suffer discrimination, white privilege speaks to the corresponding people who, whether or not they realize it, gain advantage from this dynamic. Systemic racism does not just have countless victims, but beneficiaries as well.

White privilege does not mean all white people are born into automatic money or power, and it does not mean that white people, whether or not they have these things, intend to benefit from racism. It means that they *cannot help* but benefit from it, because it is built into our culture. It means white people are free from the systemic bias, suspicion, and low expectations that racialized people must endure every day. It means that when a criminal has white skin, his actions are never connected to his race, while a criminal perceived as a brown-skinned Muslim inspires hatred and suspicion of other brown-skinned Muslims. It means that white people are not *de facto* representatives of their race (2014).

Despite its currency, the phrase "white privilege" is problematic. The idea of privilege obscures the structures of domination that perpetuate advantages (Gillborn 2006, Owen 2007) and makes it seem as though they are granted to whites at random, almost miraculously, without people themselves actively setting out to advance their own interests at the expense of others. To address this issue, critical race theorists often use the phrase **white supremacy** to describe not only the extremist, often violent political groups that lash out in racial hatred, but also, the forces that structure the more mundane behaviours, actions, and policies that shape society in favour of white people (Garner 2006). White supremacy involves a kind of "first-class citizenship" for white people; membership and a sense of belonging in the dominant, respected culture; occupation of and full ownership over the aesthetically normative body; entitlement to better social, legal, and economic treatment; and better life chances.

A potential issue with both white privilege and supremacy is that such terms redirect discussions of race back to the dominant norm of whiteness. Although this critique has long been levelled at so-called "critical whiteness scholarship," it is, in fact, a misreading of the aims of that scholarship. Properly executed and understood, critical whiteness theory is *not* centrally concerned with the needs or interests of white people. Rather, it seeks to foreground, make visible, and disrupt the unfair social structures that work to the advantage of whites and disadvantage of everyone else—structures taken for granted as "normal" and "inevitable" (Fee and Russell 2007). In other words, *critical* whiteness studies *criticize* the ways in which members of the racially dominant group have become blind to their own privileged positions.

One thing remains certain: most white people have been conditioned to view the world in dramatically different ways than people of every other skin colour or racial identity. For the dominant majority, life is made easier by that "invisible weightless knapsack" full of privileges that have become so commonplace, they are no longer recognized as such. But those denied that same set of privileges often become acutely aware of the unfair, oppressive practices that saturate life in the West (Gillborn 2006).

FINAL THOUGHTS

White, Canadian-born insiders like to think of themselves as accepting of all races and ethnicities, but research going back at least as far as Porter's *Vertical Mosaic* provides evidence of systematic racism. Canada maintains the illusion of equality while simultaneously marginalizing particular racialized minorities. Racism in Canada is so subtle that it passes almost undetected, with only its targets aware of it. As a result, most insiders think they live in an egalitarian, tolerant society, despite benefiting from a social hierarchy that places whites at its top. Despite insiders' formal commitment to multiculturalism, Canada remains a largely white society structured around white privilege.

DISCUSSION QUESTIONS

1. What trade-offs, if any, are involved in creating a truly multicultural society? Must we sacrifice a degree of equality on another dimension (say, gender equality) to improve racial, ethnic, or religious equality? If so, is multiculturalism something we should be striving to attain, or are other aspects of equality more important?

2. How might institutional completeness benefit immigrants and racialized groups? In what circumstances is self-segregation chosen, and when is it imposed by insiders? Would a reduction in the extent of imposed segregation improve life chances for immigrants and racialized groups?

3. Do you think white privilege exists? Is it useful to think about the advantages of being white in Canada today, or does critical whiteness scholarship merely redirect our focus back onto empowered white insiders? How are discussions of white privilege and critical whiteness scholarship different from discussions of the men's rights movement, which has also been critiqued for focusing attention on traditionally advantaged male insiders?

4. Why might insiders blame Aboriginal peoples, immigrants, and racial minorities for their own circumstances, as well as for broader social problems such as unemployment? How do these victim-blaming narratives allow insiders to continue believing in the myth of Canadian multiculturalism?

FURTHER READING

Jedwab, Jack. *The Multiculturalism Question.* Queen's University School of Policy Studies, 2014.

Patricia Boksa et al. "Mental Wellness in Canada's Aboriginal Communities: Striving toward Reconciliation." *Journal of Psychiatry and Neuroscience* 40: 6 (2015): 363–65.

Jennifer Heller. "Emerging Themes on Aspects of Social Class and the Discourse of White Privilege." *Journal of Intercultural Studies* 31:1 (2010): 111–120.

KEY TERMS

Assimilation. Process by which immigrant groups adopt the values and culture of the host society.

Critical race theory (CRT). Application of critical (i.e., conflict or Marxist) theory to issues of race. From the perspective of CRT, race is something that is performed rather than an innate quality of an individual.

Dissonant acculturation. Process by which second generation immigrants discard their native culture and often integrate into the existing underclass of the host society.

Ethnic enclave. Geographic area with high concentration of a particular ethnic or racialized group.

Ethnocentrism. Practice of evaluating and judging other societies through the lens of one's own cultural bias.

Institutional completeness. Condition of an ethnic group or enclave that has established various social institutions, such as schools and religious centres, tailored to the group and often delivered in their traditional language.

Institutionalized racism. Pattern of racism expressed in social institutions and power structures, deeply entrenched therefore often unnoticed.

Integration. Movement of ethnic and minority groups into the host society.

Othering. Tendency to place people into distinct categories of "us" and "them" based on perception of them as different from ourselves.

Performativity. Idea that social categories such as race or gender are not intrinsic but are acted out or "performed" in accordance with societal norms.

Racialization. Social process of assigning racial identities to a population.

Selective acculturation. Process by which second generation immigrants choose to adopt some aspects of their host culture while retaining ties to their native culture.

Social distance. According to Emory Bogardus, the willingness to allow certain ethnic groups into varying degrees of intimacy.

White privilege. Advantages possessed by white people solely because of their race.

White supremacy. System that affords privilege to white people on the basis of the belief that they are superior to all other races.

CHAPTER FIVE

Age Inequalities

LEARNING OBJECTIVES

In this chapter, you will:
1. Consider the implications of diverging from the expected or normalized life course
2. Question the assumptions underpinning disengagement and activity theories
3. Deconstruct ageist stereotypes associated with youth and older adults
4. Distinguish between numerical and functional age
5. Explore eldercare options in the face of an aging population

INTRODUCTION

In 2009, Dutch sailor Laura Dekker declared her intention to make a two-year solo journey around the world. She was 13 years old.

The local child welfare office objected, saying Dekker was too young to accurately assess and avoid danger, and that being alone for an extended period would stunt development at her young age (Kuchler 2009). Meanwhile, the media attacked Dekker's father, who supported her trip. One writer opined: "This is a bit like giving a kid with a new driver's license the keys to a Formula One car and letting them loose on the track at Monaco" (Doane 2009). "Allowing a 13-year-old girl to sail around the world on her own is plain stupid," another said (Abbott 2009). Ultimately, a family court ruled that Dekker was too young to sail alone and required her parents to share custody with the Council for Child Care.

What authorities failed to consider was that Dekker had been born on a boat, spent the first years of her life at sea, and was sailing on her own by the age of six (Kuchler 2009). In the end, after a ten-month court battle, Dekker did indeed sail around the world alone, becoming the youngest person to do so. Even then, the fact she was a child continued to be emphasized. One writer noted: "Many 13-year-olds appear frighteningly mature for their age, yet, like Laura, they are still children" (Owen 2009). And Jillian Schlesinger, who collaborated with Dekker to create a documentary film about her journey, described Dekker as "a truly exceptional human being with a very particular set of skills and life experiences that allow her to be able to do this very safely and very skillfully. . . . [The film] doesn't make an argument about what's possible for other people" (Rothman 2014).

Is Dekker an anomaly? She does seem different from other girls her age, and therefore fascinating. But why don't stories like Dekker's make us question our assumptions about age? Other teenagers have sailed around the globe alone, and while the fact that a handful of adolescents have done it doesn't mean *every* teenager could, their experiences beg the question: how many young people *may* be capable of such accomplishments, were they given the chance (and the proper training)?

Children and teenagers are routinely denied opportunities to prove themselves in far less risky situations. Until they reach certain arbitrary ages, they are deemed "too young" to vote, drive, be alone with members of the opposite sex or take part in various other activities. These rules are in place for good reason: many children would injure themselves or others were they allowed to do as they please. But others would not.

Age is another characteristic, alongside race and sex, to which people attach often unfounded assumptions. Just as not all women or Asians are the same, neither are all children or elderly people. In this chapter, we explore how young, middle-aged, and elderly people are "supposed" to lead their lives—the expectations society has placed on them—as well as the strategies people use to resist those expectations.

INSIDER VIEWS

People on the "inside"—in this case, middle-aged people with recognized jobs and social statuses—frequently underestimate the significance of age inequality and deny the persistence of ageism. Idealizing (often mistakenly) childhood as a time of carefree innocence, insiders tend to dismiss any disadvantages associated with old age as problems the elderly exaggerate or bring upon themselves. For example, in considering the difficulties older adults confront at work, insiders sometimes suggest that people should retreat gracefully from society when they are too old to be useful. In this way, insiders often imply that the elderly haven't come to terms with the life course (Johnson and Barer 1992).

The Life Course

Over time, people pass through different "phases" of life, with certain events typically occurring at certain times, such as education while young or parenting as an adult. The **life course** is a sequence of individual, age-related experiences or role transitions, guided and structured by social institutions including families, schools, workplaces, and churches (Pudrovska 2014, Elder 1994).

In each society, there is an expected or normative life course: a "standard biography" of sorts that dictates which social roles people are "supposed" to fill, and in what order (Katz et al. 2012, Sennott and Mollborn 2011). In North America, very young children are expected to enjoy freedom from responsibility; youth are meant to attend school; "emerging adults" in their late teens and early twenties are encouraged to complete their college or university degrees before transitioning into "adulthood," which is understood to involve full-time, stable employment that allows them to marry, buy a house, and have children. These individuals are also expected to care for their aging parents, who have entered the last phase of the life course, during which they are seen, from an insider perspective, as increasingly infirm dependents (Kohli 2007).

The life course becomes institutionalized as a set of rules by which most people expect—and are expected to—lead their lives (Nico 2010). These social rules are informal, including widely shared beliefs and norms; formal, including the legal rights to which only people above a certain age are entitled; and structural, comprising the institutions through which people are expected to pass as they age (Kohli 2007).

But many people experience a gap between the life course they expect and the one they experience. Sometimes people break the rules, failing to live up to age-related expectations (Ho and Raymo 2009). Such rule-breaking can be costly and dangerous: for instance, teenage pregnancy and unexpected parenthood (Elder 1994, Mossakowski 2011). At other times, diverging from the expected life course can be rewarding: married couples may delay childbearing to prioritize travel or career-building. Or people may be viewed unfavorably for breaking the rules, as when older people apply for a job or fill a role considered appropriate for those much younger (Panek et al. 2006).

Such rule-breaking is more common today than it once was. With the coming of the Industrial Revolution, the life course became more structured, secure, and predictable (Bruckner and Mayer 2005). Lives were structured around almost certain transitions, offering a sense of security because people could predict what the future held (Kohli 2007).

This is no longer the case in Canada and many other countries. To borrow Furlong and Cartmel's (1997) metaphor, social destinations were once reached by trains traveling on regular schedules. Today, most people reach their destinations using a variety of vehicles, each person tracing their own route on an individualized schedule (Higgs and Gilleard 2010). While most still finish their education before getting a job, get a job before getting married, and get married before having children, increasing numbers of individuals no longer follow the "standard" trajectory (Hogan 1985, Benson and Elder 2011). Life's journey has become less predictable, institutionalized, and orderly (Nico 2010, Sargent et al. 2012).

Because more people are diverging from the expected life course, age norms for young adults have loosened in recent decades. Society has become more tolerant of variations in the timing of life-course transitions (Sennott and Mollborn 2011). Yet age norms persist. Insiders still encourage young people to pursue a "normal," institutionalized life course, chiding them to "grow up" when they fail to move through schooling, career establishment, marriage, and child-rearing in an orderly fashion (Bosick 2009, Nico 2010). Such expectations may be difficult for young people to meet: secure, well-paying jobs are often hard to find after graduation.

Indeed, many young people themselves expect to satisfy certain markers of "adulthood" as they reach certain ages. Those who do so feel like purposeful, successful adults who are in control of their lives; those who do not are at a greater risk of depression and chronic stress (Mossakowski 2011). The discrepancy between their "ideal" and "actual" selves may give rise to impatience, frustration, and disappointment. Unfortunately, the ability to become one's ideal self—to live the "real," "adult" life we are taught to expect and desire—depends largely on social class (Benson and Elder 2011). More vulnerable youth, including those from low-income families who may not be able to afford higher education, often move into adulthood earlier than more privileged young people, who may spend as much as a decade completing post-secondary education.

From an insider perspective, the life course "should" be a one-way street with no stops, detours, or reversals. But for many (if not most) young people, that is no longer the case (Bosick 2009, Macmillan 2005). Divorcing, returning to school, changing careers, and moving back to the parental home are all examples of delays and supposedly backward steps. Sabbaticals and prolonged transitions into retirement are other examples of interruptions in what is "meant" to be a steady progression through the life course (Bruckner and Mayer 2005). Yet other people move through the phases of the life course out of order, as with women who return to school after marrying and having children (Jackson and Berkowitz 2005).

Given the growing diversity in the life courses people choose today, we cannot claim that one route is the most advantageous or even the most "normal." Nevertheless, insiders are typically reluctant to accept such divergences, especially by their own children. For example, many Canadian parents are exasperated by their children's inability to secure the kinds of jobs that they themselves obtained when graduating from university a generation ago. As

Maclean's puts it: "Most Canadian parents want their children to have white-collar office positions, not the kind of resource-based or industrial jobs for which there is still a strong demand" ("The graduate's million-dollar promise," January 16, 2013). Insiders may also criticize older adults for failing to conform to the traditional life course, with its retreat from paid work into retirement.

Disengagement Theory

Although age norms have shifted over the past several decades, the expected retirement age has remained steady at around 65 (Joulain et al. 2000). The idea that people "should" or "need" to retire serves as the basis of **disengagement theory** (Panek et al. 2006). Attributed to Elaine Cumming and William Henry (1961), this sociological theory holds that elderly people are among the socially and occupationally weakest members of the population, and that society must therefore displace them from positions of power and influence. Cumming and Henry note that, as people age, they gradually decline, both physically and mentally. Muscles weaken, bones become fragile, cognitive faculties slow, and illnesses are more likely to develop. This means that, at work, elderly people are often less productive than their younger colleagues (Garber et al. 2008, Filinson 2008).

At one time, mandatory retirement was society's way of dealing with this issue. Once they reached a certain age—traditionally 65—people no longer had a "right" to their job (Burns 1954). Even human rights codes that prohibited age-based discrimination in the workplace applied only to people aged 65 and under (Grant and Townsend 2013, MacGregor 2006).

Legislated mandatory retirement did not typically bar everyone 65 and over from the workforce. Individual workers were bound by company policies or collective agreements stating that their employment ended when they reached a certain age, after which point they were obligated to retire, regardless of their ability to perform their jobs (Gomez et al. 2002, Ibbott et al. 2006). If organizations wanted to allow employees older than 65 to keep working, they could; but if they wanted to mandate retirement at 65, employees had no legal recourse. Pensions (both public and private) and other forms of financial assistance were introduced to provide some degree of financial security for the elderly after they retired.

Only recently did mandatory retirement emerge as a legal issue, with certain jurisdictions prohibiting the practice as discriminatory (Gomez et al. 2002, Sargent et al. 2012). In some instances, mandatory retirement is still permitted—for example, when an employer can demonstrate that failure to impose a mandatory retirement age would result in undue costs or safety risks for the workers themselves, their clients, and the general public. These occupational qualifications are generally related to the physical demands of a given job (Flynn 2010, Gillin and Klassen 2000). However, many jobs in the present service and knowledge economy are not physically demanding. Instead, there is growing demand for workers with knowledge, education, and experience.

Today, most people view compulsory retirement as a form of age-based discrimination, or institutionalized **ageism** (Gomez et al. 2002, MacGregor 2006). Manitoba modified its human rights code in 1982 in an effort to restrict mandatory retirement practices; Quebec followed suit in 1983 (Grant and Townsend 2013), and Alberta, Prince Edward Island, New Brunswick, and Newfoundland and Labrador shortly thereafter. These changes, in conjunction with the 1985 Canadian Human Rights Act, meant that employers could not legally refuse to hire or continue the employment of workers because of their age (Filinson 2008). In Ontario, however, employers are still able to implement age-based retirement programs. People who feel they have been discriminated against on the basis of age—including by being forced to retire—can file a complaint with the Ontario Human Rights Commission (Ontario Human Rights Commission, Ibbott et al. 2006).

Studies show that legislation banning or restricting mandatory retirement has not affected employment rates for older workers (Grant and Townsend 2013). After mandatory retirement was banned, few workers aged 65 and over chose to continue working (Shannon and Grierson 2004). This is partly because many people continue to endorse the idea of age-based retirement, believing that it benefits society as a whole (Kohli 2007, Panek et al. 2006). As well, many people want to retire—especially from unsatisfactory and alienating jobs. Proponents of disengagement theory suggest that older adults in all societies give up their positions in the labour force and withdraw to the edges of society because such disengagement serves several purposes (Johnson and Mutchler 2013, Chen 2003).

First, age-based retirement frees up job positions, allowing younger people to move up the occupational and social hierarchy. Second, it ensures that outdated skills and ideas are replaced with newer, presumably more useful ones. Modern industrial economies value efficiency. The elderly are viewed as less efficient than younger people, and seen as a burden in a society focused on maximizing productivity and profit. Retirement, in this sense, is a vehicle for workforce quality control, allowing employers to bring new talent, skills, and knowledge into their companies (Ibbott et al. 2006, Flynn 2010).

Third, age-based retirement rewards retirees for their contributions to society, both through a moment of celebratory recognition—such as a retirement party—as well as by providing them with leisure time as a reward for a lifetime of labour (Sargent et al. 2012). Fourth, disengagement theory holds that people *want* to retire—usually even before they are expected to—and pensions are society's way of enabling this desire to disengage (Hardy 2002). By this account, elderly people disengage voluntarily, and are not excluded or abandoned.

The Digital Divide

Insiders who endorse age-based retirement have been quite successful in painting older workers as technologically inept (Mitzner et al. 2010, Rizzuto 2011). A so-called **digital divide** reduces productivity, with older workers lacking relevant skills and knowledge (Simms 2004, Gringart et al. 2005). Faced with the digital divide, employers have two options. They can hire tech-savvy young people to replace older employees who supposedly lack the necessary skills, or they can invest in upgrading older employees' skills. Both options carry costs, whether the retraining of older workers on new technologies or the significant expense of bringing new workers into the organization.

Though employers are interested in determining which option is most cost-effective, little research has been carried out to empirically test the supposed technological ineptitude of older workers, superiority of younger workers' skills, or the capacity of older workers to adapt to new technologies. What little research has been conducted indicates that older workers are often uncomfortable with digital technology, but also that they want to learn new skills and fear being excluded from such training (Woodward et al. 2013, Barnard et al. 2013). They are often versatile, adaptable, excited about tackling new challenges, and able to perform as well as younger workers when given the chance (Gringart et al. 2005). One study even found that older workers react *more* positively to new technologies in the workplace than their younger colleagues (Rizzuto 2011). Another study showed that older adults associate a variety of benefits with technology—for example, that it makes research and communication more convenient and efficient—and note fewer drawbacks. Almost no research shows that elderly people are unwilling to work with new technology, resist change or innovation, or fail at jobs that require the use of new technology (Mitzner et al. 2010).

Nevertheless, discriminatory ageist stereotypes persist. Some insiders go so far as to claim that elderly people are physiologically incapable of mastering new technology: as vision and hearing deteriorate, it becomes increasingly difficult and stressful for the elderly to use digital devices. Older workers are also said to be less capable of learning new skills as their cognitive abilities decline (Rizzuto 2011, Chaffin and Harlow 2005). These stereotypical views of what it means to grow old have led many employers to conclude that upgrading older workers' skills is costly and ultimately ineffective (Barnard et al. 2013).

Older adults subjected to ageist beliefs often internalize them (Chaffin and

Harlow 2005, Barnard et al. 2013). Often, they come to think they are incapable of learning, and that new technology is more complicated and confusing
than it really is, so they don't even try to master it. Their attitude is not only a
product of age; it is at least partly caused by the lack of support older workers
receive from colleagues and superiors (Rizzuto 2011, Loges and Jung 2001).

Widowhood

Despite the ongoing debate surrounding it, retirement is a commonplace and
predictable role change. Most retirees have thought about how to make the
transition. Other changes in the life course, such as widowhood, occur unex-
pectedly. Even when a spouse passes away after a long illness, the event and
its aftermath are stressful and frequently lead to loneliness, decreased quality
of life, anxiety, and even depression (Keene and Prokos 2008, Lindstrom and
Rosvall 2012).

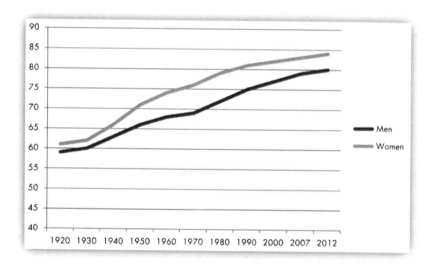

Figure 5.1: Life Expectancy in Canada

Women are more likely than men to experience these negative after-ef-
fects, for two reasons. First, because on average they live longer than men,
they often outlive their husbands. Second, it is more socially acceptable for
men to partner with women who are younger than them. These two realities
combine to make widowhood mainly a female experience (Bisdee et al. 2013,
Gillen and Kim 2009).

This fact poses challenges because, as noted in an earlier chapter, women
earn less than men and are often financially dependent on their husbands.
Women are also less likely than men to be members of workplace pension

plans, and if they were, their lower earnings result in substantially lower pension payments than their male counterparts (Gillen and Kim 2009, Young 2011). Widowhood can threaten an older woman's financial security, with some even slipping into poverty (Bisdee et al. 2013, Matthews 2011).

Other widows may find that their late husbands' health-care expenses depleted the family's savings (Gillen and Kim 2009). Although widowhood can come suddenly, it is more often preceded by spousal illness and decline, during which wives usually become the primary caregivers. Caring for a spouse in particular (as opposed to other family members) is a chronic stressor that can lead to psychological difficulties and caregiver burnout (Keene and Prokos 2008).

Some research suggests that prolonged caregiving depletes a person's emotional and physical resources, negatively affecting the bereavement process. There is, however, more evidence for a "relief model": when a spouse has been providing long-term, demanding care, the partner's death may come as a relief. Death means the end of suffering for the deceased, as well as release from a chronically stressful role for the new widow (Keene and Prokos 2008). As a result, newly widowed people often experience *less* distress and anxiety than before their spouse's death (Lee and Carr 2007).

This is particularly true of women who are widowed at a more advanced age: they cope better with the transition, likely because they expected it and were able to prepare themselves emotionally and financially (Wu and Schimmele 2007). Those widowed at younger ages—say, in their fifties—often lack both the time and the means to adequately prepare. And younger, economically disadvantaged young women are more likely to become widows to begin with, presumably because their husbands were employed in poorly paying, dangerous, difficult jobs that resulted in health problems.

For all these reasons, many older women find themselves alone and struggling financially (Angel et al. 2007). This may change as increasing numbers of "career women" attain higher earnings and greater financial independence (Bisdee et al. 2013). But the traditional gendered division of labour at home remains largely unaltered, so that bereaved partners of either sex must take on the roles and responsibilities previously held by their spouses (Wu and Schimmele 2007). Women may need to begin managing their own finances, or take on tasks their husbands had performed—gardening, car maintenance, and the like—all of which may be unfamiliar to them. Widowed men, for their part, often find cooking, cleaning, and other domestic tasks daunting: both unfamiliar and emasculating (van den Hoonaard 2010). If unable to perform such tasks themselves, widows and widowers alike may be forced to hire someone else to do—another drain on newly limited resources.

Often, younger friends and family members assist widows when and how they can, so that many widows transition from being dependent on their spouses to being dependent on their children (Ha et al. 2006). Some widows thus become closer to, or at least in more regular contact with, their children after the death of their spouse (Isherwood et al. 2012). But, since they have their own responsibilities and commitments, many younger adults cannot care for older parents adequately.

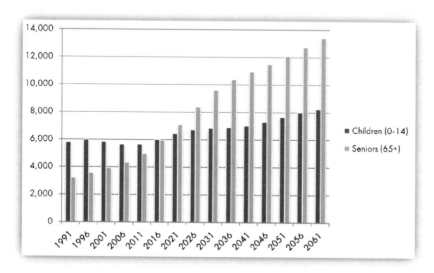

Figure 5.2: Numbers of Children and Seniors (in 000's), 1991 to 2061
ACTUAL FIGURES TO 2006, PROJECTED THEREAFTER

Widowhood can bring about a series of uncomfortable, unwelcome changes. However, the worst effects are experienced by older widows of lower socioeconomic status who are in poor health (Isherwood et al. 2012). Younger, middle-class widows who remain active may experience increased social engagement (Keene and Prokos 2008, Wu and Schimmele 2007). They may feel more inclined to socialize with others because they no longer have a companion at home, and may enjoy more free time and energy now that they are no longer caring for their spouse. These young, financially stable widows often spend more time with their children, as well as taking up new leisure activities or resuming old ones. Many also develop friendships with other elderly people, especially other widows with whom they can empathize. Staying socially engaged can help widows through the grieving process.

By contrast, elderly people without children, or whose children live far away, are at the greatest risk of isolation and loneliness after widowhood (Isherwood et al. 2012). This is especially true for men: although less likely to be widowed than women, they often find the experience more traumatizing and harder to manage (Lee and Carr 2007, van den Hoonaard 2010). In part, this is because men often rely on their wives for emotional support, to maintain social contacts, and to organize social events with their mutual friends (Lee and DeMaris 2007, Waldron et al. 2005). Without such support, some widowers lose touch with their social network.

Aging always involves change—in friendships, health, financial status, role relationships, and more. A supportive social network consisting of friends, family, neighbours, and the broader community can make these transitions smoother, increasing life satisfaction and overall wellbeing for both older men and women (Gadalla 2009, Wang 2009).

SECOND OPINIONS

Age Stratification Theory

Sociologists have long contested common assumptions made by most insiders about aging. A foundational contribution has been **age stratification theory**, which helps account for the unequal treatment of people of different ages.

Age is one of the characteristics around which all societies are structured (Dowd 1987). Age stratification theory explores how people are stratified, or vertically segregated, by age: how they are treated differently, physically segregated, pushed into different roles, supported or discounted by different social institutions, permitted to partake in certain activities and excluded from others (Marshall 2007, Uhlenberg and Giervield 2004).

A society's division of labour is structured in large part by age (as well as by gender, race, and class) (Hagestad and Uhlenberg 2005). Young people attend school; middle-aged people work, raise a family, and provide care for the young and the old, who are deemed incapable of caring for themselves; and elderly people enjoy retirement. But sociologists point out that different age groups are differentially valued and rewarded. Middle-aged insiders are lauded for their productivity, their active contributions to society, and their support for younger and older **dependents**. Children are also valued and even idealized as society's future. But they are also denied many rights, freedoms and opportunities because they are thought to be too young and immature, rendering them outsiders of sorts. Older adults, for their part, are the most significantly devalued.

All these perceptions are ageist: they rest on biased assumptions and stereotypes (Marshall 2007, McHugh 2003). Ageism both reflects and sustains the stratification of people based on age. Age discrimination resembles racism and sexism, but unlike those other forms of discrimination, it is still widely considered natural, inevitable, and harmless—even beneficial, as many insider rationalizations of age-based retirement demonstrate (Nelson 2005).

Like all discrimination, ageism has both material and psychological effects. Materially, it limits people's opportunities to secure employment (Marshall 2007, Nelson 2005). Health care and insurance provisions are determined by age, both in terms of costs and services provided. Religion is another social institution that structures services and activities according to age, as do educational institutions (Hagestad and Uhlenberg 2005). Even academics who study people of different ages are segregated: gerontologists publish in different journals and attend different conferences than researchers focusing on children.

Institutional segregation is reinforced by the spatial segregation of people of different ages: children spend their time in nurseries, daycares, playgrounds, and schools; teenagers and young adults, on university campuses, in college dormitories, and at bars and nightclubs; middle-aged people, in offices, boardrooms, and the suburbs; and elderly people, in retirement communities or assisted living facilities (McHugh 2003, Krekula 2009).

When people interact mainly with people of their own age, they can easily maintain an "us vs. them" mentality (Powell and Hendricks 2009), believing they share little in common with those older or younger than themselves. On the other hand, sustained interaction with people different from ourselves reduces prejudice, stigma, and discrimination, whether those differences involve race, class or age. Breaking down age-based barriers helps reduce the psychological consequences of ageism: its tendency to make outsiders feel rejected, excluded, and degraded (Clarke and Griffin 2008).

Canada's Aging Population

Stereotyping aside, academics offering second opinions agree with insiders that aging poses at least two central challenges for society: first, many elderly people require costly medical care and other support, and, second, that same group is considered by many to have outlived its usefulness and is therefore held in low regard (Ibbott et al. 2006). With the substantial decline in the birth rate over the past century, a greater fraction of our population is now considered elderly than ever before (Shank 2013, Barak 2009). As of 2015, 16.1 per cent of the Canadian population was aged 65 and over.

For young or middle-aged insiders, the idea of an aging population seems ominous. Some describe it as a "tsunami of seniors" (Kirkey 2012) or a "demographic time bomb" that will undermine economic competitiveness as well as the viability of health services and social programs (Gillin and Klassen 2000, Shannon and Grierson 2004). Working insiders responsible for those programs and services feel intense pressure to start making the changes necessary to accommodate the needs of older outsiders (Shank 2013).

Those older outsiders, by contrast, don't believe they pose such enormous difficulties, as many don't want to withdraw from society to become helpless dependents. Scholars offering second opinions on disengagement theory disagree with the assumption that excluding elderly people from financially rewarding and socially important roles will actually benefit society (Johnson and Barer 1992). Disengagement theory, they argue, frames humans as robots who make a 40-year contribution to society, then voluntarily jump into the social dustbin—a retirement community—where they wait patiently for oblivion (Foner 2000).

Data shows that disengagement is neither inevitable nor universal, even in modern, efficiency-conscious societies. Thanks to twenty-first century medical advances, people stay healthier much longer today than was the case when Cumming and Henry first devised their theory in the early 1960s (Sargent et al. 2012, Gomez et al. 2002). Many people are physically and mentally able to work well into their seventies and beyond, making productivity, engagement, and "usefulness"—rather than dependence and disengagement—norms for many elderly people today (Johnson and Mutchler 2013).

Even those who "need" to retire from paid employment—for health reasons, for example—often feel a sense of loss, having been stripped of a role that was central to their identity and sense of self-worth. This is especially true of people who occupy only a few social roles outside work. They depend heavily on their jobs to satisfy a variety of needs, including friendship, interest, and structure. Such people often dread retirement (Gillin and Klassen 2000). Men are more likely to hold this negative perception of retirement: their status as "man of the house" is often contingent on earning a wage and being the primary breadwinner. Such men are especially likely to continue working later in life, and once they retire, they often take up hobbies and volunteer work to provide a sense of purpose.

Then there are those people who genuinely enjoy their jobs (Gomez et al. 2002). Studies show that highly educated professionals, such as university professors, most often want to work into their seventies. These well-paid employees can usually afford to retire earlier, but continue to work because they find their jobs interesting and rewarding.

Such people are, however, in the minority. Only a small fraction of workers want to work longer than they must; most look forward to retiring, and many would do so even earlier if they could afford to (Gomez et al. 2002). When people are allowed to continue working if they want to, few of the problems posited by disengagement theory in fact result. In particular, there is little effect on youth unemployment rates (Filinson 2008). Instead, forced retirement reduces overall labour-force participation and economic productivity. As the population ages, skilled-labour shortages may result as older adults retire.

Disengagement theory has also been questioned on empirical grounds.

Cumming and Henry's research made use of a small sample of elderly people living in Kansas City in the late 1950s: healthy, middle-class adults of high socio-economic status (Fischgrund 1976). But people of different economic, educational, and social backgrounds have different views on work and retirement. Middle-class, securely employed people who can look forward to substantial pensions may dream of retirement, but the less well-off may fear it as a time of tight budgets and limited possibilities.

Finally, disengagement theory has been criticized for its implicit assumption that paid labour is the most important way in which people participate in society. In reality, older adults remain active and engaged in many other ways (Johnson and Mutchler 2013, Chen 2003). For example, retirees often become more active parents and grandparents, volunteer in their communities, participate more actively in their church, or take on leadership roles in leisure organizations. Withdrawal from the role of paid employee is not synonymous with a general withdrawal from society.

Activity Theory

The critique of disengagement theory we have just noted has, in fact, given rise to a theory of its own. **Activity theory** (Havighurst and Albrecht 1953) posits that, having been forced out of productive (i.e., paid) work, many older adults experiment with new roles and activities, or engage more deeply with already existing ones. People who remain highly engaged preserve a sense of self-worth, gain greater life satisfaction, and age more "successfully" than those who do not (Hardwicke and Sproule 2010, Bezerra et al. 2012).

Activity theorists note that insiders characterize retirement as a negative experience: a life-changing "loss" of such roles as paid worker and income-earner, requiring adjustment and reorientation (Gerber 1984). But these negative connotations are socially constructed. Although some younger people may view retirees as unproductive, older adults want to feel valued, and many make ongoing efforts to give their lives purpose.

Activity theory, however, has flaws of its own. Like disengagement theory, it is overly general, characterizing the elderly as a homogenous group with the same goals, interests, and desires. As well, it is underpinned by a neoliberal view of productivity and consumption and by the assumption that "good" citizens should be active contributors to the economy (MacGregor 2006). If older adults are not in paid employment, they are expected to contribute to society in other ways lest they be viewed as lazy or redundant.

Old Age Benefits

State benefit programs for the elderly were first enacted in Canada almost a century ago, following the establishment of such programs in the United Kingdom and other European countries. The Old Age Pensions Act was passed in 1927; it furnished federal assistance to provinces providing pensions to Canadians aged 70 and older (Canadian Museum of History). In 1952, the Old Age Security Act (OAS) made pensions solely a federal responsibility. Today, the OAS program provides a monthly payment to most people aged 65 and over (Government of Canada 2014).

In 1966, the federal government introduced the Canada Pension Plan (CPP). The CPP is an earnings-based social insurance program (Canadian Museum of History, Government of Canada 2014) that provides benefits to contributors and their immediate families in the event of loss of income due to disability, death, or retirement. Unlike OAS payments (and like its U.S. counterpart, the Social Security program), CPP is available only to those who have worked for pay and therefore have made contributions to the plan.

Programs like OAS and CPP, however beneficial, reinforce stereotypes of the elderly as helpless and dependent and therefore deserving of financial support (Binstock 2010, Roth et al. 2012). They also play into perceptions of elderly people as a burden on younger taxpayers (Tigges 1991). Neoliberal desires to reduce the size of government have contributed to the emergence of a new stereotype: the "greedy geezer." The stereotype is bolstered by the unique characteristics of the aging baby-boom generation now entering late adulthood: healthier, better educated, and inclined to work longer than previous generations, do baby-boomers really require the same degree of state support as their parents and grandparents (Roth et al. 2012)?

While **active aging** is desirable, it is also helps limit social spending. People who "age well" will not need to rely on the state (Higgs and Gilleard 2010). By privileging the personal (self-care and self-responsibility) over the collective, neoliberalism reinforces the assumption that elderly people can and should look after themselves, regardless of any structural barriers that may hinder their ability to do so (Powell and Wahidin 2005).

Another factor underlying the "greedy geezer" stereotype is the undeniable success of benefit programs (Binstock 2010). Such initiatives have reduced poverty rates among the elderly, rendering the circumstances of impoverished, under-educated, malnourished children and low-income families much worse by comparison (Higgs and Gilleard 2010). Many observers argue that support for the elderly reduces the benefits available to younger families.

Children's advocates also point out the "unfair" political advantage exercised by older outsiders: older adults can vote to protect their personal interests, but children and teens cannot. As the population ages, they reason, the elderly's political clout grows proportionately. Spending on eldercare may eventually absorb an unsustainably large fraction of national resources (Powell and Wahidin 2005), and some ask if it is "worth it" to spend so much money on people in the last years of their lives (Tigges 1991).

In debates surrounding the allocation of public resources, the elderly are demonized by middle-aged, working insiders in at least two ways. First, they are thought to use their voting power to demand ever higher payroll taxes. Retirees, who do not have to pay such taxes either personally or through their employers, thus secure benefits for themselves at the expense of working-age individuals (Giles and Reid 2005). Second, old-age benefits are characterized as "stealing" resources that would better be used to help future generations: the children and grandchildren of people who are now middle-aged (Higgs and Gilleard 2010, Tigges 1991).

These assumptions are all predicated on the **senior power model**. According to this view, seniors are thought to hold undue, even dangerous amounts of political power. This model also assumes that all elderly people view their benefits in the same way, despite differing socioeconomic situations, and will vote self-interestedly for candidates who promise to address "senior issues" like health care and pensions.

The senior power model, however, fails to account for other factors influencing elderly people's voting behaviour. Sex, gender, sexual identity, race, socioeconomic status, employment status, ethnicity, religion, and many other variables affect voting decisions (Binstock 2010). Consider, too, that many older adults are deeply invested in the wellbeing of people of other age groups, their children and grandchildren among them. For their part, younger people want to ensure their relatives are cared for as they grow old. Most people also realize they will someday grow old and come to depend on public health care, pensions, and old age benefits. Ultimately, people do not only or always vote in their immediate, age-related interests.

From this perspective, reduced spending on old age benefits would harm not only older adults but the middle-aged and young as well. Reduced healthcare spending, for example, would likely require younger people to assume greater caregiving responsibilities for older family members. Similarly, cutbacks in pensions and old age benefits might force many older people from their homes into three- or even four-generation family households.

Ideas like "active aging" that aim to encourage independence among the elderly are sometimes manipulated for ideological purposes as neoliberal politicians seek to shift responsibility for the wellbeing of the elderly from the state to individuals and their families (Shank 2013). Though empowerment and freedom are positive goals for older adults, state support is still needed and need not constitute dependency.

Feminism and Female Aging

As the senior power model suggests, old age has been constructed as a monolithic identity obscuring other characteristics such as gender, race and class (Krekula 2009). When younger people think about the elderly, their age, and associated notions of infirmity, vulnerability and helplessness, are often all that comes to mind. Yet why, for example, should a teenage girl distinguish herself *from*, rather than identify *with*, an older woman? They are both women.

We often distinguish ourselves from elderly people when it is convenient to do so and when it benefits our own interests (Krekula 2009). Privileged groups use such distinctions to maintain advantage. A case in point: young women enjoy an advantage over older women in our society (Clarke 2011). Women are valued, idealized, and portrayed as desirable while young and attractive, then dismissed as uninteresting and even repulsive when they begin to show signs of aging (Montemurro and Gillen 2013). To be sure, younger women are often objectified, while older women are usually free from the sexualizing male gaze. But within our culture's "sexual economy," young women are valued more highly than older women.

The experience of aging is different for men and women (Russell 2007). Because they are more highly stigmatized for their changing appearance, women in our culture dread getting older in a way that most men do not (Lewis et al. 2011, Montemurro and Gillen 2013). A gendered double standard is applied to the aging bodies of men and women. Some think men grow more attractive—or "rugged"—with age, but most people agree that women's beauty and desirability decline with loss of youthfulness (Muise and Desmarais 2010). Consider the epithet "mutton dressed as lamb" leveled at women who do not dress "appropriately" for their age (Krekula 2009). There is no equivalent phrase for men.

Especially in North America, women are expected to try to maintain their youthful appearance as they age (Winterich 2007, Muise and Desmarais 2010). They become increasingly concerned with, and try to avoid or conceal, grey hair, weight gain, and the facial hair that can begin to appear as hormonal levels change with age (Clarke 2011). Concern with such changes drives the market for "anti-aging" products and services. But the media themselves are at least in part responsible for the perceived need for these products by idealizing young, fit, slender women who epitomize the "thin ideal" discussed in an earlier chapter (Montemurro and Gillen 2013).

The idea that aging is something women need to "fight" implies that the natural process of growing older must be resisted, or at the very least camouflaged (Clarke 2011). Women are encouraged to "transcend" their age by disciplining their bodies and striving to attain a "fit," "beautiful" appearance that can't even be attained by many younger women. As a result, almost all Western women feel dissatisfied with their aging bodies (Winterich 2007).

Sometimes, verbally abusive husbands and intimate partners promote this process. Some men blatantly sexualize and objectify young, stereotypically beautiful women. As a result, older heterosexual women may feel stigmatized and rejected. While their younger selves may have attracted male attention, their present, older selves are dismissed and ignored (Hogan and Warren 2012).

Feminist researchers are conflicted about women's efforts to police their aging bodies. Some say that women who choose to use "anti-aging" products and undergo cosmetic surgery are empowering themselves by making their own decisions about how they want their bodies to look. But others note that women who try to "fight" the signs of aging are merely submitting to largely male-defined cultural standards of beauty (Muise and Desmarais 2010).

OUTSIGHTS

People on the "outside"—in this chapter, the young and the old—have different concerns and preoccupations than middle-aged people. They are likely to note prevalent assumptions that people of certain ages should embody certain traits and engage in certain behaviours: elderly people are wise, young people innocent and energetic. Older adults who behave "youthfully"—by dressing fashionably, or frequenting bars and nightclubs thought more appropriate for twenty-somethings—and young people who appear mature beyond their years would suggest that these stereotypes are merely social constructs.

Socially Constructing Age

A constructionist perspective considers old age, as well as any other phase in the life course, as an arbitrary category (Vincent 2006). The boundaries between youth, middle age and old age are often based on loose, poorly defined criteria and incorrect information (Kehl Wiebel and Fernandez Fernandez 2001). We cannot precisely define when someone is no longer middle-aged and has become "old," any more than we can say when someone has passed out of "youth" (Degnen 2007). Many people do experience physiological changes as they age: their hair loses its pigmentation, wrinkles appear, and their health and agility may decline. But elderly people are not always easily distinguishable, nor do all of them exhibit identical characteristics. The same is true of other age groups. By framing old age mainly in terms of the physical and mental decline that sometimes accompanies it, we engage in a type of reductionism, ignoring individual variation.

Ideas of infancy, adolescence, middle age and old age are constructed differently in different cultures. In the West, we are number-conscious: we categorize people according to their chronological age, which is thought to predict physical and mental capabilities and to correspond with "normal" developmental stages (Morrow 2013). But chronological age and psychosocial maturation do not always coincide (Barak 2009). People often diverge from expected, accepted age-related behaviours.

Some cultures focus more on **functional** and **relational age** (Morrow 2013). Children are not defined by their chronological age; rather, different children assume varying roles and responsibilities, depending on their individual capabilities and inclinations. This is to some degree true even in Canada. Adolescents who grow up in low-income, single-parent families, where they are expected to take on more responsibility at an early age, mature more quickly than middle-class youth who are the same chronological age (Benson and Elder 2011).

That childhood and adolescence are not inevitable or invariable social categories is demonstrated by the range of definitions in use around the world (Degnen 2007). The United Nations, World Bank, and various other organizations all define "youth" differently, depending on the issue at hand (Morrow 2013). Yet people continue to hold normative expectations about the "appropriate" age at which young persons "should" engage in certain behaviours and be prohibited or protected from others. North Americans often campaign to "defend" or "protect" children from "threats" to their "innocence."

Consider the popular *Because I Am a Girl* campaign. This well-meaning initiative seeks to prevent Third World girls from becoming child brides and mothers. However, the campaign sweepingly defines "child marriage" as that of any individual "before age 18" (becauseiamagirl.ca), drawing on North American standards of "adulthood" in a discussion of non-Western conjugal relations.

What's more, the campaign is concerned not only with eliminating child marriage but also with regulating adolescent female sexuality. The *Because I Am a Girl* website notes that "[g]irls who stay in school during adolescence have a later sexual debut." Possible "investors" (i.e., donors) are encouraged to "[s]end girls to school and see their futures improve as they learn valuable skills [and] delay marriage and pregnancy." At least in part, the goal is to ensure that adolescent girls extend their sexual innocence until they reach a Western standard of adulthood.

Campaigns like *Because I Am a Girl* insist on the universality and stability of the category of the "girl child" (Koffman and Gill 2013). In North America, little girls are "supposed" to be innocent and non-sexual. But just as elderly people are not necessarily infirm or incapable, young girls are not always as innocent as adults like to think: the pure, naive "girl child" is a social construction, too. Philanthropic organizations like *Because I Am a Girl* exploit this construct, playing on fears that "our" daughters may be corrupted. Little girls are portrayed as helpless, needy victims who must be "saved."

Such cultural projections are perpetuated by social institutions in every society. North American social institutions in particular use age as a benchmark for a wide variety of rights, including the right to vote, drive, rent a car, enroll in school, consume alcohol, smoke cigarettes, and have consensual sex (Giles and Reid 2005). Institutions force people into conformity with the behaviours and attitudes considered appropriate to their age (Sennott and Mollborn 2011).

For instance, some parents may be disappointed their children have failed to attain standard markings of adulthood. But outsiders argue these benchmarks are more difficult to achieve today. As one young person, Maddie Pfotenhauer, put it: "I did plan my education in a field where there were jobs but . . . two weeks before I graduated the government (both federal and provincial) decided to pull funding. . . . I've been looking in related fields but the work just isn't there."

Similarly, Katie Daniels has worked for pay since her first summer job at age 14. Her commitment to a wide range of extracurricular activities and stellar grades in high school paid off when she was offered scholarships at four universities. Two years after graduating, however, Daniels was still waiting tables. "I used to know the path," she said. "Do what you're told. Do the right thing, and good things will happen to you." But now, she says, "I feel like I was sold a bill of goods" (Sandell, 2012).

Ultimately, most people try to conform to age-appropriate norms and expectations because they want to be socially accepted and avoid ridicule, marginalization, and stigmatization (Sennott and Mollborn 2011). But what does it mean to "grow up"? Do a mortgage and car payments adequately define adulthood today? What are the implications of "acting like a child" when you're 35? The fact that such phrases exist—that people need to be pressured into "acting their age"—demonstrates that life-stage categories are *not* secure, universal or inevitable, but, rather, socially and culturally constructed.

Resisting Old Age

Older outsiders similarly contest the social constructions surrounding old age. Interviews with retirement community residents suggest that older adults often try to dissociate themselves from the negative image of being "elderly" (Roth et al. 2012). They acknowledge that younger people view retirement homes as "warehouses" for the old and infirm: places on the margins of society where people go to die (Gamliel and Hazan 2006). To counteract such assumptions, many older adults emphasize how busy they are, the variety of organized social activities in which they participate, and their physical and mental fitness. Some even resist changes designed to make their communities more accessible, such as the installation of wheelchair ramps. Such enhancements, they think, reinforce the assumption that retirement communities are designed for the disabled, sick and dying (Roth et al. 2012).

Above: The old and young, though at different ends of the life course, have in common the fact that their freedom of action is often circumscribed by societal norms set by middle-aged insiders (Chronicle Journal Times, New Thunder Bay, 1978/Girl Guides of Canada).

Below: Mobility often poses problems for the elderly, particularly if they lose the right to drive, thus jeopardizing the opportunity to age in place (Terry Ozon).

When members of an elderly community do begin to decline in physical or mental health, they are often "othered" by younger, still active members (Gamliel and Hazan 2006). For example, younger residents may question the ability of the "actually" elderly to continue driving safely. In response, elderly people with physical or mental impairments tend to isolate themselves, avoid community events, and report feeling ashamed and embarrassed when they are seen in public.

Younger and older retirees alike speak of "advanced old age," "the oldest old," or the "fourth age": a period at the end of life characterized by severe physical and mental decline (Degnen 2007). Although many elderly people experience at least some health issues in their later years, this fourth age, like other life phases, is at least in part socially constructed. Younger retirees in their late fifties or early sixties define the fourth age chronologically: once you have lived a certain number of years, you are *really* old. Other retirees, in contrast, understand the fourth age in terms of functional capacity in daily life, including the ability to remain independent.

Whether younger or older, still-active retirees aim to exclude themselves from the category of the "oldest old," doing so in different ways. Many older individuals portray themselves as anomalies, exceptions to the category of "elderly," with all its negative connotations (Barrett 2003, Gamliel and Hazan 2006). Doing so is easier for younger retirees. Though they may have been viewed as elderly and incapable by middle-aged neighbors in their former communities, these individuals feel comparatively young in retirement communities with a preponderance of older residents (Powell and Hendricks 2009).

To ensure they are recognized as young, healthy, active members of their new community, these young retirees distance themselves from older community members. They form semi-exclusive clubs, participation in which is predicated on vitality and physical ability. Activities like kayaking and golf mark them out from the more sedentary members of older groups. Older adults are thus complicit in constructing age-based identities.

Older outsiders who do not reside in retirement communities may reject stereotypes of age by seeking employment or participating in physically demanding activities. For example, 82-year-old Alan Wilson continues to teach line-dancing classes. Asked his thoughts on "being old," Wilson said: "It's just a number, it's how you feel" (Mehta 2012). Adina Lebo, 62, says she was let go from her position as a marketing services provider after 21 years: "One day when you least expect it, you find yourself out there looking for a job—and I don't think many people realize how difficult that is. . . . People weren't returning my phone calls. They weren't replying that they'd received my CV" (CBC News, "Baby boomers push back" 2012). Nevertheless, Lebo refuses to retire, insisting that her chronological age has no bearing on her skills and abilities: "I'm a very young 62. . . . I work out an hour and a half a day. I'm in better shape now than I was in my 20s or 30s. From my perspective, I'm in the peak of my power."

Because age categories are, in part, socially constructed, they are also "performed." To be socially accepted, people engage in the activities and behaviours expected of people their age. People who deviate from these norms are often stigmatized; such shaming promotes conformity to the norms.

There are a variety of approaches to aging, and few researchers maintain rigidly constructionist or essentialist interpretations. (An essentialist holds the view that certain human characteristics—for example, sex or age—are fundamental and unchanging.) Biology, culture, and the social environment all interact to shape age-related life experiences. That said, constructionist perspectives help us to better understand aging, reminding us that the definitions and meanings a society attributes to age are informed by social norms.

Conformity and Deviance

Our society views childhood and adolescence as periods of life when people are inevitably irresponsible, foolish and willing to take undue risks (Cauffman et al. 2010, Hunter et al. 2009). Some say this is because most young people have little to lose by behaving in deviant, reckless ways (Hirschi 1969). Most adults, on the other hand, are subject to four types of bonds that encourage conformity: *attachments* to significant others, *commitment* to more traditional or socially acceptable behaviours, *involvement* in traditional activities, and *belief* in the moral values of their society (Ozbay and Ozcan 2006, Fukushima et al. 2009).

"Growing up" means taking on these four kinds of bonds and "outgrowing" the deviant tendencies associated with childhood. Children who are strongly attached (the first type of bond) to their parents and teachers are less likely to commit deviant acts (Ozbay and Ozcan 2006, Morris et al. 2011) while children who don't care what their parents or teachers think of them are more likely to break the rules. Similarly, youth who are committed to traditional courses of action sanctioned by society, such as going on to university after finishing high school, are more likely to obey the social rules. Finally, children who have been socialized to value the norms of their society are less willing to defy those norms (Chriss 2007). For example, 15-year-old Asia Reid explains why she refused to drink at a party she attended: "My parents' opinion has always been a huge thing in my life. It's not so much the punishment I would get if they found out I'd been drinking. It's that, if I ever disappoint them, it makes me feel, like, weird" (Gillis 2009).

From this perspective, everyone is motivated to break the rules (Fukushima et al. 2009). Some people, however, despite such motivation, are more constrained than others to obey societal norms (Kissner 2008, Chriss 2007). Teenage outsiders are not intrinsically irrational or utterly incapable of making good decisions, but they may have little incentive to behave responsibly (Steinberg 2007). Prolonging adolescent freedom from social or economic responsibility may even encourage foolhardy behaviour. In societies where children and adolescents hold more adult social responsibilities, they behave in a more adult fashion. For example, Danish adolescents, who are given adult responsibilities relatively early, practice sex more safely, drive more carefully, and perform household tasks more reliably than their North American counterparts.

Young outsiders point out that many adults engage in the reckless behaviours for which they chastise youth. Seventeen-year old newspaper columnist Jesse Lupini (2008) argues that

> [a]dults have generated a number of teen stereotypes. Teens are irresponsible, untrustworthy, rude, sexually obsessed, loud and inclined to drink to excess, take drugs, eat badly and say "like," "random" and "dude" too much. I know a handful of teens who fit this description . . . and at least as many adults.
>
> Think of all the scandals created because adults lied, covered up, lacked manners or were caught driving drunk or doing drugs. . . .
> It's unfair to attribute personality characteristics to an age group.

We tend to overemphasize the ways in which people of a certain age are similar, and downplay the interests, behaviours, and skills they share with people of other age groups. These generalizations allow us to continue believing that the standardized life course is natural and inevitable, rather than predicated on assumptions that are often ageist.

Filial Responsibility

Inter-generational support or **filial responsibility** (the material and emotional support of older parents by their children) is practiced to different extents in different societies (Cheung and Kwan 2009, Khalaila and Litwin 2012). Norms of family obligation are weaker in countries with generous old age security systems, and stronger in countries like China where the state plays little or no role in caring for the elderly (Dykstra and Fokkema 2011, Chappell and Funk 2012).

Culture also plays a role. Asian cultures, especially those influenced by Confucian traditions, are known for their explicit espousal of filial piety. Again using China as an example, children are taught from an early age to respect, obey, and care for their elderly parents (Funk and Kobayashi 2009, Elmelech 2005). People raised in such a culture may continue to expect high levels of filial responsibility long after they have emigrated to other countries (Chappell and Kusch 2007).

American and Canadian adults also expect some degree of filial responsibility (Gans and Silverstein 2006). These expectations vary depending on the adult child's circumstances and whether the parent is perceived as deserving support. Younger adults are often more accepting of the concept of filial responsibility, perhaps because they are rarely called upon to care for older relatives and hold an idealized picture of providing such care might be like (Guberman 2003, Dykstra and Fokkema 2011). For the most part, the sense of filial responsibility decreases with age, as people begin to understand what such responsibility entails.

The elderly, on the other hand, may not endorse notions of filial piety even though they stand to benefit from it: they understand the sacrifices their children would have to make on their behalf, and want to spare them that burden (Funk 2010, Dykstra and Fokkema 2011). Even when their children want (or feel obligated) to care for them, some elderly individuals prefer to maintain their autonomy.

Those Canadians who do care for their elderly parents often claim that they see it not as a duty but as an expression of love and a way of reciprocating the sacrifices their parents made for them when they were younger (Funk and Kobayashi 2009). However, studies show that at least some caregivers are motivated by the promise of an inheritance when their parents pass away (Elmelech 2005), and that some elderly individuals promise (or threaten to deny) their children an inheritance to ensure continued care.

In Canada today, filial care tends to be provided by and for women (Cheung and Kwan 2009). Women on average live longer than men, and require care for a longer period. Middle-aged women are also more likely to care for older relatives, likely because daughters (and daughters-in-law) are socialized in most cultures to assume the role of caregiver for both their own children and any other family members in need (Chappell and Kusch 2007).

One father who participated in a study designed to assess how closely Japanese Canadian parents' views on filial responsibility aligned with those of their children declared: "Even though [my daughter] stops by to visit once a week, it's not enough. She only spends a couple of hours with us. My wife is getting older and she needs more help around the house. I figure that daughters should take care of their parents a little better than that, don't you? Show some more respect." By contrast, a Japanese Canadian mother whose son visits her several times a week said: "I don't agree [that children should care for their parents in old age]. Kids shouldn't feel burdened by this sense of obligation. That's too Japanese, too traditional" (Kobayashi and Funk 2010).

For their part, middle-aged adults are often torn between a genuine desire to support aging parents and their own demanding work and personal lives. For example, Ruth Ho has lived with her mother in Vancouver since her mother was diagnosed with Alzheimer's disease, quitting her job to care for her full-time. When Ho's sister also fell ill, she cared for both of them: "I have been told many times by people that [I] have given up too much. . . . And to a certain extent, I have. But it was my choice". Choosing to provide care for her mother was much more challenging for Barb, a retired teacher in Windsor, Ontario. Before full-time care was necessary, Barb said of her mother: "She's too difficult. . . . She argues about everything and I seriously could not take that. I would be a basket case." When Barb's mother was diagnosed with Alzheimer's, however, Barb took on the responsibility of visiting her mother's house daily: "There were days I absolutely hated going there. . . . It wasn't something I wanted to do. But it was the right thing for my mother and for me" (Anderssen 2012).

Even when adult children *want* to care for their aging parents, they may be unable to do so. Dawn Sinclair works full-time as a medical aesthetician during the week and spends weekends caring for her 85-year-old mother, who was left partially paralyzed by a stroke. An only child and single mother, Sinclair says "it almost feels like I am in survival mode. . . . There is a lot of guilt because no matter how much you do, it is never enough. . . . Family can't be expected to do it all. . . . It just isn't possible" (Church 2016).

Some form of care for older Canadians that is not based in kinship is essential (Cheung and Kwan 2009, Khalaila and Litwin 2012). But assisted living facilities or professional in-home caregivers are too expensive for many families, and may not be sufficiently supportive of older individuals' autonomy, independence, and social integration. Oosterveld-Vlug et al. (2013) interviewed 30 nursing home residents to determine which circumstances supported or undercut their sense of dignity. One respondent said: "At home you can do or not do what you want. Here . . . they say: 'get out of bed,' 'eat.'" Another declared: "I'm a burden. When you're ill you're simply a burden, that's how I see it." The bottom line is that, despite the insider-endorsed image of the "greedy geezer," the actual experiences of many older Canadians attest to the difficulties of growing old in our country today.

Protecting Rights and Limiting Risks

Older adults often have difficulty making their wishes heard by family members or caregivers. Sometimes, however, the elderly may not be the best judges of their own abilities, and where their decisions involve risk for others, collective rights must be considered. Consider two instances in which we need to respect older adults' rights while at the same time limiting the risk they pose to themselves and others. First, should seniors be able to "age in place," or be moved to assisted living facilities? Many seniors are unaware of the risks they face in their own homes, as well as precautions they can take to avoid such risks (Shields et al. 2013). Sometimes, this lack of awareness is the result of conditions like dementia that affect elderly people's memory and judgment, and, in turn, reduce their ability to move around their homes safely (Lach and Chang 2007).

When personal care and daily living become challenging and even dangerous for the elderly, they may need to move to an assisted living facility. But life in such facilities is not always the best option for either the elderly individual or the wider community (Shields et al. 2013). Older adults who remain in their homes often display better social, financial, and health outcomes, a higher quality of life, fewer depressive symptoms, and a greater sense of autonomy and independence. Assisted living facilities are also expensive for society as a whole, as well as for the individual.

For these reasons, researchers developed the concept of "aging in place" as an alternative: homes are modified to promote safety and overall ease of living. Continuing to live at home is in many cases more cost-effective, and therefore more sustainable, than moving to assisted living facilities.

To successfully age in place, older people require support from friends, family members, and the broader community; otherwise, they risk financial trouble and social isolation (Shank 2013). For example, the neighbourhood must be walkable, and transit needs to be readily accessible. However, not all adults who wish to age in place are healthy or wealthy. Many struggle with the functional aspects of daily life. Effective programs and policies are necessary to support people who wish to continue life as they know it, at home.

As well as making homes and communities accessible to elderly people with physical limitations, activities offered in the community need to cater to this population. Elderly people must be socially integrated into their wider communities. They cannot be isolated, marginalized, or even rejected when they try to take part in social or cultural activities.

A second example of the precarious balance between freedom and safety centres on elderly people's right to drive. Some older adults may no longer be capable of driving safely (Gagliardi et al. 2010), and it may be in everyone's best interest for them to stop driving, even if doing so reduces their mobility and independence. News reports frequently feature accidents involving older drivers, coverage that is often accompanied by calls for more rigorous assessments of elderly people's fitness to drive. In Ontario, for example, drivers over age 80 are required to renew their licenses every two years. In other jurisdictions, older drivers are not allowed to drive after dark, or are limited to driving within 10 kilometres of home.

But such restrictions may not be effective, and are expensive to uphold and difficult to enforce. They may also be unnecessary in some circumstances. Older drivers are injured more often and more severely in accidents, but do not necessarily crash their cars more often than younger people.

Happily, most elderly people do change their driving habits as they age: they drive more slowly, stay closer to home, drive mainly during daylight and in good weather, and drive less often. They are also much less likely to drink and drive.

Complicating matters is the fact that older people who live on their own rely on their cars to get around. If driving rights are restricted, they are forced to rely on friends, family members, or caregivers. When this happens, many elderly individuals become depressed and feel incapable and helpless. Or they may refuse to ask for help, giving up social activities and withdrawing from the world.

FINAL THOUGHTS

All societies offer people of different ages different opportunities and bind them with different constraints. People experience age-related advantages and disadvantages throughout their lives. This makes age a unique type of in-equality: *everyone* ages so long as they remain alive. Men rarely experience what it is like to be a woman; white people don't know what it's like to be black. But every old person knows what it was like to be young, and the vast majority of young people will eventually experience middle and old age. We all begin with few rights and responsibilities, acquire many of both as we reach middle age, and are divested of both as we grow old.

After decades of research and policy development, people are beginning to recognize and address the disadvantages of old age. Many of the myths of old age are being questioned, and some effort has been made to improve the elderly's quality of life and safeguard their sense of freedom and dignity. In contrast, young people continue to be understood in stereotypical terms—as irresponsible, immature children—and are denied almost all legal rights as a result. We are increasingly willing to recognize that elderly people are in fact people, and that they age in unique, individual ways. But we refuse to see children in the same sense: we still think of them as universally vulnerable, inno-cent, and incompetent, no matter what they do to prove otherwise. That's at least part of the reason why Laura Dekker's father received hate mail for sup-porting his competent, mature, experienced daughter in her dream of sailing around the world.

DISCUSSION QUESTIONS

1. Do you think older adults in Canada today are expected and encouraged to disengage, or to remain active? Do you think older Canadian adults *want* to conform to either set of expectations? Is either set of expectations more beneficial for older adults, and for society as a whole?

2. How does sex impact one's experience of age? For example, how does adolescence differ for boys and girls, and how do the physical changes that often accompany aging affect older men and women differently? In either instance, are there double standards (i.e., expectations to which women are held that men are not, or vice versa)?

3. Has anyone ever made an assumption about you, based on how old you look? Did that assumption align with your numerical age? Did it affirm or disrupt your understanding of the skills and competencies you believe you possess?

4. Should adult children be expected to provide care for their aging parents? In what circumstances would an exception to this rule be appropriate, if any? If adult children are simply unable to provide such care (for instance, if they themselves are severely ill or disabled), what are some alternatives?

5. Have you or one of your friends ever diverged from the expected life course? How did your friends, family members, or acquaintances react?

FURTHER READING

Felismina R. Mendes. "Active Ageing: A Right or a Duty?" *Health Sociology Review* 22:2 (2013): 174–85.

Erin M. Cline. *Families of Virtue: Confucian and Western Views on Childhood Development.* New York: Columbia University Press, 2015.

Matthijs P. Bal et al., eds. *Aging Workers and the Employee-Employer Relationship.* Cham, Switzerland: Springer International Publishing.

KEY TERMS

Active aging. Continued engagement by the elderly in society.

Activity theory. The theory that elderly people take on new roles as they age, such as volunteering.

Age, functional and relational. Age groups classified not by chronological age but by expected roles fulfilled by individuals.

Ageism. Discrimination based on age.

Age stratification theory. The theory of how society separates individuals into age groups, some of which experience ageism.

Anticipatory socialization. The process of preparing for the social changes that come with aging by maintaining social ties.

Dependents. Individuals who rely on others financially.

Digital divide. The perception that younger workers are more adept at the use of technology in the workplace.

Filial responsibility. Support of the elderly by their children, the degree of which varies by culture.

Life course. Social phases of life based on societal expectations.

Primary earners. Individuals responsible for providing financially for themselves and their dependents.

Senior power model. The theory that older individuals are more involved in the political process and that elderly people vote primarily in favour of initiatives and candidates benefiting their own age group.

Social bonding theory. Theory suggesting that young people are not as attached to society and are less likely to conform, participate in traditional activities, and to hold accepted moral values.

Spatial segregation. Separation of individuals geographically by age group.

CHAPTER SIX

Sexual Orientation Inequalities

INTRODUCTION

On Monday, May 4, 2015, thousands of Toronto public school students did not attend class (McGouran 2015, Renzetti 2015). It was the first day of a "strike" meant to last a week, by which angry parents were protesting changes to the Ontario sexual education curriculum. Hundreds of parents (and some of their children) rallied in front of Thorncliffe Park Public School waving signs reading "Let kids be kids," "Respect cultural and religious values," and "What's next . . . Safe animal sex?"

Despite protests like this one, the revised sex-ed curriculum was implemented in September 2015 by the province's Liberal government, led by Ontario's first female and first openly gay premier, Kathleen Wynne. Opponents included conservative Christian groups like Parents as First Educators (PAFE), which described the new curriculum as "morally contentious," "age-inappropriate," overly "explicit," and out of line "with the principles of many religious and cultural groups" (Pierre 2014, Boesveld 2015).

These concerns arose at least in part because the curriculum requires that young people be taught the correct names for genitalia, causing some to fear that "pre-pubescent children" will be "overloaded with graphic information about sex" (Pierre 2014). Opponents argue that a curriculum covering topics such as sexual consent and sex for pleasure encourages children to begin having sex at an early age (Boesveld 2015, Renzetti 2015) and that the revised curriculum fails to frame sex as appropriate only for married couples (Masson 2015). The argument has also been made that children should not be taught about same-sex relationships, sexual "orientations," gender "identities," or "deviant sexual practices." "Forcing" children to learn about these issues has even been described as "child abuse" (McGouran 2015). Similarly, teaching children that gender identities are socially constructed, rather than inevitable manifestations of one's biological sex, leads some to fear "serious sexual confusion" and the normalization of "a mental disorder" (Campaign Life Coalition).

In contrast, supporters—who constitute the majority of the population—consider the new curriculum long overdue. It was last updated in 1998 (Csanady 2015) and now covers subjects like "sexting," "cyberbullying," and easily accessible Internet pornography not even on the radar two decades ago.

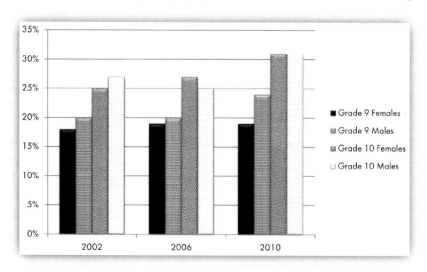

Figure 6.1: Sexual Activity among Young Canadians

One goal of the new curriculum is to help youth make informed choices: "Students," it states, "should have the knowledge and skills needed to make sound decisions about matters affecting their health and well-being before they experience real-life situations where decisions have to be made" (Ontario Curriculum). The 244-page curriculum document also covers nutrition, physical fitness, and drug addiction, barely touching on topics such as oral and anal sex that protestors claim are its focus (Coren 2015, Csanady 2015).

Although detractors worry the new curriculum will make **homosexuality** seem "permissible," the document is descriptive, not prescriptive. It notes that same-sex marriage is now legal in Canada, that some children have gay parents, others gay friends and family members, and that others still are gay themselves. These are realities many children already know or can easily discover for themselves, not an effort to promote particular types of behaviour (Coren 2015). Indeed, young people today can access far more "graphic," "explicit" sexual material on their own, outside the classroom. Many are more knowledgeable about sex than some adults would like to think. Many have also developed a highly distorted understanding of what sex is "supposed" to be like, as movies, songs, and pornography commonly portray people with specific body types, engaged in very specific sexual activities (Renzetti 2015).

Nevertheless, many parents responded to the implementation of the new curriculum by withdrawing their children from the schools teaching it: as of late May 2016, enrollment at the Toronto District School Board had dropped by more than 2000 elementary students, and one school trustee attributed part of the drop to parents' unwillingness to expose their children to the new curriculum (CBC News 2016).

Ultimately, the debate surrounding the new curriculum is about how to most effectively "protect" children: should we try to shelter them for as long as possible, withholding information they may be too young to adequately process? Or do we provide them with reliable information about sex before they begin to engage in it, educating them so they can make informed decisions (Renzetti 2015)? As we will see, the anxiety experienced by some Canadian parents over their children's knowledge of sex reflects a broader societal anxiety. This anxiety drives some to try to monitor, regulate, and control sexual behaviour, most often in an effort to enforce conformity to a **heterosexual** norm.

INSIDER VIEWS

Moral Crusades and Immoral Geographies

People on the "inside"—in this case, heterosexual adults—are likely to maintain a narrow and exclusionary view of "normal" sexual desires and activities. Very broadly, they consider monogamous, preferably marital, vaginal sex between men and women over the age of 18 as normal and appropriate. People taking part in other sexual activities, or having a different combination of partners, deviate from this standard. Insiders vary in the degree to which they view such deviation as a problem: the demonization of non-heterosexual sex was more widespread and vehement in the past, while today greater numbers of heterosexual insiders have come to accept, or at least tolerate, alternative sexual behaviours. In some quarters, however—especially, rural, isolated, religious communities where residents are less educated—hatred and fear of deviant sexual behaviour remains pervasive. And even tolerant insiders still consider alternative sexualities to be just that: *alternative*, and a deviation from the norm.

To assert their normalcy, heterosexual couples contrast themselves with those people who have "different" types of sex: that is, they define themselves in terms of what they are *not*. For this reason, functionalist sociologists, including Kingsley Davis (1937), argue that certain "inappropriate" or "deviant" sexual activities hold social value.

Consider prostitution. Davis (1937) notes that such sexual **deviance** defines the boundary of acceptable sexual activity. By labelling prostitution "immoral" and stigmatizing those who practise it, insiders distinguish themselves from these "abnormal" sexual "deviants." Yet another "us vs. them" dichotomy is established, one that is reinforced through spatial segregation (Link and Phelan 2001, Hallgrimsdottir et al. 2008). At least while they are working, prostitutes are to be found in brothels or red-light districts. By contrast, sex is rarely if ever so blatantly sold in the suburbs, where families and children predominate. Sex workers are thus othered by being confined to certain spaces—cordoned off from normal society, associated instead with what Phil Hubbard terms "immoral geographies" (1998).

The media play a role in constructing some of these immoral geographies (Hallgrimsdottir 2008) by always portraying sex workers in urban settings characterized by poverty, homelessness, and drug use. Readers and viewers are reassured that they are far removed—geographically, economically and socially—from sexual deviants.

Moral crusades against deviant sexual behaviour are another means by which insiders reinforce normative boundaries. People who denounce prostitution often worry about the breakdown of the **nuclear family**, or fear that society's morals and ethics have deteriorated. In their eyes, prostitution violates the expectations of **monogamy** and sexual loyalty that accompany traditional marriage (Weitzer 2006). Those who oppose prostitution often frame both male and female sex workers as carriers of sexually transmitted infections, threatening to transmit disease to members of "respectable" families (Wong et al. 2011).

Prostitution also represents a breakdown of traditional gender roles, something which seems threatening to socially and religiously conservative groups. With their many partners and obvious sexual experience, female sex workers upset norms of feminine sexual passivity, modesty, and chastity (Vanwesenbeeck 2013, Wong et al. 2011). In an attempt to reify such gender stereotypes, insiders stigmatize these "immoral" outsiders, taking pains to distinguish them as "deviating" from the standard ideal of the "good girl."

Moral crusades frequently succeed in vilifying prostitution, though never in eradicating it. In recent years, Canadian laws dealing with prostitution have been revisited numerous times. At one time, prostitution itself was legal, but almost all related behaviours, including pimping, running a brothel, and attempting to buy or sell sex in public places, were against the law (Lazarus et al. 2012). Today, those who freely choose to engage in sex work are immune from prosecution, but their clients may be charged with a criminal offence. The ongoing attention the issue of prostitution has received underlines widespread concern with this form of sexual deviance, and society's need to penalize and regulate it.

Even if prostitution does play a functional role in society, as Davis proposes, it carries with it negative consequences for sex workers, who are stigmatized, marginalized, and physically or emotionally abused. Some internalize the negative judgments others pass on them, reducing their ability to resist abuse from clients or compel clients to use condoms to protect against sexually transmitted infections (STIs) (Lazarus et al. 2012). Because most sex workers are aware of other people's disdain for them and their line of work, they rarely seek assistance from health care professionals, and are reluctant to be tested for HIV and other STIs. This hesitation to access health-care services, together with sex workers' reduced ability to negotiate condom use, means that stigmatization indeed contributes to the spread of STIs.

Even health-care providers who work with prostitutes are sometimes stigmatized—a phenomenon known as "stigma by association." Some employees at Peers Victoria Resources Society (PEERS) in British Columbia say they cannot discuss the work they do to help sex workers with their friends or families, for fear of disapproval (Phillips et al. 2011). Even academics studying the lives of sex workers may be personally stigmatized. Some sex-work researchers have been accused of being "obsessed with sex," and told their interest is "unworthy" of academic study (Hammond and Kingston 2014).

We will return to the issue of sex work in later sections of the chapter, first to explore the varied perspectives feminists offer on the matter and then to consider the outsider views and experiences of prostitutes themselves.

The Decline of the Family

The moral crusade against prostitution is to a large degree the product of insider anxiety about the decline (or even the "death") of the family. Since the late 1950s, the idealized nuclear family, consisting of a male breadwinner, housewife, and two or more children, has been in the decline in North America. There are several reasons for this.

First, though most people eventually marry, more women today delay marriage and childbearing to attend school and start a career (Bohnert and Milan 2012). Second, more couples live together without getting married, and these unmarried couples are increasingly likely to have children together. Third, single parenting is more common today than in the past (Employment and Social Development Canada 2007). Finally, although the vast majority of married couples are straight, the legalization of gay marriage in Canada in 2005 has led to an increase in the number of gay married couples (Rose 2011, Dnes 2007). Between 2006 and 2011, the number of same-sex married couples in Canada increased by more than 42% (Statistics Canada 2015).

Some insiders believe the decline in traditional family arrangements will have harmful consequences for society (Nell 2005, Gotell 2002). For the most traditional insiders, the decline marks a stark divergence from appropriate sexual relations, as they believe that the main purpose of marriage is to produce and raise children. If so, sex should be practiced only by married heterosexual couples.

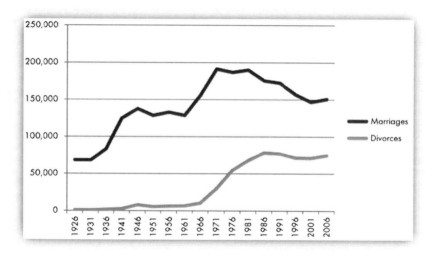

Figure 6.2: Canadian Marriages and Divorces, 1926 to 2006

For religious fundamentalists of all faiths, the nuclear family represents one of the most important structures by which strong moral values are passed down to the next generation. As the traditional family declines, they fear, so do the traditional values it embodies and promotes, threatening the collapse of the social order as a whole (Kurth 2013). For instance, many religious groups worry about the increasing popularity of premarital, non-procreative sex. If sex is supposed to produce children, people who have "unproductive" sex outside of marriage are merely indulging their sinful desires.

These are the views of a minority of insiders; over the past 50 years, sexual practices and attitudes have changed for most people (Htun and Weldon 2011). For example, a poll by Statista (2013) asked, "Do you personally believe that sex between unmarried adults is morally acceptable, unacceptable, or is it not a moral issue?" 47% of Canadians responded that it was not a moral issue, while 34% deemed it acceptable, and only 15% said they thought it was unacceptable. Canadians have also become more tolerant of divorce. In Canada today, a divorce is granted if it can be shown a marriage has broken down; living apart for one year or more ("no-fault divorce") is the most common grounds for establishing marital breakdown, though adultery or abuse also constitute grounds for divorce. By contrast, Islamic Sharia law provides men with a unilateral right to divorce their wives simply by stating that they wish to do so (Htun and Weldon 2011). Meanwhile, women are able to divorce only if their husbands have delegated this right to them, or if they are willing to forfeit some or all of their dowry in order to obtain a divorce (Mashhour 2005).

Although Canadian attitudes regarding divorce seem fair and egalitarian by comparison, we could do better. Family law remains rooted in patriarchal views that endorse various gender and sexual inequalities. Take the matter of abortion. Although legal in Canada, abortion remains hugely contentious, to the point that many politicians sidestep related issues, refusing, for example, to help improve women's access to the procedure.

Facilities that provide safe, expert abortions are unevenly distributed across the country, with almost half of Canada's 94 facilities located in Quebec (Vogel 2015). British Columbia and Ontario have only 16 facilities each, while Alberta, Saskatchewan, and Manitoba have only eight among them. Quebec and British Columbia are the only regions in which the proportion of facilities located in rural or remote areas is equal to the proportion of women living in such areas. Prince Edward Island stands alone as the sole Canadian province with no abortion facilities whatsoever. Ultimately, women seeking abortions in Canada will find an already challenging decision complicated even further by the geographical distance of providers.

In some provinces, abortion clinics are not publicly funded. The alternatives are to pay out of pocket or to seek an abortion in a hospital, but abortion clinics were opened to begin with because too few hospitals offer abortions: only one in five Canadian hospitals performs the procedure (Health Canada 2016). Many hospitals require a referral from a physician, while clinics do not, and some clinics, unlike hospitals, will perform abortions for women under the age of 18 without parental consent.

Fear of backlash from anti-abortion groups has led many hospitals and doctors to refuse to perform the procedure at all. Though less common than in the past, anti-abortion violence, protests, and harassment continue to endanger abortion patients and providers alike.

Canada's **LGBTQ** population has also struggled to secure their rights, at least in part due to protest activities in the U.S., where legalization of gay marriage took longer and remains contentious. One reason for the delay was the desire to preserve what Christian conservatives describe as the sanctity of marriage. Ironically, insiders eventually came to hope that the legalization of gay marriage would encourage married LGBTQ couples to conform to the traditional nuclear family structure (Croce 2014).

Many gay spouses report that the legalization of gay marriage has made them feel more accepted by heterosexual family members and coworkers. In this sense, gay marriage has "validated" homosexuality for people who meet heterosexual expectations (Fingerhut et al. 2011).

But not all gay people conform to traditional marital roles (nor do all straight people, for that matter). In its most traditional, patriarchal form, marriage is a fundamentally unequal relationship: husbands exercise authority over their household and its members, while wives obediently maintain the household and care for the children. Gay couples tend to maintain more egalitarian relationships: interviews with 30 married gays and lesbians in Toronto found they distribute household tasks more equitably than heterosexual couples (Green 2010). These non-heterosexual partners also had more equal say in family decisions. So, rather than "corrupting" or "degrading" the institution of marriage, LGBTQ marriages are more equitable—and in turn, perhaps healthy—than heterosexual ones.

One of the most popular arguments against gay marriage is that gay couples cannot have their own biological children (Schumacher 2014). This, in turn, has opened up a vigorous debate about same-sex parenting.

Same-Sex Parenting

Today, gay couples *can* have children through adoption, surrogacy, and artificial insemination (Mamo 2007, Pratesi 2002). Many straight couples who struggle to conceive make use of the same methods. Nevertheless, some insiders argue that children of same-sex parents will not develop as well mentally and emotionally as those with opposite-sex parents (Chevrette 2013). Critics allege that lesbian unions lack a proper father figure, threatening the psychological growth of their children; similarly, in families with two fathers, children will be harmed by the lack of a traditional mother figure (Green 2010). Some even propose that children must be "defended" from the threat posed by homosexual parents. As a result, until recently, surrogacy and artificial insemination were denied to everyone but straight couples unable to conceive through intercourse (Bryld 2001).

Such fears have not been borne out by research. In 2011, there were over 9500 same-sex families with children living in Canada (Statistics Canada 2015), and studies suggest same-sex couples are as capable of parenting effectively as heterosexual couples (Biblarz and Stacey 2010). Children raised by same-sex parents do *not* experience different behavioural and educational outcomes than children of heterosexual unions, nor do they feel any less loved or accepted by their parents (Mattingly and Bozick 2001, Schneiderman 2005).

In fact, many children of same-sex unions feel they have gained important insights into gender relations, and learned more inclusive definitions of family by growing up with same-sex parents (Crowley et al. 2008). They are also more likely to value diversity, to resolve conflicts more effectively, and to have higher self-esteem than children raised by opposite-sex parents (Gartrell et al. 2013).

Bill C-250

In contrast with religious and social conservatives, insiders more in the mainstream of society feel that blatant discrimination against members of the LGBTQ community is unacceptable. Accordingly, legislation and policies were enacted to prevent or punish it. In little more than 30 years, Canadian governments have transitioned from criminalizing the LGBTQ community to penalizing those who commit hate crimes against its members (Schmitt 2008, CBC.ca 2012).

Hate crimes, by definition, range from inciting hatred against to promoting the genocide of a group or an individual belonging to that group (CBC.ca 2011). Many such crimes involve spreading hateful or degrading messages about minority groups in public spaces. They can also involve efforts to intimidate, harm, or frighten people who self-identify as, or are thought to be, members of minority groups.

Sections 318 and 319 of the Canadian Criminal Code criminalize the spread of "hate propaganda" and the "public incitement of hatred" against a variety of minority groups (CBC.ca 2011). Bill C-250, originally intended to protect people against hate crimes perpetrated on racial, religious and ethnic grounds, was amended in 2004 to include **sexual orientation** (Grace 2005, Moore and Rennie 2006).

The amended Bill C-250 is a major step forward in promoting LGBTQ rights. However, the bill's efficacy remains to be determined. One major problem has been defining hate crimes and identifying situations where that definition applies. In many instances, perpetrators deny their actions have anything to do with the victim's LGBTQ status (Nolan et al. 2004). Because sexual orientation is not an observable feature (unlike race, for example), those who commit hate crimes can claim that they were unaware of a victim's sexuality (Moore and Rennie 2006). Others claim that alleged hate crimes are merely individual altercations, not part of a wider pattern of discrimination.

Bill C-250 may address obvious hate crimes, such as physically violent "gay bashings," but it is less effective in addressing more subtle forms of discrimination. Consider research by Lisa Jewel and Melanie Morrison (2010) on university students' treatment of their gay colleagues in Western Canada. While overt discrimination has become less prevalent, covert discrimination, including hateful speech and discriminatory jokes, has become *more* common. Some even suggest that Bill C-250 has forced anti-gay discrimination underground, resulting in a more insidious pattern of discrimination that will be even harder to address.

A third challenge to determining the efficacy of this important piece of legislation lies in the fact that victims of hate crimes often hesitate to report their attackers. Some fear they will be attacked again out of retaliation if they report an incident. Others recognize that by bringing an attack to the attention of authorities, they risk attracting attention—perhaps even shame and blame—from their communities. If the victim is not openly gay, reporting a hate crime means openly revealing his or her sexual identity, potentially attracting more stigmatization or further attacks. Finally, the police have not always dealt effectively or supportively with such complaints in the past. Victims may not think it worthwhile to report incidents only to receive inadequate assistance in return (Bell and Perry 2015, Perry 2010).

Bearing these limitations in mind, researchers have compiled considerable amounts of data about hate crimes, the settings where they are most likely to occur, and the types of people most likely to commit them. First, higher rates of anti-gay violence are found in regions where larger numbers of LGBTQ people reside (Green et al. 2001). Paradoxically, then, more hate crimes are committed in cities, where there are more gay households, even though urban dwellers tend to be more tolerant of LGBTQ people (Bell and Perry 2015). Second, men—especially young white men—are more likely to commit hate crimes than women (Herek et al. 1997, Rayburn et al. 2003). Third, non-religious people are the least likely to commit hate crimes, and the likelihood of committing a hate crime increases with the intensity of a person's religiosity (Alden and Parker 2005, Jewel and Morrison 2010).

These demographic variables combine with situational ones: in LGBTQ- and women-friendly environments, some men—especially white, religious men espousing traditional values—may feel threatened and attempt to assert their dominance through hateful or violent acts (Schmitt 2008). Finally, perpetrators of hate crimes tend to believe that non-heterosexuals are abnormal and immoral (Bell and Perry 2015). As a result, people who behave in stereotypically gay ways, or who have made their sexuality known to others, face a greater risk of victimization (Pilkington and D'Augelli 1995).

Hate crimes hurt not only the targeted individual but inspire fear throughout the entire LGBTQ community (Bell and Perry 2015, Perry 2010). In response, some LGBTQ people refuse to leave their homes; others change their behaviour, clothing, and other "markers" of sexuality in the hopes of concealing their sexual orientation or gender identity and avoiding victimization (Moore and Rennie 2006).

The amendment of Bill C-250 was an important step in securing legal rights and protection for Canada's LGBTQ community. But that community continues to suffer many different types of discrimination and disadvantage. To be effective, changes to laws must be complemented by changes to social attitudes, values, and beliefs.

Workplace Discrimination

Discrimination against members of the LGBTQ community also occurs at work. Many organizations claim to value diversity in their employees, but do not always follow through on that commitment.

Even in equal-opportunity workplaces, we continue to see anti-gay bullying, name-calling and harassment perpetrated by coworkers aware of their victims' sexuality (Gates et al. 2013). Lesbians in particular often report sexual harassment and unwanted advances from their straight male colleagues, who claim that they pursue lesbians as a "challenge" (Giuffre et al. 2008). Gay men, for their part, often report being excluded from stereotypically "masculine" business outings like golfing and visiting strip clubs.

Many gays and lesbians feel a need to hide their sexuality when applying for work and even after being hired (O'Ryan and MacFarland 2010, Nadler et al. 2014). This is especially true in predominantly masculine, heterosexualized work environments, such as the military or police force: here, LGBTQ workers are especially unlikely to disclose their sexuality (Bernstein et al. 2012). In some cases, employees have even been terminated after disclosing their sexuality. One study found that lesbians fired after revealing their sexuality were understandably less likely to disclose their sexual orientation to new employers (Ragins et al. 2007).

Those individuals who do disclose their sexuality often report being met with silence, exclusion, and stigmatization (Roberts 2010). Relationships with fellow employees suddenly change, with some coworkers becoming uncomfortable in their presence. Because colleagues treat them differently, LGBTQ workers who have come out may avoid interactions with coworkers and exclude themselves from workplace activities. Others begin to dress, speak, and behave differently than they otherwise would, to avoid drawing attention to their sexuality.

Managers, bosses, and other authority figures can make the workplace environment friendlier to gays and lesbians by backing anti-discrimination policies, providing mentoring, developing LGBTQ employee networks, encouraging teamwork and cooperation, and aiming to foster a non-hetero-sexist organizational climate (Ragins et al. 2003, Bernstein et al. 2012). LGBTQ workers themselves confirm that LGBTQ groups and networks, work-place campaigns that highlight inclusion and safety for LGBTQ employees, and sponsorship of LGBTQ events make them feel supported, included, and less stressed at work (Giuffre et al. 2008, Buddel 2011). Not surprisingly, such environments allow LGBTQ workers to feel more open about their sexuality, and less guarded in their interactions with colleagues. This, in turn, leads to greater job and overall life satisfaction, and better job performance (Colgan et al. 2007). Establishing a "gay-friendly" work environment benefits employers as well as employees.

By comparison, conditions that lead an LGBTQ person to stay "in the closet" at work include work teams that are racially imbalanced or composed mostly of men. Having a male supervisor also increases the likelihood that LGBTQ employees will try to conceal their sexuality, as people experience more discrimination and **homophobia** under male supervisors. When LGBTQ workers are unable to "come out" at work, they feel more stress, more isolated from their colleagues, and a disconnect between their work and pri-vate lives. Working in this type of homophobic environment greatly reduces job satisfaction; it even affects concentration, requiring LGBTQ workers to "prepare" themselves mentally before going to work (Colgan et al. 2007).

A variety of laws have been implemented in an effort to protect LGBTQ individuals' rights in the workplace. In 1977, for example, Quebec became the first province to include sexual orientation as a prohibited ground for dis-crimination in its human rights code (Mazur 2002). In 1996, discrimination against people because of sexual orientation was prohibited by the Canadian Human Rights Act (Gotell 2002). And by 2002, many employers had added same-sex benefits to their traditional benefit plans, making Canada one of the first countries to provide benefits to same-sex couples.

These new laws and policies have made many Canadian workplaces more LGBTQ-friendly. Insiders point out many more LGBTQ people hold high-pro-file, well-paying, high-status roles today than in the past (Klie 2009). They suggest that, since LGBTQ workers can secure promotions and raises, we are no longer struggling with discriminatory hiring, firing, and promotion prac-tices.

Despite these improvements, however, Canadian LGBTQ people still report being discriminated against in the workplace, especially in more subtle ways. One in three LGBTQ workers thinks that their employer is gay-friendly in principle or in its policies, but only one in five strongly agrees that their employer is gay-friendly in practice (Brown 2003). There appears to be an "implementation gap": laws and policies exist that are designed to prevent or punish discrimination, but they are not always implemented effectively (Drucker 2009).

Insiders argue that existing anti-discrimination laws testify to society's commitment to ending the mistreatment and marginalization of the LGBTQ community. They also suggest that, as today's young people grow up in close contact with this increasingly visible community, acceptance of LGBTQ people will only grow, and the very need for such legislation will correspondingly decline. Given the huge strides that have been made in securing and protecting the rights of LGBTQ people, insiders are optimistic that things will continue to improve.

SECOND OPINIONS

Academics offering second opinions on issues around sexuality often aim to disrupt the traditional beliefs held by those insiders who fear, dislike, or discriminate against LGBTQ people. For example, in an effort to prevent the legalization of gay marriage, some argued that gays and lesbians are incapable of maintaining long-term, monogamous relationships, and that their "natural" promiscuity makes them seek out multiple partners instead of settling down with one (Dnes 2007). These attributes, it was claimed, make gay and lesbian people less fit for marriage than straight people.

Empirical research initially supplied some support for these beliefs, indicating that gay relationships were on average shorter-lived than heterosexual marriages. A study conducted using data from the 1970s showed that most gay relationships had ended by their fourth or fifth year (Lau 2012). Compared to married couples, the relationship dissolution rates among male and female same-sex cohabiters were seven and five times higher, respectively.

More recent research, however, points toward lower relationship dissolution risks for same-sex couples. Until 2005, when same-sex marriage was legalized in Canada, cohabitation was the most intense form of traditional commitment available to same-sex partners (Dnes 2007). Earlier research had compared gay cohabiting relationships with heterosexual marriages—a problematic comparison, given that cohabitations, whether gay or straight, are on average shorter-lived than marriages or other legally recognized unions.

One California study found that unregistered gay cohabiting relationships lasted an average of 8.32 years, while officially registered gay cohabiting relationships lasted 11.02 years (Carpenter and Gates 2008). Other studies confirm that, whether partners are gay or straight, legal marriages are least likely to break down, followed by officially registered cohabitations, unofficial cohabitations, and, finally, relationships in which partners are not living together (Biblarz and Savici 2010, Lau 2012).

Some researchers suggest that people in cohabiting relationships, whether gay or straight, expect and demand less personal commitment than married people. Others note that cohabiting couples often receive less support from friends and family, making them more likely to separate when they encounter relationship difficulties. Gay or straight, married couples report a higher level of relationship satisfaction than cohabiting or unmarried couples (Lau 2012). Gay couples who married following the legalization of same-sex marriage report greater relationship satisfaction and attachment to their partners after getting married.

For these and other reasons, then, LGBTQ people were more likely prior to the legalization of same-sex marriage to dissolve their relationships than straight people. With legalization, the same obstacles to dissolving relationships now apply to them (Carpenter and Gates 2008, Alderson 2009). As a result, recent studies show no significant difference in the rates at which gay and straight relationships break down (Rosenfeld 2014).

The number of same-sex marriages nearly tripled between 2006 and 2011 (Rose 2011). Similarly, the incidence of same-sex **common law relationships** rose by 15% during the same period (Statistics Canada 2014). It would seem, then, that stereotypes of gays' sexual promiscuity are largely unfounded. Gay people are able and willing to establish monogamous, long-term commitments, just like straight people. Whether monogamy makes either straight or gay people happy is, of course, a whole other question, and one beyond the scope of our discussion here.

Queer Theory

In examining gay marriage and its impact upon the traditional institution, many academics offering second opinions have turned to **queer theory**. For many, queer theory is impossible to define. In fact, this slipperiness—the inability to capture everything that queer theory does—may be its biggest strength. Indeed, prominent feminist philosopher Judith Butler proposes that we should even try to "queer" our understanding of "queerness." She explains that to be effective as "a site of collective contestation," anything queer must never be "fully owned, but always and only redeployed, twisted, queered from a prior usage and in the direction of urgent and expanding political purposes" (Butler quoted in Jagose 2009). Some scholars thus applaud queer theory for evading the essentialism that plagues some strains of feminism.

Like queer theory itself, queer identities are fluid, constantly changing, and impossible to define, because not everyone is "queer" in the same way (Kilgard 2014). Every individual who identifies as queer is also treated differently and has different experiences. "Queer" is thus a non- or anti-label that does not refer to any one thing in particular, but is instead unstable and unpredictable.

Legalization of same-sex marriage was the culmination of a long campaign for greater legal protection and visibility for LGBTQ people in Canada and elsewhere. These scenes are from Toronto Pride activities in 2010 and 2011 (top: JasonParis/flickr; bottom: Ryan/flickr).

Queer theorists are thus interested in **plurality** and multiplicity, aiming to deconstruct the dichotomies and binary ways of thinking that shape most North Americans' perspective on life. For example, with the legalization of same-sex marriage, gay and lesbian couples have become increasingly visible (Drucker 2009). However, instead of realizing that sexuality is nuanced and pluralistic, most North Americans continue to hold a binary understanding of sexuality: humans, they believe, are either gay or straight. Homosexual relationships are just an inversion of heterosexual ones, with gay constituting the "opposite" of straight.

Queer theorists disagree, reminding us that sexualities cannot be encapsulated within a binary system. Rather, sexualities are fluctuating, indeterminate, and often hard to label or describe, something we have known at least since Kinsey carried out his landmark empirical studies of American sexuality in the 1940s and 1950s (Kilgard 2014). People who identify as **bisexual**, **transgender**, or queer complicate the hetero-/homosexual dichotomy (Oswin 2008). They occupy an ambiguous space between these two more widely accepted categories, with preferences and even anatomies that shift, and which fail to fit within traditional views of gender and sexuality as stable and unchanging (Callis 2014).

Because they evade simple categorization, bisexual, transgender, and otherwise queer people continue to make at least some heterosexuals feel uncomfortable and even confused. Some scholars claim that both queer theory and queer people themselves have the potential to subvert widespread norms and expectations, changing the ways our society views and experiences sexuality (Kilgard 2014).

However, other academics have highlighted that most queer and otherwise non-normative outsiders do not effectively challenge the status quo in practice. More often, people with these ambiguous identities experience powerlessness and various types of mistreatment (Callis 2014). Many are ignored: unable or unwilling to understand less familiar sexualities, many in the mainstream population disregard them altogether.

Queer, bisexual, and transgender people may also be subjected to an even greater degree of exclusion than gays and lesbians. Bisexuals suffer the same disadvantages and mistreatment that self-identified gays and lesbians experience when openly involved in same-sex relationships. But even some members of the gay community discount bisexuality, claiming that it is not a legitimate orientation and that self-identified bisexuals are "confused" or unwilling to come out (Botswick 2012).

Bisexual women are often more strongly rejected by the lesbian community than are bisexual men by the gay (male) community (Eliason 2001, Ault 1996). In part, this is because heterosexual men are more likely to "pardon" female bisexuals for deviance from the heterosexual norm. Excited by fantasies of female-female sex, some heterosexual men view female bisexuals as ideal sex partners. In return, believing these individuals enjoy some degree of heterosexual privilege, the lesbian community may come to distrust and resent them. In this sense, then, people who identify as bisexual, transgender, or queer may be considered "outsiders" when compared with gays and lesbians who maintain more traditional, monogamous marriages.

Finally, queer people have failed to effectively challenge the status quo because, for the most part, they are lumped into the single broad category of "non-heterosexual." Just as we conceive of race in terms of white vs. non-white, we conceptualize sexuality in terms of straight vs. non-straight. Even the acronym LGBTQ reflects this: heterosexuality stands alone as an independent category, set in contrast to every other type of sexuality represented by the acronym. A binary understanding of sexuality continues to prevail, despite the hopes of some queer theorists (Chevrette 2013).

Queering the Nuclear Family

One of the more effective ways in which queer theorists have questioned the status quo is by drawing attention to the impact that LGBTQ partners have had on views of the family. Instead of viewing LGBTQ sexualities as types of deviance from the norm of heterosexual **conjugality**, queer theory sees them as forms of active resistance against such expectations (Jagose 2009). Same-sex partners, especially those with children, "queer," or undermine, traditional understandings of the family. Their mere existence disrupts and therefore forces us to re-examine established views on what families are and do. They achieve this in two ways, both of which have been championed by certain queer scholars and questioned by others.

First, some same-sex families "normalize the queer" by demonstrating they behave in the same ways as "normal" heterosexual families, a process known as the **similarity/difference (S/D) framework** (Chevrette 2013). Straight parents and gay and lesbian parents resemble each other in two important ways: both practise child-centred parenting and both try to parent children according to socially produced scripts. Lesbian families, in particular, display strengths many straight couples would do well to adopt (Moore 2009, Röndahl et al. 2009); for example, these families are more likely to exhibit an egalitarian decision-making structure (Savin-Williams and Esterberg 2000).

The S/D framework has been criticized, however, for continuing to use heterosexual monogamy as the standard or even ideal against which all other sexualities are measured. In addition to perpetuating a binary opposition between heterosexuality and all other sexualities (Callis 2014), the S/D framework compares a historically marginalized, disadvantaged group with a group that continues to be privileged even today. In other words, these "alternative" sexualities are made to seem more "normal" and "acceptable" because they do not deviate from our heteronormative expectations as much as originally feared. The S/D framework recognizes and validates non-heterosexual people, as opposed to ignoring them, but does not always challenge or even acknowledge the problem posed by **heteronormativity** (Chevrette 2013).

The second way in which LGBTQ families queer the nuclear family is by questioning the relevance of this traditional family structure. Merely by existing, LGBTQ families challenge the way we have chosen to organize society—that is, into small pods consisting of heterosexual, monogamous parents and their children. Queer families construct their own forms of social organization, which stand in contrast with and thereby challenge the broader heteronormative lifestyle (Drucker 2009).

This formulation of queer theory potentially sidesteps the issues associated with the S/D framework. Rather than trying to render LGBTQ relationships acceptable by heteronormative standards, radical queer theorists point out that LGBTQ relations destabilize that standard.

But as we have seen, LGBTQ relationships often resemble straight relationships. One of the stumbling blocks that queer theory has yet to overcome is how LGBTQ relationships can be characterized independently from the heterosexual norm. Nonetheless, queer theory has allowed us to reconsider the debate on the decline of the family from a different perspective. Queering the family exposes the family's socially constructed, ideological nature: it reveals that the nuclear family is not a "natural" arrangement determined by human biology, but rather, a culturally shaped social arrangement. In turn, we can begin to question what arrangements may best meet our sexual, material, emotional, and social needs (Drucker 2009). The ultimate manifestation of this queering of the family would be the realization that people can be defined independently of their reproductive capacities: they can have identities that do not foreground their sexuality or familial role.

Sex, Gender, and Sexuality

In many ways, queer and feminist theory are closely related. Both seek to challenge commonly held assumptions and subvert traditional norms. But in other ways, the two theories differ. Most importantly, sex and gender, often the focus of feminist inquiries, are not the same as sexuality, the focus of queer theory (Jagose 2009).

In the popular mind, sex, gender and sexuality map onto each other in straightforward, simple ways. We are socialized to think that all human bodies may be neatly categorized as belonging to one sex or the other, and that the male and female sexes are exact opposites of each other. Within these discretely sexed bodies are what Judith Butler (1988) describes as binary gender "cores" or "identities." Gendered behaviours, ways of dressing, and ways of speaking are thought to be expressions or manifestations of the masculine or feminine "essence" within. In turn, these inner gender "cores" are thought to determine the sex to which people are sexually attracted (Butler 1988).

However, sex, gender and sexuality do not always align in this straightforward way (Jagose 2009). On the contrary, Butler holds that interior "gender cores" and "natural" heterosexuality are "punitively regulated cultural fiction[s]" (1988), socially constructed and passed along through social learning. What it means to be a man or a woman, gay or straight, is defined by one's society. Concepts of sexuality and gender change across cultures and over time, even within individual lifetimes.

Science and medicine sometimes contribute to popular mythology. Beginning with the nineteenth-century medicalization of homosexuality, non-heterosexuals were widely regarded as having "a nature gone awry." Whether deliberately or subconsciously, non-heterosexuals were thought to exhibit "a kind of interior androgyny, a hermaphrodism of the soul," "a certain way of inverting the masculine and the feminine in oneself" (Foucault 1978). The gender "within" the homosexual is thus considered the inverse of the gender that naturally corresponds to his or her sex. By framing heterosexuality as a biological given, the sex-gender system conceals heteronormativity and compulsory heterosexuality, rendering them invisible—seemingly inevitable products of human hardwiring.

Researchers are growing increasingly confident that sexuality itself—that is, attraction to people of the same sex, another sex, or both—is inborn (though all the evidence is not in). The expression or performance of sexual desire, however, is not innate nor is it dictated by biology. It is a product of social context, the result of a complex interaction between physiological, psychological, cultural and social factors.

Popular culture encourages the idea that sexual desires and actions are unmediated expressions of uncontrollable urges, but nothing could be further from the truth. To think this way is to ignore the significant role played by social context in shaping human sexuality. Social norms and expectations pressure people to mate in traditional ways with people similar to them in age, social class and education, but of a different sex. We are taught that these mating patterns are normal, natural, and even healthy. By contrast, prostitution is socially constructed as a deviant practice, despite the fact it is universal.

Feminists have taken issue with the idea (discussed earlier) that female prostitution fulfills an essential social function (Järvinen 1993). Instead, they argue that it is an oppressive patriarchal institution that perpetuates male domination over women. But, like Davis's functional theory, this feminist perspective wrongly assumes that all prostitution is heterosexual, involving male clients and female sex-workers (Robinson 2007). As such, both theories take the heterosexual nuclear family as a given, and both assume that men have uncontrollable sexual urges that must be satisfied, while ignoring the fact that women may also harbour sexual needs or fantasies that may not be met by traditional family structures. Both theories ignore the existence of male sex-workers and female clients, as well as people who provide sexual services to lesbian, gay and transgender clients.

To be sure, not all feminists share this view. Some propose that prostitution, along with other deviant activities, should not be considered "bad" or "abnormal," or set in opposition to "good," "normal" practices. They note that, by framing prostitution in opposition to heterosexual marital sex, Davis's theory "others" commercial sex work: it marginalizes sexual activities that do not fit within socially determined boundaries. Yet other feminists focus on the exploitation of women of colour, noting their restricted access to education and jobs makes them more likely to be forced into sex work (Robinson 2007).

Some scholars offering second opinions have set out to expose the assumptions, stereotypes and constructions that shape the popular understanding of sex work. They note that socially constructed hegemonic masculinities protect male sex workers from experiencing the same degree of stigmatization faced by female sex workers. Heterosexual male prostitutes can reframe their work as an expression of stereotypical masculinity: they enjoy sex with numerous women, making prostitution a means of demonstrating their sexual prowess. On the other hand, male sex workers with male clients may be doubly stigmatized because they participate in commercial sexual activity while at the same time violating the norm of heterosexuality (Vanwesenbeeck 2013). Male clients who buy sex from either men or women are also stigmatized. Many report feeling emasculated because others assume they are unable to find sexual partners in any other way. Men who buy sex are thus shamed for the specific act of buying sex, often through reminders that sex is "supposed" to take place in either a marriage or loving relationship (Sanders 2008). On the other hand, female sex workers and women who buy sex are more often stigmatized for their "identity" (Sallmann 2010). Selling or buying sex is widely thought to make women "sluts" or "whores": that is, it is presumed to change who they are, or at least, how they are seen.

Views of prostitution are, in the end, shaped by a variety of social constructions, including popular conceptions of what it means to be a man or woman—and those perceptions are determined by the society we live in.

Power and Repression

Many insiders and even academics believe that heterosexuality remains the norm because it is sanctioned by powerful institutions such as organized religion and the state. By condemning homosexuality as a sin, the church has discouraged openly gay relations, as has government by refusing until recently to legally recognize gay marriages. French philosopher Michel Foucault has offered a second opinion, suggesting *not* that power structures repress sexuality, but, rather, that ideas about sexuality are produced through social interaction and discussion. According to Foucault, the ideas, norms, values and goals of authority figures and rebels alike are socially constructed, not imposed unilaterally from above.

In his discussions of power and sexuality, Foucault explores the roles of the church, the state, and the medical system, as well as the people who rebel against these institutions. A good deal of evidence exists that shows that religiosity is often associated with negative attitudes towards gay people (Hooghe 2010, Woodford 2012a). Some Christians are explicitly and vocally homophobic, and other faiths, including Islam, Hinduism and Buddhism, have also refused to accept alternative sexualities (Adamczyk 2009).

Many religious texts explicitly condemn homosexuality, while promoting heterosexual marriage, childbearing and the nuclear family (Hooghe 2010, Neitz 2014). Many people learn what is sexually (and socially) acceptable from religious teachings (Adam 1998). Not only can such teachings lead heterosexual believers to develop homophobic beliefs; they can also make non-heterosexual believers fear exclusion from their religious community and rejection by their friends and family members (Henrickson 2009).

It should be noted that many religious people hold more complex and nuanced views on homosexuality (Henrickson 2009). Some are open-minded about and tolerant of gay people, though they strongly oppose the legalization of same-sex marriage (Woodford 2012a). Others agree that the civil rights of gay people should be upheld, but find the practice of homosexuality itself to be immoral. Still others distinguish between gay people's characters and their behaviour, claiming that one can "love the sinner, but hate the sin" (Wright 2014). Finally, some Christians accept gay people who do not actively "practice" homosexuality and remain celibate, though they reject people who "give in" to their urges and are sexually active (Rosik 2007).

There are also some religious people with no qualms about homosexuality whatsoever (Henrickson 2009). Unlike those who interpret religious texts literally, as condemning all sexualities except heterosexual, conjugal relations, they think the meaning of these texts may have been lost or altered when they were translated and recopied. They suggest that sacred texts should be reinterpreted to best understand their intended meaning. For example, during debates over the legalization of same-sex marriage in Canada, the Metropolitan Community Church in Toronto stated that "a variety of Christian denominations think the Christian church has misinterpreted the Scriptures to condemn homosexuality" (Young 2010).

In *The History of Sexuality* (1978), Foucault challenges the widespread notion that religious institutions are mainly responsible for repressing sexual freedom. While religion continues to influence the way people think about sexuality, science and medicine now play a more important role. Scientific and medical discourses around sexuality constrain us because they teach us to look at sex in specific ways. Most people internalize the norms laid down by science and medicine, and, often unconsciously, aim to conform to them. As a result, we become self-monitoring, self-disciplining sexual actors.

Consider the ways that members of different societies think about masturbation. Though the practice is ubiquitous, every society has constructed views about whether it is normal or abnormal. Well into the twentieth century, even medical doctors promoted the idea that masturbation while young could lead to mental or physical infirmities in adulthood. Today, we recognize there is no evidence supporting these beliefs and no reason for anyone to feel ashamed of these sexual practices.

Science and medicine, however, provide only two of the many frameworks through which sexuality may be viewed, though they are frameworks privileged and endorsed by most people in contemporary society. Foucault (1978) notes that the now dominant, scientific view of sexuality arose from the nineteenth-century medicalization of sexuality. Previously, some sexual practices, such as "sodomy" (i.e., anal sex) were understood as temporary aberrations: isolated acts of deviance, or short lapses into unusual, unexpected behaviour with no longer-term significance for a person's identity. But with the medicalization of homosexuality, the "homosexual" became a type of person with a particular lifestyle, whose sexuality affected their entire being: homosexuality was "everywhere present in him . . . written immodestly on his face and body because it was a secret that always gave itself away" (Foucault 1978).

This way of thinking gradually led to the binary view of sexuality discussed earlier, consisting of heterosexuality on the one hand and all other forms of "deviant" or "abnormal" sexualities on the other. However, this binary view, as Kinsey would show, is inaccurate. We live in a world where (to borrow Foucault's term) a "mosaic" of genders and sexualities proliferate and multiply (1978).

Other scholars, including Butler (1988), disagree with Foucault, arguing that while sexualities may be pluralistic, social institutions struggle to force them back into simple binaries. Butler proposes that "taboos and a punitive regulation of reproduction" perpetuate the traditional family structure by making us think the only acceptable expression of sexual desire is marital sex aimed at producing children. To channel sexuality in this heterosexual way,

gender performances are "punitively regulated," "compelled by s
tion" and forced into conformity by the threat of marginalizatioɪ
punishments.

Foucault, for his part, claims that power structures expose "the various
forms of sexuality," drawing attention to the variety of sexual preferences,
behaviours and acts in which people engage. Rather than prohibiting, excluding or erasing non-heterosexual sexualities, the forms of power and control
exercised in modern societies ensure the proliferation of the "peripheral sexualities" they were intended to contain. Despite the mistreatment they attract,
these non-normative sexualities hold subversive potential. Attempts to
"evade," "flee from," and "fool" the people in power constitute a type of pleas-
urable power in itself. This means the *target* of power can *exercise* its own
power by "showing off, scandalizing, or resisting" attempts at control. For
Foucault, these "evasions" and "resistances" can gradually undermine the
"machinery of power" that seeks to scrutinize, label and contain them.

The Gay Village and Gay Marriage

Today, marginalized sexual minorities are often said to have "fought back"
against oppression through the establishment of "safe," LGBTQ-friendly
neighbourhoods, such as the gay villages that have emerged in major Canadian cities like Toronto, Montreal, and Vancouver. Many LGBTQ people see
these villages as expressions of their sexuality that help subvert the heterosexual norm.

And yet, these gay villages can also be seen as ghettos for LGBTQ populations. Consider Toronto's gay village as an example. Historically, before its
establishment as a safe community for sexual minorities, the Church-Welles-
ley area was beset by crime, poverty and prostitution. Even today, it continues
to house large numbers of disadvantaged people, with many subsidized housing projects and a concentration of homeless people living on the streets.
Nearby Jarvis Street remains infamous for prostitution. Many middle- and
upper-class Torontonians avoid the area.

In short, sexual minorities in Toronto are segregated in an area widely
regarded as a "bad" neighborhood. People who identify as LGBTQ flock to the
neighbourhood in search of a community where they will be accepted and allowed to "express themselves" without censure. But the felt need for such a
"safe place" testifies to the fact that sexual minorities still experience stigmatization, discrimination, and rejection by the broader society. Similarly, this
spatial segregation means that the heteronormative majority don't "have" to
see or interact with the LGBTQ community.

In the end, "gay villages" may not symbolize acceptance and inclusivity as
much as insiders might like to think; instead, they reinforce heteronormativity

by isolating and effectively hiding the LGBTQ population from the rest of the population. Similarly, gay marriage may not be as destabilizing as some opponents believe. Same-sex married couples express their "alternative" sexualities in traditional ways; in the end, these seemingly "non-normative" marital and familial arrangements conform to tradition, rather than departing from it.

OUTSIGHTS

People on the outside—in this case, LGBTQ people and others whose sexual roles and identities differ from heterosexual norms—hold different views on some of these issues than heterosexual insiders. Take prostitution: sex workers themselves understand and talk about their work differently than do insiders or even scholars offering second opinions on the matter.

Some academic research and most political and philanthropic campaigns frame female sex workers as passive victims, forced or even sold into the sex industry (Jacobsen and Skilbrei 2010). This places them in opposition to their heterosexual male clients, who possess the ability to choose their course of action. Indeed, for many, sex work is not a freely made choice: many workers *are* victims, forced to sell their bodies because they have no alternative means of survival.

But some sex workers insist they are engaged in legitimate "work" by their own choice (Vanwesenbeeck 2013). They note that sex work provides them with an income, allows them to support their families and even offers opportunities for personal growth (Jacobsen and Skilbrei 2010). For instance, escort Nikki Thomas (2016) writes:

> I'm a Toronto-based companion, as well as the former Executive Director of the Sex Professionals of Canada (SPOC). I'm also a three-time graduate from the University of Toronto. I have degrees in Political Science, Sexual Diversity Studies, and Psychology (specifically Cognitive Science, with background in neuroscience as well). Despite my academic background, I find that my career as an independent, self-employed escort has taught me more about human behaviour than any university course ever could.

Others view sex work as a form of entrepreneurship. Carmen Shakti of Vancouver describes sex work as her "calling," but says she also wants people to understand that she and other sex workers "have communities and families and hopes and dreams and we're complex people. We're not just 'whores'" (McCue 2015). Similarly, a sex worker who blogs under the name Juliet November writes:

When folks think about labour, they often struggle to understand how sex could be a "real job" and why we do it . . . . *We do sex work because it is a job and so our decisions about sex are primarily economic.* As with your job, money is not the only factor (e.g. we need work that our bodies can physically do, that accommodates our child or parent-care, we want to enjoy our work too) but it is certainly one of the main factors! (November 2013)

Asked to describe some of the misconceptions about sex work, 24-year-old Amber Rose, an independent escort in Montreal, explains:

. . . some of the most harmful ones [are] that no sex worker enjoys this type of work, that all are looking for way out, that the majority of sex workers are exploited or trafficked (sex work and human trafficking are not the same thing), that it's degrading and demeaning work, that it's "not a real job." Every sex worker is an individual and complex, and their reasons for being in this industry are all different, so lumping everyone into the same category is dangerous. . . . From the way media portrays sex work you expect for the men to be disgusting and creepy, and the women to be hooked on drugs and not doing well in life. This was not the case at all, and I think that's what made me start to love this profession. The men are completely normal, and the majority are respectful, fun and personable, and the women are some of the most intelligent, down-to-earth, organized individuals I've met in my life (Smith 2015).

Leaving the matter of choice aside, some sex workers argue that if their work is understood as legitimate, they will suffer less stigma, marginalization, discrimination, and physical and sexual abuse (Weitzer 2007). From their point of view, it may be better to think of sex work as a profession, not a form of slavery. For instance, "G," a 40-year-old sex worker in Toronto, says she wishes that sex work would be legalized: "We just want to be contributing, tax-paying members of society and step out of the shadows. It would also improve escort safety, public health and potential tax revenue through regulation and licensing. When sex work is out in the open, it is easier to find and help the trafficked" (Smith 2015).

Many sex workers highlight the need to have their voices heard, rather than allowing advocates or politicians, even well-meaning ones, to speak on their behalf. In an interview for a popular blog, university student Naomi Sayers, an Indigenous feminist and former sex worker, notes the importance of including "a spectrum of voices when addressing the issues a broad group like sex workers may face . . . not just the voices that are considered to be important by dominant discourses and discussions" (Black Coffee Poet 2013).

Heteronormativity

Sex workers are often portrayed as a homogenous group, despite their diversity. Recall that feminist scholars have highlighted a similar tendency for the mainstream public to assume that all sex work is conducted within heterosexual boundaries. These assumptions are products of a **heteronormative** mindset, or what sociologists call the institutionalization of heterosexuality: the tendency to take heterosexuality for granted as natural, "right" and the standard against which all other sexualities are measured (Kilgard 2014).

In the past, homosexuality was seen as a disease or disorder (Ryder 1991). Today, LGBTQ people are considered abnormal only in a statistical sense: insiders might suggest that because their numbers are relatively small, they can safely be excluded from broad theories about human sexuality.

Heteronormativity is more subtle than homophobia, but it too is built into every facet of our society. For the most part, however, the heterosexual majority fails to notice the heteronormative nature of our institutions, assumptions, and practices. LGBTQ outsiders are best able to identify heteronormativity and the exclusion it perpetuates. For example, in a column titled "Dear Straight People," undergraduate Austin Bryan (2015), who identifies as queer, lists some of the disadvantages faced by LGBTQ people in a heteronormative society:

> I have learned to love you straight people, for who you are. Even when you think it is a compliment to assume everyone is straight like you. Straight people, your sexual orientation is not a default. It is not a compliment to say "I didn't think you were gay when I first met you." Your heteronormativity is not what I strive for nor want.
>
> I have learned to love you straight people, even though you don't have to defend your heterosexuality. You don't have to sit and listen to others in your class debate your right to get married. . . . [You] don't even realize that your sex education is the only one actually taught in school. Your people are not disproportionately affected by HIV. People don't ask you how you have sex. Your community isn't accused of being pedophilic. Your sexual orientation is not criminalized in over 78 countries. . . . [You] can walk in public with a significant other without people staring, yelling, whispering, cringing or avoiding you. . . .
>
> Straight people, no one looks in your eyes to tell you that you're going to hell for being straight. No one tells you they want straight people to burn to death. People don't try to convince you to change your sexual orientation. People don't ask you why you "chose" to be straight. You don't have to pronounce your sexuality and "come out" to anyone (Bryan 2015).

Such commentaries expose the subtle, often overlooked ways in which insiders continue to enjoy hidden advantages, and point to the similarly subtle, implicit processes through which these advantages are endorsed and perpetuated. Consider social learning as an example. Parents perpetuate heteronormativity by framing heterosexuality as normal, natural and inevitable for their children (Martin 2009). Most parents take their children's heterosexuality for granted, assuming they are straight until told otherwise. Parents engage in a second set of practices for managing heteronormativity when facing the possibility their children may not be straight. Though some prepare to "deal" with this possibility, a few still hope their children will "turn out" straight, while others try to "prevent" homosexuality in their children.

By privileging heterosexuality as "normal," parents construct their children's sexual attitudes and experiences. But they are not the only ones contributing to the reproduction of heteronormativity. Traditional male-female marriage remains a cultural norm in our society. For the most part, it is even considered an ideal—a desirable arrangement most people strive for (Callis 2014). Children raised in a family headed by different-sex parents learn to think that this is the arrangement they themselves should seek when they grow up.

Butler, who has explored the role of the nuclear, heterosexual family in reproducing heteronormativity, notes that sex, gender, and sexuality are constructed in binary terms to serve "reproductive interests" (1988). In particular, we learn to force a wide range of human sexualities into "the confines" of heterosexual marriage. In turn, the institution of marriage guarantees that children are socialized to perform gender and sexuality in traditional ways, ensuring that the existing kinship system will be reproduced from one generation to the next.

The Media

The media, like other social institutions, endorse certain sexual behaviours while discouraging others, deeply influencing the ways in which we understand sexual roles and activities (Raymond 2013).

Case in point: the enormously popular Disney animated features enjoyed by countless children around the world. *Cinderella, Snow White and the Seven Dwarfs, Beauty and the Beast, Frozen*, and other Disney films portray marriage as the norm: the most satisfying way to conclude a narrative. The same is true of popular books such as the Harry Potter series, which concludes with the hero and his friends marrying and raising children. Mainstream media tend to perpetuate heteronormativity, socializing people to think that heterosexuality and conjugal monogamy is the norm, as do most classic films and works of literature (Rich 1980).

That said, LBGTQ people, once seldom seen in movies and on television, are more visible today (Gayoso et al. 2009). The hosts of some popular television shows, such as Ellen DeGeneres, are openly gay. Many dramas and comedies also feature at least one gay character; in fact, the token gay has become a predictable motif, much like the token black of a generation or two ago. Newscasts also frequently include stories dealing with so-called "gay issues."

These media portrayals can have a positive effect on the way youth view their own sexuality. In particular, they can make some LGBTQ youth feel that society accepts them as they are. Television shows that have LGBTQ characters can also provide LGBTQ teenagers with fictional personas to whom they can relate.

Positive portrayals of sexual minorities in the media also make heterosexuals view those minorities more favourably. One study found that more than two-thirds of heterosexuals surveyed regarded gay television or movie characters in a positive light (Bonds-Raacke et al. 2007). The same participants also reported feeling positively towards gay people in reality (Riggle et al. 1996).

People within the LGBT community agree that any representation at all in the media is a step forward, especially in comparison with earlier depictions of non-heterosexuals. In the 1920s, gay men were often used in films as comic relief, their gender-bending effeminacy emphasized. Later, in the 1950s, gay characters in Hollywood films were portrayed as sexual deviants. And in the 1980s, gay characters were most often associated with AIDS, and viewed as diseased and repulsive (Gayoso et al. 2009, Benshoff and Griffin 2006). In comparison to these negative portrayals, present-day media represent the LGBTQ population far more favourably.

That being said, many LGBTQ people feel that television programs such as *Glee* promote an unrealistic, "sanitized" image of gay men (Greenlee 2005) as asexual, white, feminized and financially secure (Gayoso et al. 2009). A report issued by GLAAD (The Gay and Lesbian Alliance Against Defamation) indicated that on broadcast networks, 69% of gay characters are white, 19% black, 7% Latino and 6% Asian (Moylan 2015). Although some viewers are more accepting of gay characters who are "like them" in terms of their whiteness, others become less sympathetic towards LGBTQ people represented in this way (Hettinger and Vandello 2014). If the straight mainstream thinks that LGBTQ people belong to a privileged elite made up of mainly white, wealthy men, they may be less likely to support LGBTQ rights. Moreover, these depictions don't accurately represent gay men—at least, not all of them. There are as many kinds of gays and lesbians as there are heterosexuals.

For their part, few lesbians, bisexuals, transgender people and **asexual** people are represented in the mainstream media at all (Oakenfull et al. 2008).

Courtney Ehrenhofler (2014), who identifies as asexual, writes:

> Every day, people who don't identify as heteronormative are forced ¡
> live in a culture that isn't ours, but is increasingly forced upon us.
> Take it from an asexual (ace): Living in a very heteronormative and
> increasingly sex-enthusiastic culture is very isolating if you don't
> conform to it. From TV shows and movies—like graphic sex scenes on
> HBO and plots that revolve entirely around trying to hook up with
> members of the opposite sex—to walking down a supermarket aisle
> and seeing covers of magazines like *Cosmo* boldly showing headlines
> like "101 Sex Tips to Please Your Man," or *Sport Illustrated*'s "Sexiest
> Swimsuit Models!" sex is everywhere.

By depicting LGBTQ characters in terms of stereotypes, the media also encourage people to think that all members of this community are identical, with similar interests, values and mannerisms (Gayoso et al. 2009). Such a depiction lends credit to the assumption that LGBTQ people are fundamentally different from heterosexuals (Pickering 2004). As gay columnist Owen Jones (2015) explains:

> Let's face it: representation of LGBT people on our screens is com-
> parable to . . . those one-dimensional, insulting portrayals of black
> people that used to be so widespread in mainstream popular culture.
> Not that I'm saying that battle has been won either. . . . The enter-
> tainment industry remains institutionally racist. But many gay writ-
> ers have suggested that the portrayal of gay characters is sometimes
> analogous to those old minstrel shows, which are now rightly seen as
> unacceptable. Silly, cardboard cut-out gay men, comically mincing
> around for our general amusement.

Public awareness and understanding of LGBTQ people is increasing, yet heteronormativity persists.

FINAL THOUGHTS

Insiders are likely to think that homophobia is no longer a pressing social issue, but outsiders continue to experience violence, abuse, and stigmatization. The LGBTQ community has made impressive strides in recent years, most notably in the legalization of same-sex marriage (Anderson 2008). On the whole, more Canadians accept non-heterosexuality. In 2006, one year after same-sex marriage was legalized, 59% of Canadians said they supported it, up 10 percentage points from a decade earlier (Woodford 2012b).

Still, many Canadians continue to oppose LGBTQ rights. Nor is acceptance of same-sex marriage synonymous with support for LGBTQ people and relationships in general. Many people think that others should be free to do as they please, without interference from the state. Others allow that same-sex marriage does not harm them personally, or interfere with their lives in any way, so they are more or less indifferent on the matter. Yet neither of these perspectives indicates support for, or even an understanding of, non-hetero-sexuality.

Consider, as an example, the Accepting Schools Act introduced in Ontario in 2011. The act aimed to reduce bullying in schools (Shipley 2014), and as one of its provisions required schools to accept student clubs aimed at fostering gay-straight alliances.

Many people were dissatisfied with these new requirements. Catholic school boards in particular questioned how such clubs and alliances could be reconciled with the church's teachings against homosexuality. Follow-up studies showed that after the implementation of the legislation, students still suffered discrimination because of their sexuality. Few educators were willing to advocate for the rights of LGBTQ students; in particular, vice-principals and other senior staff members were reluctant to offend the parents of other students, especially religious parents who had already spoken out against the new measures (Shipley 2014).

In a sense, insiders and outsiders are *both* right: many Canadians now support the LGBTQ community, but others denounce it, and others still engage in subtle forms of discrimination against non-heterosexuals. People holding more traditional religious and social values continue to oppose LGBTQ relationships and rights (Bramlett and Jefferson 2010), something that is problematic because of high rates of immigration from countries that are religiously and socially conservative.

Because LGBTQ people continue to be mistreated, it is clear that inclusive laws and policies do not immediately translate into social change (Ryder 1991). LGBTQ people have finally been granted the right to legally marry, to raise children together and to be protected from violence and discrimination (Gotell 2002), but few would deny that we continue to live in a heteronorma-tive society (Moreau 2004).

DISCUSSION QUESTIONS

1. How do gay villages promote acceptance of LGBTQ people? How might they hinder it? By focusing on their potential to change mainstream, insider views of sexual minorities, are we overlooking the ways LGBTQ people understand and experience these spaces?

2. What rules and regulations, if any, do you think should be imposed on sex work? Would legalization make sex work safer for those who freely choose to participate in it, or would legalization merely make this form of "deviancy" seem acceptable, encouraging more people to participate?

3. Have you ever realized you were making a heteronormative assumption (for example, by assuming a friend was straight until they told you otherwise)? Have you ever had someone else make a heteronormative assumption about you? Are these assumptions problematic?

4. Do you think LGBTQ couples effectively queer the nuclear family? Or, by expressing their love in traditional, institutionally endorsed ways, are same-sex married couples conforming to a heterosexual norm?

FURTHER READING

April Callis. "Bisexual, Pansexual, Queer: Non-binary Identities and the Sexual Borderlands." *Sexualities* 17:1–2 (2014): 63–80.

Susan Driver. Queer Girls and Popular Culture: Reading, Resisting, and Creating Media. New York: Peter Lang Publishing Inc., 2007.

Mark Henrickson. "Sexuality, Religion, and Authority: Toward Reframing Estrangement." *Journal of Religion and Spirituality in Social Work: Social Thought* 28:1–2 (2009): 48–62.

KEY TERMS

Asexual. Low or absent desire for or interest in sexual activity.

Bisexual. Attraction to both the male and female sexes.

Common law relationships. Relationships where people live together but are not officially married.

Conjugality. Pertaining to marriage.

Deviance. Norm breaking, or the stigmatization and labelling of certain groups as deviant.

Discrimination. Unfair mistreatment of groups of people because of factors such as ethnicity, skin colour, sex, etc.

Gender. Socially constructed aspects of femininity and masculinity, as opposed to SEX *(see below)*, which deals with biological aspects.

Heteronormativity. Institutionalized belief that heterosexuality is normal.

Heterosexuality. Sexual attraction to members of a different sex.

Homophobia. Fear of homosexuality.

Homosexuality. Sexual attraction to members of the same sex.

LGBTQ. Acronym: lesbian, gay, bisexual, trans and queer/questioning.

Minority groups. Groups of people stigmatized because of race, ethnicity, sexuality, etc.

Monogamy. Form of relationship in which an individual has only one partner at any given time.

Moral crusades. Social movements that deal with symbolic problems (e.g., alcohol).

Nuclear family. Family unit composed of two parents and their children.

Plurality. In this chapter, the belief sexuality encompasses more than just two orientations (straight and gay).

Queer theory. Sociological approach that challenges assumptions of heterosexuality and a binary view of gender (i.e., only masculine and feminine).

Sex. Biological and physiological aspects of being male and female (for example, males and females have different sex organs).

Sexual orientation. A person's sexual identity (e.g., bisexual, heterosexual, homosexual).

Sharia law. Islamic legal system, including regulations for daily living.

Similarity/difference framework. Comparison of LGBTQ (non-heterosexual) with heterosexual relationships.

Social reproduction. Renewal of structures, cultural ideas, etc., allowing societal conditions (e.g. inequality) to be transmitted from one generation to the next.

Transgender. Person with a gender identity that does not correspond normatively to his or her biological body (e.g., a person with a male body who identifies as a female). *Also* TRANSGENDERED, TRANS.

CHAPTER SEVEN

Consequences of Inequality for Health

LEARNING OBJECTIVES

In this chapter, you will:
1. Consider the social determinants of health alongside genetic and behavioural ones
2. Question whether Canada's health care system is universally accessible
3. Examine the evidence for the absolute and relative income hypotheses
4. Learn how outsiders are disproportionately affected by issues like long wait times

---

INTRODUCTION

Yaimy had just emigrated from Mexico to Toronto to join her Canadian husband, Joel, when the couple discovered they were pregnant (Bambury 2015). Yaimy had applied for permanent residency under Joel's sponsorship, and was told she would have access to Canada's renowned public health care system. She was *not* told, however, that newcomers to Ontario must wait three months before enjoying these services. In the meantime, Yaimy had to deliver her baby by caesarean section. When the couple learned that procedure's cost of between $10,000 and $15,000 would not be covered, Joel arranged with the hospital to pay in advance.

The day of Yaimy's scheduled delivery, and once she was lying in the hospital bed with an IV in her arm, the anesthetist requested $800 in cash from Joel (Bambury 2015). The doctor reportedly refused to give Yaimy any medication until being paid. Without an alternative, Joel left his confused wife—who spoke little English—to withdraw the cash from an ATM.

Fortunately, Joel had instant access to $800 in cash, but other immigrants are not so fortunate. Pamela (not her real name) lacked the $10,000 she was told it would cost to deliver her baby in the Vancouver hospital moments away from her apartment. Instead, she was forced to deliver the baby at home with a midwife. She recalls: "It was so hard, with no painkillers or drugs. I was so scared. And I just kept thinking, should I have gone to the hospital in the first place?" (Bambury 2015).

Not every province requires a three-month waiting period for health insurance, but a great many immigrants do come to Ontario. As a result, Yaimy and Pamela are just two of thousands of pregnant women who lack access to health care in Canada. In part, this situation is the result of negative insider views of immigrants: since newcomers have not paid Canadian taxes their whole lives, why should they immediately enjoy access to taxpayer-funded health care services?

Prenatal care is, however, not only something that many Canadians would consider an ethical imperative; research shows it is also fiscally prudent. Pregnant women who do not receive prenatal care are seven times more likely to experience complications during pregnancy and delivery. Because lack of care can result in serious consequences for both mother and baby later in life, every dollar spent on prenatal care is estimated to save the health care system four dollars down the line (Bambury 2015).

These two examples show that, although Canada is known for its system of universal, government-paid health care, the system does not cover everyone equally. Although exact figures are hard to come by, researchers estimate that somewhere between 500,000 and one million people living in Canada are uninsured (Bambury 2015). Moreover, the same inequalities that result in lack of coverage also produce poor health.

The more unequal a society is, the greater the incidence of preventable health problems. This chapter will examine how the various social inequalities considered so far—class, gender, race, age, and sexuality, and others—compromise outsiders' health and wellbeing. Inequality places marginalized groups in double jeopardy: they suffer poorer health in the first place, including preventable illnesses, and then are denied access to the health services they need to get well.

INSIDER VIEWS

Insiders tend to ignore or deny the relationship between inequality and poor health. In this case, insiders are those whose privileged status keeps them in largely good health, but who are able to easily access health care services should they require them. These privileges tend to blind insiders to the negative health outcomes associated with disadvantage, as well as to flaws in the health care system that disproportionately affect outsiders.

The Social Determinants of Health

This chapter will focus on health, which many people wrongly believe to be solely a result of good and bad personal choices, so it is useful to begin with a brief discussion of the factors that social scientists and public health researchers call the **social determinants of health** ("SDOH" for short). These factors are beyond the control of any single individual, yet often have a far greater effect on people's health than many of the individual determinants—like healthy eating and regular exercise—that are commonly associated with good health. We briefly discuss the SDOH before going on to consider insider and outsider views of health as well as second opinions.[*]

Income and Income Distribution. Perhaps the single most important social determinant of health is how much money a person makes. Diet, exercise and alcohol and tobacco use all vary by income, which also has a direct impact on other social determinants, including shelter, education, and early childhood development.

Education. The more education a person has, the healthier they are likely to be. It is not hard to see why. As Mikkonen and Raphael point out, "level of education is highly correlated with other social determinants of health such as the level of income, employment security, and working conditions." Better-educated individuals can also access information about how to improve one's health more readily.

Employment and Job Security. Work provides not only income but a structure for people's daily lives and a ready-made sense of identity. Unemployment, by contrast, leads to financial pressures as well as mental health issues, including stress and higher-than-average risks of depression, anxiety, and suicide. As well, people who have lost their jobs often take up coping behaviours—smoking and drinking, for example—that in and of themselves have negative consequences for health.

Employment and Working Conditions. The nature of one's work also affects health. Factors to take into account include "1) employment security; 2) physical conditions at work; 3) work pace and stress; 4) working hours; [and] 5) opportunities for self-expression and individual development at work" (Mikkonen and Raphael 2010). Stressful jobs can increase the risk of both physical and mental illnesses.

Early Childhood Development. What happens to us in childhood (and even before we are born) can hold serious consequences for our health later in life. In some cases—for instance, a pregnant mother's poor diet or use of alcohol or tobacco—those experiences can affect health throughout the life course, regardless of the socioeconomic circumstances of a person's later life.

---

[*] For a more thorough discussion of these determinants, we direct the reader to Juha Mikkonen and Dennis Raphael, *Social Determinants of Health: The Canadian Facts* (2010). The discussion here is based largely on that study.

Food Insecurity. As Mikkonen and Raphael put it, "[p]eople who experience food insecurity are unable to have an adequate diet in terms of its quality or quantity. . . . People experiencing food insecurity consume fewer servings of fruits and vegetables, milk products, and vitamins than those in food-secure households."

Housing. Not surprisingly, adequate shelter is a prerequisite for health. Environments that are too crowded may be disease-ridden; even today, some Canadians (particularly Aboriginals living on reserves) lack access to clean drinking water; and if housing is too expensive, people have less to spend on other basic needs.

Social Exclusion. People who are socially excluded or disadvantaged find it more difficult to secure good jobs and to access social services, including health care. As a result, they run a higher risk of poor health, and are less likely to be adequately treated when they do fall ill.

Social Safety Net. Mikkonen and Raphael define the "social safety net" as those "benefits, programs, and supports that protect citizens during various life changes that can affect their health." (Such life changes include both expected events, such as having children or retiring from work, as well as unexpected occurrences, such as losing one's job or being injured in a car accident.) If the social safety net is comprehensive, there is less likelihood of these events resulting in permanent health problems.

Health Services. An important factor in keeping people healthy is access to good health care. A universal health care system like Canada's spreads the costs across all members of society and ensures low-income individuals still have access to health care, although inequities persist.

Aboriginal Status. First Nations peoples in Canada experience worse health outcomes than other Canadians because of continuing income inequalities, inadequate housing, and numerous other factors.

Gender. Because of the various gender inequalities discussed earlier, women tend to experience more health problems than men (although they also live longer on average). Gender inequality intertwines with income inequality in having negative consequences for women's health.

Race/Immigration. As Mikkonen and Raphael note, "Racialized Canadians experience a whole range of adverse living circumstances that threaten not only their health but also the overall health and well-being of Canadian society," including lower-than-average incomes, persistent unemployment, and difficulty in accessing high-quality health care. At one time, there was little or no difference in the health of immigrants compared to people born in Canada, but more recent immigrants from non-European backgrounds experience poorer health than individuals born here or who came to Canada from Europe.

Disability. Disabilities can, of course, have an immediate impact on an individual's health, but also important is the level of government support for people with disabilities. Compared to many other developed countries, Canada underfunds programs that provide support to people with disabilities and has also made less progress in integrating them into the broader society.

The SDOH provide a useful framework to discuss this chapter's main topic, the relationship between inequality and health in Canadian society.

Defining Sickness and Health

The proposition that social inequality has negative effects on people's health—and that health is a societal matter, not just the responsibility of individuals—would at one time have been strongly questioned. A century ago, social programs in Western countries were still in their infancy, and it was only after the Second World War that most people in Western societies came to think that governments held a significant degree of responsibility for ensuring the well-being of their citizens. In Canada, this new way of thinking led first to provincial health insurance plans (the first was in Saskatchewan) and then, in the 1960s and '70s, to a federal medicare program.

Since then, public expenditures on healthcare have continued to grow. Indeed, because of effective but costly new medical treatments and technologies and the fact people live longer, spending on health care is much higher today than 50 years ago. In Canada, although the public sector's proportion of total health care spending fell from 76% of all expenditures in 1975 to 71% in 2009, absolute levels of spending increased enormously, from about $30 billion (as measured in constant 1997 dollars) in 1975 to about $94 billion by 2009—much faster than either the Canadian population or economy grew during the same period. As well, the enormous increase in the use of prescription medicines, which are mainly covered in Canada under private health plans, has increased the share of costs borne by private health insurance plans and individuals.

Although the postwar commitment to public health has not vanished, the ascendancy of neoliberal ideologies in political discourse from the 1980s onward brought enormous pressure to bear on governments to restrain spending on what were deemed "private" or "personal" aspects of people's lives (Raphael 2006). Indeed, many people today think that each individual has a personal responsibility to maintain his or her health. Though the federal and provincial governments continue to spend large amounts of money on health care, there is growing unease about the balance between public and private (or individual) responsibility in this realm. For this reason, we cannot ignore the harmful consequences of insiders over-emphasizing individual responsibility for health. Doing so decontextualizes people's real-life needs, ignores the importance of the SDOH, and indulges in victim-blaming (Korp 2008, Minkler 1999).

Where does this focus on personal responsibility come from? In part, it comes from the practice of medicine itself. Underpinning these individualistic beliefs are **biomedical** and **behavioural** models of health and medicine (Raphael 2006). From the biomedical perspective, poor health is the product of a person's physiological and genetic traits. The behavioural model likewise puts responsibility for good health on the shoulders of the individual. This theory frames bad choices, such as smoking, a poor diet, or a sedentary life-style, as the causes of poor health, and notes that such choices are entirely within an individual's control (Baranowski et al. 2003).

No doubt, a healthy lifestyle is better for people than an unhealthy one, and personal responsibility is preferable to personal irresponsibility. The issue is whether society has a responsibility to help people achieve a healthy life-style, to reduce the harm associated with an unhealthy lifestyle, and to assume collective responsibility when people are unable—for various reasons—to exercise personal responsibility.

And, too, healthy behaviour and personal responsibility are not simply a matter of knowing more about one's health and choosing to act on it. Increased health knowledge does not always lead to better health behaviours because those behaviours are complex and contradictory. Most importantly, people face other demands on their time and resources: earning an income, caring for their families, and so on.

Michel Foucault, whose ideas about sexuality were explored in the pre-vious chapter, considers these popular perceptions of health in his theory of neoliberal **governmentality** (Lemke 2002). Foucault suggests that govern-ment discourses tend to enforce the insider notion that health is a personal concern, not a political one. Starting in childhood, we are exposed to cam-paigns that encourage us to think it is our personal responsibility to eat the right foods and exercise regularly. Such campaigns may play a role in pro-moting healthy behaviours, though often they don't: as an example, consider the long-running Participaction campaign, which has been shown to have little or no benefit. Foucault's point is that by emphasizing personal responsibility, the state is freed from any obligation to care for the health of its citizens in other, potentially costly ways. Indeed, research suggests that behavior and lifestyle modifications have less effect on people's wellbeing than the SDOH; in fact, some studies suggest they may be only one-third as important.

The biomedical and behavioural models—currently the most popular per-spectives on health—are supported by scientific evidence, but they do have their flaws. Most importantly, they fail to address a vast range of social and economic factors that influence people's health. These models also give short shrift to the idea that good health is more than just the absence of illness. There are a variety of emotional, mental and physical aspects of health that contribute to overall wellbeing and a high quality of life. Nevertheless, many North Americans only seek medical help once they fall ill or injure themselves, and our health care professionals focus on curing sickness, not preventing it (Wade and Halligan 2004, Izquierdo 2005).

Because in Canada health care is paid for by the state and ability to pay for services is supposedly not a factor, insiders tend to think that everyone has an equal chance of enjoying good health: everyone, rich and poor alike, can access the services they need to treat any illnesses or diseases that may arise. But research reveals that this view misrepresents reality in at least two ways: first, in terms of individuals' ability to maintain good health, and, second, in equalizing health outcomes among those of different income levels. In one study, Atler et al. (2011) tracked the health status and health care use of 14,800 participants for more than a decade. They controlled for preexisting cardiovascular risk and for demographic factors such as age, sex, and income that the biomedical model has shown to predict poor health. As one might expect, people of lower income used health care services the most.

Nevertheless, this group had much worse health outcomes than higher-income participants. The researchers drew two conclusions from this analysis. First, aiming to prevent the onset of illness is more effective than treating illness once it has occurred; and, second, universal health care does not negate the negative health outcomes associated with low income. A 2010 investigation by the Hamilton *Spectator*, for instance, found a difference in life expectancy of 21 years between residents of well-off and impoverished neighbourhoods only five kilometres apart.

Another study throws into question the extent to which access to health care, compared to other social factors, actually affects health outcomes. Prus (2011) found the health of both Canadians and Americans was heavily influenced by socioeconomic status, sex, race, and marital status. Ready access to health care did little to improve people's health in either country, though such access was far easier in Canada.

A third study highlights a major flaw in the behavioural health model. Reid and Herbert (2005) examined the risk behaviours of disadvantaged Canadian women. They found that, because of limited financial resources, these women were *unable* to make healthy choices: for example, they could not afford to buy fresh produce. To cope with the stigma and discrimination they experienced because they were poor, many of these women turned to smoking and binge eating; their outsider status encouraged unhealthy behaviours.

To address the shortcomings of the biomedical and behavioural models, researchers developed a more comprehensive **biopsychosocial** approach to health. In addition to physiological factors, this model takes into account the way in which social factors influence wellbeing (Boudreau et al. 2007, Strumberg and Martin 2009). As we have seen, these SDOH include safe, affordable housing, social and economic integration, and a supportive social network (Yip et al. 2007, Prus 2011). Lower income people are typically in worse health, which research on social determinants attributes to sub-standard housing, economic segregation, social isolation and precarious employment (Frohlich et al. 2006).

Considering one case in particular, the biopsychosocial model has helped us understand the link between heart disease and lack of education. Less-educated people are more likely to experience depression and anxiety, and to smoke and eat unhealthily to cope with those feelings; in turn, these habits place greater strain on their hearts (Diez Roux 2007, Blanchflower and Oswald 2008). While the biomedical model attributes heart disease to genetics, and the behavioural model attributes it to an unhealthy lifestyle, the biopsychosocial model reveals a variety of interconnected factors that combine to increase the likelihood of heart disease, including experiences of inequality and disadvantage.

In other words, various socio-demographic factors (including sex, age and race) interact to influence a person's exposure to stressors. People who are persistently subjected to discrimination, for example, are more prone to suffer anxiety, poor sleep, and even depression. These experiences are damaging in themselves, reducing a person's quality of life. But in addition, they make them more susceptible to disease.

Most Canadians continue to endorse the biomedical and behavioural models of disease, but many health care professionals have come to embrace the biopsychosocial approach (Gatchel et al. 2007). As early as 1986, two key texts emerged out of the first international conference on health promotion, held in Ottawa. First, the Ottawa Charter of Health Promotion stressed the need to restructure public policies on health, create supportive environments, strengthen communities, and reorient health services to address the SDOH (Lee et al. 2009). Second, the Epp Report singled out economic status as a significant determinant of health. It called for efforts to reduce economic inequalities, increased disease-prevention initiatives, and programs to help people cope better with economic disadvantage (Rutty and Sullivan 2010).

Nonetheless, political leaders and the general public have been slow to catch up with researchers (Rutty and Sullivan 2010) and remain especially resistant to calls for reduced inequality as a health-promotion strategy. Among the provinces, British Columbia and Ontario have been least likely to address structural factors contributing to poor health (Gore and Kothari 2012). The more a given initiative focuses on reducing inequality, the less government support and funding it receives. The growing acceptance of the biopsycho-social approach as a theory does not translate into its adoption in practice.

Measuring Sickness and Health

To understand the effects of different factors on people's health, we must be able to reliably measure sickness, health, and their incidence among various groups. **Epidemiology** is an applied science that examines the distribution and causes of disease across a population. Epidemiologists draw on many disciplines, including medicine, public health, sociology, psychology and economics, to study patterns of health and illness in a society (Rothman 2012). Instead of trying to evaluate potentially vague, subjective notions like well-being, most epidemiologists measure health using standard quantitative measures. One of the most common is **life expectancy**.

Advances in medicine, technology and public health have led to a dramatic increase in global life expectancy over the past few decades. Fifty years ago, average world life expectancy was 47 years, but by 2012 it had increased to 73 years for women and 68 years for men (World Bank 2011, World Health Organization [WHO] 2014). Now as then, developed countries continue to enjoy the highest life expectancies; of these, Japan has the highest life expectancy, at 83.2 years (OECD 2012). By contrast, the southern African nation of Angola has the world's lowest life expectancy, at 38.2 years. For its part, Canada ranks thirteenth in the world, at 81.4 years (WHO 2016).

Such differences are hardly surprising. Japan is a wealthy country whose people have access to clean, safe housing, high-quality schools, advanced health care systems, and many other health-promoting institutions. By contrast, Angola is a relatively poor country, with a per-capita gross domestic product only one-eighth that of Japan, and to make matters worse, the country's wealth is shared unequally. Poor Angolans struggle to meet their daily needs, including those for food and shelter, and the health care system is inadequate and underfunded.

A gap in life expectancy between rich and poor is also evident within Canada itself. Overall, Canadian life expectancies continue to rise. But life expectancy varies by region: in wealthier southern areas, Canadians tend to live longer; in the north, where impoverished groups such as the Aboriginal population are concentrated, life expectancy is lower (Labonte et al. 2010, O'Donnell and Wallace 2011).

Maternal mortality rates—the number of mothers who die in childbirth for every 100,000 births—are also linked to income inequality. Most pregnancy and childbirth-related deaths occurring in low-income nations (Labonte et al. 2010). In 2013, Canada's maternal mortality ratio was 11, while Sierra Leone's was 1,100 (World Health Organization 2015).

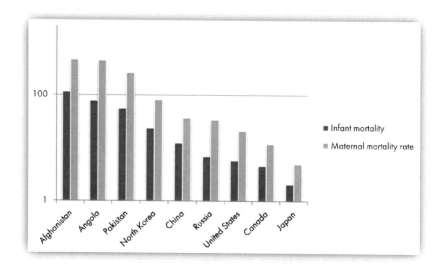

Figure 7.1: Infant and Maternal Mortality, Selected Countries

The **infant mortality rate** and **under-five mortality rate (u5mr)** are two other measures of population health that correlate with global economic inequality. Infant mortality rates indicate the number of children for every 1,000 live births who die before reaching one year of age. In Denmark, a highly developed nation with one of the smallest gaps between rich and poor, the infant mortality rate is 3. The rate in Canada is slightly higher, at 5. In Haiti, infant mortality is much higher, at 55, and in Afghanistan it sits at a staggering 70 (World Bank 2015).

The under-five mortality rate measures the number of children per 1,000 live births who die before reaching their fifth birthday. In 2013, Canada and Denmark had rates of 5 and 4, respectively, while rates in Haiti and Afghanistan that same year were 73 and 97 (World Bank 2015).

The Absolute and Relative Income Hypotheses

This brief review of selected studies shows clearly that inequality and poor health are correlated: they show up in the same places, among the same populations. But is this correlation causal? Does inequality *cause* poor health?

To answer that question, we need to find out two things. First, we need to learn whether the people suffering poorer health are the same people suffering the greatest health losses because of increased inequality. Second, we need to confirm that it was inequality that was to blame for the decline in health, as opposed to poverty and its associated stressors.

The absolute and relative income hypotheses are two widely adopted explanations for poor health. The **absolute income hypothesis** holds that poverty—bluntly put, lack of money—causes poor health. People begin to experience negative health outcomes when they become so impoverished they can no longer afford necessities like food, shelter and medicine. According to the **relative income hypothesis**, on the other hand, it is inequality—being poorer than your neighbor, even if you do have enough money to secure the necessities of life—that is the root cause of poor health (Collin and Campbell 2008, Boodoo, Gomez, and Gunderson 2014). People who can meet their daily needs may still suffer negative health effects, having failed "to meet the desirable standard of living set by the rest of society" (Adjaye-Gbewonyo and Kawachi 2012).

The two theories point toward different sets of social policies as the solution for poor health outcomes in society. If absolute poverty is the cause of bad health—if the absolute income hypothesis holds true—then the most effective solution would be to grow the economy so that enough money to survive trickles down to even the least well-off members of society. But if inequality is to blame—the relative income hypothesis is true—a better solution would be to raise taxes on high-income earners and redistribute income through social programs so as to close the gap between rich and poor.

Of course, it is important not to create a false dichotomy. A certain level of income is needed to survive at all. However, just as obviously, inequality causes stresses that lead to poor health. The goal here is to call attention to the effect of inequality on health. While almost everyone acknowledges that poverty is bad for one's health, insiders have been more reluctant to accept the proposition that in this regard inequality is bad, too—even inequality in the midst of relative prosperity.

As a result, insiders, who have a vested interested in perpetuating the unequal status quo, tend to emphasize the absolute income hypothesis, citing research that provides support for it. For instance, studies show that mortality decreases as individual income increases, since better-off people can afford to invest in their health (Gerdtham and Johannesson 2004). On the other hand, the relative income hypothesis recognizes that different social groups in different cultures may have different lifestyles and standards of living. In wealthier societies and social circles, a "normal" standard of living requires an income higher than subsistence level. The standard of living for low-income Americans may be equivalent to that of middle- or even upper-class individuals in developing countries. Nevertheless, because they live in a wealthy society and are surrounded by people better-off than themselves, low-income Americans are less content with what they have than middle- or upper class citizens of poor nations (Sanders 2010, Adjaye-Gbewonyo and Kawachi 2012).

Similarly, endemic poverty is not the only cause of widespread poor health; even in poor countries, a greater degree of relative inequality has a negative effect on health (Beckfield et al. 2013). Angola has the lowest life expectancy in the world, but its per capita GDP is far from being the world's lowest: indeed, it is more than five times higher than Benin's, yet in Benin average life expectancy is nearly 22 years longer than in Angola (WHO 2016). The fact Angola is poor reduces life expectancy; but the fact that Angola's wealth is so unequally shared makes a bad situation much worse.

Research shows that social hierarchies can cause illness when low-income people experience poor self-esteem and high levels of stress because of their lower incomes (Coburn 2004). People sort themselves into reference groups consisting of others like themselves in terms of income, status and quality of life. If, in comparing ourselves with others in our reference group, we feel we come up short, we experience psychosocial stresses that lead to poorer physical and emotional health. Middle-aged people still in the workforce experience such comparisons most acutely. Every day at work, they encounter people who are positioned above them on the pay, social and bureaucratic hierarchies (Boodoo et al. 2014).

As a result, they compare their income and status with those of other people more often than do retirees. Relative income has been found to accurately predict life satisfaction among middle-aged working people, while increases in absolute income have a greater effect on the life satisfaction of retired people who can no longer compare their incomes to their peers as easily (Sun and Stengos 2008).

Social comparison studies provide strong evidence for the relative income hypothesis, because they show that health inequalities exist even among the well-off. The so-called Whitehall studies (named after the seat of the British government) explored the health of British civil servants. All enjoyed a sufficient income, so that material deprivation could not account for differences in health. Instead, participants experienced different opportunities in and degrees of control over their work lives—differences that affected their health by causing stress and psychological strain that accumulated over time.

The original study, "Whitehall I," which began in 1967, indicated a correlation between social class and mortality. After ten years, workers at the highest employment grade had lower mortality and morbidity rates than those in the lowest employment grade. In other words, higher-status workers lived longer, healthier lives than their lower-status colleagues. Behavioural risk factors, such as smoking, low physical activity and high blood pressure, only partially explained these differences (Marmot et al. 1991).

From 1985 to 1988, a second study, "Whitehall II," was conducted. British civil servants remained the focus, but this time women were included. (The first study had included only men.) Once again, participants in higher-paying, higher-status positions enjoyed better health; those in lower-status jobs ran a higher risk of heart disease in particular. As found in Whitehall I, obesity was more prevalent among participants in lower-status jobs, especially clerical ones. They also drank more heavily, while those in higher-status jobs exercised more frequently and followed healthy diets.

The second study also found that participants in lower-status jobs reported less control over their work lives. They were less likely to experience variety or stimulation in their day-to-day tasks, and were offered few opportunities to learn new skills. Most were dissatisfied with their jobs, and were also more likely than workers in higher-status jobs to have experienced two or more stressful life events in the previous year. Finally, these lower-status workers were less likely to have a confidante with whom they could discuss their problems or who could provide advice and support.

In summary, the Whitehall studies showed that poor health is more prevalent among people working in lower-status positions. These people were more than able to meet their needs; variables other than material deprivation were responsible for their higher risk of heart attacks, cardiovascular disease, gastrointestinal disease and stroke. These other variables related to social inequality and occupational stress.

Factors related to absolute poverty, such as the spread of infectious disease, poor sanitation, a lack of sewage, or lack of clean drinking water, are not the only causes of poor health; even people who are comparatively well-off suffer from poor health when exposed to job-related stressors and income inequalities (Marmot et al. 1991). And we should also note the problem of food insecurity and nutritional inequality. Increasing food prices disproportionately affect the poor, who are then less likely to consume fruits and vegetables.

Most researchers stand somewhere in the middle in the debate over the absolute and relative income hypotheses, recognizing the harmful effects of both absolute poverty and inequality. Consider, for example, how both theories illuminate the reasons that many Canadian women experience poor health. Absolute poverty has been shown to most forcefully impact female-led households: these families are likely to have low incomes, and sometimes family members even go hungry for lack of sufficient food (Gori-Maia 2013). The widespread poverty of female-led households is, however, in part the product of gender inequality: the barriers to education, employment, and career advancement discussed earlier in this book make it challenging for women to support families independently (Beckfield et al. 2013).

The challenge, then, is to disentangle the many factors that affect people's health and wellbeing. Not surprisingly, having more money benefits individuals, but there are also significant psychosocial benefits associated with reduced income inequality at the societal level (Ellison 2002). It remains to be seen where the effects of absolute income end and those of relative income begin. Consider, for instance, the relationship between inequality and obesity.

Obesity

Obesity is a topic widely discussed in North America whose causes (and consequences) have been widely disputed. In 2012, the Public Health Agency of Canada estimated that 25% of the adult Canadian population was obese, a marked increase from just a few decades ago: in 1970, obesity affected just one-tenth of Canadian adults (Byles 2009, Hajizadeh and Campbell 2014).

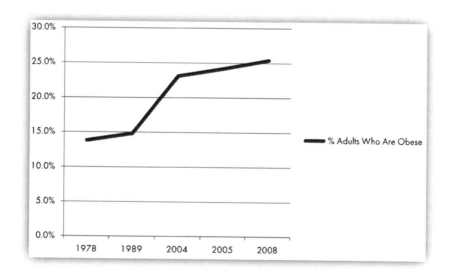

Figure 6.2: Rate of Adult Obesity in Canada

These numbers are of concern because obesity has been linked with other dangerous conditions, including heart disease, cancer, and diabetes (Hajizadeh and Campbell 2014, Byles 2009). Obesity has also been correlated with negative educational and occupational outcomes. It should be noted, however, that the numbers themselves are in dispute. As discussed in an earlier chapter, some researchers contest the validity of the widely used Body Mass Index (BMI) and suggest the increased incidence of obesity may be in part a result of changes in how the BMI is calculated.

Of greater interest to many scholars has been the issue of weight stigmatization. Research shows that in North America and elsewhere, fat people are discriminated against, earn less money, and are less likely to be promoted (Saguy 2013). Obese children perform more poorly in high school and are less likely to go on to post-secondary education (Gortmaker et al. 1993, Carpenter 2006). When limited educational attainment is combined with stigmatization, many of these youth also have difficulty securing employment. Obese women are stigmatized to an even greater degree; they are less likely to go on to higher education or good jobs, and are also unlikely to marry (Burkhauser and Cawley 2009, Devaux and Sassi 2013). Obese men and women alike often suffer from chronically low self-confidence, and are often poorly integrated into their communities.

Some efforts to combat obesity—so-called "yo-yo dieting," for instance—may be worse for people's health than obesity itself. Some wonder about the degree to which notions of obesity are a medicalized form of discrimination and stigmatization, directed at people with greater-than-average weights.

Insiders tend to subscribe to the behavioural model when discussing obesity: they argue that it is the product of individual choices, including an unhealthy diet, lack of exercise, and too much television-watching (Arkes 2009). The average-weight mainstream is so intolerant of obesity that the term "fat-shaming" has been developed to describe the vicious ways in which obese outsiders are publicly tormented.

To a considerable degree, however, overweight people are not to blame for being obese. Genetic determinants play a part in determining weight, as do social determinants (Raphael 2006, 2008). An especially important predictor is the neighbourhood in which one lives. Low-income families usually live in less desirable areas where nutritious food choices are more difficult to come by, and which lack pedestrian-friendly environments like parks, playgrounds, and hiking trails (Frank et al. 2007, Griffith et al. 2011). Lower-income individuals are also more likely to experience stress because they cannot provide for their families. Others, working long shifts or several different jobs to make ends meet, cannot provide emotional support for their children, who themselves run a higher risk of obesity (Garasky et al. 2009).

The link between weight and stigma became more salient in the 1990s, at precisely the same time that precarious labour arrangements grew more prevalent and obesity rates began skyrocketing (Lee et al. 2011, Burkhauser and Cawley 2009). As deep cuts were made to welfare programs, fewer low-income families could afford costly produce and were forced to turn to calorie-dense packaged foods (Galea et al. 2005, Raphael 2008).

What's more, research shows that high rates of obesity correlate with high rates of relative inequality (Pickett et al. 2005). Evidence shows the greater the gap between rich and poor, the higher the level of obesity in that society. But who ends up obese may vary from country to country. In developing nations with high rates of inequality, the highest levels of obesity are concentrated among the wealthy, who can afford to buy all the food they want (Pampel et al. 2012). By contrast, in wealthy developed nations with high rates of inequality, obesity is concentrated among the poor. In Canada, for instance,

Aboriginals, especially those living on reserve, are more likely to be obese than non-Aboriginal Canadians (Public Health Agency of Canada 2011).

A synergistic relationship thus exists between obesity and inequality: social and economic disadvantage predicts obesity, and obese people are subject to greater discrimination in both social and workplace settings, leading to further disadvantage.

SECOND OPINIONS

Problems of Access

Scholars offering second opinions contest the insider view that inequality and health are unrelated, aiming instead to expose the negative outcomes that inequality exerts upon public health.

Conflict theorists, for example, view health and medical services as commercial "goods" that are unequally distributed among different social classes. From this perspective, health inequalities are largely the result of economic and social inequalities that render disadvantaged populations more vulnerable to harm, while hampering their access to medical services and health-affirming lifestyles (Graham 2008).

Cardiovascular disease and cancer are both more prevalent among outsiders with lower incomes (Alter et al. 2011, Booth et al. 2010). After diagnosis and treatment, these people also experience poorer outcomes than their better-off counterparts, who enjoy readier access to health services and treatments. Similarly, Aboriginals face racism and discrimination when dealing with the health care system (Allan and Smylie 2015).

Insiders often question how this situation could arise, given Canada's universal health care system. But academics offering second opinions point out that merely because health care is state-funded does not mean that everyone is equally able to access or utilize it (Alter 2011).

Consider the amount of time required for an annual medical checkup. Travel time, waiting for the doctor and the appointment itself can add up to several hours. It is more difficult for an outsider working long shifts at several jobs to fit in such an appointment than it is for an insider so privileged she need not work at all. The appointment itself may be "free," but related services and costs often are not: patients must pay for their own transportation and parking, and many lack employee benefit plans to cover the cost of medications their doctors prescribe.

Health care providers may also discriminate, perhaps unconsciously, against patients with lower incomes. This is especially true when it comes to finding a family doctor, as primary care is in high demand but short supply. Since the government pays for the service, patients' financial position and ability to pay should not factor into providers' decision to take them on. A study conducted in Toronto explored whether health care providers' personal views of potential clients' social standing influenced their willingness to offer them an appointment. The researchers made telephone calls to a random sample of 375 general practitioners, pretending to be patients seeking an appointment.

Following scripts, they played the role of either a high socioeconomic status patient (such as a bank employee recently been transferred to the city) or a low socioeconomic status patient (such as someone who was receiving social assistance). While 22.6% of the phone calls from high socioeconomic status patients ended with an offer of an appointment, only 14.3% of those from low socioeconomic status patients did the same. Patients presenting as being of higher socioeconomic status thus gain preferential access to primary care (Olah et al. 2013).

To improve public health, academics offering second opinions recommend that opportunities and resources be equalized for all citizens. Redistributive taxation and increased social spending would help low-income Canadians access health care services more easily, allowing them a better chance of preventing and treating illness and injury (Marmot 2005, Frohlich et al. 2006). Neighbourhood clinics would also make a wide range of services more easily accessible to low-income people, immigrants, and other disadvantaged groups.

Those offering second opinions also point to the problematic and selective ways in which health-related messages are often constructed and delivered (McPherson and Armstrong 2009, Bern-Klug 2009). When poor health is attributed largely to individual choices and behaviours, and the impact of social determinants is downplayed, the dominant insider behavioural-biomedical view of health is perpetuated (Gasher et al. 2007.)

Such messages can also contribute to the medicalization of certain health conditions. This may be beneficial to the public, as when doctors and other practitioners draw attention to serious illnesses, but the medical-device and pharmaceutical industries may also be complicit in medicalization for less positive reasons. After all, they stand to profit from the "discovery" of new diseases to research and treat. In other instances, social and cultural biases, rather than actual health risks, lead claims-makers to construct certain conditions as health problems (Pieterman 2007). Some even think this to be the case with obesity as a health issue, as we discussed above.

The media play a large role in the construction of health problems, and sometimes distort the issues in question. According to a study of media reports on second-hand smoke, most reports focused less on the actual science involved than on moral narratives concerning the battle between individual liberty and public health (Malone et al. 2000).

Sociologists have long been interested in the processes through which we isolate the ill and reintegrate them back into society after they become "well" again. Talcott Parsons' notion of the "sick role" (1951) is a classic example, giving the individual patient specified "rights" (e.g., to skip work) and "obligations" (i.e., to take his or her medicine). People who fall ill are to be accorded sympathy, help, and exemption from their normal roles, but the ill, in turn, are expected to try to recover. Patients should seek medical help from competent practitioners, and follow their advice.

But sick people generally receive sympathy only when they are not to blame for their ailment. Victims of obesity, for instance, may not only be denied sympathy or help, but are often shamed and marginalized. As well, the concept of the "sick role" fails to adequately account for psychological issues and the social construction of diseases.

Psychological and Emotional Abuse

For many years, psychological and emotional abuse was viewed a personal, private issue, to be addressed on an individual level. Scholars offering second opinions on public health question this view, drawing attention to the role of social factors in causing such abuse. Both victims and perpetrators are more likely to be members of low-income families, and to be living in communities with high rates of unemployment and poverty (Iadicola and Shupe 2012, World Health Organization 2014). Psychological abuse early in childhood reduces life chances: mistreated children are more likely to remain disadvantaged as adults, which increases the likelihood the cycle of abuse will continue.

As already noted, Canada's Aboriginal population has been subjected to a great deal of psychological abuse, the damaging consequences of which persist today (Bombay et al. 2009). Psychological as well as physical and sexual abuse was visited upon many First Nations children attending residential schools. The children of those onetime students report that their parents' traumatic experiences negatively affected their ability to care for them. Thus, although they themselves never attended a residential school, the cycle of psychological abuse or neglect continued, contributing to the development of depression and suicidal thoughts in this next generation and resulting in high rates of suicide among Aboriginal Canadians.

Psychological abuse of children can lead to developmental, learning and behavioural problems (Hibbard et al. 2012). Emotionally neglected children often withdraw socially (Erickson and Egeland 2011, Odhayani et al. 2013). Combined with the delayed cognitive development and learning difficulties that can develop because of psychological abuse, this withdrawal can result in poor academic performance, affecting victims' opportunities for employment

(Hildyard and Wolfe 2002). Adults who are psychologically abused often struggle to focus at work and do their jobs well, leading to absenteeism or termination (Government of Canada 2015b).

People who were emotionally abused as children often suffer from anxiety, low self-esteem, fear of abandonment and depression, all of which can lead to difficulties forming healthy friendships and romantic partnerships and to lower-than-average incomes (Odhayani et al. 2013, Riggs and Kaminsky 2010). Children who repeatedly witness their parents fighting are more likely to become involved in abusive relationships themselves as adults. Witnessing their mothers being abused teaches young boys that it is normal and acceptable to behave violently, even towards loved ones, while girls are socialized to expect and tolerate such abuse (Government of Canada 2015b).

For all these reasons, sociologists offering second opinions argue that psychological abuse is not an isolated, individual problem but, rather, one that negatively affects society as a whole. The widespread incidence of mental illness results in decreased economic productivity and increased health care costs (Government of Canada 2015b, Hibbard et al. 2012).

Private Health Care in Canada

Insiders and academics offering second opinions are also divided on the benefits and drawbacks of private health care, although both groups recognize that Canada's present health care system has several shortcomings, including long wait times and a shortage of family doctors (Statistics Canada Health Services Access Survey 2009).

Insiders suggest these problems can be overcome by privatizing the health care system, at least to some degree. From this neoliberal perspective, privatization will engender competition between service providers, forcing them to become more efficient and reducing wait times and overcrowding (British Columbia Ministry of Health 2007). Proponents of privatization also think that it will promote innovation, provide more choice, and optimize the quality of care because for-profit service providers realize patients may go elsewhere if their needs are not met (Canadian Health Services Research Foundation 2005, Woolhandler and Himmelstein 2004).

On the other hand, scholars offering second opinions question the role that for-profit health services can or should play in Canada's supposedly universal system (Contandriopoulos and Bilodeau 2009). Research shows that privatization does *not* reduce wait times or overcrowding (Canadian Health Services Research Foundation 2005). By shifting the focus toward maximizing profits, privatization also increases the costs of services, and may increase mortality among people unable to pay for those more expensive services (British Columbia Ministry of Health 2007). Private hospitals sometimes try to increase revenue by keeping patients for longer stays than necessary, and performing superfluous procedures. Some private service providers charge more for the same services: in a 2008 Ontario study of medical laboratory services, for-profit laboratories charged $33 per patient, while the cost in non-profit hospital laboratories was only $22 per patient (Sutherland 2012). For-profit health care institutions also have greater administrative costs, including higher salaries for senior executives.

Even a partially privatized health care system threatens to reduce the quality of public health care, which in a so-called "two-tier system" will suffer from the gradual loss of resources to the for-profit tier. Some doctors will leave the public system for higher-paying jobs in the private sector. In turn, wait times and waiting lists in the public sector will lengthen even further. In the end, privatization may worsen inequalities in health care access (Madore and Tiedemann 2005, Glauser 2011).

Under the terms of the Canada Health Act, provincial health insurance programs are obliged to cover all necessary medical services. Private health insurance plans—those funded by premiums paid by individuals or employers—cover pharmacological and other treatments not deemed "medically necessary" (Madore and Tiedemann 2005, Canadian Institute for Health Information 2014).

The Canada Health Act does not, however, define the term "necessary," allowing variations in the coverage provided by different provincial health insurance plans. For the most part, dental services, eye care, physiotherapy, and most prescription drugs are *not* covered by provincial plans. People must pay for these services out-of-pocket or through private insurance. Some employers offer benefits packages to cover these services, at least in part, but low-paying, contract and otherwise precarious workers often lack such coverage and may not be able to afford these services.

Canada is the only developed country with universal health coverage that does not provide universal coverage for prescription drugs (Morgan et al. 2015). As a result, some patients are routinely unable to fill prescriptions for medically necessary drugs because they cannot afford to do so, something that further exacerbates the "health divide" between high- and low-income people. So, contrary to popular belief, private health care does exist in Canada already, and, in some cases, it restricts outsiders' access to services and treatments they need (Deber 2003, Srebrolow and Tremayne-Lloyd 2007).

OUTSIGHTS

Outsiders—those most disadvantaged by inequalities—are more likely to see serious flaws in Canada's health care system. They are, after all, the ones who tend to experience the negative health effects of inequality, and struggle to access health services and treatments. In fact, outsiders with physical and mental disabilities, racial minorities, and sexual minorities are among the most in need of high-quality health care, yet are most likely to struggle to access such services.

Long Wait Times

People talk a lot about long wait times for health services, and these remain a pressing problem, whether we are referring to the hours spent in overcrowded emergency rooms, doctor's offices or walk-in clinics, or the months spent waiting for an appointment with a specialist. Of course, wait times can never be cut to zero in a world of finite resources, and although studies show that they do have a significant effect on health outcomes, they are likely less important than some of the other factors discussed in this chapter.

Nonetheless, we must ask why many people become so frustrated with waiting and try to devise ways to make it more tolerable. Several factors make waiting irritating. First, some people are waiting for significant, potentially life-saving treatments. For them, waiting is upsetting because they are in pain, their lives are in danger, their daily routines have been disrupted by illness, and they fear what may happen if they do not receive treatment in time (Wellstood 2005). In an extreme case, 56-year-old Cathie Burnup of Alberta waited more than a decade for a surgery to relieve incapacitating pain in her neck and back: "It's such a waste of my life, when I know it could be fixed. It's so frustrating. I sit around and do nothing and watch life pass me by." Unable to work because of pain, Burnup remains largely housebound: "Life is awful. It's chronic pain, so it's lonely, because you really don't fit in with society, you can't interact with people so you kind of become a hermit" (Marchitelli, 2016).

In the case of medical emergencies, long wait times may force people to suffer pain and endure humiliating symptoms in plain view. For example, 29-year-old Christine Handrahan of Peakes, P.E.I., was nine weeks pregnant when irregular bleeding made her worry she might be losing her baby. She and her husband spent three hours waiting in an emergency room as she bled through her jeans: "Somebody should have cared enough to say 'Oh my goodness, you're going through a miscarriage, do you need some quiet time?' What bothered me the most was the fact that I had to sit in public going through a miscarriage" (Thibedeau 2010).

Waiting is even more frustrating when it appears others have jumped the queue. Certain groups consistently experience longer wait times than others. Female patients are less likely than male patients to be scheduled for a first consultation with a specialist within one month (Carriere 2010). Similarly, immigrants, undereducated people, and low-income earners waited longer than average for their first appointment (Petrelli 2012, Gregory 2013).

These delays often contradict outsiders' expectations of Canada's medical system. In a study that investigated immigrants' views of the health care system, one participant contrasted this idealized picture with his actual experiences:

> [A] new immigrant . . . [thinks] everything will be free, sponsored by government. They don't have a clear picture. . . . There should be information about waiting for a family doctor, what options if you need services, waiting in emergency three to six hours. You need to mention things clearly so people don't have a flowery idea in their minds (Pollock et al. 2011).

Two problems exist. First, the system is overburdened: it cannot always provide timely, efficient, high-quality care to everyone who needs it, when they need it. Second, the services that are available are unevenly distributed across the population, with Canadians who are insiders on every dimension being more likely to access specialists and treatments in a timely fashion.

Aboriginal people are among the most severely disadvantaged. In 2008, 45-year-old Brian Sinclair went to a Winnipeg hospital emergency room seeking treatment for a blocked urinary catheter. The Métis man had lost both legs a year before when his landlord locked him out in freezing February weather, resulting in frostbite. Upon arriving at the hospital, Sinclair spoke with a triage aide, but was not registered, and did not receive an evaluation from a nurse. In the absence of attention from hospital staff, a janitor mopped the floor in front of Sinclair's wheelchair where Sinclair had repeatedly vomited, and left him with a bowl. After other patients asked hospital staff to assist Sinclair on no less than four separate occasions, a security guard found that he had died awaiting treatment. Sinclair had waited for 34 hours, and died of a bladder infection that was treatable (Macdonald 2015)

In the legal proceedings that followed, no fewer than 17 hospital staff members admitted that they had seen Sinclair in the waiting area. Several said they assumed Sinclair was either intoxicated or homeless and seeking shelter. Sinclair's cousin Robert declared: "Stereotypes are at the root of why Brian was ignored for 34 hours" (Macdonald, 2015). Indeed, a poll shows that one Prairie resident in three thinks "many racial stereotypes are accurate."

Because of prejudice and discrimination, at least some outsiders are subjected to longer-than-average wait times, the consequences of which can be fatal. The inquest into Brian Sinclair's death found it was not homicide and did not require a public inquiry—perhaps a correct conclusion legally, but the wrong one from the standpoint of social justice and health inequality.

Disability and the Canadian Health Care System

As Sinclair's experience demonstrates, people with disabilities are among those outsiders who struggle most to access health services in Canada. Considering that more than four million Canadians have a disability—that is, they are limited in their ability to take part in certain activities, or struggle to perform daily functions (McColl et al. 2011)—their challenges throw into question the equality and universality of the health care system (Devaney et al. 2009).

Moreover, many people with disabilities are in greater-than-average need of health services. They are more likely to seek appointments with their family doctors, require various forms of therapy, and hire homemaking or attendant-care service providers. The first of many barriers they face in accessing these services is physical: some find it challenging to travel to doctors' offices if they lack access to reliable public transportation, have difficulty finding someone to drive them, or struggle to find parking near the building. Waiting rooms, change rooms, washrooms, and even equipment may not be wheelchair-friendly. For example, research shows that women in wheelchairs are screened less often for breast cancer, even though they face the same risk of developing it, because some mammography machines cannot be adjusted to the proper height (Devaney et al. 2009).

Similarly, doctors are more likely to rely on verbal explanations of symptoms when assessing people with certain disabilities, rather than performing physical examinations (McColl et al. 2008). Sometimes, this is because their schedule is tight, and it takes longer than usual for people with certain disabilities to undress. Or doctors may suppose that people with physical disabilities are ashamed of their bodies, and would prefer to avoid an examination (Raymond et al. 2014). Ideally, doctors will have the time and patience to consult with each of their patients, explain the importance of physical examinations, and ask about patients' comfort levels. Their inability (or, sometimes, unwillingness) to do so is just one of the ways in which our overburdened healthcare system can fail the people who need it most.

Prejudicial attitudes towards disability can also reduce the quality of care that these patients receive. Some doctors do not think they are obliged to spend time and money modifying facilities to meet the needs of people with disabilities (McColl et al. 2008). Others feel inconvenienced and burdened by such patients, and, to reduce the time spent with them, avoid discussing preventive services (Gibson and Mykitiuk 2012).

Some medical school instructors promote negative views of disability. For example, one participant in Vertrees' (2012) study said that when she was in medical school, the word "disabled" was understood to mean there was something wrong with the patient. Disabilities were viewed as incurable illnesses—problems doctors could do nothing about. Increasingly, however, the medical community is recognizing that disabilities are not illnesses, but rather, part of daily life (McColl et al. 2008). Some outsiders view their disabilities as harmful, but many do not. They strive to maintain lifestyles and pursue goals similar to those of able-bodied people. Others view their disability as just another personal characteristic, like hair colour or height, and do not let that one feature define them (Raymond et al. 2014).

People with disabilities often report being involved in a broader range of activities than medical professionals anticipate. In one study of Canadian women with disabilities, participants said they experienced fewer limitations and restrictions on their activities than the researchers themselves perceived. In other words, researchers sometimes make assumptions about the capacities of people with disabilities that those people themselves do not think hold true. Such assumptions may negatively affect the quality of health care they receive.

For instance, the sexual health of patients with disabilities often goes unaddressed by doctors who feel uncomfortable with the subject or do not think they received enough training about it in medical school (Devaney et al. 2009). Instead of providing accurate information and being supportive, some doctors discourage patients with disabilities from having children, believing they may pass their disabilities on to the next generation, or that people with disabilities may be poor parents. For example, one patient with impaired vision needed her doctor to complete documents so that she could apply to become a foster parent. She reported that her doctor declined, saying he could not see someone like her becoming a parent.

Similarly, some physicians wrongly think that women with disabilities are uninterested in sex, or are asexual altogether, and are therefore at lower risk of developing cervical cancer. Many Canadians with disabilities report they feel compelled to coordinate their own care because their doctors lack the knowledge to assist them (Donnelly et al. 2007). Path Danforth, who uses a wheelchair and is vice-chair of the Council of Canadians with Disabilities, points out "the reality is that [people with disabilities] are sexual beings. It's an issue that remains seldom talked about, which I find quite bizarre" (Loriggio 2015).

Many outsiders with disabilities report frustration with the health care system's repeated requests that they provide documentation of their condition to prove eligibility for certain treatments or financial aid (Gibson and Mykitiuk 2012). Many view these requirements as invasions of their privacy. They may also be costly, as the administrative fees associated with applications for parking permits and disability benefits add up over time (McColl et al. 2010). People with disabilities living on low incomes are especially likely to struggle to gain access to the help they need (Casey 2015). Some report that administrative and organizational barriers, not their disabilities themselves, limit their ability to take part in activities and get involved in their communities (Raymond et al. 2014).

Darlene Veinot of Thunder Bay, Ont., is unable to maintain a job due to a severe back injury: "I'm missing two discs," she says. "And I have a muscle on the right side wrapped around the sciatic nerve. So that's very, very painful." Veinot receives provincial assistance, but claims it is so little that she can afford to eat only once a day. She is eligible for a program that would provide larger payments. However, because she does not have a family doctor, no one has been able to track down her medical records. Lacking documentation of her condition, her application for benefits was twice denied (CBC News 2012).

Effective communication with doctors and other medical practitioners poses a challenge for some patients with disabilities. Sometimes it is simply a matter of not listening carefully. When Margaret Lumchick was diagnosed with rectal cancer, her doctor told her that surgery was the standard treatment, but that because she suffered from post-polio syndrome and accompanying muscle weakness, she would only receive radiation therapy: post-polio syndrome, which can cause breathing problems, increased her risk of being left dependent on a respirator if she underwent the surgery. Lumchick tried to explain that her post-polio weakness affected only the lower regions of her body, and that travelling to the hospital five days a week for radiation therapy would be extremely difficult because of her mobility challenges. When she said she wanted surgery instead, Lumchick reports that the doctor "became irritated. . . . He signed a prepared form and told me I *would* go for radiation. Then he abruptly got up from his desk and opened the door signal for me to leave. . . . I am a woman. I am 74 years old. I am handicap I am alone. I am disposable" (Goar 2015).

After returning to her family doctor, seeking another referral, and I the tumor removed by a different surgeon, Lumchick says she wants vent other people with disabilities from suffering in the same way she c filed a complaint against the first surgeon, but the College of Physici Surgeons of Ontario took no punitive action, merely reminding hi "importance of a full discussion of treatment options, including liste patient's concerns and obtaining comprehensive expert advice when necessu., to help the patient make an informed decision." Lumchick says of the outcome: "A little tap on the fingers to tell him he's been a naughty boy won't change anything" (Goar 2015).

Indeed, many doctors admit they find it challenging to communicate with patients with disabilities. Cognitive disabilities can pose even greater communication challenges, often causing frustration for both parties, and leading some doctors to avoid discussing preventive care so as to cut the appointment short (Devaney et al. 2009). Other health care providers are unsure how to explain and gain consent for certain examinations, and may opt to avoid conducting sensitive preventive tests like mammograms altogether.

These communication challenges can make it difficult for Canadians with mental disabilities to exercise their right to be involved in making choices that affect their health (Raymond et al. 2014). Some doctors think that intellectual disabilities render people incapable of such decision-making. But because there is such a wide range of mental disabilities, decision-making capacities vary greatly. Some people are able to make informed, responsible decisions, while others need support and guidance from caregivers familiar with their unique needs. Like all patients, those with cognitive disabilities must be presented with the full range of choices available to them, and the potential ramifications associated with any given choice (Fyson and Cromby 2013, Bach and Kerzner 2010).

Sometimes, people with physical or mental disabilities are placed in long-term care facilities, where they are supposed to receive ongoing care from qualified, carefully trained experts. Those who have lived in such facilities, however, suggest that they are neither as safe nor as supportive as they are supposed to be. Paul Caune, who has muscular dystrophy and uses an electric wheelchair, lived in the George Pearson Centre in South Vancouver for two years in an effort to better manage challenges related to mobility. "Pearson is an extended care hospital based on a nineteenth-century industrial model of delivering care and it's impossible to have freedom and dignity in such a model," he said, citing as an example an overly rigid curfew. When a nurse tried to make him go to bed at 9 p.m., Caune says, "I kept on disagreeing with her, and I had had a bowel movement. And she threatened me, that if I didn't go to bed at nine o'clock from now on, then she would leave me laying in my own bowel movement. And she did." After he filed a complaint the next morning, the nurse apologized, and a note was placed in her human resources file. Nevertheless, Caune describes the incident as "scary," "disgusting," and "infuriating," and has since moved out of Pearson (CBC News 2015).

To improve the quality and accessibility of health care for Canadians with disabilities, health care providers must receive better information and training about the needs of this population (Donnelly et al. 2007). Today, some people with disabilities end up educating their doctors on the challenges associated with their disabilities, their abilities, and their needs. Often, physicians "offload" patients with disabilities onto occupational therapists, when collaboration among various specialists would be more useful (Turcotte et al. 2015). Improved awareness and understanding of the needs of people with disabilities will help them get the health care they need.

As noted above, time constraints pose another problem. To adequately address the concerns of patients with disabilities, doctors might book two appointment slots for these people, reducing the pressure they may feel when another patient is waiting.

Restricted access to health care services for Canadians with disabilities can result in more health problems later in life. For example, when doctors who feel rushed or unable to communicate fail to provide preventive advice, patients are put at a higher risk of developing chronic conditions associated with aging, such as poor cardiac health (McColl and Shortt 2006). Improving the quality of health care provided to Canadians with disabilities right now will also improve their long-term health.

Sexual Minorities and the Canadian Health Care System

Governments are showing increased concern about fair and equal treatment for the LGBTQ population. In 1997, for example, the Quebec Ministry of Health and Social Services established a committee to assess the health problems commonly experienced by, and services offered to, members of the LGBTQ community (Clermont and Sioui-Durand 1997). They found these outsiders to be at a heightened risk of mental illness, including depression, anxiety, suicide, self-harm, post-traumatic stress disorder and substance abuse (CMHA 2015, Tjepkema 2008).

Some of these conditions were attributable to the psychological trauma associated with the fear of coming out, anticipated negative treatment from friends and family, or attempts to hide one's sexual identity altogether. LGBTQ people may turn to substance and alcohol abuse as a way of coping with homophobia (CMHA 2015). Hate-motivated harassment and attacks cause physical, mental and emotional suffering among many members of the LGBTQ population. And gay males continue to make up the largest HIV/AIDS-infected group in Canada (Public Health Agency of Canada 2012).

Despite these challenges, the Quebec ministry found that lesbians and LGBTQ youth used health care services less often than the heterosexual population (Clermont and Sioui-Durand 1997, Tjepkema 2008). Some health care providers had reacted negatively when they disclosed their sexuality, others had breached confidentiality agreements, while still others had been verbally hostile or physically rough (Mimeault 2003).

For their part, health service providers reported feeling poorly trained to treat non-heterosexual patients. Health care services had been designed with a heterosexual clientele in mind, making the system less supportive of and accessible to the LGBTQ community. The ministry recommended new measures to reduce homophobic and heteronormative attitudes among health care workers, and to improve education and training around LGBTQ health care needs.

In 1999, the British Columbia government issued a similar document,

Caring for Lesbian Health, which aimed to identify the barriers lesbians face in accessing health care services and examine the quality of their interactions with providers. Some of the issues this report identified stem from the labelling of homosexuality as a disease in the mid-twentieth century, and efforts to create diagnostic criteria for lesbianism that included physical traits or behaviours such as broad shoulders or an interest in sports. These misconceptions continue to inform practices and policies today.

The report also provided recommendations to improve the quality and accessibility of care for lesbians. Forms and policies were to be revised to use inclusive, unbiased language to reduce their obvious heteronormativity. Policy-makers recommended challenging the use of offensive and discriminatory language, holding training on inclusiveness and teaching front line workers how to use gender- and sexuality-inclusive language when discussing medical and sexual histories with patients. Creating a safe and welcoming atmosphere is expected to encourage patients to disclose their sexuality, allowing service providers to screen for health concerns to which LGBTQ people are especially vulnerable.

Despite huge steps forward, sexual minorities continue to struggle with a variety of health concerns. Transgender people—those identifying outside the normative male-female binary—are especially vulnerable. Their gender identity may not align in traditional ways with the sex they were assigned at birth. Many different identities fall under the transgender umbrella, including crossdressers, drag queens, transsexuals, gender-queer people, and two-spirit people (Namaste 2000).

Transgender people report they continue to feel marginalized, feared, hated, altogether ignored or otherwise subjected to "transphobia" (Obedin-Maliver 2015, Wallace and Carter 2003). Some of these issues stem from the medicalization of transgender identities, which were framed as "problems" that had to be "fixed" (Namaste 2000). The 1994 edition of the *Diagnostic and Statistical Manual of Mental Disorders,* best known by its abbreviated title "DSM-IV," employed the term "gender identity disorder" (GID) in relation to transsexual people seeking to transition. Diagnostic criteria for GID included "a strong and persistent cross-gender identification" and "persistent discomfort with his or her sex" (Kurzweil 2014).

Members of the transgender community felt the DSM-IV's treatment of GID pathologized transgender people, making them appear to have a mental disorder; it also reinforced dominant, binary understandings of sex and gender (Wallace and Carter 2003). In 2013, the newly published DSM-V sought to remove the stigma by introducing the term "gender dysphoria" (GD). This is a condition in which there is a "marked difference between the individual's expressed/experienced gender and the gender others would assign him or her"

(American Psychological Association 2013). While the earlier definition stresses a discordant "identity," the revision focuses on a person's distress as the reason for diagnosis.

Despite increased acknowledgment of transgender people by the medical community, the mainstream population has tended to ignore them because they do not fit tidily within our binary sex-gender system. More recently, with transgendered people like Caitlyn Jenner appearing on magazine covers and television programs, the general public seems inclined to view them as entertaining abnormalities. They may no longer be invisible, but they are not viewed as "normal," either. They remain subjects of physical violence, sexual harassment and assault, discrimination in the workplace, and bullying at school (Bauer et al. 2009). The consequences of this are higher high-school dropout rates and more mental health issues, among other things.

Because they are considered to make up a small, even insignificant portion of the overall population, programs, policies and institutions have not yet been developed to meet their health care needs (Snelgrove et al. 2012). Transgender people may, however, not be as small a minority as sometimes thought. A single community health centre in Toronto reports serving more than 615 transgender clients (Bauer et al. 2009). These numbers include only those people who seek sex reassignment surgery, and, as such, do not reflect the entire transgender population.

Perhaps because of beliefs about their relatively small numbers, certain health services for transgender people are not considered medically necessary, and are not covered under provincial health plans (Obedin-Maliver 2015). In Alberta, Manitoba, Prince Edward Island, Nova Scotia and New Brunswick, for instance, gender affirming surgery is not covered (Mandlis 2011).

Surgery aside, other medical care is sometimes difficult to access for the transgendered. Will Rowe, transgender outreach and advocacy coordinator at the LGBTQ Community Wellness Centre in Hamilton, Ont., notes that it is "difficult for us to find family doctors who are willing to prescribe hormones" (Young 2012). Some resort not only to taking non-prescribed hormones but also performing "do-it-yourself" surgical procedures, such as mastectomies and orchiectomies (i.e., testicle removals), on themselves.

Another group of outsiders whose unique health care needs are often poorly understood or ignored altogether are immigrant women who underwent female circumcision in their countries of origin. In a study of 432 Somali women living in Ontario who had recently given birth, Chalmers and Omer-Hashi (2000) found that many health care providers were not only unfamiliar with female circumcision and unable to provide adequate care during and after pregnancy, but also acted in prejudiced and offensive ways toward the women. Several patients said they felt as though they had been inappropriately put on display. One recalled: "I had ultrasound in early pregnancy. They all called each other and laughed so hard. I was scared lying down with a gown in a dark room with these humiliating people around me. My genitals were on display—a group of white-coated staff will come and look and talk to each other with disgust."

Participants in this study also reported that doctors and nurses were unapologetic about their lack of knowledge of the patients' condition. One remembered: "The doctor called his secretary and support staff. They said to each other 'how could she possibly get pregnant?'" Health care providers also offered unsolicited opinions unrelated to the care being provided. "I was repeatedly told my mother was a child abuser," one patient recalled. "That traumatized me and affected my pregnancy. They refer to me as a barbaric woman with low intelligence."

Canadians turn to health care providers for support and information. Yet some of the most vulnerable outsiders continue to be denied care and are also subjected to discrimination and mistreatment that may compromise their mental health. In this chapter we have only been able to provide an overview of these contentious issues. Much more remains to be said—and done.

FINAL THOUGHTS

To sum up, research consistently links better health to higher socioeconomic status (Gershon et al. 2012). The unemployed, homeless, Aboriginals, single parents and certain groups of immigrants and ethnic minorities suffer comparatively poor health because of their lower socioeconomic status (Hiscock et al. 2012). Many outsiders feel they lack control over their health, or are unable to engage in healthy behaviours. Partly as a consequence of this, lower-income people also tend to smoke more, leading to higher rates of heart disease, stroke and lung cancer (Hiscock et al. 2012, Gershon et al. 2012).

In Canada, objective and self-reported measures of health improve as income rises (Canadian Population Health Initiative 2008). If high-income households are defined as those with annual incomes of more than $80,000 and low-income households as those with yearly incomes of less than $20,000, the contrast is striking. Only 39% of low-income men and 40% of women rate their overall health as good or excellent, while 69% of high-income men and 72% of women do so. Infant mortality rates are 40% higher in Canada's poorest neighbourhoods than in the country's wealthiest neighbourhoods (CPHI 2008), and death rates are also far higher.

Part of the reason for these skewed health outcomes is unequal access to health care. Low-income people are more likely to use emergency-room services and be hospitalized, but less likely to visit a doctor (Tozer 2014, Allin and Stabile 2012). In other words, they fail to obtain the preventive care that would allow them to avoid serious health issues requiring emergency-room visits. Even middle-class people suffer by comparison with the wealthy. Canadians with average incomes—those, say, between the fortieth and sixtieth percentiles—are twice as likely to experience difficulties filling prescriptions and paying for medical expenses than above-average earners (Mikkonen and Raphael 2010). Canada's health care system is clearly neither as universal nor accessible as we would like to think (Reinier et al. 2011).

Moreover, it has long been understood that low income and socioeconomic status negatively affect people's health by reducing the ability to pay for material necessities such as food, shelter and medicine. Low socioeconomic status also causes chronic stress by stigmatizing and marginalizing people who are made to feel less worthwhile than their higher-status counterparts (Wilkinson 2006b). Constant, chronic stress harms one's health. Lower-income people who endure such stress for weeks, years or even their entire lives become more vulnerable to a wide range of ailments.

In the end, two things are clear. First, outsiders consistently suffer worse physical and mental health than insiders. Second, outsiders struggle to access the health care services necessary to prevent or treat the conditions they are suffering from.

DISCUSSION QUESTIONS

1. Why might privileged insiders—those who are generally healthy and easily able to access health care—deny that inequality is related to public health?

2. Do you think obesity is the product of poor choices, such as an unhealthy lifestyle? If the social determinants of health explain obesity more effectively, what measures should health care providers take to reduce it?

3. Is hormone therapy and/or sex reassignment surgery medically necessary? Should (at least some degree of) government funding be provided to trans people who want these services?

4. Given that our health care system does not cover "medically unnecessary" services or prescription drugs, do you think it's fair to say Canada provides its citizens with free and universal health care?

FURTHER READING

C. Bambra et al. "Tackling the Wider Social Determinants of Health and Health Inequalities: Evidence from Systematic Reviews." *Journal of Epidemiology and Community Health (1979–)* 64:4 (2010): 284–91.

Mel Bartley. *Health Inequality: An Introduction to Theories, Concepts, and Methods.* Polity Press, 2004.

M.L. Hatzenbuehler et al. (2013). "Stigma as a Fundamental Cause of Population Health Inequalities." American Journal of Public Health 103:5 (2013): 813–21.

KEY TERMS

Absolute income hypothesis. Theory holding that absolute poverty—lack of money—causes poor health; i.e., people experience poor health when they become so impoverished they cannot afford necessities like food, shelter, and medicine.

Behavioural model. Medical model focusing on lifestyle choices as the causes and treatments of illnesses.

Biomedical model. Medical model focusing on the biological nature of illnesses, their physical causes and treatments.

Biopsychosocial approach to health. Approach to health taking into account psychological, biological and social factors.

Epidemiology. Study of causes, spread, pattern and effects of disease within a defined population in order to identify risk factors for different diseases.

Governmentality. Complex set of processes through which human behaviour is systematically controlled in ever-wider areas of social and personal life. For Foucault, governmentality is not limited to the body of state ministers, or even to the state, but permeates the whole of a society and operates through dispersed mechanisms of power.

Heteronormativity. Belief that heterosexuality is normal.

Infant mortality rate. Risk of an infant's dying in the first year of life, measured in deaths per 100,000 births.

Life expectancy. Statistical measure of the average time a person is expected to live, based on year of birth, current age and other demographic factors, including sex.

Maternal mortality rate. Risk of a mother's dying in childbirth, measured in deaths per 100,000 births.

Relative income hypothesis. Theory holding that economic inequality, rather than absolute poverty, causes poor health. Stands in contrast with the ABSOLUTE INCOME HYPOTHESIS by suggesting that even people who can afford necessities such as food and shelter will suffer negative health outcomes if they do not meet the desired standard of living in place in their society.

Social hierarchy. Implicit or explicit rank order of individuals or groups with respect to a valued social dimension, conferring on people different amounts of prestige and power.

Social integration. Interconnection of individuals in society.

Under-five mortality rate (u5mr). Risk of a child's dying in the first five years of life, measured in deaths per 100,000 live births.

CHAPTER EIGHT

Consequences of Inequality for Crime

LEARNING OBJECTIVES

In this chapter, you will:
1. Consider how economic inequality spurs survival-motivated property crimes
2. Explore the link between violent crime and class, race, and gender inequalities
3. Learn how the media shape popular perceptions of crime rates and criminals
4. Question why racial minorities are overrepresented in Canada's criminal justice system
5. Evaluate prison conditions and their connection to recidivism

INTRODUCTION

Tina Fontaine, from the Sagkeeng First Nation, was only 15 years old when she was murdered, wrapped in plastic, and her body dumped into the Red River in Winnipeg. When her remains were recovered after she had been missing for several weeks, police were able to confirm Fontaine's death but little else surrounding the circumstances of her murder. In fact, her discovery was a complete accident: at the time, police had been searching for the remains of a homeless man who had drowned.

Fontaine's aunt, Thelma Favel, had cared for the girl since she was three: her mother had abandoned her, and her father had been diagnosed with lymphoma (although he later died of a fatal beating in a dispute over money). Fontaine's short life was tainted by crime from beginning to end. The girl's murderers "treated her like garbage, wrapping her up in a bag and throwing her into the river," her aunt said (Macdonald 2015). "She wasn't garbage. She was my baby. . . . It's not safe out there for Aboriginal girls."

Fontaine is but one of many Aboriginal girls and women who have gone missing or been confirmed dead. Between 1980 and 2012, 1,017 Indigenous women were murdered in Canada, making their homicide rate 4½ times higher than that of non-Aboriginal women (Amnesty International 2015).

In this chapter, we will consider why disadvantaged outsiders are more likely to be victims of crime than privileged insiders, as well as the ways in which our criminal justice system repeatedly fails these victims. We will also consider the social factors, such as extreme poverty, that lead many outsiders to commit crimes. As we will see, social inequality drives criminal behaviour and deeply compromises public safety for everyone, insiders and outsiders alike.

INSIDER VIEWS

Causes of Crime

Insiders—people who endure few, if any, significant social disadvantages—are likely to ignore or deny the relationship between inequality and crime and punishment. Insiders in this context include those who lack motivation to commit crimes: they benefit from the status quo, and do not need to take illegal measures to improve their already privileged circumstances. Those insiders who *do* commit crimes feel fairly confident that they will not be caught, or, if they are, will not be subjected to the same harsh penalties as lower-income individuals, racial minorities, and other outsiders who typically lack the resources to defend themselves effectively against criminal charges. For both kinds of insiders, the decision to engage in criminal activity is personal; social factors are not seen as playing a role. When discussing crime as a social problem, insiders conclude there are many factors causing crime, but inequality is not a significant one.

Indeed, inequality *is* but one of many causes of crime. Numerous other social variables also play a role. These alternative variables are, however, often linked to inequality in some way, and the most convincing explanations of crime recognize the role of inequality.

Alcohol consumption, for instance, has repeatedly been connected to crime (Graham et al. 2011, Browning and Erickson 2012). Alcohol reduces inhibition and self-control, increasing the risk of physical violence (Public Health Agency of Canada 2012). Men who drink heavily are more likely to physically and verbally abuse their wives (Johnson 2001). This correlation holds even when we control for class, age and relationship type—other variables that predict domestic violence. The relationship between domestic violence and alcohol is especially strong for men who view women as inferior and subordinate. Heavy drinking alone does not always cause abuse; feelings of dominance and ownership over women contribute, too.

Because drugs, like alcohol, affect self-restraint and decision-making capacities, insiders often blame drug use for criminal behaviour. Law enforcement officials, who may be regarded as members of powerful, authoritative insider institutions, contribute to the widespread belief that drug use is among the strongest predictors of crime. For example, on its website, the Toronto Police Service declares that "marijuana grow operations . . . have brought the criminal element into our neighbourhoods jeopardizing our safety," implying that public safety will be enhanced by catching and punishing those who break drug laws.

One study did find that drug use predicted criminal activity (Manzoni et al. 2007) but the same researchers found that access to social support played a role as well (Manzoni et al. 2006). People living in cities with easier access to welfare committed fewer income-generating crimes (such as participating in the sex-work industry or dealing drugs). Moreover, income is typically the link between drug use and criminality. Poorer people who become dependent on drugs are often driven to shoplifting, burglary, and forgery to feed their addictions. Wealthier users are typically able to fund their habit through non-criminal means. Drug use in and of itself may predict some instances of criminal behaviour, but others are the product of the combination of drugs and economic disadvantage.

Mental illness is a second variable associated with crime—violent crime in particular. Insiders are likely to blame the mentally ill for high crime rates and to suggest that measures targeting individuals, such as imprisonment, are sufficient to reduce crime, as opposed to broader social policies such as gun control. Republican presidential candidate Donald Trump blamed a 2015 school shooting on the shooter's mental illness: "This isn't guns, this is about mental illness," he declared (Elkin 2015).

To be sure, studies show that inmates at correctional facilities are more likely to suffer from mental illness than the general population, and offenders with mental disorders are more likely to serve time for violent offences (Stewart and Wilton 2014, Abracen et al. 2014). Former convicts suffering from mental illness also have higher rates of **recidivism**. But at least part of the problem is the lack of mental health services available to such people. Both in correctional facilities and the "outside" world into which former prisoners are eventually discharged, mental health service providers are hard to locate, have long waitlists, and are unaffordable for many people. In any event, blaming people with mental illnesses for violent crimes merely exacerbates their stigmatization (Powers 2015) and reinforces a false perception of them: in fact, less than 5% of the 120,000 gun-related murders that occurred in the U.S. between 2001 and 2010 were committed by people with mental illnesses (Wolf 2014). The tendency for insiders to blame crime on the mentally ill seems to some degree nothing more than a scapegoating strategy, directing attention away from issues like gun control and accessible mental health care.

Children who are neglected, abused, brought up in violent homes or otherwise traumatized are more likely to become involved in criminal activity as adults (Pellerin et al. 2003, Haapasalo and Moilanen 2004). So-called "dangerous offenders"—people who commit the most dangerous crimes—typically have survived such traumatic, abusive childhoods (Langevin and Curnoe 2014). Once young people reach their teen years, peer influences begin to outweigh familial ones. One study revealed that Toronto teens whose friends approved of delinquent behaviour were much more likely to commit property and violent crimes (Strohschein and Alvinelle 2015). Youth are susceptible to gang recruitment, and gang membership almost always entails involvement in violent, often serious crimes (Stys and Ruddell 2013). Once again, however, research confirms that the young people most likely to grow up in troubled households and, in turn, to join gangs are outsiders who suffer from inequality-related disadvantages (Public Safety Canada 2016).

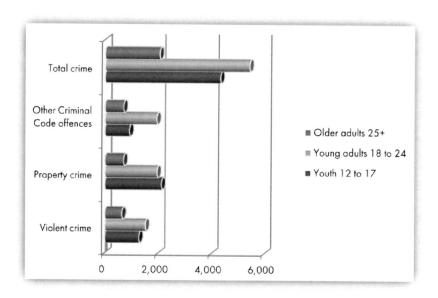

Figure 8.1: Person Accused of Crime by Age Group, 2014
RATE PER 100,000 POPULATION

Young people who perform poorly in school or drop out altogether run a higher risk of criminal involvement, both immediately and later in life. Thirty-seven percent of criminal offenders in the 2012–13 reporting year had a grade 8 level of education or less (Government of Canada 2014). Lacking adequate education, these people are left with fewer opportunities to pursue viable employment, driving many to illegal alternatives. On the other hand, higher levels of education predict higher levels of criminal victimization. One study found that participants with post-graduate degrees were twice as likely as those lacking high school diplomas to be the targets of property crimes (Gabor and Mata 2004). Because higher levels of education typically correlate with higher incomes, the underlying correlation may be between income and risk of becoming a target for burglary and theft.

Access to weapons also drives up the rate of violent crime. Efforts to control the use of firearms in Canada have been in place for over a century, and include restrictions on firearm and ammunition businesses and the stipulation that individuals meet licensing requirements before acquiring firearms. Research attributes the significant drop in gun violence in Canada, including homicide, suicide, and accidents, to these measures (Blais et al. 2011). By contrast, gun violence in the U.S., where laws controlling access to firearms are less stringent, is among the most widespread and deadly in the world.

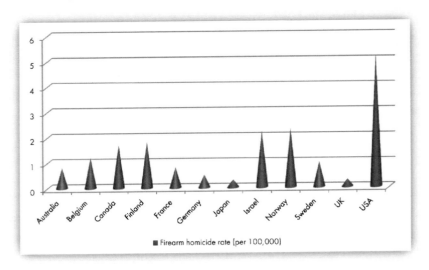

Figure 8.2: Firearm Homicide Rates for Selected Countries

Six out of every ten murders in the U.S. in 2012 were committed using firearms, double the Canadian rate. Ease of access to firearms has been proposed as one of the many factors that causes especially violent crime.

Findings on the impact of the media on crime are mixed. Some studies suggest that violent movies, TV shows and video games inspire violence by desensitizing viewers and by sending the message that violence is an appropriate way to solve problems (Anderson et al. 2003, Huesmann 2010). Others, however, suggest a causal relationship cannot be proven; so far, it has not been shown that media violence alone exerts a significant effect on violent behaviour (Savage 2004, Savage and Yancey 2008).

Overall, insiders are likely to endorse explanations for crime that blame individual rule-breakers rather than the unequal, unfair society in which those rule-breakers were raised. They argue that the poor decisions of uneducated young people to drink, do drugs, drop out of school and join gangs account for much of the crime in our society. Indeed, research confirms that a disproportionate number of young, uneducated, substance-dependent Canadians engage in criminal activity. But to blame these individuals alone for crime is to ignore the inequalities and disadvantages that often motivate their poor decisions.

SECOND OPINIONS

Scholars offering second opinions are less likely than insiders to downplay the importance of inequality in explaining crime. Rather, they suggest that many crimes are caused at least in part by inequality; that inequality structures the support and protection people receive from the criminal justice system; and that the physical, emotional, financial and social consequences of crime are felt more deeply by certain segments of the population than others.

Income Inequality and Crime

Most sociological and criminological studies find that economic inequality predicts the incidence of both property crime and violent crime (Kelly 2000, Hipp and Yates 2011). As early as 1938, sociologists drawing on Robert Merton's **strain theory** argued that poverty pushes people to commit crimes out of a need to survive and inability to access traditional means of earning a living—that is, a "strain" between one's goals and the means available through which to pursue those goals (Pratt and Cullen 2005, Pare and Felson 2014).

Merton's (1938) concept of **anomie** stood in stark contrast with the previously prevalent misconception that crime occurs when the social order fails to restrain individual criminal impulses (Murphy and Robinson 2008, Chamlin and Sanders 2013). Instead, Merton proposed that society itself engenders crime and causes people to deviate from normative behaviour (Sharma 1980).

According to Merton, people are normally socialized to aspire to goals deemed culturally desirable. They are also taught the accepted means by which to attain those ends. For example, North Americans are taught to aspire to make enough money to live comfortably and support their families. Ideally, they will reach this goal by securing a good job. But as we have seen, not everyone enjoys equal educational and occupational chances in life. For these people, socially unacceptable routes to wealth—such as theft or fraud—may be more readily accessible.

Societies discourage these deviant routes to success through punishments such as fines, imprisonment and other types of formal **social control**. These efforts to deter crime, however, often prove inadequate. In a society like ours, where more emphasis is placed on the goal than on the means by which it is attained, many people come to believe that the possible rewards of criminal activity outweigh its potential risks (Murphy and Robinson 2008). This is especially true for the desperately poor, who have little to lose if they are caught (Janko and Poplin 2015, Wu and Wu 2012).

Despite stereotypical conceptions of the criminal poor as morally bankrupt, crime (according to Merton) is not the result of some innate drive or lack of ethics (Featherstone and Deflem 2003). The broad societal goal of financial success, combined with unequal access to conventional means of achieving that success, promotes crime (Merton 1938, Agnew 1980). By denying significant numbers of people the opportunity to succeed through socially acceptable channels, conditions are created that result in high crime rates (Murphy and Robinson 2008, Chamlin and Sanders 2013).

In societies with high levels of inequality, the poor are likely to doubt they will ever become financially successful (Agnew 1980). Merton (1938) described such people as "retreatists," noting that they may "resign" or try to "escape" from society, rejecting culturally sanctioned goals and means alike (Hilbert 1989, Sharma 1980). This resignation helps to explain self-destructive behaviour such as alcoholism and drug addiction, which are not the causes of their poverty but consequences of it.

Recent studies confirm the validity of Merton's theory. Consider the connection between unemployment and crime rates: when people lose their jobs, some turn to crime to make ends meet (Fougere et al. 2009, Gronqvist 2013). Young people are especially likely to be driven to crime if the economy is in recession as they complete their schooling. One study found that young adults were 5.5% more likely to be incarcerated if they graduated during a period of high unemployment (Bell et al. 2014). At the same time, increased wages at the bottom end of the income distribution have been shown to reduce crime rates (Machin and Meghir 2004).

Survival-motivated crimes aside, studies show that burglary and auto-theft rates soar as the gap between the rich and the poor grows (Dahlberg and Gustavasson 2008, Reilly and Witt 2008). This indicates a link between inequality and crime as well as absolute poverty and crime: while the desperately poor are forced to steal out of material necessity, better-off but still comparatively disadvantaged people commit property crimes at a higher-than-average rate, even though they already possess the means to survive.

Sociologists Clifford Shaw and Henry McKay developed **social disorganization** theory (1942) to try to better understand these issues. They gathered demographic information on people with criminal records living in Chicago, and plotted their residential locations on a map. This map showed concentrated pockets of delinquency around railroads, stockyards and other industrial districts—areas characterized by overcrowding, physical deterioration and economic segregation. As diverse collections of people with diverging values, beliefs and customs crowded in upon each other, suspicion and fear grew, limiting the neighbourhood's sense of cohesion (Hipp 2007). Adding to this lack of **integration**, residents were continually moving out of the neighbourhood in an effort to escape the hostile environment. Social networks were rendered almost non-existent, resulting in social disorganization: community members were unable to collaborate to achieve common goals such as providing support and supervision for neighborhood youth (Kelly 2000).

In such areas, crimes were committed not only out of economic desperation but also because of a lack of informal social control (Kelly 2000). Lacking were tightly integrated networks of neighbours who observed each other's behaviour, held one another accountable and united behind shared objectives (Hipp 2007). Over the years, different racial and ethnic groups moved in and out of the area, yet crime rates remained consistently high. On the other hand, the level of criminal behavior fell among people who moved away, relocating to more socially cohesive areas. Recent studies confirm that moving out of a disadvantaged neighborhood reduces a person's risk of criminal behaviour (Sciandra et al. 2013) even with no change in the individual's financial status. A combination of poor economic circumstances and racial or ethnic inequalities intersect to produce the social disorganization that breeds deviant behaviour.

These findings support the idea that relative as well as absolute poverty breeds crime. As the gap between the rich and the poor widens, fewer people can afford to live in wealthy, socially cohesive neighbourhoods, and many are relegated to disadvantaged communities where delinquency flourishes because of social disorganization.

The incidence of violent offences also supports the notion of a link between income inequality and crime. The poor have more incentive to steal than the rich: financial desperation motivates property crime (Becker 1973, Ehrlich 1973). But if thefts are committed out of material necessity, what motivates violent crime?

Robert Agnew's **general strain theory** (1985, 1992) aims to answer this question by focusing on the negative emotions evoked by the strains outlined in Merton's original theory. When people fail to obtain socially valued goals (like money or status), they develop coping mechanisms to manage the negative emotions that result. Not everyone who experiences these strains turns to delinquency as an outlet, leading Agnew to suggest that criminality ensues only in certain circumstances. Specifically, when conditions are seen as unjust, unfair or beyond a person's control, feelings of anger and frustration are likely to result, potentially causing aggressive outbursts. Agnew proposed that social and income inequalities may be especially likely to elicit these negative reactions, as low-income earners living in highly unequal societies will likely become frustrated with their circumstances.

Like Merton, Agnew suggests that some people cope with their frustration through escapist coping mechanisms, such as alcohol or drug use. Others, however, turn to retaliatory behaviours, committing violent offences as an outlet for their anger. Young people are especially likely to act this way: they may be less able to access the substances typically relied upon by escapists, and also less bound by responsibilities—romantic partners, children, mortgage payments—that tend to discourage violent outbursts among adults.

In an effort to test this theory, Boggess et al. (2014) examined how **gentrification** affects crime rates. The study revealed that if several bordering neighbourhoods were all undergoing economic improvements, fewer assaults occurred in each community. But if one isolated neighbourhood began gentrifying, surrounded by communities that remained disadvantaged, aggravated assault rates rose. The same increase was not observed for property crimes, such as burglary and robbery, suggesting the rise in aggravated assault rates might be due to heightened feelings of hostility rather than attempts to acquire valuable possessions. Violent crimes against middle- and upper-class people tend to be concentrated in areas where wealth and affluent lifestyles are highly visible and contrast starkly with surrounding poverty.

These patterns can be observed on a larger scale as well. Provinces characterized by higher levels of income inequality have higher homicide rates compared to provinces where the gap between the rich and the poor is narrower (Daly et al. 2001). Similarly, homicide rates in Britain and the U.S.—countries with large income inequalities—are higher than in the more egalitarian Nordic countries (Lappi-Seppala and Tonry 2011).

Racial Inequality and Crime

Social disorganization theory also demonstrates that individual demographic features, such as race, do not adequately account for crime. Shaw and McKay conducted their research at a time when many people still thought that racial minorities were inherently predisposed to violent, deviant behaviour. Although statistics do show that racial minorities are more likely to be accused and convicted of crimes than whites, various problems, including **racial profiling**, skew these figures, as we will see below (Warren 2010, Robinson 2000). Indeed, because of the widespread stereotyping of racial minorities, especially young black men, as dangerous, violent criminals, many insiders overestimate the amount of criminal activity occurring in black neighbourhoods (Wright and Younts 2009).

Where racial minorities do carry out criminal activity, inequalities often play a role. Racial inequalities tend to correlate with economic ones, making racial minorities more likely to commit the survival-motivated crimes described above (Warren 2010, Wright and Younts 2009). Low-income earners, who are more likely to be members of racial minorities to begin with, are also more likely to live in socially disorganized neighbourhoods where crime proliferates. After moving to safer, more affluent and cohesive neighbourhoods, crime rates among these same groups drop. It's not that racial minorities are somehow intrinsically criminally inclined; rather, because of the structural barriers discussed earlier, these groups are more likely to be trapped in disadvantaged states, lacking legal opportunities to improve their circumstances (Bauder 2003).

Financial desperation is not the only motivator of delinquency. Violent crime rates again draw attention to the influence of inequality on deviance. Feelings of injustice are strongest in the economically disadvantaged communities where racial minorities are likely to reside. These areas are where we find most violent crimes committed (Hipp 2007, Steffensmeir et al. 2010).

Gender Inequality and Crime

Similar arguments have been made for the link between gender inequality and crime. Violence against women—especially sexual violence—is a prime example of criminal behaviour typically driven by unequal power relations. Such violence is especially prevalent in regions characterized by extreme gender inequality, where women hold low social status (Yodanis 2004, Jewkes 2002). In these societies, men are more likely to attempt to assert what they view as their innate right to women's bodies, and to use physical force to enforce obedience or settle arguments.

In addition, however, Gartner et al. (1998) found that **femicide**, the killing of women by men, is most common in societies in the middle of a transition from traditional to modern ways. When the status of women is starting to rise, threatening men's traditional standing, some men lash out violently. They men may be striving to reassert their former positions of authority, or they may be taking out their frustrations on those they hold responsible for the loss of their privileged positions.

The Media and Crime

In drawing attention to the ways in which economic, racial, and gender inequalities structure crime, academics offering second opinions challenge popular stereotypes about criminals and their behaviour. The media play a central role in constructing and perpetuating those stereotypes. For instance, the crimes most often featured in news reports are violent street crimes (Williams 2008, Collins 2014). Other crimes and criminals receive less attention. Academics specializing in media studies suggest that the colonial past continues to shape the types of content disseminated by the media today (Gosine and Teelucksingh 2008, Wortley and Owusu-Bempah 2012). Media treatment of crime reveals some of society's more deeply entrenched biases: certain types of criminals are highlighted, leaving the impression that they are responsible for most of the crime in our communities (Ezeonu 2010, Collins 2014). Movies and TV shows depict minorities using overly simplistic stereotypes, casting them as pimps, drug-pushers, delinquents or otherwise deviant and dangerous (Mahtani 2001, Tamang 2009).

Though racial minorities are characterized as the most common perpetrators of crime, in fact members of these groups are most likely to be victims of crime when compared to white insiders (Wortley and Owusu-Bempah 2012). Nevertheless, these characterizations exert enormous influence on popular beliefs about crime. By painting minorities as criminals or villains, the media contribute to maintaining their social, political and economic disadvantage (Ungerleider 1991, Collins 2014).

The media also paint a false picture of the magnitude of the threat posed by crime. News reports leave readers and viewers believing that crime is on the rise and that violent crime poses the biggest threat to the average person's wellbeing, even though statistics show other dangers are far more common. About 12 people are killed by strangers each year in Toronto, making one's chances of being a victim of such a crime roughly one in 220,000 (Loriggio 2008). By contrast, 1 in 440 Canadians dies of cardiovascular disease each year, and every year about 3,000 Canadians die in car crashes.

As well, the media lead people to adopt problematic understandings of the motivations behind crime. A content analysis of Canadian news reports over three decades found that stories about minority offenders were more likely to emphasize their poverty and lack of education. Articles describing white offenders, by contrast, characterized their crimes in more individualistic terms. Collins (2014) proposes that these patterns frame "white crime" as isolated and random, but "minority crime" as typical and commonplace.

Popular perceptions of criminals often centre on their race without acknowledging that poverty may motivate crime. Half of all Ontario residents think that crime is linked to ethnicity, with blacks being blamed most often (Wortley and Owusu-Bempah 2012). Many factors contribute to these distorted beliefs, but media coverage is a significant one. A documentary film about a Toronto community housing project, Regent Park, prominently featured the views of a white activist who complained the area had descended into lawlessness because of police commitment to political correctness and respect for racial diversity. Ignored in the documentary were decades of strained relations between black residents and the police, grounded in allegations of racial profiling, excessive surveillance and even police brutality.

Rather than exploring how poverty and racism may lead to higher crime rates in a neighbourhood, the documentary focused instead on the views of people from outside the neighbourhood who had never experienced life there (Purdy 2005, Tamang 2009).

The media depict crime as the product of individual pathologies. An analysis of Canadian and American crime coverage found that news stories typically foreground the young age, minority status and low incomes of alleged perpetrators, but ignore broader social patterns, such as poverty, that may lead such people to commit crimes (O'Grady et al. 2010, Tamang 2009). Audiences were reportedly more engaged by this approach (Wortley and Owusu-Bempah 2012).

Sensationalizing violent crimes also resulted in large audiences (Dowler 2004). Even coverage of victims tends to cater to insider preferences, with victims belonging to racial minorities receiving less sympathy than whites.

While violent crime receives widespread coverage, the **white-collar crimes** of the elite remain largely hidden (Williams 2008). If these "crimes of wealth"—that is, those committed out of greed or insatiable desires (Bonn 2014, Kempa 2010)—are covered at all, they are often framed as the result of government or corporate negligence or personal immorality. By ignoring white-collar crime, the media effectively erase the possibility of corporate criminality from public consciousness, rendering street crime even more prominent in its absence.

Since Edwin Sutherland's classic work *White Collar Crime* was first published in 1949, scholars offering second opinions have valued the study of crimes of wealth for its ability to "redress the imbalance in criminology's obsession with crimes of the working class" (Oxford Dictionary of Sociology). Sutherland notes that traditional theories about crime that focus solely on poverty, lack of opportunity, personality defects or bad family experiences cannot explain white-collar or corporate crime. He argues that all crime—including corporate crime—has an important cultural aspect. Criminals are taught to adopt criminal values and to hone their criminal skills, whether they are petty thieves or Wall Street financiers. Deviance is learned through ongoing interactions with others who define it in positive terms.

Despite fraud, embezzlement and extortion committed by elites, we continue to think that violent street crime is the "real" threat. White-collar crimes are typically non-violent, so they do appear less threatening than violent street crimes (Matsueda and Grigoryeva 2014). However, white-collar crimes are much more costly to society as a whole (Bonn 2014, Robinson 1998). For instance, a million Canadians have lost money because of white-collar crimes such as investment fraud (Kempa 2010).

Above: Although social problems like homelessness and drug use are often viewed by insiders as causes of crime, it may be more useful to view them as consequences of inequality (Andy Burgess).

Below: Paradoxically, mass shootings like that at Sandy Hook in 2012 tend to increase sales of firearms across the United States (Patrick Feller).

Consider another example: the 1992 Westray mine explosion in Nova Scotia. In its wake, most media coverage avoided painting the disaster as a state or corporate crime (McMullan 2006). Reports did include accusations of severe negligence, and news stories were critical both of the company and government involvement in the project. Nevertheless, the catastrophe was framed as the result of "political immorality"; by spoonfeeding reporters information, Westray was able to manipulate coverage to its advantage. Though the media do not control the criminal justice system, they do shape people's perceptions of criminal activity, often by painting white collar crimes and criminals in one way and theft and violent crimes in another.

The stereotypically racialized, impoverished people depicted in the media as violent delinquents are often arrested and punished, while white-collar criminals frequently walk away with no more than a slap on the wrist (Robinson 2000). In general, the criminal justice system is less suspicious of insiders with friends in high places. As a result, few white-collar criminals are convicted, and those who are tend to receive light sentences, although there are, as always, exceptions.

The fact that police officers are common sources of information for reporters also shapes media coverage of crime. Some officers view criminality as a pathological predisposition among racial minorities, especially young black men, and their personal views may seep into accounts of criminal actions provided to the media.

The Social Construction of Deviance

The media aside, many other social institutions help to construct popular perceptions of deviance (Boda and Szabo 2011). Academics offering second opinions contest insider assumptions that deviance is the product of individual immorality; rather, they suggest that it occurs when social controls fail to enforce the expected degree of conformity (Bryant and Higgins 2010, Jackson and Gray 2010). The standards to which we are expected to conform are themselves socially constructed: members of a society collectively decide to make the rules and laws that structure that society today, and then to enforce some of them more strictly than others.

For the most part, deviant acts are hidden. They come into view only when we look for them, and most of the time, we aren't looking very hard. For every documented act of rule-breaking, there are hundreds or even thousands of comparable acts that go undocumented.

The best estimates of overall crime rates are based on reports of incidents by victims. Yet victims of certain crimes are less likely to report them to police. The proportion that is reported depends on the nature of the crime: most homicides, attempted homicides and major property losses are reported. By comparison, few petty thefts, threats and minor assaults are reported. There is much debate about what fraction of sexual assaults are reported, but as noted in a previous chapter, the number is thought to be low (Rich and Seffrin 2012).

Fewer crimes are therefore reported than committed. Nor do police act on every report. Some alleged crimes are investigated; others are not. Some but not all of these investigations will turn up suspects and result in charges being laid. And of those people charged, some will be convicted, others acquitted. Finally, some of those convictions will result in punishment, while others will not.

During the 1950s and 1960s, symbolic interactionists began asking how deviance was defined, and who got to decide what was branded as "deviant." They concluded that deviance was a social label that some groups used to describe and stigmatize the behaviour of other groups. For the most part, white, well-off insiders are the ones in Canadian society who enjoy the power of defining deviancy (Alicke and Rose 2012, Anomaly and Brennan 2014). They do so based on their own collective beliefs, values and morals, and then try to hold the rest of society to account through the criminal justice system.

The very act of identifying deviance, symbolic interactionists suggest, may result in further deviant behaviour, as being labeled deviant harms a person's social status, life chances, and sense of self (Asencio and Burke 2011, Alarid and Vega 2010). After serving time in prison, released convicts tend to maintain their deviant identities, and the general public typically reacts to them negatively. Indeed, many view "ex-cons" as unruly, dangerous, irresponsible or lacking good judgment, and employers are usually reluctant to hire them. Many former prisoners return to the poor neighbourhoods where they lived before being incarcerated to face straitened economic circumstances, living at the margins of the labour market, precariously employed in jobs with few prospects of advancement. Many reoffend, either because they have few alternatives, or because they have internalized the criminal identity projected upon them by community members (Opsal 2012).

According to symbolic interactionists, deviance and crime are learned through processes of socialization. Beginning in childhood, we learn how to participate in society—how to take on the roles expected of us, and to anticipate the ways in which others will play their roles. Sutherland (1939) proposed that:

- Deviant behaviour is learned in association with others in intimate social relationships.
- Views about deviance are learned from others who share the cultural meanings ("definitions") of particular deviant behaviours.

- Deviant behaviour occurs when people share an excess of favourable definitions of deviance, in comparison to unfavourable ones.

Sutherland called this approach **differential association theory**, because deviant (or criminal) communities are "differentially organized" **subcultures**, with their own values, traditions and norms of behaviour. According to the theory, members of a deviant community—for example, a delinquent gang—interact regularly, participating in and communicating about delinquent acts. They hold and express positive views of these acts, unlike people outside their circle, and deny their activities were harmful (Young et al. 2014). In other words, they behave conventionally in exercising unconventional values.

Symbolic interactionism has also been used to examine how social problems are constructed as problematic. Herbert Blumer (1971) proposed that social problems develop in stages. The first stage is social recognition, the point at which a given condition or behaviour (such as drug use) is identified as a potential social concern. The second stage is social legitimation, the point at which society and its various institutional elements formally recognize the social problem as a serious threat to social stability. At both stages, many people discuss, define, and build a shared sense of "the problem." In other words, social problems are social constructs. From the social-constructionist viewpoint, even the most catastrophic social acts—genocide, for example—need to be thrust into public view and constructed as problems before action can be taken.

Moral Panics

In their capacity to shape popular perceptions of crime, the media also have the power to incite a **moral panic**: any popular controversy or dispute provoking fears so intense they threaten the social order. Stanley Cohen, author of *Folk Devils and Moral Panics* (1972), is credited with coining the term. According to Cohen, a moral panic occurs when a "condition, episode, person or group of persons emerges to become defined as a threat to societal values and interests" (1972).

Typically, moral panics are sparked (and fuelled) by **moral entrepreneurs**: people who stand to gain from the panic, and therefore help define the issue as a social problem. They frequently feed off already prevalent fears that a certain group—say, poor people, racial minorities or LGBTQ people—negatively affect society (Garland 2008, Collins 2013). Moral entrepreneurs stir up further hostility towards the group, often suggesting they threaten society's values, beliefs and best interests. Doing so may prove an easy task, as the "problematic" groups are typically already disadvantaged (Klocke and

Muschert 2010, Garland 2008). Moral entrepreneurs may also try to further legitimate or rationalize already widespread assumptions about these marginalized groups by presenting their claims as scientifically grounded (Young 2009).

The media are typically quick to become involved, and often sensationalize the imagined threat by emphasizing the supposedly harmful behaviours of the group in question (Krinsky 2013). Clear divisions form between "them" and "us," as the group comes to be viewed as "folk devils" and is scapegoated as the sole cause of the given threat (Alexandrescu 2014). When many come to believe the group in question poses a genuine threat to society, actions may be taken (or urged) that are disproportionate to the threat posed by the accused group. Public concern about the issue ebbs and flows quickly and unpredictably, and often ends suddenly as media attention shifts to another topic (Klocke and Muschert 2010). Occasionally, moral panics drive positive change, but more often they deepen existing social divisions and increase systems of control and regulation (Goode and Ben-Yehuda 2009, Garland 2008).

Sociologist Émile Durkheim argued that crime is universal and unavoidable, regardless of the nature of a society or its laws. Functionalist sociologists following in Durkheim's footsteps have resisted insider attempts to incite moral panics around crime and deviance: instead, they hold that all social structures and processes exist because they fulfill some purpose or perform a necessary function. Crime is simply one of these processes. In a classic essay on the normality of crime, Durkheim (1958) wrote:

> What is normal, simply, is the existence of criminality. . . . [This] is not to say merely that it is an inevitable, although regrettable phenomenon due to the incorrigible wickedness of men; it is to affirm that it is . . . an integral part of all healthy societies. . . . [I]t is bound up with the fundamental conditions of all social life and by that fact it is useful.

It would seem that Durkheim believed that people pursue their own self-interests, and as a result are naturally inclined towards criminality. Social controls, including the criminal justice system but also close attachments to other people, keep most from engaging in crime (Dollar 2014). Durkheim proposed that when criminals—and deviants more generally—violate social boundaries, they reinforce society's commitment to those boundaries (Agnich et al. 2010). The collective disapproval of an especially shocking crime brings society together and fosters greater social integration. The very existence of crime and deviance—and the fact they are punished—strengthens social bonds and reminds people of the need to obey the rules.

Recent research by Agnich et al. (2010) supports Durkheim's view. The researchers measured levels of student solidarity—"strongly and widely held sentiments of attachment to the collective"—on campus at Virginia Tech University, both before and after the 2007 mass shooting. Results showed a significant increase in student solidarity five months after the tragedy.

Some scholars hold that crime can foster solidarity not only through the punishment of the criminal, but also through rehabilitation. One researcher analyzed the writings of Pennsylvanians involved in the creation and maintenance of the Eastern State Penitentiary between 1829 and 1850 (Aubuchon-Rubin 2009). Early nineteenth-century Pennsylvania was found to be an optimistic society, preferring redemption of criminals over retribution. This belief in the redemptive capacity of criminals contributed to a heightened sense of solidarity in the community as a whole, a sense that was expressed in their writings.

In general, people agree which crimes are unacceptable. Because of this agreement, people who break the rules and commit deviant acts are subjected to censure and, depending on the offence, punishment. These social controls are meant to deter future offences, yet some delinquents become locked into deviant or criminal "careers." Sampson and Laub (2002) show that a process of cumulative disadvantage can cause long-term deviant behaviour. Early involvement in crime weakens social bonds to significant others and conventional institutions. For example, as insiders point out, inner-city youth are at a heightened risk of gang involvement. Scholars offering second opinions note that involvement in such gangs allows teens to develop their own subcultural rules, values and beliefs. They do this in part to overcome economic disadvantage—by stealing, for example—but also in an effort to resist middle-class norms (Dollar 2014, Ziyanak and Williams 2014). Regardless of initial motivations, criminal behaviour flourishes in communal settings where everyone holds similar, positive views of delinquency, and there are no negative perceptions to deter deviant activity (Baumer 2007).

Researchers suggest, however, that people may transition out of this criminal lifestyle after a key life event, such as marriage or entering the workforce. These events can lead to the formation of new social bonds that impose controls on behaviour and reduce the risk of further criminal activity. Existing relationships, such as those with a family member or spouse, can also help offenders leave criminal activities behind (Cid and Martí 2012).

OUTSIGHTS

Outsiders—people disadvantaged and marginalized as a result of inequalities grounded in class, race, sex, age or sexuality—are the most likely to understand the consequences of those inequalities for crimes of all types. After all, they are the most likely to be affected by those crimes, both as victims and perpetrators.

Racial Profiling

Outsiders, for example, are most likely to have experienced racial profiling: the tendency to interpret people's behaviour differently, based on their race, language or religion (Millar and Owusu-Bempah 2011). The best-known example involves the police pulling over cars driven by young black or Aboriginal men, expecting to find alcohol, drugs, weapons or other grounds for arrest (Parmar 2007). The police practice of **carding**—random street checks that result in the personal details of those who are stopped being entered into a database for future reference—has also come under scrutiny. Again, potentially biased criteria appear to determine who is selected for questioning; the fact that personal information is retained leads many to complain of privacy violations (Ross 2015).

Toronto resident Knia Singh claims he has been carded 11 times, on some occasions while driving. He says he is always stopped to undergo a "general investigation"—not for committing a specific traffic offence—and that he was not initially aware that his personal information was being entered into a database. Eventually, Singh launched a challenge against the police under the Charter of Rights and Freedoms for what he sees as racial profiling, as well as a Freedom of Information request to see what details about him have been recorded (Cole 2015). He says he assumes that police thought he was a foreigner because he's black; indeed, the Freedom of Information request revealed that the police had repeatedly recorded his birthplace as Jamaica, even though he was born in Toronto. He says of the experience: "Police seem to assume that if you're not white, you're born somewhere else, and my contact cards confirm that." Singh also says that on one occasion he tried to challenge an officer who attempted to card him. In response, the officer allegedly asked: "Would you like me to put you in handcuffs in the back of the cruiser, and we can call immigration to find out if you're here legally or not?" (Gillis 2015).

Insiders and outsiders agree that certain racial groups are over-represented in the Canadian criminal justice system, but they disagree on the reasons for this over-representation (Carrington and Fitzgerald 2011, Bracken 2008). Insiders think that racial minorities are more likely to commit crimes, and thus more likely to be caught and prosecuted (Corrado et al. 2014). From this perspective, the police are well-advised to search young black and Aboriginal men more often than young white men, since this approach will increase their chances of apprehending offenders (Thomsen 2011, Ryberg 2011).

In contrast, outsiders are more likely to see racial profiling and carding as differential, discriminatory treatment by the police and broader criminal justice system. Because police searches are discretionary, outsiders suggest, racist officers can indulge their prejudices by opting to search people of a despised ethnicity (Ilić 2013). There is some empirical evidence that confirms this assertion: racial minorities are far more likely to be stopped and searched than would be expected from prior rates of arrest and conviction (Neil and Carmichael 2015). In comparison to whites, members of certain minority groups are also more likely to be arrested and formally charged, regardless of their involvement in a crime.

Aboriginals and the Criminal Justice System

Aboriginal people in particular are disproportionately represented in the Canadian criminal justice system (Bracken 2008). Aboriginals make up only about 4.3% of the overall Canadian population, but they account for 20% of the federal and 27% of the provincial and territorial prison populations (Statistics Canada 2013, 2014). Canadian Aboriginals are imprisoned at a rate roughly ten times that of non-Aboriginal Canadians (Office of the Correctional Investigator 2013).

And things are only getting worse. Since 2000, the Aboriginal federal inmate population has grown by more than 56% (Office of the Correctional Investigator 2013). Aboriginal women now account for one-third of all federally sentenced women in Canada, and Aboriginal youths are eight times more likely to be imprisoned than white youths (Corrado et al. 2014). Young Aboriginals are also more likely to receive long sentences, regardless of their criminal history and the severity of their offense (Jeffries and Stenning 2014). In comparison to non-Aboriginal Canadians, Aboriginals are more likely to be denied bail, charged with multiple offences and spend additional time in pretrial detention (Bracken 2008).

Nonetheless, insiders continue to endorse largely stereotypical, biased explanations for the disproportionate number of criminally charged Aboriginals. Many blame fetal alcohol spectrum disorder (FASD), which results in physical and mental disabilities, internal organ problems, learning disabilities, and many other issues resulting from fetal exposure to alcohol (Bracken 2008). Children affected by FASD are at an increased risk for developing substance abuse problems of their own, performing poorly in school, and running into trouble with the law. Evidence shows an over-representation of Aboriginal people with FASD at different levels of the Canadian criminal justice system, especially in the Prairie provinces.

While FASD is a serious problem for the Aboriginal community, and no doubt plays a significant role in giving rise to behaviours that ultimately result in criminal charges, the causal chain does not stop there. FASD and other alcohol-related issues are not simply the results of individual shortcomings. Rather, they are products of a legacy of discrimination against Aboriginals dating back to colonial times (Tait 2003). Residential schools caused widespread trauma by forcibly removing Aboriginal children from their parents, tearing Aboriginal families apart (Neeganagwedgin 2014, Saunders 2015). Many children were physically and sexually abused in these schools, which operated in some regions of Canada as late as the 1990s. Those who survived suffered long-term mental health challenges, leading many to develop unhealthy coping behaviours such as alcohol abuse. Survivors of the residential school system lacked any sense of a healthy, positive childhood, rendering them unable to provide such a childhood for their own children. Their trauma has been transmitted to the next generation, who grow up in communities characterized by high rates of suicide, domestic abuse, poverty, family conflict, physical and sexual abuse, and substance use (Brazeau et al. 2013).

Many white Canadian insiders maintain negative, even racist attitudes towards Aboriginals: they consider them inferior, treat them unfairly and endorse negative stereotypes about them. Such discrimination reduces educational and occupational opportunities for First Nations peoples; as low-income earners, they are more likely to fall into survival-motivated delinquency (Jeffries and Stenning 2014, Gutierrez et al. 2013).

Other minorities are similarly over-represented in the criminal justice system (Carrington and Fitzgerald 2011). Young blacks are more likely to attract police attention than whites, and to receive harsher sentences if convicted (Wortley and Tanner 2005). The proportion of blacks in federal prisons is three times that in the Canadian population overall. Not surprisingly, black Canadians are more likely to think the country's criminal justice system is discriminatory than are whites or Asians.

A case in point: in 2015, the Durham Regional Police Service was ordered by the Ontario Human Rights Tribunal to pay Joesph Briggs $10,000 to compensate for what it deemed to be racial profiling. The 29-year-old had stopped at a fast-food restaurant. While he ate, two police officers checked his car's licence plates, believing he was a prohibited driver, and refused to allow him to leave the restaurant in his car. When Briggs came back later to retrieve the car, the officers followed him as he drove off, pulled him over, and detained him. Briggs says of the incident: "I didn't do anything. . . . Me being a black man is what made them investigate." After the human rights tribunal issued its ruling, he said: "I feel vindicated. I just hope this brings more attention to what black men go through in North America" (Taekema 2015).

The insider stereotype of young black men as would-be criminals destined to spend at least part of their life in prison (Kearney 2006) fails to take into account the mutually reinforcing nature of black unemployment, lack of education and incarceration. Once released from prison, many former convicts struggle to secure a job, as most employers conduct criminal record checks on potential hires and refuse to employ former convicts.

Nevertheless, some insiders and even scholars offering second opinions suggest these arguments are merely excuses used by outsiders to justify criminality. Some studies suggest that racial minority status and poverty do not adequately account for the higher crime rates among Aboriginal populations. Instead, these studies point to individual criminal history, an antisocial personality and ties with other delinquents as the main predictors of criminality among both Aboriginals and non-Aboriginals (Gutierrez et al. 2013). Similarly, some claim that past abuses committed by the Canadian government cannot fully account for the poor decisions and delinquent behaviours of individual Aboriginal people today (Jeffries and Stenning 2014). Others argue that First Nations people should not continue to blame historical colonialism for their plight. As a Winnipeg teacher put it in a Facebook post:

> [H]ow long are aboriginal people going to use what happened as a crutch to suck more money out of Canadians? The benefits the aboriginals enjoy from the white man/Europeans [sic] far outweigh any wrong doings that were done to a concurred [sic] people. . . . My ancestor[s] migrated here [in the] early 1900s [and] they didn't do anything. Why am I on the hook for their [i.e., Aboriginals'] cultural support? (CBC News 2014)

This issue is one on which non-Aboriginal insiders and Aboriginal outsiders are sharply divided. Academics have struggled to provide convincing evidence for one side of the debate or the other. It is difficult to collect empirical data that would allow us to demonstrate a causal link between the historical mistreatment of Aboriginal peoples and their ongoing marginalization and disadvantage today.

What we *can* prove is that besides being more likely to serve time, Aboriginals are more likely to be victims of crime (Monchalin 2010). The same structural variables that push people toward delinquency—poverty, social disorganization and poor social support—also place them at a higher risk of victimization. People who experience such disadvantages are more likely to spend time in "hot spots" where delinquency flourishes, including the socially disorganized, marginalized neighborhoods studied by Shaw and McKay.

It can also be shown that Aboriginal delinquents are treated differently by the criminal justice system than non-Aboriginals, suggesting some degree of discrimination against them. Aboriginal youths are less likely to get pre-arrest warnings from police officers than non-Aboriginals accused of similar offences—that is, they are more likely to receive "real" punishments than a slap on the wrist (Neil and Carmichael 2015). Overall, Aboriginal youth are eight times more likely than whites to be sent to prison (Corrado et al. 2014). They also receive longer sentences than average, even when individual criminal histories and the severity of the offences are taken into consideration.

The same holds true of Aboriginal adults (Neil and Carmichael 2015). Sentences for Aboriginal women in the federal prison system are on average nine times longer than those of non-Aboriginal women; Aboriginal men's sentences are more than six times longer than those of their non-Aboriginal counterparts (Owusu-Bempah et al. 2014).

Aboriginal people victimized by crime are also less likely to receive support from the criminal justice system. To cite one example, two Aboriginal sisters from Winnipeg were found dead in February 2000 (CBC 2004). They had been stabbed to death, but only after they had called 911 five times seeking help. A police car was dispatched in response to the first call, but the subsequent calls were disregarded, as the 911 operators allegedly believed the women were intoxicated (Macdonald 2015). The subsequent investigation blamed inadequate training and the challenges associated with being a 911 operator for what happened; prejudice and discrimination were not considered as explanations for the incident.

Such differential treatment suggests the criminal justice system is biased against racial minorities in general and Aboriginals in particular. Insiders may even feel threatened by progress made towards racial equality, and may try to maintain their privileged position by strengthening a criminal justice system that tends to keep large numbers of minorities behind bars. Interestingly, the staffing levels of local police departments increase in proportion to the size of minority populations in the municipality (Neil and Carmichael 2015), perhaps because of a belief that more law enforcement officials are needed to "manage" people expected to behave in a criminal fashion.

There is some evidence to suggest that the documentation practices of police officers may obscure the extent of discrimination embedded in our justice system. Police and court records may not indicate whether an offender or victim is of Aboriginal status if that information is not thought relevant to the case. Many observers assume this lack of information about the ethnicity of offenders will reduce the danger of stereotyping, prejudice and racial profiling. It may, however, be the case that non-disclosure of the race data that is available is intended to conceal the extent of racial profiling. Police may choose not to report race "because they do not see it to be in their interests" to reveal hard evidence of the practice (Millar and Owusu-Bempah 2011).

Suggestions for reducing incarceration rates among Aboriginal populations include the reconsideration of culturally insensitive laws. Some Aboriginal peoples and supporters suggest that they cannot be expected to obey laws imposed upon them long after they had already established their own way of life. Insiders rightly note flaws in this argument, particularly the practical impossibility of incorporating the cultural views of every minority group into federal law (Tomm 2013). Similarly, it does not seem feasible to exempt certain populations from obeying laws that do not correspond with their beliefs or values, as some approaches to cultural sensitivity would recommend.

The justice system has, however, overlooked opportunities to practice more cultural sensitivity in situations that do not involve these complications. For example, throughout the 2000s, the Kitchenuhmaykoosib Inninuwug (KI) First Nation of Ontario tried to prevent a mining company from drilling on what the KI considered to be their property. The judge acknowledged the KI were trying to protect their traditional land, culture and beliefs, but in the end ruled that the company was permitted to drill on the land (Tomm 2013).

The ruling directly infringed upon Treaty 9, which KI leaders had signed in 1929 to maintain their right to hunt, trap and fish on their land, and which had specifically been designed to prevent early loggers and miners from encroaching (Ariss 2009). Although Ontario's controversial Mining Act allows claims to be staked anywhere on Crown land (CBC News 2008), the Supreme Court has affirmed that the government must defer to and make an effort to accommodate First Nations peoples before acting in a way that might infringe upon their treaty rights. In the end, however, the court opted to uphold the outdated and contested Ontario Mining Act rather than a valid treaty with First Nations people. Having failed to make their case in the mainstream judicial system, the KI attempted physically to block the company from drilling. As a result, those involved in the protests received six-month-long jail sentences. The KI claimed the ruling and related punishments further weakened the Aboriginal community.

Another proposed means of combating the over-representation of Aboriginals in the criminal justice system is to enable Aboriginal communities to control their own children's education. Canadian schools have made progress in addressing Canada's history of marginalizing Aboriginals; Canada's Truth and Reconciliation Commission, which included Aboriginal and non-Aboriginal leaders and released its final report on residential schooling in June 2015 (Tremonti 2015), recommends that all children in kindergarten through grade 12 be taught about residential schools. Some Aboriginal activists want their communities to set up independent child welfare systems and implement community and school programs that educate young people about First Nations' cultures and languages (Neeganagwedgin 2014).

Prison Conditions

No matter their offence, all prisoners are entitled to adequate food and shelter while incarcerated. Outsiders' complaints that these human needs are not being met have recently caught the attention of the mass media.

Although it endorsed a tough-on-crime stance that would have presumably entailed increased spending on the prison system, the Conservative government led by Stephen Harper also cut the correctional system's budget as part of an overall deficit-reduction program (Paperny 2012). Spending on food services was slashed and a cost-saving "cook-chill" program was implemented, in which food is prepared, cooked and chilled at a central kitchen before being delivered to penitentiaries for storage until it is eventually served. Defending these new practices, a spokesman for the public safety minister declared that prisons "are meant to correct criminal behaviour, not serve as a vacation home" (Clancy 2015). Such views are not uncommon among the general public, many of whom similarly think of jails as "country clubs" for pampered criminals (Goar 2013).

Jean-Paul Aubee is an inmate at the medium-security Mission Institution in British Columbia who has already served 14 years of a life sentence for murder (Clancy 2015). He speaks from personal experience in describing the problems caused by the new food-service system. "I shake a lot because of malnutrition," he says. "The food is causing people to experience diarrhea, nausea, vomiting. I have experienced this myself many times." The Mission Institution is one of four prisons whose full kitchens were closed as cost-saving measures; prisoners' meals are now delivered using the cook-chill program. When the carts that are supposed to heat the food do not work or are not properly sterilized, inmates reportedly fall ill because of food-borne illnesses. Others claim the kitchen runs out of food before everyone has had a chance to eat. "That is extra protein," another inmate was told after discovering worms in his food. "Just move it out. It's fine." In a complaint the inmate subsequently filed, he argued that "to continue this deplorable cycle is refusing to provide the necessities of life."

Other cost-saving measures include refusing to bring night trays to prisoners, as they are costly to deliver and not required under prison policy (Clancy 2015). Sometimes, however, this means prisoners go without food for more than 20 hours, as when the prison is on lockdown. Diabetic prisoners are denied food between supper and the next day's breakfast because of the new policy.

Although many insiders privileged enough to never come into personal contact with the criminal justice system believe that harsh sentencing effectively deters and punishes crime, the reality is that incarceration is costly. It costs more than $100,000 to imprison one adult for a single year (The John Howard Society of Ontario). The salaries of prison guards and administrative costs account for the bulk of expenditures, with food and shelter making up a relatively small fraction of the budget. When two of Aubee's fellow inmates filed complaints regarding the quality of food, they said prison officials responded by telling them that food costs were capped at $4.91 per inmate per day (Clancy 2015). Trying to slash these already low costs even further will not make much difference in the federal prison budget, but it may very well compromise prisoners' health.

FINAL THOUGHTS

One of the biggest problems caused by crime is that it justifies—some would say *demands*—punishment. Fear of crime tends to incite moral panics and, in turn, calls for harsher sentencing, increased police funding and the building of more prisons. This system, built at least in part on fear and stereotypes, then segregates and punishes people differently, according to class and race. Existing class and racial conflict grounded in an "us vs. them" mentality is exacerbated.

The most common form of punishment for serious offenders is imprisonment. The damaging experiences prisoners endure leave them less able to deal with life on the outside after they are released. Another consequence of imprisonment is that inmates learn the prison subculture, especially its anti-administration values and codes of conduct. Through contact with more experienced inmates, prisoners gain new criminal skills, often learning to behave in even more undesirable and violent ways. **Prisonization**, as Donald Clemmer calls this process, produces prisoners who have been effectively socialized into prison life—people who fit perfectly into the inmate society but cannot function outside it. As their release dates approach, inmates often feel great stress. Once released, many commit new crimes—sometimes even more violent crimes—and are returned to prison in a process known as recidivism. The extent of recidivism is difficult to measure, but studies consistently find large numbers of offenders returning to the criminal justice system—some over and over again.

Recidivism may also be a product of the reduced life chances of inmates after release. The stigma of a criminal conviction, diminished human capital because of absence from the workforce and weakened social connections all limit the employment opportunities open to ex-prisoners. Jobs requiring high levels of trust, skills or credentials are largely out of reach. Former inmates are channeled into the secondary labour market where employment is precarious and there are few prospects for mobility. In this way, the penal system reinforces social disadvantage.

What is it that we hope to accomplish through the criminal justice system? The system has not been effective in teaching people the error of their ways so that they may return to "normal" life in their communities. We seem more invested in a retributive approach to justice: criminals who have brought suffering upon others should themselves suffer in turn.

This punitive approach is exceptionally costly. In the 2010–11 fiscal year, the adult correctional system cost more than $4 billion to operate, excluding the capital costs of building new facilities (Statistics Canada 2013). Incarceration also places financial strain on prisoners' families. Most prisoners are unable to pay child and family support while incarcerated. This leaves their families dependent on welfare, leading to a new generation of children raised by low-income single parents. In turn, these youth are more likely to slip into criminal careers, lacking alternative means by which to improve their circumstances, and so the cycle continues.

In the absence of a viable alternative to incarceration, we should aim to reduce crime itself. As we have seen throughout this chapter, unequal societies are breeding grounds for crime. By reducing inequalities of all types, we would be diminishing one (of many) motivating factors that currently push people towards deviant behaviour.

DISCUSSION QUESTIONS

1. Are random checks and carding useful law enforcement practices? Should people be expected to submit to these inquiries willingly, in order to defend public safety?

2. Should we care about poor prison conditions, given that one of the aims of incarceration is to make criminals suffer in retribution for the suffering they have caused others? What about inmates who have been convicted of "victimless crimes," such as marijuana possession, but who are sentenced to endure these substandard conditions all the same?

3. How might the media change the way they portray crime in order to more accurately represent the types of crime and criminals in our society?

4. What are some of the ways in which the police and other law enforcement officials perpetuate stereotypes about criminals? How do other law enforcement officials challenge those stereotypes?

FURTHER READING

Sasha Abramsky. *American Furies: Crime, Punishment, and Vengeance in the Age of Mass Imprisonment*. Beacon Press, 2008.

Chester L. Britt and Michael R. Gottfredson, eds. *Control Theories of Crime and Delinquency*. Transaction, 2003.

John Hagan and Bill McCarthy. *Mean Streets: Youth Crime and Homelessness*. Cambridge University Press, 1998.

Thomas Grisso. *Double Jeopardy: Adolescent Offenders with Mental Disorders*. University of Chicago Press, 2004.

KEY TERMS

Anomie. Absence, breakdown, confusion, or conflict in the norms of a society.

Carding. Controversial random street checks that result in the personal details of those who are stopped being entered into a database for future reference.

Differential association theory. Theory developed by Edwin Sutherland positing that crime is a learned phenomenon rather than a biological predisposition.

Femicide. Form of sex-based hate crime. Most commonly, the killing of women by men.

Gentrification. Upgrading of decaying, usually inner-city neighbourhoods, involving physical renovation of housing stock, displacement of low-status occupants by higher-income groups, and often change in property type from rental to ownership.

Moral entrepreneurs. Those who stand to gain from a moral panic, and therefore help define an issue as a social problem.

Moral panic. Any popular controversy or dispute that provokes feelings and fears so intense that they threaten the social order; occurs when a "condition, episode, person or group of persons emerges to become defined as a threat to societal values and interests" (Cohen 1972).

Racial profiling. Tendency to interpret people's behaviour differently, based on their race, language, or religion.

Recidivism. Committing a crime on more than one occasion; reoffending.

Social control. Social processes by which behaviour of individuals or groups is regulated; mechanisms for ensuring conformity to social norms, and for dealing with deviance from those norms.

Social disorganization. Breakdown of social institutions, frequently associated with poverty. First explored by urban sociologists of the Chicago school, especially Clifford Shaw and Henry McKay, who analyzed it by correlating rates of truancy, tuberculosis, infant mortality, mental disorders, adult crime, and juvenile delinquency in the poorest areas of the city.

Strain theory. Posits that deviance occurs when individuals or groups are conditioned to desire and pursue certain ends, but lack access to culturally acceptable means to attain those ends. Alternative, even criminal action may be taken to reach socially acceptable goals.

Subculture. Group that is distinct from the larger culture but borrows (and often distorts, exaggerates, or inverts) its symbols, values, and beliefs.

White collar crime. Term introduced by Edwin Sutherland to draw attention to the illegalities and misdeeds of 'captains of industry' and other middle-class members of the business world.

CHAPTER NINE

Consequences of Inequality for Conflict

INTRODUCTION

On November 13, 2015, three coordinated teams of gunmen and suicide bombers staged a series of attacks in Paris. A concert venue, major sports stadium and several bars and restaurants came under fire, leaving 130 people dead and 368 injured, many seriously in the deadliest attacks in France since the Second World War. **ISIS** (Islamic State in Iraq and Syria), a radical Islamist militant group, claimed responsibility.

In the wake of the attacks, anti-Muslim acts were reported across Canada and the U.S. as well as in Europe. Mosques were defaced and set afire, Muslims were threatened upon leaving their places of worship, and Muslim women wearing hijabs were subjected to verbal and physical abuse. In December 2015, Republican presidential candidate Donald Trump called for all Muslims to be banned from entering the United States, whether as immigrants or tourists.

Terrorism is, at least in part, both a cause and consequence of inequality. Few would deny that terrorists act out of frustration and rage. Feeling they lack other means to protest their disadvantaged status, terrorists resort to murder. But in addition to being one of the most devastating consequences of inequality, terrorism also exacerbates existing racial, ethnic and religious tensions. It intensifies feelings of fear and hatred between "us" and "them," evidenced in the **Islamophobia** that has intensified across the West since the November attacks.

Mainstream, insider responses to terrorism can have troubling implications, too. Canadians and Americans were made instantly aware of the Paris attacks. Updates on the attackers' whereabouts, the death count, the sites under attack, the measures that were being taken to rescue hostages, and endless other details were broadcast as they happened. Facebook turned on its "Safety Check" feature, allowing 4.1 million people to confirm to friends and relatives they were safe from harm. There was an instant outpouring of sympathy, support and solidarity for victims and their families. Thousands of North Americans posted photographs of Parisian landmarks with the hashtag "#prayforparis," and filtered the French flag over their Facebook profile pictures.

One day earlier, a double suicide bombing in Beirut, Lebanon that killed 43 civilians failed to elicit a similar outpouring of sympathy, despite being covered by major news organizations. There was no Facebook safety check and Instagram wasn't flooded with tourists' photos of Beirut. "When my people died, no country bothered to light up its landmarks in the colors of their flag," blogged one Lebanese doctor (Bernard, 2015). To be sure, there are numerous reasons for the disparate reactions. There were fewer casualties in Beirut; Paris is a tourism magnet familiar to millions of North Americans firsthand; and North American television networks maintain heavily staffed bureaus in London, making coverage of the Paris attacks relatively straightforward.

But these factors alone do not account for the greater intensity of North Americans' reactions to the Paris attacks. In 2014, the ongoing conflict in the Gaza Strip left 2,314 Palestinians dead (about two-thirds of them civilians, according to the UN) and 17,125 severely injured; again, despite significant amounts of coverage by Western news organizations—the conflict was the lead story on the *CBS Evening News* for several nights in July 2014—the Western public was largely apathetic.

Outpourings of sympathy from North Americans don't do much to help people at the centre of violent conflicts, but they do speak volumes about dominant Western views on such conflicts. Our reactions indicate who we think deserves sympathy and who doesn't; where conflict is considered a normal part of life and where such events seem shocking and horrifying; and how we characterize some perpetrators as inhumane, savage murderers and others as "freedom fighters." North Americans (and Westerners in general) usually stand in solidarity with people we view as being most "like us," while we paying far less attention to the suffering of people who we see as fundamentally different from ourselves.

So, inequality causes conflict, but also conditions responses to it. In this chapter, we frame war as a social problem that has harmful consequences for everyone. But unless we change the way we view and react to war, we risk allowing such conflicts to continue.

INSIDER VIEWS

Causes of Conflict

Insiders—people who suffer from few if any significant social disadvantages— are likely to ignore or deny links between inequality and conflict. In this case, insiders include those who believe themselves safe from war: North Americans who are free to imagine that large-scale violence is a common occurrence in distant, underdeveloped nations, but rarely plagues their own communities. As well, there is disproportionate hysteria about the likelihood of attacks to the homeland.

What factors do insiders cite as causes of conflict? Some endorse the theories of evolutionary biologists. This line of thought frames aggression as an innate aspect of human nature, inherited not only from our human ancestors but a characteristic of many animal species, borne of a world where only the strongest, fastest and smartest organisms secure access to limited resources such as food and shelter. According to evolutionary biologists, conflicts that arise today are sparked by similar factors, and especially by conflicts over limited or unevenly distributed resources (Navarrete et al. 2012).

A second insider perspective on war is grounded in psychoanalysis. Freudian analyses suggest that humans are inherently violent: they harbour innate drives, including cruelty, aggression and selfishness, that education and socialization struggle to constrain in modern, "civilized" society (Sampson 2005). Wars, according to psychoanalysts, are the expression of these internal drives on a large scale (Parens 2013, Meloy 2012).

Third, historical analyses stress the capacity of charismatic, assertive leaders to initiate conflict. Adolf Hitler is undoubtedly the most often cited example. After losing World War I, Germany fell into economic and social disarray. Recovery was barely underway when the 1929 crash of the New York stock market threw the world economy into depression, causing massive unemployment throughout Europe, including Germany. Hitler seized on the climate of fear, blaming Jews and other minorities for the problems plaguing Germany, and using his skills as an orator and propagandist to support his claims. Hitler's claims that he could solve the country's economic and social problems and restore Germany to a place of primacy in world affairs brought him to power, beginning a series of events that would lead to the outbreak of the Second World War, the most destructive conflict in all of human history (Schwabe 2014).

Fourth, some political scientists emphasize the decision-making that unfolds prior to violent conflicts as an explanation for war. Cost-benefit calculations take into account the potential status and power gained from victory against the potential loss in the event of defeat (Dafoe et al. 2014). It has been suggested that such calculations—mistaken, as history would show—led Germany and the Austro-Hungarian Empire to take actions that precipitated the First World War in August 1914.

Fifth, **Malthusian theories** hold that population growth will always outstrip the limited supply of natural resources. By Malthusian theories, we mean those that highlight social problems arising from a growing excess of population in relation to food and other resources. Competition for food, water, and other increasingly scarce necessities lead to violent conflict (Felix and Okumoko 2014). Indeed, many leaders wage war in foreign nations in pursuit of resources they no longer have (Reuveny and Barbieri 2014).

Marxist theorists also focus on the role played by resources, but suggest that conflict arises when powerful groups struggle to establish a monopoly over them. The resources in play include not only basic necessities like water but underpinnings of modern industrial economies, such as oil, and luxury items like diamonds and gold. Still, the mere presence of valuable resources is not enough to trigger violence: were that the case, Alberta would be rife with civil conflict. Struggles over natural resources arise in areas where the state's law-enforcement capabilities are limited (Koubi et al. 2014).

Canada is a modern nation-state with the means (acting alone or in conjunction with its allies) to protect its resources from external powers and internal threats; indeed, Canada partners with other nations to develop its natural resources. Other countries, including many in Africa, have not been so lucky. The likelihood of such countries falling into civil war, with one side or the other being supported by foreign interests, has risen dramatically since the 1970s (Ross 2006). Armed rebel groups derive considerable income from natural resources that come under their control (Le Billon 2001); for instance, ISIS earns hundreds of millions of dollars from black-market oil exports from the territories it controls. As a result, regions where valuable resources are abundant tend to experience longer civil wars.

Finally, extensive evidence shows that young people—especially young men—are especially likely to initiate or engage in violence (Nordås and Christian Davenport 2013). The **youth bulge theory** suggests that conflict is likely to arise when large cohorts of young people are unable to find jobs (Bricker and Foley 2013). Many developing countries with relatively young populations face this challenge, but growing levels of youth unemployment and precarious employment in North America and Europe are of concern as well.

As you can see, there is no shortage of theories to account for conflict. Many incorporate the issue of inequality in one way or another—for example, unequal access to limited resources. Indeed, researchers have gathered statistical and ethnographic data that makes the connection between inequality and conflict impossible to overlook.

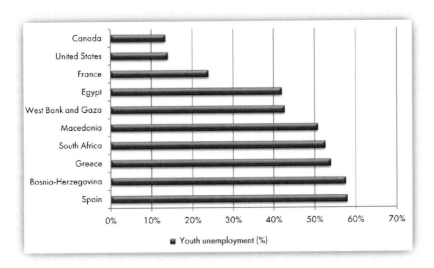

Figure 9.1: Youth Unemployment in Selected Countries, 2014
% OF TOTAL LABOUR FORCE, AGES 15 TO 24

SECOND OPINIONS

Scholars offering second opinions have attempted to show with greater precision how inequality produces violence and conflict. They also stress the wide range of negative consequences associated with war. Foremost among these negative consequences is, of course, the large number of casualties caused by violent conflict.

Although more than 70 years have passed since the end of World War II, that period has scarcely been free from armed conflict: more than 160 wars have occurred since 1945, killing more than 24 million people. Civilian casualties have greatly increased, now accounting for 90% of war-related deaths (Pedersen 2002). And war continues to plague survivors long after the actual fighting has ended. Physical injuries require ongoing treatment and rehabilitation; families are torn apart; and mental health issues such as post-traumatic stress disorder, anxiety, depression and substance abuse haunt survivors, soldiers and civilians alike (Joly 2015, Wheaton et al. 2015). A study of 1,000 Iraqi children who had been exposed to conflict found that 92% of them suffered from developmental delays stemming mainly from insecurity and fear (Salvage 2007).

Another study found that migrants who left their home countries during wartime and fled to Canada were more likely to suffer from depression, anxiety and chronic stress than Canadian-born citizens and migrants not exposed to conflict (Joli and Joly 2015, Wheaton 2015). Finally, a survey of Canadian veterans found that 42.5% had been diagnosed with PTSD, and a further 48.4% with a mood disorder (Pittman et al. 2012).

The most disadvantaged communities and nations feel the negative effects of conflict most acutely. These regions are disproportionately likely to become involved in armed conflict in the first place, and their citizens are the most likely to become refugees, seeking asylum in other, safer places (Pedersen 2002). Making matters worse, poorer countries are often poorly equipped to manage the negative health effects of war. In countries where a large gap exists between rich and poor, private health care services catering to elites garner most of the available resources, and the rest of the population enjoys only limited access to health care—a pressing problem in the aftermath of violent conflict (Ghobarah et al. 2004).

Gender inequality can limit women's access to health care during and after periods of conflict. For example, in Afghanistan under the Taliban, female health care providers were sometimes barred from practice though custom stipulated that women be treated only by other women. This posed a particular problem for women who had become pregnant: only 10% of deliveries during this period were overseen by competent health care practitioners (Salvage 2007).

Women and children are also disproportionately susceptible to malnutrition during wartime. In many countries, cultural customs hold that men are to eat first, while women and children are expected to make do on whatever is left. Women and children are also at a high risk of malnutrition because they constitute 80% of all refugees and internally displaced persons. Within refugee camps, poor sanitation and inadequate water supplies foster the spread of diseases such as cholera, tuberculosis and even the plague (Jansen 2006).

The Revolutionary Impulse

As noted above, many scholars offering second opinions have analyzed the mechanisms by which inequality causes conflict (Dutta et al. 2014). Karl Marx was among the first to propose that class inequalities could spark violent conflict, as the exploited working classes rose up against the owners of the means of production. The link between inequality and violence would seem straightforward: extreme inequality frustrates the disadvantaged, who turn to violence to try to improve their lot (Bartusevicius et al. 2014).

In an effort to test this theory, economist Robert Macculloch (2005) asked 250,000 randomly sampled people in 12 different countries about their desire for revolution. In countries where inequality was acute and net incomes were low, more people favoured revolution. The unemployed voiced the greatest support, even after controlling for personal variables such as sex. On the other hand, members of the highest income quartile were least likely to support a revolt. Other studies confirm that economic inequality tends to spark unrest (Deiwiks et al. 2012, Flores 2014), including the World Values Survey, which canvassed 130,278 people across 61 countries. It was also found that measures that improved an individual's personal circumstances even slightly reduced his or her support for revolution.

Macculloch and other scholars have struggled, however, to show that a stated desire for revolt will actually translate into violent action, even under the worst possible conditions (Cramer 2003, Esteban and Ray 2011). In many countries, action against an oppressive regime is not feasible, and failed attempts at revolt may even result in a crackdown and greater oppression (Deutsch 2006). More often, frustration caused by social inequality manifests itself in other forms. Among men, it often surfaces as aggression against wives and children; and in women and children, frustration may result in psychosomatic illnesses and even suicide (Prilleltensky 2003).

People violently resist oppression only under certain circumstances. They are unlikely to rise up violently against authority if they have been taught throughout their lives that their actions will fail to alter their circumstances. People must think they have at least some chance of winning before waging war (Besancon 2005). Second, when people have few opportunities or resources to draw upon, revolutions are also unlikely regardless of the level of oppression. When people have higher expectations and can draw on greater resources, uprisings are much more likely, even if the injustices are less extreme. Violent resistance to unfair and oppressive conditions is, in the end, highly dependent on a population's opportunities, resources and expectations (Staniland 2012, Bartusevičius 2014).

Several conclusions can be drawn from all of this. First, rebellion is most likely to occur when outsiders have risen above abject poverty, but remain substantially disadvantaged in comparison to insiders (Staniland 2012). At this stage, outsiders have both the resources needed to rebel, and the motivation to do so. This suggests that it is **relative poverty,** not **absolute poverty** that motivates many instances of violent resistance (Østby 2008). In a study of 77 popular rebellions, Bartusevičius (2014) found relative income and education levels to be better predictors of conflict than absolute income levels. Even in societies that are prosperous overall, perceptions of injustice and unfair treatment can propel the relatively disadvantaged towards rebellion.

Second, rebellion may be driven by expectations that are rising faster than change is in fact occurring (Cramer 2003). Outsiders often want immediate change: they want to see their demands met in the course of their own lifetimes. But actual rates of social change are typically slow, which may result in feelings of disappointment and frustration among outsiders, leading them to rebel (Deiwiks et al. 2002).

Expectations are less likely to be met in some societies than in others. Where people have no legal or legitimate opportunities to voice their grievances, they may express their frustrations through violent uprisings, including terrorist attacks (Mousseau 2002). Targets may include wealthy citizens of the country itself, who they see as responsible for their disadvantage, or people in more privileged nations because they feel their government has failed to protect their interests. Of course, terrorism is also motivated by other factors, such as religious fundamentalism or hatred towards a particular group or nation. Economic inequality can, however, exacerbate these factors (Bloomberg et al. 2008). Where inequality is high, both outsiders and insiders alike are motivated to engage in conflict, the former to improve their status, the latter to maintain their dominance (Dutta et al. 2014).

In contrast, a population's "taste for revolt" may be restrained by a government's ability to respond to demands for change (Besancon 2005). Governments who wish to control people's revolutionary urges must avoid disproportionately violent responses (Deutsch, 2006). Excessively severe punishments may even encourage rebellions, providing rebels with compelling evidence of the government's misdeeds and making it easier for them to recruit new members to the cause.

Finally, governments may try to strengthen feelings of nationalism to quell rebellious impulses. They may invest in spectacular celebrations of national holidays, demand that high points in the nation's history be stressed in school curricula, erect imposing monuments, and rename buildings and streets after national heroes and symbols (Solt 2011). When feelings of nationalism are strong, people are less likely to question the status quo, instead feeling a sense of unity and solidarity with their leaders and fellow citizens (Hayes 1926).

Nationalism also assuages concerns about economic inequality. It uses a shared national identity to veil the extent of inequality among citizens. In turn, citizens view each other as equal members of one community, even though in economic terms they are unequal (Solt 2011). Second, nationalist policies portray inequality-related social problems, such as unemployment, poverty and unequal access to education, as special-interest issues that pertain only to a small segment of the population.

Studies show that as income inequality increases, nationalist sentiments also increase, suggesting that many governments use nationalism to their advantage, to gloss over inequalities. When income inequality is at its lowest, the chances that a citizen will be "very proud" of his or her nation are about 47% (Solt 2011). But when inequality is at its highest, this figure rises to 83%.

Inequality can, and often does, spark a desire for revolt. But this desire does not always translate into action. Only in certain circumstances will violence erupt. More often, insiders use nationalist sentiments to conceal inequalities that would otherwise enrage outsiders and make them demand change.

Horizontal Inequalities

So far, we have focused on how economic or class-related inequalities—so-called vertical inequalities—produce conflict. Researchers have also considered **horizontal (ethnic-, regional- or religious-based) inequalities**—that is, inequities between culturally defined groups who engage in so-called "identity wars" (Dutta et al. 2014, Stewart 2009).

Horizontal inequalities occur when power and resources are unequally distributed between groups differentiated by race, ethnicity, religion, sex, gender, sexuality, age and so on (Annan 1999, Østby 2008). In different societies, some identity categories may be more relevant than others. Religion may be considered an important aspect of personal identity in one society but not in another (Stewart 2009). Where religion is an important element of identity, people who belong to the dominant religion enjoy social acceptance while those who identify as members of alternative religions may be discriminated against and disadvantaged (Stewart 2014). But if religion is seen as unimportant to people's identities, the same inequalities do not emerge.

Race, ethnicity and religion are the horizontal inequalities that preoccupy most scholars offering second opinions. Ethnic minorities are often subject to economic, political and social discrimination. Many suffer poorer life chances, reduced political power and social marginalization (Gurr 2000, Cederman et al. 2011). Just as the poor are motivated to protest economic disadvantage, so too are ethnic minorities motivated to protest their discriminatory treatment.

Ethnic grievances may prove even more potent motivators than class-based ones, for several reasons. First, minorities are more likely to strongly identify as members of a racial or ethnic group than the poor are to identify as members of the working class (Stewart 2009). Second, members of certain ethnic, racial and religious groups are likely to share similar class backgrounds. This further encourages feelings of solidarity (Esteban and Ray 2011). The result is often **polarization**, where clusters of people sharing similar attributes come to identify strongly with one another, to the exclusion and alienation of others (Motiram and Sarma 2014). The more different that members of each cluster are (or *perceive* each other to be), the stronger will be the feeling of alienation and the greater the degree of polarization (Bhavnani and Miodwnik 2009).

Third, the racial differences underlying horizontal inequalities can become more intractable than the income differences behind vertical inequality (Gubler and Selway 2012). There is at least some evidence that in parts of pre-colonial Africa, racial and tribal variations were not enormously important until Europeans arrived and made them important, partly as a means to divide and conquer.

Although you cannot change your race, you can change your income status (difficult though it may be). Recall that insiders believe hard work and dedication can help people rise from a low- to a high-class status. Many outsiders have also adopted this view, as it allows them to maintain hope for a better future. In contrast, racial discrimination may seem impossible to overcome: because they cannot change the colour of their skin (although, of course, cultural constructions of what skin colour means are open to change), people who feel disadvantaged because of their race may feel they will always face discrimination.

When people feel they cannot overcome structural barriers through legitimate means, they are more likely to turn to illegitimate, potentially violent ones. Such violence is particularly likely to erupt in highly polarized societies, since members of an isolated and discriminated-against ethnic group identify so strongly with each other: they possess the unity, cohesion and group organization needed to mobilize (Østby 2008, Cederman et al. 2011). A "taste for revolt" grounded in racial or ethnic grievances is more likely to erupt into actual violence than discontent grounded in class inequalities alone. Indeed, ethnic grievances have caused the most civil wars since 1945 (Gubler 2012).

Surprisingly, in societies where racial or ethnic inequality is extreme, conflict is more likely to arise when economic conditions are more *equal* (Besancon 2005). This is because, under such circumstances, racial and ethnic minorities have access to the economic resources needed to wage war. Also, in more equal societies, minorities are better able to assert that their disadvantages are a result of their race or ethnicity, rather than their class. Studies show that when governments make an effort to accommodate the demands of racial and ethnic minority groups, the incidence of violence decreases.

Racial, ethnic and religious minorities are also at greater risk of being violently targeted by dominant groups seeking to perpetuate their power and privilege. **Genocides,** in which a racial, ethnic or religious group is deliberately destroyed, are the most brutal consequences of horizontal inequalities (Stewart 2014). The United Nations deems five genocidal acts to be international crimes: killing members of a racial, ethnic or religious group; causing serious bodily or mental harm to members of the group; imposing conditions on the group calculated to destroy it; preventing births within the group; and forcibly transferring children from the group to another (Schabas 2011).

The first step toward genocide occurs when the dominant group forcibly imposes polarization (or isolation) on a minority group. Racial or ethnic minorities are othered, classified as a "them" pitted against the dominant majority, or "us." This othering typically involves segregating the target population geographically, politically and socially, so that they are made to seem as different from the majority as possible (Levy 2006). This segregation is intended to make the minority group seem less than human and legitimize attacks upon it.

Not all racially, ethnically and religiously diverse societies engage in violent conflict (Lipset and Rokkan 1967). Academics offering second opinions account for this fact with **cross-cuttingness** theory, which explains how two cleavages, or social divisions, relate to and sometimes intensify each other (Simmel 1955, Selway 2010). These cleavages can be between individuals, groups or organizations, and are typically based on different ethnic, religious or economic characteristics (Taylor and Rae 1970).

A society in which each ethnic group belongs to its own unique religion does not have any cross-cuttingness. In this society, the social cleavages between each ethnic group are reinforced along religious lines. Conversely, in a society with perfect cross-cuttingness, there is *no* link between individuals' memberships in various groups: citizens "cross over," and belong to more than one group. In such a society, for instance, knowing what racial group a woman belongs to would tell us nothing about her religious affiliation.

Cross-cuttingness reduces the likelihood of conflict in several ways. First, it diminishes the strength of people's ties to any one group (Lipset 1960, Bormann 2015). Instead, people spread their sense of commitment across a variety of groups that compete for their loyalties (Blau 1977, Selway 2010). Second, cross-cuttingness reduces in-group communication and facilitates communication with members of other groups. This "external" communication can weaken the influence that rebel leaders have in appealing solely to ethnic ties, since members of a variety of groups can see that they have things in common with people in the other groups to which they are loyal. Communication with members of these other groups can also expose people to alternate views and perspectives, making them less likely to "other" these different groups (Selway 2011). Thus, cross-cuttingness encourages members of different groups to trust each other more (Fineraas and Jakobsson 2012).

When ethno-linguistic identity is crosscut by additional social cleavages such as religion, socioeconomic class, and geographic region, the likelihood of a rebellion drops. Specifically, Gubler and Selway (2012) investigated cross-national data from over 100 countries and found that when ethnicity is crosscut by socioeconomic status, geographic region, and religion, civil war is only one-twelfth as likely.

Lack of cross-cutting can divide a society and promote conflict (Gusfield

1962, Raleigh 2014). When several social differences overlap and reinforce each other, it becomes easier for rebel leaders to spur these groups into violent action. Few members have cross-cutting loyalties to other groups, making them feel more unified with and committed to their own group, as well as less hesitant to rise up against other groups. For instance, an ethnic group that practices a different religion than most others, is significantly poorer, and is geographically isolated will be easier to unify and mobilize both physically and psychologically (Gubler and Selway 2012).

Philanthropy and Humanitarian Aid

Scholars offering second opinions have faced many complexities in trying to prove that inequality and conflict are connected. Nevertheless, they have successfully shown that disparities in wealth have caused at least some wars, past and present. Accordingly, they have concluded that redistributing wealth will encourage peace. To date, however, there have been no efforts made to reduce global economic inequality, for various reasons.

First and foremost, it is unlikely that people in prosperous nations will readily agree to lower their standards of living to benefit less wealthy societies. While many North Americans are willing to donate small sums of money to select projects in the developing world on occasion, only a very few would be willing to substantially reduce their own comfort and privilege to establish a more equal distribution of wealth worldwide. In this sense, the Global North is home to many "insiders" on an international scale, whereas the Global South is home to many of the world's most disadvantaged "outsiders."

Second, even if North Americans were willing to make such sacrifices, redistributing wealth from rich to poor nations would not guarantee an increased standard of living in those poor nations. Detailed rules must be implemented and carefully enforced to ensure that citizens benefit from foreign aid (Hudson 2004). Otherwise, politicians and state elites may appropriate the funds to further their own interests at the expense of their citizens (Sachs 2006).

Third, much of what is said to be foreign aid is in fact support of client states and close allies, and is often directed towards military spending (LeRiche 2004). For example, the biggest single recipient of U.S. foreign aid is Israel, whose GDP per capita is about the same as Japan's. While there may be good reasons to support Israel, reducing global inequality is not one of them.

For these and many other reasons, no efforts have been made to establish a more equal distribution of wealth across the world. Instead, various charities and humanitarian organizations have been established, and military interventions staged, in efforts to quell conflict or alleviate the suffering of civilians living in war zones. However, academics offering second opinions have shown that these well-intentioned efforts do not always succeed in establishing peace or reducing suffering (Baines and Paddon 2012).

Consider the 1994 Rwandan civil war. Despite the presence of United Nations peacekeeping forces, 800,000 Tutsis—a Rwandan ethnic group—were slaughtered en masse by the Hutus, another local ethnic group. As the violence escalated, U.N. officials declined to send more troops, and eventually withdrew Belgian forces (Dallaire 2003). The Rwandan government and some Western journalists even accused the United Nations' aid contractors and its High Commissioner for Refugees of aiding Hutu war criminals (Narang 2015).

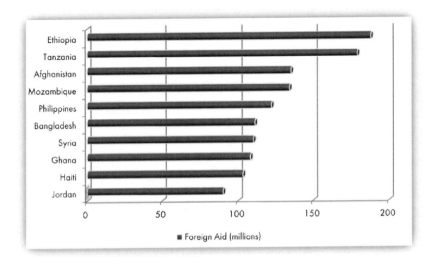

Figure 9.2: Canadian Foreign Aid, 2012 (millions of dollars)

These accusations highlight the many subtle ways in which foreign interventions can inadvertently prolong conflict (Nunn and Qian 2014). Scholars offering second opinions refer to this effect as **the paradox of humanitarian action:** efforts genuinely intended to ease suffering can actually extend it. Foreign economic aid, supplies, medical assistance, and so on make war less costly to the combatants. By providing needed material resources to one or both sides, such aid can allow wars to drag on longer than they otherwise would (Humphreys 2005, Boutton 2014).

In the former Yugoslavia, for example, over half of the donated resources meant to alleviate civilian suffering were instead redirected to feed and supply soldiers. In other instances, local rebels have stolen aid donations meant for civilians (Nunn and Qian 2014). In Somalia, bandits would steal food and then protect themselves from allegations of theft by forcing villagers to attest they had received their share of food aid. Some estimate that as much as 80% of food aid was looted or stolen during this conflict alone (Keating 2012).

Similarly, in the case of civil wars, humanitarian aid organizations will often side with the state, and provide food, shelter, water and medical supplies to citizens who are not rebelling. However, non-uniformed insurgents typically intermingle with citizens in such conflicts, making it impossible for relief workers to avoid providing rebels with resources. This is what happened during the Rwandan civil war, after which aid organizations discovered that Hutu forces had made use of supplies donated to relief and refugee camps (Keating 2012).

As part of their work, aid organizations establish protected areas, including refugee camps, where combatants and citizens can receive medical assistance and recuperate without the threat of attack. However, these spaces are often abused, providing uninjured combatants with the opportunity to recruit, regroup, strategize and launch new attacks while enjoying protection from their opponents (Humphreys 2005, LeRiche 2004). Conflict analysts have proposed that such humanitarian safe zones protected Bosnian troops in this fashion, inadvertently extending the duration of the Bosnian war.

Empirical tests of these theories have been carried out. In a statistical analysis of civil wars since 1945, Narang (2015) found that civil wars where more aid was distributed lasted longer on average than those where there was little or no aid. In an examination of conflict in developing countries between 1972 and 2006, Nunn and Qian (2014) found that food aid both promotes the incidence of and sustains armed civil conflict in the recipient nation.

Evidence also suggests that foreign aid can increase income inequality, likely because dominant groups appropriate most of the resources for themselves. Van Rensselaer et al. (2005) found that as a given nation receives more aid, its income inequality grows proportionately.

This is not to say that foreign aid is always bad. Even if it causes a war to last longer than it otherwise would have, the aid may save many civilian lives (Hultman et al. 2013). All too often, however, foreign aid is deployed ineffectively. Facing tight timelines, philanthropic organizations rush into conflict zones without considering how or why previous interventions failed. They are, of course, rightly desperate to put an end to suffering as quickly as possible. These organizations are also competing against hundreds of other charities to secure donations, and are helping the suffering, to assure people that they are most deserving of funds.

Most global insiders (i.e., privileged members of the Global North) view philanthropy as an unalloyed good. But such interventions are not foolproof solutions to conflict and suffering, and sometimes even increase inequality. Some scholars offering second opinions argue that humanitarian aid has another, less obvious purpose: to establish the reputation of intervening countries as peacekeepers.

This argument follows from the lack of concern most insiders have for the ways in which their donations are used (Keating 2012). Once they've given money, many insiders forget about the conflict. Charities are well aware of people's short attention spans, and therefore implore would-be donors to take immediate action. Analyzing these calls to action, Thomas Keenan argues that the compulsion to act arises not purely from a desire to help, but instead, from a desire to avoid *criticism* "for 'doing nothing'" and engaging in "an inaction bordering on voyeurism" (Keenan 2000). Humanitarianism thus tends to idealize "acting" in and of itself; doing *something* must be better than idly standing by and "allowing" people to suffer.

And yet, the ways in which the general public is called to action can be more harmful than productive. First, they may reinforce the power imbalances that generate the "need" for these campaigns in the first place, reproducing inequalities between the privileged Global North and the disadvantaged South. Philanthropic campaigns play off stereotypical understandings of aid, with a prosperous citizen of the First World benevolently helping an impoverished Third World resident (Dragotesc 2011). Keenan argues such an exchange is not grounded in the feeling that "we're all humans here" and should help one another when in need; instead, charity is an "asymmetrical" exchange between the people in "need" of help and their fortunate, privileged "helpers."

Rony Brauman et al. (2004) make a similar point, proposing that the recipient of humanitarian aid is typically defined "by his deficiencies and disempowerment. It is his fundamental vulnerability and dependency, instead of his agency and ability to surmount difficulty, that is foregrounded by humanitarianism." The most effective means of securing donations is to paint people in war-torn nations as helpless victims desperate for assistance (Dragotesc 2011). Donors are rewarded with images of victims recovering from their injuries, receiving food and water, or returning to school, thanks to their help. Instead of promoting more equality between the First and Third Worlds, some humanitarian campaigns unintentionally reinforce disparities in global power and privilege.

Advertisements for many charities lead donors to think they can make a genuine difference in the world through donations as small as $5 or $10. By doing so, contributors may feel they have done their duty as responsible global citizens and can return to their comfortable lives. Such initiatives alleviate any guilt global insiders may feel about the unequal distribution of resources, power and privilege, and discourage prolonged, critical thinking about global inequalities—which is precisely what's needed to make a significant impact.

In attempting to secure donations, charities also imply that Westerners have few concerns compared to people in the Third World, distracting attention from the many social problems that still trouble our own society. Many North Americans are willing to donate hard-earned money to a "good cause" in Africa, yet are reluctant to support initiatives designed to alleviate problems like poverty in their own countries. The wealthiest insiders are especially unwilling to support redistributive taxation, but many are happy to make large donations to charities, for which they receive favourable media attention as well as a welcome tax break. This suggests that at least some philanthropic work is performed out of a desire to improve one's reputation: to be viewed as a benevolent, compassionate person, instead of a greedy insider.

Peacekeeping

Canadians proudly view themselves as citizens of a nation that works for peace instead of waging war. Since Prime Minister Lester B. Pearson won the Nobel Peace Prize for his role in resolving the Suez Crisis in 1956, Canada has participated in many successful peacekeeping operations: indeed, until the mid-1990s, we contributed to every one of the UN's peacekeeping missions.

But just as charitable donations can make an individual *feel* socially responsible, the Canadian peacekeeping identity has become more of a self-flattering construct than a reality. Canada has been absent on the peacekeeping front for more than a decade: we have not contributed a single soldier to a UN peacekeeping mission since 2001 (Rowland 2015). When we do send troops abroad today, it is for military purposes. But politicians, echoed by the media, frame these missions as being in defence of democracy and freedom. Canadians are so proud of their reputation as peacekeepers that this social construct is easy to exploit (Jeffress 2015).

Western values have been similarly exploited to marshal support for military ventures. Foreign aid and military intervention are claimed to encourage the spread of democracy in the developing world. Since the end of the Cold War, humanitarian aid distributed by OECD countries has increased fourteen-fold, to well over $11 billion (U.S.) (Narang 2015). The U.S. Agency for International Development (USAID) claims this increase in aid has contributed to the spread of democracy: "[T]here were 58 democratic nations in 1980. By 1995, this number had jumped to 115 nations. USAID provided democracy and governance assistance to 36 of the 57 nations that successfully made the transition to democratic government during this period" (Knack 2004).

Academics offering second opinions, however, suggest that foreign interventions may in some cases derail democratization (Downes 2013). Intervention can lead to nationalist backlash; as well, interventions by their very nature create instability that may erupt and undo any progress that has been made, once the foreign troops pack up and go home.

Canada also tends to be selective in deciding which nations deserve help. Until 2012, a "tied aid" policy dictated that foreign aid would be provided to countries on the condition that they spend it on Canadian goods and services. Foreign aid could be seen as an effort to boost the economy here at home as much as an expression of humanitarianism.

In addition, military intervention can undermine the sovereignty of the recipient state. **Sovereignty** is a nation's right to control its territory and the population within it. When foreign troops intervene in a conflict, citizens of the country in question may come to question the authority and ability of their leaders, and social disorganization (with all its negative consequences) may be the result. On the other hand, many believe that state sovereignty is not absolute, and *should* be restricted under certain conditions—for example, if the state is deliberately harming its citizens (Ayoob 2002).

There are good arguments for and against such interventions. As UN Secretary-General Kofi Annan put it: "[I]f humanitarian intervention is an unacceptable assault on sovereignty, how should we respond to a Rwanda, to a Srebrenica—to gross and systematic violations of human rights that affect every precept of our common humanity?" At the same time, it has been suggested that interventions by developed nations in the Third World are primarily exercises in neo-colonialism. What has become clear is that if a country's armed forces are strong enough—as in North Korea, which has developed nuclear weapons—the odds of foreign intervention are much diminished, no matter how poorly that country treats its citizens. As well, the problematic nature of recent interventions in Afghanistan and Iraq has led many Western nations, including the United States, to lose their appetite for further such ventures.

OUTSIGHTS

Like scholars offering second opinions, outsiders recognize that the effects of war fall most heavily on the poor and the socially disadvantaged.

Gendered Warfare

In wartime, the "normal" gender inequality that exists across all societies becomes intensified. Conflict pushes men and women into deeply stereotypical roles, and encourages people to believe that conventional gender roles are intrinsically "right." As men wage war, they come to be viewed even more strongly as protectors and defenders. Women, for their part, are typically constructed as weak, helpless and in need of protection. With firearms readily available in periods of conflict, rates of violence against women and domestic abuse often rise (Jansen 2006).

Women's vulnerability increases further when enemies target civilians, brutalizing women in particular to destroy morale. Despite the fact that these acts constitute war crimes, rape, forced prostitution, sexual assault and sexual slavery continue to be used as instruments of war (Legal Information Institute 2015, Henry 2014).

Mistreatment of women during wartime has long been considered a demonstration of soldiers' masculinity and strength (Wachala 2012). Women were viewed as "booty," valuable goods wrested from one's opposition as rewards or tokens of success (Kirby 2012). Rape was considered an unpreventable *consequence* of war (Red Cross 2015).

But rape is also a means of waging war, not just a reward for victory (Henry 2014). Sexual violence is much less costly for attackers than weapons, which are expensive, difficult to acquire, and risky to transport and distribute. Sexual violence also does great harm to both the immediate victims but also their families, communities and the broader society (Kirby 2012, Heit 2009). Muslim women were systematically raped during the war in Yugoslavia (United Nations 1998), while children, elderly women, nuns, and even female corpses were raped throughout the Rwandan genocide (Wachala 2012). In both instances, rape was a premeditated strategy intended to diminish enemy morale. In recent conflicts, military officials have even distributed condoms and performance-enhancing drugs to soldiers in an effort to explicitly encourage the rape of enemy civilians (Schneider et al. 2015).

In addition to breaking the enemy's resolve, rape can be used to express hatred of a racial or ethnic group. Consider the brothels established by Japanese forces during World War II. The Japanese government justified the use of foreign **comfort women** as necessary to fulfill Japanese soldiers' "inevitable and uncontrollable" sexual desires—desires that could lead to the rape of Japanese women, if not otherwise assuaged (Cohen 2013). But these brothels also served to degrade the Korean women who composed 80% of the sex slaves raped by Japanese troops (Pilzer 2014). Their rape and murder was a strategy by Japanese forces to erode Korean morale, as well as an effort to erase Koreans' ethnic identity—an extension of Japan's occupation of Korea.

Soldiers with HIV/AIDS may try to spread the disease through rape, hoping that it will either kill enemy women or discourage them from having children to whom they would pass the disease (Mokhtanzadeh 2013). In other cases, forced impregnation is used to alter the racial or ethnic composition of a hated population (Watson 2007). After Serbian soldiers raped and impregnated Muslim women during the conflict in former Yugoslavia, they detained them in "rape camps" until their pregnancies were too advanced to terminate. The objective was to brutalize and "dilute" the Muslim population.

In extreme cases, the resulting mixed-race children may be abandoned or even killed by their mothers; if they survive, they are typically ostracized and despised, viewed as "the enemy" (Lee 2011). Interviews with teenagers born of war rape in Bosnia and Herzegovina found that these mixed-ethnicity youth felt "scapegoated" by their communities, blamed for reminding their neighbours of the war and their own mothers of their assault (Erjavec and Zala 2010, Watson 2007). "I am kind of . . . available for everyone to hate me," said 15-year-old Zerina. "I am guilty for their misery. . . . [N]o one likes me, everyone avoids me, everyone hates me."

In the contemporary world, women are increasingly involved in violent conflict themselves. Women in armed groups are usually assumed to fill supporting roles, but reports from civilians and soldiers alike reveal that female combatants have perpetrated physical and sexual violence in the Congo, Liberia, Haiti, Rwanda and the Abu Ghraib prison during the Iraq War.

In interviews with ex-combatants who had fought in the civil war in Sierra Leone, Dara Kay Cohen (2013) found that female combatants both participated in and facilitated the gang rapes of their opponents. Women made up 24% percent of the membership of the Revolutionary United Front (RUF), the organization responsible for most of the rapes carried out during the conflict. Of all reported rapes, 76% were reported as being perpetrated by gangs; of those gang rapes, three-quarters were committed by all-male groups, the remainder by mixed groups of men and women.

However, neither individual women nor groups of female combatants were accused of perpetrating wartime rape, suggesting that this tactic continues to be male-led. Female combatants also fall victim to sexual violence themselves. Fully 93% of women who fought in the RUF reported they did not join voluntarily, but were abducted (Cohen 2013). One former female RUF member said that "[m]ost of the RUF women were raped when they first joined." Another, who was 14 years old at the time of her interview, reported that at first she "helped with domestic work. . . . I was about ten years old when I became part of the fighting forces. The RUF thought that once a girl had attained puberty and started having sex, she was physically mature enough to become a soldier" (Denov 2006).

Cohen (2013) proposes that these female combatants tried to gain acceptance from their male RUF colleagues—and deflect their sexual advances—by finding them "alternatives." One female RUF member said: "Women would tell the men that 'I found a beautiful woman for you.' We would help capture her and hold her down." Participating in a gang rape reportedly allowed female fighters to "bond" with their male peers, creating feelings of solidarity.

Child Soldiers

A **child soldier** is any person under 18 years of age associated with an armed force or group in any capacity (UNICEF). Child soldiers include not only those who commit violence or carry weapons, but also cooks, porters, spies and messengers recruited by rebel forces, as well as sex slaves and sexual partners. UNICEF estimates approximately 300,000 children under the age of 18 are associated with armed forces and groups around the world today. Most are located in Afghanistan, Myanmar, Chad, Columbia, India, Iraq, Occupied Palestinian Territories, Philippines, Sri Lanka, Sudan and Thailand (Mouthaan 2015).

Children join armed forces and groups for a variety of reasons. Many are abducted and forced to enlist against their will, or conscripted by the government. Often, their parents are killed in front of them, so they know they have no family to return to even if they escape captivity. Cut off from their old life, they are sometimes given new names with militaristic themes, creating the sense that they are now part of a new "family" (Thomason 2015).

Children who "voluntarily" enlist are coaxed with promises of food and shelter, or the protection of the armed group. Some girls enlist after fleeing domestic mistreatment or sexual violence (and, as we have seen, many are often subjected to further abuses once they enter the rebel group) (Mouthaan 2015). Others actively seek membership to avenge the loss of family members (Grady and Jones 2013), while others still genuinely support the cause for which the group is fighting (Sinha 2013). Armed groups, for their part, target children because they are thought to be less likely to question or disobey adult commanders, easy to persuade, and inexpensive to keep because they eat less and can be paid little or nothing (Mouthaan 2014).

Income inequality also has a bearing on the likelihood of children being recruited. In societies with high levels of income inequality and large numbers of impoverished citizens, many young people are displaced and vulnerable. With nothing to lose, they are easy to recruit. Poverty, lack of education, and un- or under-employment all increase the chances of children joining an armed group to obtain protection, health care, shelter, and sustenance. In contrast, children from well-off families have no incentive to enlist. If rebels try to abduct them, their wealthy parents can afford to pay them off, or to send their children out of the country altogether (Lasley and Thyne 2015).

Once recruited, rebels exploit age inequalities, viewing child soldiers as more expendable than adults and using them as human shields, to sweep minefields, or on suicide missions. Gender inequalities also become more pronounced. Girls account for 40% of all child soldiers, and are often made to perform stereotypically gendered labour, such as cooking, cleaning, washing clothes, and providing medical care. However, as we have seen, active participation in hostilities is not reserved entirely for men; one study found that girls and boys were exposed to violent events to about the same degree, including being forced to fight at the front lines (Betancourt et al. 2011). That said, female child soldiers are disproportionately affected by **gendered violence**. Girls are at a much higher risk than boys of sexual violence, exploitation, domestic or sexual slavery, and forced marriage (Betancourt et al. 2011). Male child soldiers, for their part, are socialized to think that sexual violence is normal and acceptable, either by observing the rape of female child soldiers or by being encouraged or forced to participate (Mouthaan 2015).

The long-term physical and psychological effects of exposure to such violence at a young age are staggering (Hermenau et al. 2013). When a child is under intense stress for a prolonged period, the resources normally put towards growth and development are redirected towards survival (Grady and Jones 2013, Klasen et al. 2010). Child soldiers are often rendered unable to establish secure, healthy relationships and to regulate their own emotions and behaviours.

One study of former child soldiers in Uganda found that, for many years following their traumatic experiences of combat, participants continued to suffer ongoing intrusive memories (Klasen et al. 2010). Nearly all reported post-traumatic stress symptoms. Other mental health issues affecting former child soldiers include depression, anxiety disorders, dissociation, somatic complaints and behavioural problems (Grady and Jones 2013). These youth are likely to perform poorly in school, struggle with social interactions, suffer from sleep problems, and behave aggressively (Simo-Algado et al. 2005).

The amount of time spent with an armed force or group also affects mental health and behaviour (Hermenau et al. 2013). Boys who spent one year or less as a child soldier maintained a trust in people as well as their social values, and described themselves as "victims" (Boothby and Thomson 2013). Boys who spent more than a year as a child soldier displayed disobedient and uncooperative behaviours during their first few months in a rehabilitation centre and continued to use aggression in an effort to exert social control and influence. These boys described themselves not as "victims" but as "members" of the armed group they were associated with, and often reported that they had been given some amount of power in the form of leadership positions. All participants in the study experienced recurrent thoughts or memories of traumatic events more than a decade and a half after leaving the rehabilitation centre.

Post-conflict factors also contribute to mental health issues in former child soldiers (Betancourt et al. 2010). Upon returning to their original homes, many former child soldiers report feeling rejected by their communities, and even by family members. In a study of former Colombian child soldiers, experiences of labeling, stereotyping, status loss and discrimination were found to negatively affect their ability to successfully reintegrate into their communities and lead a normal, productive life. Many could not return home to their families and former lives, since discrimination made it impossible for them to find housing and employment on which they could support themselves independently.

Income inequality also influences post-conflict experiences (Vindevogel et al. 2013). Among former child soldiers, post-traumatic resilience—the absence of behavioural and emotional problems—is associated with higher socioeconomic status and more education (Klassen 2010). In other words, children from more privileged backgrounds are better able to cope with the traumatic experience of child soldiering. But child soldiering can also contribute to the perpetuation of income inequality. Former child soldiers interviewed by Boothby and Thomson (2013) reported that one of the most damaging aspects of being associated with an armed group was a loss of economic opportunities; they had spent their formative years fighting instead of obtaining an education or work experience. One of 48 northern Ugandan former child soldiers interviewed by Vindevogel et al. (2013) lamented, "I was still disappointed that much of my life was wasted in the bush."

In patriarchal societies, female former child soldiers are typically expected to resume traditional gender roles instead of seeking out opportunities for education or employment. In Sierra Leone, many girl child soldiers were excluded from rehabilitation programs and education and livelihood packages, with obvious negative consequences for their mental health and socioeconomic circumstances. For these and other reasons, females affected by war and conflict-related trauma have been found to experience higher rates of psychosocial distress and mental health problems than males.

Despite expectations for them to assume the stereotypical roles of wife and mother, many female former child soldiers are stigmatized and rejected by their communities. In one study, Ugandan and Sierra Leonan men refused to marry women who were child soldiers, describing them as "sexually tainted" and "unpredictable" (Betancourt et al. 2011). Others rejected these women because their sexual victimization was thought to render them incapable of bearing children (Mellis 2014).

Female former child soldiers are acutely aware of these realities, as well as the economic and social problems that life as an unmarried woman will pose. For example, Maria, who was abducted at the age of 12 and interviewed about her experiences with RUF at the age of 15, said: "I'm afraid I won't get a husband to marry me because of my past with the rebels. . . . My aunt told me that no man will marry me now [that I am no longer a virgin]. I feel a sense of despair. What will happen to me? How will I manage?" (Denov 2006).

In an effort to alleviate some of these issues, child soldiers are typically placed in **disarmament, demobilization, and reintegration (DDR)** programs following their removal from an armed force or group. The term **disarmament** refers to the removal of children from the military organization and control of their captors. Through demobilization, armed groups downsize or disband, and through reintegration, former child soldiers transition back into their old lives and communities (Denov and Marchand 2015). These programs thus aim to provide physical and psychological rehabilitation and help reintegrate children back into their communities (Thomason 2015).

Some question whether children should be afforded special treatment not provided to those over the age of 18 also exposed to violence at the hands of armed armed groups (Gretry 2011). The idea that children require special protection is common, and is incorporated in domestic law and international conventions. In 1989, the United Nations adopted the Convention on the Rights of the Child (CRC), which stipulates that children under 15 years of age should not be recruited into an armed force or group, or forced to take part in conflict. It also declares that every state must take all possible measures to ensure the protection of children involved in armed conflict (United Nations Human Rights Office of the High Commissioner 1989). Canada has also taken measures to intervene globally on behalf of children's rights, hosting the first International Conference on War-Affected Children in 2000 (Moynagh 2014). Most broadly, Article 25 of the Universal Declaration of Human Rights states: "Motherhood and childhood are entitled to special care and assistance. All children, whether born in or out of wedlock, shall enjoy the same social protection."

Such "special care and assistance" may be problematic in the international context of war, given that Western conceptions of childhood are socially constructed and not universal. Regardless of their actual experiences, participation in violence, or crimes they commit, children are first and foremost regarded as victims (Gretry 2011), viewed as especially vulnerable and unaware, open to exploitation at the hands of monstrous warlords.

In reality, however, these young people have lived through such challenging experiences that they no longer fit the mold of the naïve, innocent child (if they ever did to begin with). Many have proved themselves capable of making decisions and taking action in the face of enormous adversity (Gretry 2011). Nevertheless, child soldiers are often denied the opportunity to inform us of their experiences: their court testimonies are often doubted by adults and deemed inaccurate or incomplete, because they are young.

These issues of childhood innocence and naïveté have also prompted some to question how freely youth can "choose" to enlist. Many propose this choice can never be truly voluntary, because children are too young to understand the weight of their decisions and to legally provide consent (Sinha 2013). In turn, they should not be held responsible for any wrongdoing.

On the other hand, if a child joins an armed force because it is the only way he will be able to eat, was his choice entirely voluntary? These same push factors—such as the need for sustenance and physical protection from other armed groups—pressure adults into military service. If **coercion** renders someone deserving of "special protection," many adults would be entitled to similar treatment.

In most instances, it is difficult to conclude whether a child was forced to join an armed group or enlisted voluntarily. Standing in contrast to the popular media image of the naïve child soldier who is an absolute victim is the complete reverse: children who have been rendered monstrous perpetrators of violence. Both representations are inventions of the Western media. The lived realities of child soldiers are much more complex, making it difficult to fit them into these media-constructed categories.

For example, after interviewing 45 former child soldiers in the Democratic Republic of Congo, Lucille Gretry (2011) found that although they are typically represented as passive victims, their own statements suggest they are mature, independent decision makers in trying circumstances (much like their adult counterparts). One boy named Blaise said: "I volunteered. They needed us, because of our strength. There was no other way to get in. We were lost. We did not have any choice. We joined the army."

Western standards of "child" and "adult" are arbitrary, and the fact that a chronological age of 18 years marks the beginning of adulthood in some parts of the world may not be culturally relevant in others. Some children are able to make fully autonomous decisions, and as a consequence, bear moral responsibility for their actions. Krista Thomason (2015) found that former child soldiers do report feelings of guilt, shame and remorse for their actions while involved with an armed group. The outsights of child soldiers themselves suggest that they are simultaneously victims, perpetrators and resistors of violence (Hermenau et al. 2013), but international child protection laws classifying children as "victimized combatants" currently dominate the discussion (Denov 2012).

FINAL THOUGHTS

Sometimes violent conflict seems the only means by which to resist oppression, and in certain circumstances it can bring about political, social or cultural change, reducing social inequalities. But large-scale violent conflicts damage a nation's infrastructure and institutions, force civilians to flee war zones, and cause immeasurable pain, suffering and loss.

The **just war theory** holds that a justifiable war must spare the innocent, be declared by a legitimate authority, and be fought in the name of a valid cause (Kumar 2012). But since war inevitably entails the loss of human life and often fails to achieve the stated goals, is it ever justifiable? With the intro-duction of weapons of mass destruction, some suggest that a "just war" is no longer possible.

Violent conflict may also reinforce the inequalities it set out to reduce. This is especially true of racially, ethnically, and religiously motivated terror tactics. As we noted at the start of this chapter, many Muslims living in sup-posedly multicultural societies across the world were subjected to acts of Is-lamophobia in the wake of the Paris attacks. Ola Mobarak, 17, who lives in Milton, Ont., observed that after the Paris attacks, "the backlash against Mus-lims started pretty much right away, and it was overwhelming. . . . [S]ince I was a Muslim, I wasn't allowed to have my own space to be affected by an international tragedy" (Boesveld 2015). The violence of a few is projected onto every member of a racial, ethnic, or religious group, all of whom are assumed to share the same extremist beliefs. Inequality not only causes oppression, but also treats the advantaged and disadvantaged differently when they either exploit or try to resist that inequality.

Disadvantaged groups with the requisite education and resources have increasingly turned to nonviolent forms of protest in an effort to have their voices heard (Campante and Chor 2012). **Civil or nonviolent resistance**, for example, is a mode of conflict where unarmed civilians use various coordi-nated methods, such as strikes, protests, demonstrations, boycotts, civil dis-obedience and mass non-cooperation, to express discontent without directly harming (or threatening to harm) their opponent (Chenoweth 2014). Often, they work towards a better-defined political, social or economic goal, such as challenging an autocrat or contesting discriminatory practices (Chenoweth and Cunningham 2013, Nepstad and Erikson 2011).

Civil resistance campaigns may succeed for several reasons. For one, they attract a larger and more diverse base of supporters. Instead of limiting par-ticipants to young, able-bodied men willing to perpetrate extreme violence, peaceful campaigns are more likely to attract women, professionals, religious figures, civil servants, and others from a range of cross-cutting groups. His-torically, these larger, more diverse campaigns have a better chance of suc-ceeding because they demonstrate a widespread lack of support for the oppressor, be it the government or some other institution. Since protestors are not engaged in illegal or violent activity warranting punitive action, the likeli-hood of a crackdown is lessened (Chenoweth and Stephan 2014).

Nonviolent resistors are also more difficult to demonize than violent combatants. Rebels who terrorize civilians are easily framed as villains, and their destructive tactics overshadow the cause for which they fight. Nonviolent resistance, in contrast, can draw attention to the power of civilians to deny their support for unjust regimes. They show a lack of support for the status quo, shifting power dynamics by withdrawing their consent to an exploitative or oppressive government (Hallward et al. 2012). Nonviolent forms of protest more effectively challenge inequality than violent conflict, and entail none of the devastating consequences of warfare.

In the end, there is a significant amount of research to suggest that inequality promotes conflict, but the connection between the two is far from simple or linear. Conflict does not arise in every society that is unequal; if it did, all societies would be in a perpetual state of war. Nor does it always arise in those societies where inequality is most pronounced. The most extreme inequalities deny disadvantaged groups the resources they need to protest, thus perpetuating the status quo.

What we know for certain is that the suffering of some draws more attention and sympathy than the suffering of others. Privileged global insiders are more likely to stand in solidarity with people most like them—that is, other members of white, Western societies. By contrast, support from the Global North is much less likely to reach members of the Global South, unless it is in the form of pity. Even attempts to address violent conflict contribute to perpetuating the inequalities that help drive such conflict to begin with.

DISCUSSION QUESTIONS

1. Have you ever been part of a group that has wanted to rebel against something? Did you translate your "taste for revolt" into action? What factors motivated your decision?

2. Think about a time you've donated to a philanthropic organization. Was it for a cause at home or abroad? If you were to donate money again, do you think it would be better spent on "Third World Problems" or problems here in Canada?

3. Do you consider Canada to be at war today? Are the wars Canadians have fought during your lifetime justifiable? Do stated goals of peacekeeping or spreading democracy make military interventions justifiable?

4. Are child soldiers more deserving than adult soldiers of sympathy, support, and state-funded rehabilitation and re-integration efforts?

FURTHER READING

Rony Brauman et al. "From Philanthropy to Humanitarianism: Remarks and an Interview." *The South Atlantic Quarterly* 103:2 (2004): 397–417.

Jeffrey D. Sachs. *The End of Poverty: Economic Possibilities for Our Time.* Penguin, 2006.

KEY TERMS

Absolute poverty. Extreme deprivation, including lack of food, drinking water, sanitation, health care, shelter, education and information.

Child soldiers. Any person under 18 years of age who is associated with an armed force or group in any capacity.

Civil (nonviolent) resistance. Mode of conflict in which unarmed civilians use various coordinated methods, such as strikes, protests, demonstrations, boycotts, civil disobedience, and mass noncooperation, to convey their discontent without directly harming (or threatening to harm) their opponent.

Coercion. Use of force or intimidation to obtain compliance.

Cross-cutting theory. A theory that explains the relationships between different types of social divisions.

Comfort women. Estimated 200,000 women from China, Guam, Korea, Malaysia, the Philippines, Indonesia, and the Netherlands who were kidnapped or lured to Japanese brothels with phony promises of employment, and then held as sex slaves by Japanese soldiers during the Second World War.

Disarmament. In this context, the removal of child soldiers from the military organization in which they serve and from the control of their captors.

DDR programs. Rehabilitation programs for child soldiers focusing on disarmament, demobilization, and reintegration.

Gendered violence. Gender-specific violence. Forced impregnation is an example of a gendered violent act towards women.

Genocide. Deliberate elimination of a racial, ethnic, or religious group.

Group polarization. Emergence of clusters of people sharing similar attributes who strongly identify with one another, to the exclusion and alienation of others.

Horizontal inequalities. Inequalities occurring when power and resources are unequally distributed between groups differentiated by their race, ethnicity, religion, sex, gender, sexuality, age, and so on.

ISIS. Islamic State in Iraq and Syria, a radical Islamist militant group.

Just war theory. Theory that defines a war as "just" if it spares the innocent, is declared by a legitimate authority, and is fought in the name of a valid cause, such as rights vindication.

Non-violent campaign. Campaign of social resistance carried out by unarmed civilians who do not directly threaten the well-being of their opponent.

Paradox of humanitarian action. Efforts genuinely intended to ease suffering that actually extend conflict.

Relative poverty. Condition in which people lack the minimum income needed to maintain the average standard of living in the society in which they live.

Sovereignty. A state's right to control its territory and the population within it.

Youth bulge theory. Theory holding that conflict will more likely arise when there are more working-age youth in a given society than there are available job opportunities.

CHAPTER TEN

What Is to Be Done?

LEARNING OBJECTIVES

In this chapter, you will:
1. Consider why redistributive taxation is denounced by insiders and supported by outsiders
2. Determine whether under-taxing the wealthy is good or bad for the economy
3. Learn why some outsiders internalize insider views, and vote against their own interests
4. Listen to outsiders' recommendations for reducing vertical and horizontal inequalities

INTRODUCTION

Throughout this book, we have examined how different types of people—insiders, academics offering second opinions, and outsiders—experience and interpret inequality. The views of insiders are widely disseminated through such social institutions as the media, families, and the education system. Because these views receive the most attention, they effectively perpetuate the status quo. These ongoing performances of inequality create the unequal opportunities that all of us confront every day in making our life choices.

Yet inequality carries heavy costs. Research links it to heightened risks of illness and mortality, crime and punishment, and violent conflict within and between nations. These social problems demand attention for self-evident reasons.

Given the negative consequences of social inequality, why does it persist? This question can best be answered by considering some of the myths insiders have used to justify the status quo. First, insiders have successfully convinced most people that inequality—even extreme inequality—is natural and inevitable. According to insiders, inequality exists to reward hard workers for their dedication and perseverance. Reducing inequality would diminish the incentive for people to work hard and carry out demanding jobs that are vital to society as a whole. Inequality is not only natural; it is necessary.

Academics offering second opinions have shown this view of inequality to be unfounded. There are other ways to incentivize hard work, encourage people to take demanding jobs, and stimulate the economy than by rewarding the rich to an ever-increasing degree and entrenching disadvantage ever more deeply. Scholars have identified viable ways to reduce inequalities and their harmful consequences—ways we know will work because they have been successfully implemented in other societies, where there is now greater equality, and, in turn, less sickness, crime and conflict. The problem is to convince the wealthy, powerful insiders who are the main decision-makers in our society to put such measures in place.

Insiders use various strategies to make the status quo seem normal, inevitable and justified. Many do so because they benefit from the existing system of inequality. That said, it has been shown that greater equality would benefit not only disadvantaged outsiders, but also insiders themselves, by promoting health, peace and order. Most people would likely endorse more equality if they realized its advantages.

That is the task we will undertake in this final chapter. By presenting empirical evidence gathered by academics offering second opinions together with the views of outsiders on what should be done to address inequality, we hope to make a compelling case that practical action can be taken to reduce the degree of inequality in Canada today.

A Caution

Before proceeding, however, a note of caution is in order. We want to stress that, despite some similarities, we are not making the same argument that nineteenth-century German philosopher Friedrich Nietzsche did in his essay, *On the Genealogy of Morality*. That is, we are not arguing about the difference between a "master morality" and "slave morality."

Like Nietzsche, we recognize that two moralities or worldviews exist when it comes to examining inequality. Nietzsche equated the so-called "master morality" to classical Greek and Roman values, which prized strength, pride, and nobility; and he equated the so-called "slave morality" to Christian values, which prized sympathy, kindness, humility, and forgiveness. Like Nietzsche, we recognize these two "moralities" signify different cultural systems—one preindustrial and aristocratic, the other modern and democratic. As Nietzsche points out, the master morality confidently views the self as the source of all values: "what is good for me is good." The slave morality, created in opposition to the master morality, is, on the other hand, obsessed with freedom, equality, and the collective good.

Unlike Nietzsche, we do not view the democratic, so-called "slave morality" as weak or degenerate, or the aristocratic "master morality" as pure and preferable. Indeed, we believe the opposite. Because we live in a civilization persuaded by democratic values and so-called "slave morality," and because we think a rational case can be made for the greater human benefits of democratic equality, we mount an argument against "aristocratic" and self-centred insiders. But like Nietzsche, we do understand that in the modern world there are two worldviews (or moralities) that need to understand each other and come to terms on issues of inequality. To bring about this understanding, we think, is the role of the sociologist. So, we begin, once again, by re-examining the views of "insiders"—the "masters" (or would-be masters) in present-day civilization.

INSIDER VIEWS

Economic insiders—that is, middle- and upper-class people with stable, well-paying jobs—benefit from the status quo. Most would therefore prefer to maintain it, rather than reduce the inequalities that afford them power and privilege.

These insiders often oppose equalizing measures such as **redistributive taxation.** The CBC's online voter engagement survey, "Vote Compass," unsurprisingly revealed that lower-income Canadians are more likely to support higher taxes on better-off Canadians (2015). Asked "How much should wealthier people pay in taxes?" only 27% of Canadians earning more than $100,000 a year responded "much more." By contrast, 37% of those earning between $60,000 and $100,000 and 45% of people making less than $60,000 a year said "much more." Support for higher levels of taxation increases as one's personal income decreases.

Of course, it makes sense for higher-income earners to want to pay as little in taxes as possible. Many insiders argue that high incomes and comfortable lifestyles are just rewards for hard work, and see no reason to sacrifice their own standard of living to improve that of lower-income outsiders they view as lazy, unmotivated, or untalented. Aaron Wudrick, a former corporate lawyer who is now federal director of the Canadian Taxpayers Federation, claims that

> punitively higher taxes reduce the incentive for people to work harder: why put in that extra hour at work or open that second location of your coffee shop, if the government is going to take 75 per cent of what you make? As for business taxes, in an increasingly globalized world, putting them up too high can trigger some companies to cease doing business in Canada, or move away altogether—and take would-be tax revenues with them (2015).

Because insiders influence public policy more than outsiders, their views have played a major role in shaping social assistance programs in Canada over the past several decades. During that period, Canada's **welfare system** has been reformed in ways that disadvantage the poor (Nelson 2013); in particular, employment insurance coverage has been curtailed, as have **child care subsidies** and other forms of income support (Forouzin 2010).

Beginning in the late 1980s, Canada experienced high unemployment rates due, in part, to a universal shift towards the precarious forms of labour discussed earlier in this book. The number of families living in poverty rose dramatically as a result, but at the same time, the general economic downturn and fear of budget deficits led governments to cut spending on social services. Politicians began to reduce the size of government (Himelfarb 2014), market forces were allowed to play out, and deregulation became the norm (Forouzin 2010). Some insiders advocated strongly that the welfare state be abolished altogether.

In the face of economic challenges, insiders argued that by cutting taxes on high-income individuals as well as businesses, the economy would grow more quickly and all Canadians, even the poor, would reap the benefits as they "trickled down." Although the most extreme plans to scrap the social safety net were not carried through, deep cuts were made to many social programs. Consider changes made to the Canada Assistance Plan (CAP). It was established by the federal government in 1966 to provide funding for health and social welfare programs under a 50/50 cost-sharing arrangement with the provinces (Forouzin 2010). CAP guaranteed Canadians the right to an adequate income when in need without being required to work or take part in training programs while receiving assistance.

In 1985, a new Employment Enhancement Accord allowed the Progressive Conservative federal government and the provinces to build work incentives into social assistance programs (Forouzin 2010). Receipt of social assistance was no longer based only on need: employability became a requirement, with only people who were working or seeking work being eligible (Eardley et al. 1996, Nelson 2013). Soon, the federal government placed a "cap on CAP," agreeing to pay only 30% of expenditures and transferring a larger fraction of the cost to the wealthier provinces (Ontario, Alberta, and British Columbia).

A decade later, in 1995, the CAP was replaced with the Canada Health and Social Transfer (CHST). This program offered the provinces a set amount of money for spending on social services, promising them more leeway to change their health care and social programs as they saw fit. In theory, this afforded provincial governments greater flexibility, but in practice, it meant the provinces could put in place more conditions for receiving social assistance, including welfare-to-work programs. These changes were part of a broader movement away from social funding. Since the 1980s, social programs have undergone restructuring, decentralization, and downsizing. Some have even been dismantled (Ayala and Rodriguez 2006). At the same time, public support of such programs has plummeted. This trend is perhaps the strongest example of how claims-making by insiders can have significant consequences for everyone's life chances, insiders and outsiders alike (Himelfarb 2014).

Some economically disadvantaged outsiders have adopted views similar to those of insiders, opposing the very redistributive policies from which they stand to gain. Even though an enhanced social support system would improve their quality of life, as well as mitigating the harmful effects of inequality for health, crime and conflict, outsiders have come to believe (like insiders) that such a system would be unfair, harmful to the economy, or impossible to put in place. But these beliefs are erroneous. Other societies have convinced their citizens of the benefits of a strong social support system, and have prospered by implementing one. Doing so, however, requires a shift in values. Only in societies where most people think that economic outcomes are beyond the control of any single individual do we find strong support for redistribution. There, even wealthy insiders recognize that poor people lack the ability to prevent or alter their circumstances, and are thus more open to redistributive policies (Smyth et al. 2010). The challenge is to accomplish a similar "mindshift" here in Canada.

SECOND OPINIONS

As funding for social support programs was cut, scholars offering second opinions explored how these changes affected outsiders. Many grew interested in determining whether lower taxes on the wealthy actually stimulated economic growth.

Research shows it does not, contrary to popular (insider) opinion. In fact, under-taxing the wealthy harms the economy. Researchers Jonathan Ostry, Andrew Berg and Charalambos Tsangarides of the International Monetary Fund analyzed pre- and post-tax data, and found that lower net inequality stimulates economic growth and promotes longer periods of economic expansion (Beltrame 2014). Redistributive taxation does not hold back growth, contradicting the insider belief that such redistribution compromises economic prosperity by deterring well-off, self-styled "job creators" from continuing to work hard and invest.

Academics offering second opinions also question whether welfare turns outsiders into "lazy dependents," as insiders like to suggest. Instead, they find that even the most generous support fails to meet the needs of low-income families. There is too little state support to promote laziness, let alone glamorize dependency.

Studies tell us that many welfare recipients are employed, but require additional support because their precarious jobs provide insufficient income to support their families. Minimum-wage workers are severely underpaid, here in Canada and elsewhere, especially when compared to senior executives. For instance, the CEO of restaurant chain McDonald's was paid $9.5 million in 2013, while most of the chain's workers in Ontario received the then minimum wage of $10.25 per hour (Bittman 2014). So even if a McDonald's employee flipped burgers for 40 hours a week, she would only earn $21,320—1/446 what the CEO earned.

By underpaying workers, corporations shift the responsibility for supporting the poor onto taxpayer-funded social programs and well as charitable initiatives such as food banks. From this point of view, public assistance is not a means of encouraging laziness among recipients but, rather, a transfer of public funds to wealthy corporations and their highly paid executives (Bittman 2014).

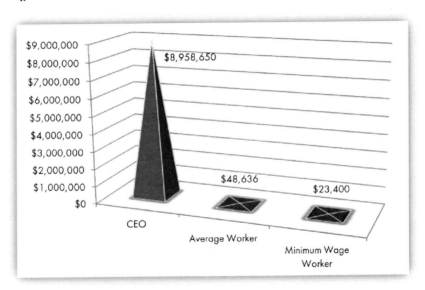

Figure 10.1: Comparative Annual Incomes

In any case, social assistance programs fail to provide adequate benefits (Nelson 2013). The various forms of provincial and municipal social assistance all leave recipients beneath generally accepted poverty thresholds (Eardley et al. 1996). It has also become increasingly difficult to generate support for these programs, however meagre. In sum, then, academics offering second opinions have shown that social support in today's Canada is far from "generous." And although insiders argue that social programs providing, at most, subsistence-level benefits will motivate outsiders to find jobs as quickly as possible, researchers have actually shown that more generous welfare support *facilitates* (rather than discourages) job-seeking.

As these scholars note, it is not always in people's best interests to take the first job they are offered. Insiders are right in one respect: people who receive inadequate benefits remain unemployed for shorter periods of time. Out of desperation, they are forced to accept almost any job they are offered, even if that also means accepting lower wages (van Berkel 2007, Nelson 2013). But, as a result, these people are often over-qualified and over-educated for that job, and earn less money than they otherwise might (Pollmann-Schult and Buchel 2005). By forcing people into immediate employment, inadequate social benefits trap skilled workers in lower-income brackets for prolonged periods. This underemployment of talented people is costly for society as a whole. Because they are earning less than they "should be," given their credentials, they are also paying less in taxes than would otherwise be the case.

In contrast, research has shown that Canadians who receive the maximum amount of unemployment benefits available will eventually enjoy greater long-term job stability. These recipients can afford to carry out longer job searches, allowing them to find positions better suited to their skills and level of education (Pollmann-Schult and Buchel 2005). Rather than a "hammock" that facilitates learned helplessness and dependency, unemployment benefits and other forms of social assistance serve as springboards, propelling recipients into better jobs and better lives.

OUTSIGHTS

Some outsiders internalize the victim-blaming narratives disseminated by insiders, but others do believe they are disadvantaged because of systemic inequalities and barriers hindering their upward mobility. These people are therefore invested in restructuring the status quo. They recognize that redistributive policies and social assistance programs have been put in place to that end, but tell us that these measures are not adequately addressing their problems.

In particular, many Canadians who receive social support report that it is insufficient. John, who receives benefits under the Ontario Disability Support Program (ODSP), writes:

> People do not choose to be disabled and live in poverty. Things happen in life and that we are all subject to . . . such as illness, prolonged loss of job, etc. The current system (ODSP) does not meet the needs of the people who use it. For example, to rent an apartment in Toronto costs at least $800 a month. To this you must add food and transportation, which is another roughly $400 month. It takes at least $1200 a month to live in the city of Toronto. The present level of support for an individual is nowhere

near this. This causes great hardship for the disabled. The government must do the right thing and raise the ODSP rates. Remember, most people are one pay cheque away from poverty. This can happen to anyone—even YOU (Income Security Advocacy Centre 2011).

Because it is inadequate, few people rely on social assistance for extended periods of time (Ayala and Rodriguez 2006). More often, low-income earners transition in and out of dependence on social support as their work arrangements fluctuate (Backman and Bergmark 2011, Hansen 2009). These so-called **"cyclers"** who return repeatedly to welfare dependence are most often young, single parents with young children (van Berkel 2007, Gough 1997). However, many eligible people do not even apply for social assistance, possibly because of the stigma attached to being labeled a "welfare bum" or "on the dole" (Eardley et al. 1996). Consider as an example the experience of Meghan, a single mother in Ontario:

I was hoping, as all of us hope, to be employed soon and in a position where I could leave welfare after more than two years. . . . [I feel] that I could get by on the meagre amount I receive, not because it's adequate for a single mom, but because I don't like to complain. I've been self-sufficient all my life and I like my independence. . . . Well, I don't think I'm so proud anymore. I often say that you can't know an experience like welfare or disability until you have lived it. . . . The system did what it does well. It beats us down. It tears into our spirit. It robs us of dignity. The system, at its best, should support people in times of crisis and encourage us, through adequacy, to help preserve our sense of self-worth and dignity. It doesn't. Rather, it's punitive. And it depends, in part, upon people like me, who despise being made to ask, being made to beg, for no less than the dignity we all deserve. After a lifetime of meaningful, rewarding work. I've fallen far. I've fallen far because there was far to fall. And because, in retrospect, there were no supports to grab hold of on the way down. . . .

Instead of being comforted, I am directed to a program designed to get me off the system as quickly as possible. One where I can wait by the phone, inexplicably with child care available to me at a moment's notice, to take a job as a dishwasher and have half of my minimum wage clawed back to punish me even further. Or I'm directed to a resume writing course. Or to a seminar on how to achieve the post-secondary education I already possess. No. The dignity I've built and known all my life is not for sale. I won't beg you to strip me of it. I'll get by on food vouchers and food banks and inadequate amounts of support until I land that job again, hopefully before my health gives way (Income Security Advocacy Centre 2011).

Above: Inequality in North America is visible perhaps nowhere more than in the city of Detroit, where thousands of abandoned homes, factories and public buildings are mute evidence of the fact the city has lost almost two-thirds of its population since the 1950s. But a rebirth of residential and commercial activity in the downtown provides some measure of hope for the future (Rick Harris).

Below: Only in a dialogue between insiders and outsiders is there hope for mitigating the harmful effects of inequality (Shutterstock).

Non-Vertical Inequalities

Class inequalities are more readily observed than those related to sex, race, age and sexuality, and easier to measure in **quantifiable** terms. Certain segments of the population obviously enjoy greater material comfort than others. Because they cannot deny its existence, insiders try to justify the present system of class inequality, arguing that people merely get what they deserve.

In considering inequalities grounded in sex, race, age and sexuality, insiders claim that enough has already been done to address these inequalities, and further efforts are unnecessary. This book has explored the many laws, programs, policies and other official measures that aim to protect outsiders against discrimination, remove barriers to their advancement, and promote their overall wellbeing and social integration. Citing these initiatives as evidence, insiders hold that Canadians have successfully built an inclusive, tolerant society where everyone is equal (or at least, enjoys equal opportunities).

Outsiders disagree with this assessment. People who suffer the disadvantages of social inequalities say the discussion is far from closed, and we still have considerable distance to go before enjoying the egalitarian society insiders think already exists.

How are we to resolve these conflicting viewpoints? Academics offering second opinions can act as intermediaries. They have provided empirical data showing that at least some social inequalities persist today. They also propose that those inequalities are often overlooked because of the influence of insiders. By contrast, the outsiders who experience the consequences of these inequalities firsthand are ignored, unable to voice their opinions on matters with which they are deeply familiar. As a result, those efforts that *are* made to address inequality all too often fall flat, having been developed for the most part without input from the very people they are meant to help.

Acting as intermediaries, scholars offering second opinions suggest that political leaders, policy-makers and other influential insiders try to listen more carefully to outsiders. Throughout this book, we have attempted to do just that, giving voice to people who are otherwise silenced, marginalized and ignored during discussions of social problems they experience personally. Since many outsiders feel that existing policies and programs are not doing enough to combat inequality, scholars offering second opinions propose that we ask them what *they* think should be done.

That is what we aim to do in this book's final pages: explore suggestions from outsiders on how to reduce the inequalities that disadvantage them. We cannot (and do not) provide a comprehensive solution to every kind of social inequality, nor do we suggest that the few outsiders cited below speak for all women, members of racial minorities, LGBTQ people, or young people and the elderly. Instead, this overview is meant to serve as a starting point for more productive discussions about inequality, in which more outsiders feel able to speak out about the changes they would like to see, and more insiders feel compelled to listen respectfully to those requests.

Gender Inequality. One of the most visible manifestations of gender inequality is domestic violence against women. In an effort to alleviate that abuse and provide protection to women in its aftermath, charitable and community organizations have long provided shelters and support programs. Many women who have suffered abuse testify to the usefulness of these programs, yet others think that more could be done.

In a 2015 study, Tutty interviewed 282 women who had been abused about their experiences in shelters, the services they felt were most needed, and those they had found lacking. A majority of women said they wanted "emotional support or counselling from shelter staff" immediately upon arrival, including information about how to cope with their stress and anger as well as assistance in improving their self-esteem. The vast majority also noted that having "a safe, secure place to stay" was important, and many women felt it was important for shelters to provide referrals for housing. A little more than half the women surveyed said they wanted shelter staff to understand their need to take a "break" from their abusive partners; they wanted time removed from their home lives to weigh the costs of staying in as opposed to dissolving their relationships. In all these regards, shelters proved useful for many women. Others, however, acknowledged that shelters served as only temporary Band-aids for their problems, as lack of money and permanent housing, combined with fear, would likely lead them to return to their abusive homes.

Almost all the women interviewed had children, and half said that they wanted some form of support in their capacity as mothers. About four in ten women said they would have found counselling for their children to be useful, and that having child-care services available would have been helpful during their stay in the shelter.

Most of the women reported positive, supportive experiences with shelter staff, but some felt they were being blamed for their suffering. One woman said: "A couple of the staff members need to rethink their choice of jobs. We are made to feel like we've done something wrong." Another woman highlighted the fact that shelters become overcrowded: "Basically it was full house, during the whole stay." And it should be remembered that such shelters, however well-run, merely respond to damage already done; less progress has been made in preventing physical and sexual abuse to begin with.

One specific example of emotional abuse to which women are disproportionately subject is fat-shaming as well as other efforts to regulate physical appearance. When Kara Waite, a community college professor who says she has struggled with body image issues her whole life, learned that a friend's eight-year-old daughter was being body-shamed by her classmates, she gave some thought to what might be done:

> "I don't want to make her feel bad," my friend said. "What do I do?"
> Take her outside. Plant a garden. Play in the snow. Play tag. . . . Buy her art supplies and show her all of the bodies that artists have celebrated throughout history. Feed her good stuff, but have conversations with her while she eats it. . . . Tell her she is beautiful, but say it half as much as you say that she is kind and generous and hysterically funny and at the top of your list of favorite people. Talk about anything but bodies. . . .
> Love her exactly as she is. Accept her exactly as she is. Like her, too, and let her know it. Fill her up with love and like and acceptance so she doesn't learn to get it from cookies and Doritos and sundaes and pizza.

Unlike physical and emotional abuses, which are blatant examples of gender inequality, people are likely to dismiss the **second shift** as a popular "choice" among modern women. As we have seen, women who pursue full-time careers are often forced to choose between their work and their families at some point, leading many former "career women" to speak out about the impossibility of "having it all." Anne-Marie Slaughter, the first female director of policy planning at the U.S. State Department, says she left that dream job when being away from her teenage kids became too tough to manage. Slaughter argues:

> The best hope for improving the lot of all women, and for closing what Wolfers and Stevenson call a **"new gender gap"**—measured by well-being rather than wages—is to close the leadership gap: to elect a woman president and 50 women senators; to ensure that women are equally represented in the ranks of corporate executives and judicial leaders. Only when women wield power in sufficient numbers will we create a society that genuinely works for all women. That will be a society that works for everyone (2012).

Before that can happen, Slaughter recognizes that society must address the glass ceiling and other barriers that prevent women from assuming such high-power positions. She suggests traditional work-patterns be overhauled to the benefit of men and women alike:

> Long hours are one thing, and realistically, they are often unavoidable. But do they really need to be spent at the office? To be sure, being in the office *some* of the time is beneficial. . . . Still, armed with e-mail, instant messaging, phones, and videoconferencing technology, we should be able to move to a culture where the office is a base of operations more than the required locus of work. . . .
> One way to [do] that is by changing the "default rules" that govern

office work—the baseline expectations about when, where, and how work will be done.

For instance, an organization might set a policy of holding in-office meetings only during hours corresponding to a normal school day, "a system that might normalize call-ins for those (rarer) meetings still held in the late afternoon." Slaughter suggests that everyone could benefit from being more willing to acknowledge their parenting or family-related needs in the workplace, concluding that:

> Ultimately, it is society that must change, coming to value choices to put family ahead of work just as much as those to put work ahead of family. If we really valued those choices, we would value the people who make them; if we valued the people who make them, we would do everything possible to hire and retain them; if we did everything possible to allow them to combine work and family equally over time, then the choices would get a lot easier (2012).

Another manifestation of gender inequality often attributed to female "choice" is that of sexual abuse. Survivors are sometimes made to feel as though they are to blame for abuse, having chosen to wear "revealing" clothing that "invites" sexual advances.

Many think that the problem of rape culture can be addressed by shifting popular understandings of the reasons why rape and sexual assault occur. In addition to awareness-raising campaigns, there are concrete actions that could accomplish this. Consider, for example, the dress codes in place in many middle schools and high schools that prohibit girls from wearing "revealing" or "form-fitting" clothes. Some teachers and school administrators try to rationalize these rules by proposing that scantily clad girls constitute "distractions" for their (male) peers, undermining their ability to learn (Deschamps 2015).

Female students suggest they are unfairly targeted by such dress codes. In May 2015, Alexi Halket, 18, arrived at Toronto's Etobicoke School of the Arts wearing a sleeveless crop-top. Rather than attending class, she was sent to the principal's office to be lectured on "appropriate clothing." Instead of going home to change, Halket called on female students across the Toronto area to wear crop tops to school the next day in a show of resistance. She said: "We wanted to stand in solidarity against people making women cover their bodies because it's 'offensive' and 'inappropriate'" (Deschamps 2015).

Lauren Wiggins, a 17-year-old attending high school in Moncton, N.B., reports a similar experience. She received a detention for wearing a floor-length halter dress that exposed her shoulders, upper back, and bra straps. In a letter to the school's vice-principal, she wrote: "The fact that authority figures, especially males, can tell young women they must cover up their shoulders and their back because it is 'inappropriate' and 'a distraction' is very uncomforting . . ." (Frisk 2015). She was then given a one-day suspension.

Punishing women like Halket and Wiggins for their clothing choices means blaming victims for their sexual harassment—even before it happens. By resisting dress codes, some women show that they are aware that these restrictive rules may actually promote rape culture. By challenging them in highly publicized ways, it may be possible to shift the focus away from women's bodies and clothing, and deal instead with the problematic notion that sexual harassment and abuse is "okay" if it is "provoked."

Sexual harassment and abuse is a problem not only in schools but also in the workplace. Insiders often argue that employees need to be empowered to report such mistreatment (Wear et al. 2007). Outsiders who have endured harassment note two difficulties with this view. First, the onus should not be on victims to report events that should not have happened in the first place; we should instead be concerned with altering harassers' behaviour so that these incidents never occur.

Second, harassers are often in positions of power and authority, making it difficult and professionally risky for women to report harassment. Wear et al. (2007) interviewed 30 female medical students attending five different medical schools in the U.S. Most had either experienced or observed sexual harassment during their placements, but felt unable to report it for fear that their grades or professional reputations would suffer as a direct result. The students emphasized that encouraging women to report harassment was not the answer:

> They don't need a better way for people to report it, they need to start at the top and make an impression that this is wrong, and infuse this into people because they've been doing it for so long they think it's fine and then residents see the attendants acting this way and they think "Oh, it's acceptable," and it's a kind of vicious cycle because no one at the top says "*No*, you *can't* make comments like that."

Others who have been subjected to sexual harassment argue that a stronger female presence in the workplace could help stop the practice. Fasting et al. (2007) interviewed 25 elite female athletes about their experiences of sexual harassment perpetrated by male authority figures. One athlete, Hanne, said that she thought female support, such as a harassment officer, might reduce further mistreatment:

> If we had had that kind of woman in our club, I think she would have heard a lot from the girls and women surrounding her, if sport clubs had

had persons whom it would have been easy to go and talk to if one needed help or advice, I think that would have helped. Maybe one just could have used such a woman to talk with, and maybe one could have used her to get advice about whether one should continue with a case or not. But I didn't have anything like that, I was in an environment with only boys and men, and it was impossible to talk to anyone.

By reducing the obstacles to women securing high-level positions, we might address two problems at once. Not only would more women be able to move up the corporate ladder, fulfilling their personal aspirations; those women would also be in positions of power that would allow them to improve life at work for other women.

Racial Inequality. You may recall that racialized women are more likely to be targets of abuse than others. In particular, immigrant women who strive to maintain certain cultural practices may be criticized by native-born Canadians, and encouraged to assimilate.

Outsiders have responded to this debate by arguing that it shouldn't be a public debate to begin with. Zarqa Nawaz, a British-Canadian of Pakistani origin who created the sitcom *Little Mosque on the Prairie* (and who wears a hijab), said she thinks there are other, more important issues that should be addressed. "We're in a recession, what is the plan to go forward? Those are the things I want to talk about. Not about women in [the] niqab. . . . That's just stupid."

What many racialized women say *is* a problem is their inability to access health care and other public services without encountering discrimination. Earlier, we considered the experiences of female Somali immigrants who had previously been the subject of female genital mutilation and who now required prenatal care here in Canada. One woman said she hoped "health care professionals will be trained in this issue so they will treat us with respect and not like animals." Another said she wanted her visitors to be respected by hospital staff: "My friend prayed at my bedside. The nurse walked on the prayer mat with her shoes. When I asked how she could do that she responded: 'You people are so barbaric.'" In all, the women felt that their quality of care could be greatly improved if health care professionals treated them with the same degree of professional respect shown in interactions with other patients.

Also related to racial inequalities are the barriers to employment faced by many skilled, highly educated immigrants upon arrival in Canada. Habiba Zaman (2010) interviewed 12 highly educated, skilled Pakistani women who had emigrated to Vancouver, asking each if she had recommendations for the provincial or federal governments. One woman, Tara, responded:

> Please don't think the new immigrants are illiterates. They are all well-

292

educated. They may have a language barrier, but they are more educated or smart than a lot of locals [Canadian-born]. They should not be assessed on these grounds. They should be evaluated on the basis of their degrees and there should be proper counselling. The government should work beforehand on where they require the work force, and accordingly the new immigrants should be adjusted. If there are any lacks, the immigrants should be asked to upgrade their education or skills. The government should give new immigrants direction. The government should communicate with immigrants so that they can be properly placed.

Improved communication between Canadian immigration authorities and immigrants *before* they arrive in Canada would reduce the shock many immigrants report feeling upon arrival, and allow them to make plans in advance for retraining or upgrading their skills, if needed.

Immigrants and other members of racial minorities are also likely to experience racial profiling. Rohan Robinson, a 32-year-old black elementary school teacher, says he's lost count of how many times he has been pulled over by police without being ticketed. "Policing is important," Robinson says:

> I totally support the police, but I support them when they go at it from an objective perspective, where, no matter who you are, if you did the crime, you get the consequences. If I am speeding, I'm supposed to get the same consequence as someone else who is speeding, no matter what. If I'm driving and I get pulled over for no reason, it should happen to everybody, not just me (Rankin 2010).

Robinson's comments fall short of a concrete plan to eliminate racial profiling, but they do show that, despite being targeted, perhaps unfairly, by police, he does not advocate a reduced police presence or restrictions on the ability of police to conduct random checks. Rather, he opposes the insider rationalization of racial profiling: that racial minorities *should* be stopped and searched more often than white Canadians, since they supposedly commit a disproportionate number of crimes. If random checks are to be permitted, Robinson proposes they should be genuinely that: *random*.

Aboriginal youth are especially likely to be subjected to racial profiling, among a range of other discriminatory practices. One Métis woman, âpihtawikosisân, has written extensively about inequalities suffered by Aboriginals. She notes:

> Many Canadians have been asking, "What can I do to help?" This is something you can do. Understand the issues yourself, and help other Canadians understand them better too. Don't let these beliefs remain "common knowledge" any longer. Challenge them, and challenge the

politicians who rely on these stereotypes in order to justify ongoing colonialism. Support Idle No More. . . . Demand change.

More specifically, âpihtawikosisân calls on non-Aboriginals to drop the notion that **assimilation** of Aboriginals into mainstream Canadian culture would solve "the Aboriginal problem":

> Many Canadians are still clamouring for assimilation. You can see this again in all those comment sections, in all of the dialogues about 'how to fix the Aboriginal problem'. The solutions are invariably, "Make them more like us! Private property! Get them out of isolated communities and into the cities with the rest of us! No special rights! No differences! Treat them the same!" and so on. . . . It's all been tried. It really has. Pretty much every suggestion currently being given to assimilate native peoples has been actively tried before, with disastrous results and ultimately, a failure to actually assimilate us.
>
> Stop it. It didn't work, and it isn't going to work. . . . Accept the fact that we are here, and we aren't leaving, and that we recognise you aren't leaving either. It would do us all a world of good if we could be on the same page on this one.

Progress towards greater equality for Aboriginal people should begin, she argues, with Canadians educating themselves about Aboriginal history and becoming familiar with aspects of Aboriginal culture, including First Nations languages. "I see language learning as a 'way in' to a deeper and more respectful (and healthier) relationship [that] has incredible potential for fostering understanding and cooperation."

Interestingly, âpihtawikosisân is not proposing anything new; her suggestions are very much in the mainstream of the "cultural mosaic" approach to multiculturalism that many Canadians hold to be one of the cornerstones of our culture.

Age Inequality. In the West, children and adolescents are typically viewed as immature and naïve, and many adults strive to defend their "innocence" for as long as possible. Yet youth account for an increasing fraction of the homeless population in Canada. These outsiders—in terms of both their age and their economic circumstances—are forced to show a degree of resourcefulness and maturity "beyond their years." Their circumstances are extreme, but what they have to say about their struggle to survive homelessness suggests that we might do well to reconsider some of the ways we think about young Canadians.

Pandora Parks, now 21, has been homeless since she was 15. Asked what is needed to get her off the streets, the Winnipeg native said: "Government assistance. Having them raise the rates so that I can afford maybe a bachelor [apartment] in a neighbourhood that's not full of crack dealers" (Spurr 2015). Being homeless, Parks said, is "better than staying in a youth shelter—all the arbitrary rules that they have, and being treated like a child. You don't feel any safer, and you're no less likely to have your stuff stolen. As for women's shelters, it feels like it's where Amazons go to die. There's so much sadness, it's really, really painful. It's a toxic environment. I've only stayed at any shelter for 12 hours, 24 hours at the most."

Saleem Hill, 22, has also been self-sufficient since age 15. Asked what people should know about homeless youth, he responded: "This is the misconception—I worked last year full time. People would think that a person in a shelter would probably be up to no good, and not doing anything." He added: "I've always been on social assistance since high school. Even though I work, I always use that service. When you're staying in a shelter, you receive less. They say, you're not paying rent, we're going to take that away from you. I wouldn't be here for more than two months if they did not do that."

Parks and Hill's words indicate that, despite the disadvantages with which they struggle, neither wants to be treated like a helpless "child." Parks wants to establish a home for herself, so she can focus on completing high school. Hill, for his part, wants to be recognized for making ends meet on his own. Insiders might say both have been robbed of their childhoods, but neither Parks nor Hill seem interested in bemoaning their loss of innocence or framing themselves as victims.

At the other end of the age spectrum, older Canadians are also often treated in infantilizing ways. Many are told they are no longer physically or mentally capable of living independently. This is no doubt true of some, but others would benefit from aging in place, as discussed earlier. To support this goal, a Canadian organization called Seniors for Seniors offers in-home support and care, provided by younger seniors for older ones (Kazia 2013). Dorinne MacNab, an 88-year-old who was diagnosed with Alzheimer's disease more than ten years ago, uses their services. Over the last decade, MacNab has had several older adults who work for Seniors for Seniors visit her at home up to five times a week. Her visitors are only slightly younger than she is, but they can help her prepare meals, run errands, and assist with other aspects of her care. MacNab recognizes that a much younger person could also support her in these ways, but she says the most helpful part of the service is the meaningful conversations she's able to have with people of her generation: "To talk to somebody who is in their 20s, they can't talk about the same history as I can, they weren't even here. . . . I have to have somebody that has a little more background, that we have something in common."

The "junior seniors" who provide support agree with MacNab. Sandra Davidson, a 67-year-old employee of Seniors for Seniors, says the people she works with "can relate to me because even though there is a generation gap, it's still very similar to our upbringing and our values and morals."

Organizations like Seniors for Seniors are helping to keep older adults in their homes, but some seniors must still be placed in assisted living facilities. One senior interviewed by Sarah Wood (2012) who has lived in such a facility for three years said that she would prefer to be at home, but appreciated the advantages of living in what are still popularly known as "nursing homes": "If something goes wrong, if you have an 'accident' or anything, somebody is here to help you." But, she added, "it takes them so darn long to get to you. Sometimes I wonder if it really matters to have the nurses here at all." Asked what improvements could be made to assisted care facilities, this particular senior was adamant: "Hire more nurses! The nurses are always saying that they are short-handed. That they've got too many people to take care of and not enough of them to go around. . . . Most of the time in the evening and at night, there are only two nurses here." She added: "I'd PAY the nurses more, too. Most of these girls said they don't make enough to make ends meet."

Because aging in place is not yet an option for all older adults—and likely never will be for those who suffer from acute dementia or other debilitating ailments—assisted living facilities and other support systems must be made as effective as possible. An obvious way to improve residents' quality of life would be to hire more support staff.

Another (admittedly less drastic) practice that makes many Canadian seniors feel infantilized is the revocation of their driver's licenses. More sensitive rules and regulations are needed in this area. True, some older adults eventually become unfit to drive, and to ensure the safety of everyone else on the road, their licenses should be revoked. But rather than automatically assuming that every individual over some largely arbitrary age is unfit to drive, individualized assessment systems that give older adults the chance to demonstrate their abilities need to be put in place.

Sexuality Inequality. Sex workers are among the most outspoken of outsiders. They have publicly discussed their work, their views on the legislation that regulates it (or fails to do so), and their belief that such legislation is often developed without their input. For example, insiders claim that Bill C-36, the "Protection of Communities and Exploited Persons Act," was passed in an effort to protect sex workers (Smith 2015). But sex workers themselves say they do not feel the legislation protects their interests. Jean McDonald, the executive director of Maggie's, a project run by and for sex workers in Toronto, said:

> Sex workers across the country—thousands of us represented by 20 to 30 different organizations, as well as individuals—were not listened to in the development of this legislation. . . . The Bill criminalizes adult consensual

sex.... [I]t's not dealing with anything about being forced into the industry or underage workers. Even if we scrapped the entire legislation,
we still have laws in the books that deal with underage persons, we still
have laws that deal with rape and sexual assault, we have laws around
trafficking.

McDonald suggests that sex workers would enjoy safer working conditions
if the industry were decriminalized and the public educated about sex work in
ways that would help reduce the stigma surrounding it:

> Even if the laws start to change overnight, there's still not a concerted
> effort to see sex work as a valuable and viable work option, and to see sex
> workers as respected members of our community with access to the same
> kinds of labor protection and legal rights that everyone in Canada should
> have.... We should feel like we can call the police should something
> happen to us. People say, *Oh, you know, prostitution isn't the oldest
> profession, it's the oldest oppression*, and I say, well, if people are op-
> pressed in any form of work or any part of our lives, the way to address
> that is not to criminalize these aspects of our lives: it's to ensure legal
> rights and labour protection so that oppressions can be challenged
> (Smith 2015).

In an interview about her Vice documentary, *A New Era of Canadian Sex
Work*, former stripper-turned-musician Lowell said: "[I] think there are a lot
of rich, white Christian people with power trying to step into the lives of people who don't have those privileges. And they do all this without identifying
any of the social reasons why people might do sex work. Saving people who
don't want to be saved doesn't work."

Lowell visited Nevada to investigate how that state's legalized, regulated
sex-work system contrasts with Canada's more restrictive framework:

> They call the place I visited a "sex resort," because you can stay there
> over night. Contrasting with Canada, it was so much better. It's clearly a
> safer way to deal with sex work. I saw women there who had been vic-
> timized in the past but wanted to continue doing sex work—they were
> taught how to empower themselves and given the means to do it safely.
> That's huge.
>
> But the thing is, when you talk about legalization, it's complex. You
> still have people who are running things and it's still selective and can
> alienate certain groups. Decriminalization is for sure the safest way to
> approach sex work, but it doesn't solve everything. ... Laws like Bill C-36
> make it seem like you have to choose who you want to support—the vic-
> tims, or the people out in the streets who like their work. But you don't
> get to choose who has human rights. Everyone has rights. It's the gov-

ernment's job to treat every person equally when it comes to safety and their rights.

Some sex workers feel that Bill C-36 could increase the risks they face at work by restricting their ability to negotiate with clients, ensure the venue they will be using is safe, and clearly communicate which services they offer and which they do not. Kerry Porth, a former sex worker who is now the board chair of Pivot Legal Society, said: "Canadians need to understand that this new law will not protect sex workers or communities. Instead, C-36 will impoverish them and deepen their vulnerability to exploitation and violence" (Hollet 2014).

Constantly being treated like a victim detracts from their sense of agency, say some sex workers. Rather than focusing on new laws, they say they are more interested in changing the public's perception of sex work. One woman says the best thing you can do is to treat her like everyone else. April Adams (2015) writes:

> There are absolutely women in the world who are trafficked, who are doing sex work for reasons that are terrible and coercive and highly traumatizing. If you encounter someone with a story like that socially, do your level-best to help them. . . . But if you meet a self-identified sex worker (or dancer or hooker or cam girl), especially in a big city, and you don't see someone standing behind them holding a gun, do them the favor of assuming that they have control over their own life. Do them the favor of assuming that they make decisions according to an idiosyncratic but valid analysis of their choices and consequent financial outcomes.

According to Adams, at least some sex workers freely choose to participate in the industry, but her comment that they do so only after a "valid analysis of their choices" highlights the fact that some women are left with few alternative means of survival. Adams (2015) recommends improving women's financial stability, so they are not forced to choose between impoverishment and sex work: "I can tell you that all the people I know who got into sex work early had one thing in common: financial instability. They don't all have daddy issues, sexual abuse, or early childhood divorce in their backgrounds (I don't have any of those). I had a choice: hooking or drop out of college."

Adams' advice regarding sex workers—"do them the favor of assuming that they have control over their own life"—is, in some sense, applicable to other outsiders, too. Many members of the LGBTQ community have expressed a desire to have their individual choices respected and accepted. For instance, Tré Easton (2015) says that he would like people to stop signposting his sexuality when referring to him:

The time has come for the gay best friend (or perhaps you prefer "GBF") to, once and for all, experience a quick, clean and unequivocal death. . . . [T]he GBF is a narrow interpretation of the beautiful array of personalities that comprise the LGBTQ community. It's the unfair distilling of gay men to just one of the many things that makes him the guy who you want to be around because of his wit, sparkling personality or great taste in music. . . .

The notion of the "gay best friend" works to calcify the idea of gay as *other*. It may seem to be a minor issue of nomenclature, but what you call something has meaning, in my most humble opinion. I don't want to be limited by my sexual orientation. Nor do I wish to have undue expectations placed on me because of aforementioned orientation.

Erin Tatum (2014), a self-identified queer person, is also concerned with the language used to refer to LGBTQ people, and the ways they are addressed:

People in queer relationships are often subjected to a barrage of ignorance from the straight community. Whether it be invasive sexual questions or unwanted criticism, nothing seems to be off limits to the innocently inquisitive straight. Inevitably, one of the more repetitive and annoying debates will be the age-old question *"Who is the man and who is the woman?"*

. . . [A]sking about anyone's sex life without their permission is just rude and creepy. We're not here for your titillation. . . . Instead of asking who's the man and who's the woman, ask yourself why that question matters to you in the first place.

People who fall outside of heteronormativity—outsiders on the dimension of sexuality—are understandably concerned by insiders' refusal to listen to them. Sexuality and the law have a long, messy history, with legislators failing to consider sex workers' input when drafting policies meant to protect them, and trying to forestall LGBTQ people's desire to legally marry. Progress has undeniably been made, including the recent legalization of same-sex marriage, yet many outsiders continue to feel the effects of heteronormativity.

FINAL THOUGHTS

With few exceptions, outsiders of all types want acceptance. First, many want insiders and academics to recognize that they do indeed continue to face unequal life chances, unequal opportunities, and barriers to success and inclusion, despite insider claims that we have successfully built an egalitarian community. Second, when it comes to resolving these issues and obtaining a greater degree of equality, outsiders say they do not want to be pitied as helpless victims. Many want to be accepted as they are—permitted to live their lives as they see fit, without pressure to conform to the standards of others, or assimilate into mainstream Canadian society.

In response, insiders ask whether and to what degree such acceptance threatens society as a whole. While a majority of Canadians favour the legalization of same-sex marriage, for example, some continue to claim that it undermines the traditional institution of marriage between a man and a woman. A slightly larger minority opposes same-sex parenting, asserting that this non-traditional arrangement could harm the children of same-sex couples. Similar arguments have been made regarding almost every other instance of inequality discussed in this book, with insiders striving to show the dangers of certain outsider behaviours in an attempt to eradicate them.

In some cases, academics offering second opinions have intervened, using empirical evidence to show that some outsider behaviours are entirely harmless and may even have benefits (such as same-sex marriage and child-rearing, for instance). They have also been able to show that certain policies and programs would reduce inequality and improve people's quality of life.

Nevertheless, where there is inequality, there will always be competing narratives that aim to explain, justify, or challenge it. Sociologists should (and often do) ensure the voices of outsiders permeate these public debates about inequality. Through careful data collection and analysis, sociologists can reduce the widespread ignorance that results from lack of empirical information. As sociologist Anthony Giddens wrote in *New Rules of Sociological Method* (1976):

> The sociological observer cannot stand outside the society he or she studies, but instead constantly draws on his or her knowledge of it as a resource. . . . Ironically, only by immersing oneself in life can one watch and study it, to create an understanding of the social rules. Therefore, all sociological theories . . . reveal both the organization of society and the organization of the viewer. . . . Therefore, the tasks of sociological analysis are to reveal the structures of society in the conceptual language of social science; and specifically, to explain how human actors manage to produce and reproduce society, under constraints.

The purpose of this book has been to draw attention to the many competing narratives put forward about inequality, and the reasons—often self-serving—why some people endorse certain narratives over others. Many people view these narratives as unquestionably true statements of fact. But when considered in a new light, juxtaposed against the data presented by academics offering second opinions or the voices of outsiders, these dominant narratives can begin to unravel. This comparative exercise has practical value: the first step in any change is to become conscious of our currently unconscious attitudes and beliefs. Only by recognizing there are many views of and potential solutions for inequality can we begin to address it.

To that end, we must become more aware of our tendency to distinguish between different "kinds" of people based on characteristics like sex, age, race, ethnic ancestry, social class, and sexual orientation. The habit of categorizing people based on these features is related to the more problematic habit of ascribing unequal value to them—of valuing masculinity over femininity, youth over old age, whiteness over non-whiteness, rich over poor, and heteronormativity over alternative sexualities. By showing that these categories are socially constructed, as is the power of traditionally dominant groups, we are better able to value the standpoints and opinions of outsiders—of the disadvantaged and disregarded. Taking their views seriously, as well as those offered by insiders and academics, is crucial if we are to achieve the best understanding of inequalities, their causes, and their consequences. To come to grips with the enduring issue of inequality, we must not only acknowledge its existence, but also listen to outsiders when they tell us how they would like to address it.

DISCUSSION QUESTIONS

1. Is inequality fair and justifiable, or unfair and harmful? How would insiders and outsiders alike benefit from reducing inequality? Conversely, what drawbacks might be associated with reduced inequality, for members of either group?

2. Of the recommendations for reducing inequality listed in this chapter, which do you think are reasonable, or most likely to be enacted? Which do you think would lack sufficient public support?

3. After reading about inequality from the perspective of outsiders who experience it first-hand, have your views of these people changed? Consider, for example, how you thought about homeless people and welfare support before reading this book. Are your views on these issues the same, or have they changed?

4. Do you think we can achieve greater social inequality just by talking to and about outsiders in different, more respectful ways? Or are laws and policies the most effective way to drive change?

FURTHER READING

Rony Brauman et al. "From Philanthropy to Humanitarianism: Remarks and an Interview." *The South Atlantic Quarterly* 103:2 (2004): 397–417.

Miles Corak. "Income Inequality, Equality of Opportunity, and Intergenerational Mobility." *The Journal of Economic Perspectives* 27:3 (2013): 79–102.

David Green et al., eds. *Income Inequality: The Canadian Story*. Institute for Research on Public Policy, 2016

Wayne Lewchuk. *The Precarity Penalty: The Impact of Employment Precarity on Individuals, Households and Communities—and What to Do about It.* McMaster University, 2015.

David Macdonald. *Outrageous Fortune: Documenting Canada's Wealth Gap.* Canadian Centre for Policy Alternatives, 2014.

Laura McDonough et al. *The Opportunity Equation: Building Opportunity in the Face of Growing Income Inequality.* United Way of Toronto, 2015.

N. Ruiz and N. Woloszko. "What Do Household Surveys Suggest about the Top 1% Incomes and Inequality in OECD countries?" OECD Publishing, 2016.

Jeffrey D. Sachs. *The End of Poverty: Economic Possibilities for Our Time.* Penguin, 2006.

KEY TERMS

New gender gap. Theory suggesting that while women's lives have improved over the past 35 years, there has been a parallel decline over the same period in women's happiness compared to that of men.

Redistributive taxation. Tax system designed to reduce inequalities in wealth and income, by taxing well-off people more heavily.

Welfare system. Government programs providing financial and other assistance to the needy.

Acknowledgements

The topic of social inequality has gained great public interest over the past ten years or so. We wanted to add our voices to the debate about its causes, correlates, and consequences. The result is *Outsights*, the book you are looking at. It builds on one author's experience of teaching an undergraduate course on inequality over the past five years, and writing about social inequality and related social problems for more than two decades. It also builds on the other author's experience of studying and writing about inequality—especially gender inequality—over the past half-decade.

We have enjoyed writing this book together—the second book we have co-authored and the most recent of many projects completed together. We were helped in our work by several talented University of Toronto undergraduates, among them Emily Berry, Lina Contreras, Nabi Dressler, Hélène Emorine, Emma Graham, Sania Hameed, Richard Kennedy, Yasmin Koop-Monteiro, Catherine Maitland, Emily Povse, Ashley Ramnaraine, Marrium Sahar, Sarah Tan, Sylvia Urbanik, and Alice Wang. They assisted us in sourcing and reviewing the published academic literature on social inequality. A special thanks to undergraduate Zoe Sebastien, who assisted in the research process and also found us interesting visual materials (including graphs, charts, and diagrams) that illustrated the messages of our text. Undergraduate Teddy Avramov edited and simplified one draft of our chapters, while doctoral student Laura Upenieks offered encouragement and very useful suggestions for the improvement of our penultimate draft. We are also grateful for comments received from University of Toronto colleagues during and after a seminar presentation of the book. We got the most thorough comments from colleagues Christian Caron, Scott Schieman, and Geoff Wodtke. Thanks, everyone, for terrific help with our thinking on this project.

Equally important was the help we received from the people at Rock's Mills Press. Publisher David Stover encouraged this project from the outset, found able reviewers for the manuscript chapters, and edited the final version of the book. In the process, David made many valuable suggestions for improvement and helped us shorten and tighten what had become a too-large manuscript. So, thank you, David. You made the writing and publication of this book almost quick and almost painless. We are also grateful to six anonymous expert reviewers who, we now learn, included Stephen Mcbride (McMaster University) and John Winterdyk (Mount Royal University). Invariably helpful, they forced us to clarify our thinking and add appropriate research references.

We dedicate this book to Canada's young people—students and otherwise—who are struggling to understand the (often malevolent) forces that control their access to education, jobs, income, and dignity. We hope this book will enhance their understanding of social inequality and, more important, lead them to question what they hear from self-interested insider sources about this inequality and its supposed inevitability.

NICOLE MEREDITH

LORNE TEPPERMAN

Toronto, August 2016

References

INTRODUCTION AND CHAPTER 1

Alexander, Jeffrey. The Meaningful Construction of Inequality and the Struggles against It: A 'Strong Program' Approach to How Social Boundaries Change. *Cultural Sociology* 1:1 (2007): 23–30.

Almas, I. et al. Fairness and the Development of Inequality Acceptance. *Science* 328:5982 (2010): 1176–1178.

Alwin, Duane. Distributive Justice and Satisfaction with Material Well–Being. *American Sociological Review* 52:1 (1987): 83–95.

Armstrong, Nancy. Some Call It Fiction: On the Politics of Domesticity. In Julie Rivkin and Michael Ryan (eds.), *Literary Theory: An Anthology* (pp. 567–83). Malden, MA: Blackwell Publishing, 2004.

Arneson, Richard J. Equality of Opportunity: Derivative Not Fundamental. *Journal of Social Philosophy* 44 (2013): 316–30.

Bénabou, Roland and Jean Tirole. Belief in a Just World and Redistributive Politics. *The Quarterly Journal of Economics* 121:2 (2006): 699–746.

Bilge, Sirma. Intersectionality Undone. *Du Bois Review: Social Science Research on Race* (2013): 405–24.

Bjornskov, Christian et al. On the Relation between Income Inequality and Happiness: Do Fairness Perceptions Matter? *Center for European, Governance and Economic Development Research* 91 (2009): 1–56.

Bowleg, Lisa. When Black Lesbian Woman ≠ Black Lesbian Woman: The Methodological Challenges of Qualitative and Quantitative Intersectionality Research. *Sex Roles* (2008): 312–25.

Breen, Richard. A Weberian Approach to Class Analysis. *Alternative Foundations of Class Analysis* (2002): 42.

Brown Parlee, Mary. Situated Knowledges of Personal Embodiment: Transgender Activists' and Psychological Theorists' Perspectives on 'Sex' and 'Gender.' *Theory and Psychology* 6:4 (1996): 625–645.

Carbado, Devon W. Colorblind Intersectionality. *Signs* (2013): 811–45.

Choo, Hae Yeon, and Myra Marx Ferree. Practicing Intersectionality in Sociological Research: A Critical Analysis of Inclusions, Interactions, and Institutions in the Study of Inequalities. *Sociological Theory* (2010): 129–49.

Clarke, Averil Y., and Leslie Mccall. Intersectionality and Social Explanation in Social Science Research. *Du Bois Review: Social Science Research on Race* (2013): 349–63.

Cozzarelli, Catherine, Anna V. Wilkinson, and Michael J. Tagler. Attitudes Toward the Poor and Attributions for Poverty. *Journal of Social Issues* 57:2 (2001): 207–27.

Crenshaw, Kimberle. Mapping the Margins: Intersectionality, Identity Politics, and Violence against Women of Color. *Stanford Law Review* 43:6 (1991): 1241–99.

Croucher, Sheila. Constructing the Image of Ethnic Harmony in Toronto, Canada: The Politics of Problem Definition and Nondefinition. *Urban Affairs Review* 32:3 (1997): 319–47.

Cullen, John B. and Shelley M. Novick. The Davis–Moore Theory of Stratification: A Further Examination and Extension. *American Journal of Sociology* 84 (1979): 1424–37.

Davis, K. Intersectionality as Buzzword: A Sociology of Science Perspectives on What Makes a Feminist Theory Successful. *Feminist Theory* (2008): 67–85.

Deslauriers, Marguerite. Two Conceptions of Inequality and Natural Difference. *Canadian Journal of Political Science* 37:4 (2004): 787–809.

Deutsch, Morton. Equity, Equality, and Need: What Determines Which Value Will Be Used as the Basis of Distributive Justice? *Journal of Social Issues* 31:3 (1975): 137–49.

DeVault, Marjorie L. Introduction: What is Institutional Ethnography? *Social Problems* 53:3 (2006): 294–98.

Eells, Laura Workman. So Inequality Is Fair? Demonstrating Structured Inequality in the Classroom. *Teaching Sociology* 15:1 (1987): 73.

Eurostat. Gini Coefficient of Equivalised Disposable Income. http://epp.eurostat.ec.europa.eu/tgm/table.do?tab=table andlanguage=enandpcode=tessi190.

Fourcade, Marion and Kieran Healy. Classification Situations: Life–Chances in the Neoliberal Era. *Accounting, Organizations and Society* 38:8 (2013): 559–72.

Gainer, Mitch. Assessing Happiness Inequality in the Welfare State: Self–Reported Happiness and the Rawlsian Difference Principle. *Social Indicators Research* 114 (2013): 453–464.

Geerts, Evelien, and Iris Van Der Tuin. From Intersectionality to Interference: Feminist Onto–epistemological Reflections on the Politics of Representation. *Women's Studies International Forum* (2013): 171–78.

Grahame, Peter R. Ethnography, Institutions, and the Problematic of the Everyday World. *Human Studies* 21 (1998): 347–60.

Hafer, Carolyn L. and Laurent Bègue. Experimental Research on Just–World Theory: Problems, Developments, and Future Challenges. *Psychological Bulletin* 131:1 (2005): 128–167.

Haines, Herbert. Cognitive Claims-Making, Enclosure, and the Depoliticization of Social Problems. *The Sociological Quarterly* 20 (1979): 119–130.

Hancock, Ange–Marie. Intersectionality as A Normative And Empirical Paradigm. *Politics and Gender* (2007).

Haraway, Donna. Situated Knowledges: The Science Question in Feminism and the Privilege of Partial Perspective. *Feminist Studies* 14.3 (1988): 575–99.

Harris, Scott. Social Constructionism and Social Inequality. *Journal of Contemporary Ethnography* 35:3 (2006): 223–235.

Hedgehog Review. Editorial: The American Dream. *The Hedgehog Review* 15:2 (2013): 7.

Hekman, Susan. Truth and Method: Feminist Standpoint Theory Revisited. *Signs* 22:1 (1997): 341–365.

Hilgartner, Stephen and Charles Bosk. The Rise and Fall of Social Problems: A Public Arenas Model. *American Journal of Sociology* 94:1 (1988): 53–78.

Hinton, Pita. 'Situated Knowledges' and New Materialism(s): Rethinking a Politics of Location. *Women: A Cultural Review* 25:1 (2014): 99–113.

Hoelter, Lynette F. Fair is Fair—Or is It? Perceptions of Fairness in the Household Division of Labor. Ph.D. diss., Pennsylvania State University, 2001.

Joseph, Lawrence B. Some Ways of Thinking about Equality of Opportunity. *The Western Political Quarterly* 33 (1980): 393–400.

Kenworthy, Lane, and Jonas Pontusson. Rising Inequality and the Politics of Redistribution in Affluent Countries. Syracuse, NY: Maxwell School of Citizenship and Public Affairs, Syracuse University, 2005.

Kirk, John. Using Intersectionality to Examine the New Complexities of Work Identities and Social Class. *Sociology Compass* (2009): 234–48.

Ku, Hyejin, and Timothy C. Salmon. Procedural Fairness and yhe Tolerance for Income Inequality. *European Economic Review* 64 (2013): 111–128.

LaGory, Mark and Kevin Fitzpatrick. Life Chances and Choices: Assessing Quality of Life among the Homeless. *The Sociological Quarterly* 42:4 (2001): 633–651.

Lasswell, Thomas E. Social Stratification: 1964–1968. *The Annals of the American Academy*.

Lépinard, Éléonore. Impossible Intersectionality? French Feminists and the Struggle for Inclusion. *Politics and Gender* (2014): 124–30.

Lindsay, Keisha. (Re)reading Intersectionality and Identity in the Discourse on Marginalized Black Men. PhD diss., University of Chicago, 2009.

Longino, Helen. Feminist Standpoint Theory and the Problems of Knowledge. *Signs* 19:1 (1993): 201–212.

Lovell, Peggy A. Race, Gender, and Work in Sao Paulo, Brazil, 1960–2000. *Latin American Research Review* 4:3 (2006): 63–87.

Lovell, Peggy and Charles Wood. Skin Color, Racial Identity, and Life Chances in Brazil. *Latin American Perspectives* 25:3 (1998): 90–109.

Martens, Nicholas. What's So Fair about the Status Quo? Examining Fairness Criteria as Moderators of System Justification. PhD diss., Florida Atlantic University, 2011.

McCall, Leslie. The Complexity of Intersectionality. *Signs* (2005), 1771–1800.

Melamed, David. The Effects of Legitimacy and Power on Perceptions of Fairness. *Sociological Focus* 45:2 (2012): 125–142.

Moellendorf, Darrel. Equality of Opportunity Globalized? *Jurisprudence* (2006): 301–318.

Nash, Jennifer C. Re-thinking Intersectionality. *Feminist Review* (2008): 1–15.

Niemi, Laura and Liane Young. Blaming the Victim in the Case of Rape. *Psychological Inquiry* 25:2 (2014): 230–233.

Osberg, L., and T. Smeeding. Fair Inequality? Attitudes toward Pay Differentials: The United States in Comparative Perspective. *American Sociological Review* 71:3 (2006): 450–473.

Richards, Janet. Equality of Opportunity. *Ratio* (1997): 253–279.

Rodriquez, Jason. Product Review: The American Dream and the Power of Wealth: Choosing Schools and Inheriting Inequality in the Land of Opportunity. *Contemporary Sociology: A Journal of Review* 36:5 (2007): 438–9.

Roemer, John. Defending Equality of Opportunity. *The Monist* 86 (2003): 261–282.

Roemer, John. Equality of Opportunity: A Progress Report. *Social Choice and Welfare* 19 (2002): 455–471.

Rubin, Zick and Letitia Anne Peplau. Who Believes in a Just World? *Journal of Social Issues* 31:3 (1975): 65–89.

References

Sachs, Benjamin. The Limits of Fair Equality of Opportunity. *Philosophical Studies* 160 (2012): 323–343.

Shields, Stephanie A. Gender: An Intersectionality Perspective. *Sex Roles* (2008): 301–11.

Shipp, Mel. Income and Inequality in the U.S.: A Matter of Envy, or Fairness? *The Nation's Health*, March 1, 2012.

Stoetzler, Marcel and Nira Yuval–Davis. Standpoint Theory, Situated Knowledge and the Situated Imagination. *Feminist Theory* 3:3 (2002): 315–333.

Trump, Kris-Stella. The Status Quo and Perceptions of Fairness: How Income Inequality Influences Public Opinion. Ph.D. diss., Harvard University, 2013.

Tumin, Melvin M. Some Principles of Stratification: A Critical Analysis. *American Sociological Review* 18 (1953): 387–394.

Valentine, Gill. Theorizing and Researching Intersectionality: A Challenge for Feminist Geography. *The Professional Geographer* (2007): 10–21.

Van Kempen, Eva. Poverty Pockets and Life Chances. *American Behavioral Scientist* 41:3 (1997): 430–449.

Wagmiller, Robert, et al. The Dynamics of Economic Disadvantage and Children's Life Chances. *American Sociological Review* 71:5 (2006): 847–966.

Walby, Kevin. On the Social Relations of Research: A Critical Assessment of Institutional Ethnography. *Qualitative Inquiry* 13:7 (2007): 1008–1030.

Walby, Sylvia, Jo Armstrong, and Sofia Strid. Intersectionality: Multiple Inequalities in Social Theory. *Sociology* (2012).

Wilkins, Vicky M. and Jeffrey B. Wenger. Belief in a Just World and Attitudes Toward Affirmative Action. *Policy Studies Journal* 42:3 (2014): 325–343.

Williams–Myers, A.J. Biological Differences, Social Inequality, and Distributive Goods: An Exploratory Argument. *Journal of Black Studies* 13:4 (1983): 399–416.

Williams, Walter. Income Inequality, Income Distribution, Economic Models. *The Examiner* (Washington), January 13, 2013.

Wood, Julia. Feminist Standpoint Theory and Muted Group Theory: Commonalities and Divergences. *Women and Language* 28:2 (2005): 61–64.

Woolgar, Steve and Dorothy Pawluch. Ontological Gerrymandering: The Anatomy of Social Problems Explanations. *Social Problems* 32:3 (1985): 214–227.

World Fact Book, Country Comparison: Distribution of Family Income: Gini Index.https://www.cia.gov/library/publications/the–worldfactbook/rankorder/2172rank.html.

Wrong, Dennis H. The Functional Theory of Stratification: Some Neglected Considerations. *American Sociological Review* 24 (1959): 772–782.

Yule, Rod. Global Inequality–'That's Not Fair!' *Ethos* 20:1 (2012): 18–19.

Zilinsky, Jan. Learning about Income Inequality: What is the Impact of Information on Perceptions of Fairness and Preferences for Redistribution? Research Paper, University of Chicago, 2014.

CHAPTER 2

Abdul–Sathar, E.I., R.P Suresh and K.R. Muraleedharan Nair. A Vector Valued Bivariate Gini Index for Truncated Distributions. *Statistical Papers* 48 (2005): 543–557.

Agnew, Robert S. Success and Anomie: A Study of the Effect of Goals on Anomie. *The Sociological Quarterly* 21:1 (1980): 53–64.

Alcott, Blake. John Rae and Thorstein Veblen. *Journal of Economic Issues* 38:3 (2004): 1–18.

Almeida, Felipe. Thorstein Veblen and Albert Bandura: A Modern Psychological Reading of the Conspicuous Consumer. *Journal of Economic Issues* 48: 1 (2014): 1–12.

Anner, Mark. 2001. The Impact of International Outsourcing on Unionization and Wages: Evidence from the Apparel Export Sector in Central America. *Industrial and Labor Relations Review* 64:2 (2001): 305–322.

Aubry, Tim, Fran Klodawsky and Daniel Coulombe. Comaring the Housing Trajectories of Different Classes within a Diverse Homeless Population. *American Journal of Community Psychology* 49 (2012): 142–155.

Ayala, L. and M. Rodriguez. What Determines Exit from Social Assistance in Spain? *International Journal of Social Welfare* 16 (2006): 168–182.

Backman, Olof and Ake Bergmark. Escaping Welfare? Social Assistance Dynamics in Sweden. *Journal of European Social Policy* 21:5 (2011): 486–500.

Baker, Maureen. Working Their Way Out of Poverty? Gendered Employment in Three Welfare States. *Journal of Comparative Family Studies* 40:4 (2009): 617–34.

Barrientos, Armando, Mark Gorman and Amanda Heslop. Old Age Poverty in Developing Countries: Contributions and Dependence in Later Life. *World Development* 31:3 (2003): 555–570.

Basran, Gurcharn S, and Zong Li. Devaluation of Foreign Credentials as Perceived by Visible Minority Professional Immigrants. *Canadian Ethnic Studies* 30:3 (1998): 7–23.

Belcher, John R. and Bruce R. Deforge. Social Stigma and Homelessness: The Limits of Social Change. *Journal of Human *Behaviour in the Social Environment* 22 (2012): 929–946.

Bennmarker, Helge, Kenneth Carling and Bertil Holmlund. Do Benefit Hikes Damage Job Finding? Evidence from Swedish Unemployment Insurance Reforms. *Labour* 21:1 (2007): 85–120.

Bergmark, Ake and Olof Backman. Stuck with Welfare? Long–Term Social Assistance Recipiency in Sweden. *European Sociological Review* 20:5 (2004): 425–443.

Bittman, Mark. Is it Bad Enough Yet? *The New York Times*, December 13, 2014.

Bourdieu, Pierre. Cultural Reproduction and Social Reproduction. In Jerome Karabel and A. H. Halsey (eds.), *Power and Ideology in Education* (pp. 487–511). New York: Oxford University Press, 1977.

Bourdieu, Pierre. The Forms of Capital. In Nicole Woolsey Biggart (ed.), *Readings in Economic Sociology* (pp. 280–291). New York: John Wiley & Sons, 2008.

Bourdieu, Pierre. *Distinction: A Social Critique of the Judgement of Taste.* Cambridge, MA: Harvard University Press, 1984.

Boyles, Michael, and Rick Tilman. Thorstein Veblen, Edward O. Wilson, and Sociobiology: An Interpretation. *Journal of Economic Issues* 27:4 (1993): 1195.

Brady, David. Reconsidering the Divergence between Elderly, Child, and Overall Poverty. *Research on Aging* 26:5 (2004):487–510.

Breen, Richard and Kristian B. Karlson. Education and Social Mobility: New Analytical Approaches. *European Sociological Review* 30:1 (2013): 107–118.

Breen, Richard. Educational Expansion and Social Mobility in the 20th Century. *Social Forces* 89:2 (2010): 365–388.

Brennan, Barry. Canadian Labor Today: Partial Successes, Real Challenges. *Monthly Review* 57:2 (2005): 46.

Brown, Jason, et al. Challenges Faced by Aboriginal Youth in the Inner City. *Canadian Journal of Urban Research* 14:1 (2005): 81–106.

Brown, Louise. Foreign Whiz Kid Endured Homelessness to Graduate Top of Class at U of T. *Toronto Star*, June 9, 2015.

Brown, Phillip. Education, Opportunity and the Prospects for Social Mobility. *British Journal of Sociology of Education* 34:5 (2013): 678–700.

Burns, Katharina Kovacs and Solina Richter. Alberta's Urban Homelessness Research Capacities: A Comprehensive Environmental Scan from 1990–2010. *Canadian Journal of Urban Research* 20:2 (2011): 71–90.

Byrom, Tina and Nic Lightfoot. Interrupted Trajectories.The Impact of Academic Failure on the Social Mobility of Working-Class Students. *British Journal of Sociology of Education* 34:5 (2013): 812–828.

Caldbick, Sam, et al. Globalization and the Rise of Precarious Employment: The New Frontier For Workplace Health Promotion. *Global Health Promotion* 21:2 (2014): 23–31.

Campbell, Don. Meet U of T's Top Student, Anh Cao: Long Road to Peak Honours at Convocation. *University of Toronto News*, June 9, 2015.

Carr, Stuart C. and Malcolm MacLachlan. Actors, Observers, and Attributions for Third World Poverty: Contrasting Perspectives from Malawi and Australia. *Journal of Social Psychology* 138:2 (1998): 189–202.

CBC News. Outsourcing Bank Jobs Is Common Practice, Say Employees. CBC News, April 9, 2013.

Chamlin, Mitchell B. and Beth A. Sanders. Falsifying Merton's Macro-Level Anomie Theory of Profit–Motivated Crime: A Research Note. *Deviant Behaviour* 34 (2013): 961–972.

Chan, Jenny, Ngai Pun and Mark Selden. The Politics of Global Production: Apple, Foxconn and China's New Working Class. *New Technology, Work and Employment* 28:2 (2013): 100–11.

Chan, Tak Wing and Vikki Boliver. The Grandparents Effect in Social Mobility: Evidence from British Birth Cohort Studies. *American Sociological Review* 78:4 (2013): 662–678.

Chaykowski, Richard P. 2002. Globalization and the Modernization of Canadian Labour Policy. *Canadian Public Policy* 28:1 (2002): 81–91.

Coates, John and Sue McKenzie–Mohr. Out of the Frying Pan, into the Fire: Trauma in the Lives of Homeless Youth Prior to and during Homelessness. *Journal of Sociology and Social Welfare* 37 (2010): 65–96.

Cohen, Nicole S. Negotiating Precarious Cultural Work: Freelance Writers and Collective Organization in Media Industries. Ph.D. dissertation, 2013.

Cormier, David and Harry Targ. Globalization and the North American Worker. *Labor Studies Journal* 26:1 (2001): 42–59.

Cranford, Cynthia J., Leah F. Vosko, and Nancy Zukewich. Precarious Employment in the Canadian Labour Market: A Statistical Portrait. *Just Labour* 3 (2003): 6–22.

CTV News. Sears Canada Eliminating 800 Jobs at Montreal Call Centre. January 16, 2014.

Digiorgio, Carla. Capital, Power, and Habitus: How Does Bourdieu Speak to the Tenure Process in Universities? *The Journal of Educational Thought* 44:1 (2010): 27–40.

Dilts, David A., R. Mike Rubison, and Robert J. Paul. Unemployment: Which Person's Burden? Man or Woman, Black or White? *Ethnic and Racial Studies* 12:1 (1989): 100–114.

DiMaggio, Paul. On Pierre Bourdieu. *American Journal of Sociology* 84:6 (1979): 1460–1474.

References

Doberstein, Carey. Applying European Ideas on Federalism and Doing It Better? The Government of Canada's Homelessness Policy Experiment. *Canadian Public Policy* 38:3 (2012): 395–410.

Dooley, Martin D. Children and Poverty in Canada. *Canadian Public Policy* 20:4 (1994): 430–43.

Dribe, Martin, Jan Van Bavel, and Cameron Campbell. Social Mobility and Demographic Behavior: Long Term Perspectives. *Demographic Research* 26:8 (2012): 173–190.

Eardley, Tony, et al. Social Assistance in OECD Countries. Department of Social Security Research Report No. 46 (1996).

Erickson, Bonnie H. Culture, Class, and Connections. *American Journal of Sociology* 102:1 (1996): 217.

Everett, Jeffery. Organizational Research and the Praxeology of Pierre Bourdieu. *Organizational Research Methods* 5:1 (2002): 56–80.

Featherstone, Richard and Mathieu Deflem. Anomie and Strain: Context and Consequences of Merton's Two Theories. *Sociological Inquiry* 73:4 (2003):471–489.

Fine, Gary Alan. The Social Construction of Style: Thorstein Veblen's *The Theory of the Leisure Class* as Contested Text. *Sociological Quarterly* 35:3 (1994): 457–472.

Flavelle, D. Canada's Inequality Growing: Stats Can. *Toronto Star*, September 11, 2014.

Fong, Eric, and Kumiko Shibuya. Economic Changes in Canadian Neighborhoods. *Population Research and Policy Review* 22:2 (2003): 147–70.

Fong, Eric, and Kumiko Shibuya. The Spatial Separation of the Poor in Canadian Cities. *Demography* 37:4 (2000): 449–459.

Gaetz, Stephen, et al. *The State of Homelessness in Canada 2013*. Toronto: Canadian Homelessness Research Network Press, 2013.

Gaetz, Stephen. *Making Knowledge Matter: Mobilizing Homelessness Research through the Homeless Hub*. Toronto: Canadian Homelessness Research Network Press, 2013.

Galarneau, D., and Sohn, T. (2015). Long Term Trends in Unionization. *Statistics Canada*. 2015.

Gardner, Florence C. Redefining Flexibility: How Precarious Work Is Changing Employment Relations. Ph.D. dissertation, 1998.

Gonick, Cy. Precarious Labour. *Canadian Dimension* 45:3 (2011): 24–25.

Gough, Ian, et al. Social Assistance in OECD Countries. *Journal of European Social Policy* 7:1 (1997): 17–43.

Grant, Tavia. Precarious Employment Still Rising in Toronto, Hamilton. *The Globe and Mail*, May 21, 2015.

Hajnal, Z.L. The Nature of Concentrated Urban Poverty in Canada and the United States. *Canadian Journal of Sociology* 20:4 (1995): 497–528.

Halli, S. S., and A. Kazempiur. Neighbourhood Poverty in Canadian Cities. *Canadian Journal of Sociology* 25:3 (2000): 369.

Hamilton, David. Thorstein Veblen: Theorist of the Leisure Class. *Journal of Economic Issues* 34:4 (2000): 981–983.

Hanks, William F. Pierre Bourdieu and the Practices of Language. *Annual Review of Anthropology* 34:1 (2005): 67–83.

Hannif, Zeenobiyah and Felicity Lamm. When Non–Standard Work Becomes Precarious: Insights from the New Zealand Call Centre Industry. *Management Revue* 16:3 (2005): 324–350.

Hansen, Hans–Tore. The Dynamics of Social Assistance Recipiency: Empirical Evidence from Norway. *European Sociological Review* 25:2 (2009): 215–231.

Hardaway, Cecily R. and Vonnie C. McLoyd. Escaping Poverty and Securing Middle Class Status: How Race and Socioeconomic Status Shape Mobility Prospects for African Americans During the Transition to Adulthood. *Journal of Youth and Adolescence* 38 (2009): 242–256.

Hilbert, Richard A. Durkheim and Merton on Anomie: An Unexplored Contrast and Its Derivatives. *Social Problems* 36:3 (1989): 242–250.

Hollis, Shirley A. Blaming Me, Blaming You: Assessing Service Learning and Participants' Tendency to Blame the Victim. *Sociological Spectrum* 24 (2004): 575–600.

Horgan, Goretti. 'That Child Is Smart Because He's Rich': The Impact of Poverty on Young Children's Experiences of School. *International Journal of Inclusive Education* 13:4 (2009): 359–376.

Huschka, Denis and Steffen Mau. Social Anomie and Racial Segregation in South Africa. *Social Indicators Research* 76 (2005): 467–498.

Iannelli, Cristina. Educational Expansion and Social Mobility: The Scottish Case. *Social Policy & Society* 10:2 (2011): 251–264.

Jedrzejczak, Alina. Decomposition of the Gini Index by Sources of Income. *International Advances in Economic Research* 14 (2008): 441–447.

Jenkins, Craig J., Stephen J. Scanlan, and Lindsey Peterson. Military Famine, Human Rights, and Child Hunger: A Cross-National Analysis, 1990–2000. *Journal of Conflict Resolution* 51:6 (2007): 823–847.

Jereb, Eva and Marko Ferjan. Social Classes and Social Mobility in Slovenia and Europe. *Organizacija* 41:6 (2008): 197–206.

Jones, Marion E., Michael L. Shier and John R. Graham. Intimate Relationships as Routes into and out of Homelessness: Insights from a Canadian City. *Journal of Social Policy* 41:1 (2012): 101–117.

Kachi, Yuko, Toshiaki Otsuka, and Tomoyuki Kawada. Precarious Employment and the Risk of Serious Psychological Distress.A Population–Based Cohort Study in Japan. *Scandinavian Journal of Work, Environment and Health* 40:5 (2014): 465–472.

Kahane, Adam. Alex Himelfarb on Austerity, Inequality and 'Trickle–Down Meanness.' *The Globe and Mail*, December 19, 2014. Online.

Kaida, Lisa. Policy Briefs: English and French Language Lessons Help New Immigrants Exit Poverty. *Population Change and Lifecourse Strategic Knowledge Cluster* (2014).

Kalleberg, Arne L. Precarious Work, Insecure Workers: Employment Relations in Transition. *American Sociological Review* 74:1 (2009): 1–22.

Kane, Thomas J. Giving Back Control: Long-Term Poverty and Motivation. *Social Service Review* 61:3 (1987): 405–419.

Kazemipur, Abdolmohammad, and Shiva Halli. The Invisible Barrier: Neighbourhood Poverty and Integration of Immigrants in Canada. *Journal of International Migration and Integration* 1:1 (2000): 85–100.

Kazemipur, Abdolmohammad, and Shiva S. Halli. The Colour of Poverty: A Study of the Poverty of Ethnic and Immigrant Groups in Canada. *International Migration* 38:1 (2000): 89–108.

Kazemipur, Abdolmohammed, and Shiva S. Halli. Immigrants and 'New Poverty': The Case of Canada. *International Migration Review* 35:4 (2001): 1129–1156.

Kendall, Joan. Circles of Disadvantage: Aboriginal Poverty and Underdevelopment in Canada. *American Review of Canadian Studies* 31:1–2 (2001): 43–59.

Klodawsky, Fran, Tim Aubry and Susan Farrell. Care and the Lives of Homeless Youth in Neoliberal Times in Canada. *Gender, Place and Culture* 13:4 (2006): 419–436.

Klodawsky, Fran, et al. What Happens Over Time: Researching Homelessness Longitudinally. *Canadian Journal of Urban Research* 16:1 (2007): 93–111.

Lambert, Thomas. Thorstein Veblen and the Higher Learning of Sport Management Education. *Journal of Economic Issues* 33:4 (1999): 973–984.

Lareau, Annette. Invisible Inequality: Social Class and Childrearing in Black Families and White Families. *American Sociological Review* 67:5 (2002): 747–776.

Lareau, Annette. *Unequal Childhoods: Class, Race, and Family Life.* (2nd ed.) Berkeley, CA: University of California Press, 2011.

Leo, Christopher and Martine August. National Policy and Community Initiative: Mismanaging Homelessness in a Slow Growth City. *Canadian Journal of Urban Research* 15:1 (2006): 1–21.

Lewchuk, W., Clarke, M., and de Wolff, A. Working without Commitments: Precarious Employment and Health. *Work, Employment and Society,* 22:3 (2008): 387–406.

Liao, Tim F. Measuring and Analyzing Class Inequality with the Gini Index Informed By Model–Based Clustering. *Sociological Methodology* 36 (2006): 201–226.

Lindsey, Duncan and Sacha K. Martin. Deepening Child Poverty: The Not So Good News about Welfare Reform. *Children and Youth Services Review* 25:1 (2003): 165–173.

Lipina, Sebastian J., Jennifer Simonds and M. Soledad Segretin. Recognizing the Child in Child Poverty. *Vulnerable Children and Youth Studies* 6:1 (2011):8–17.

MacKinnon, Shauna. The Politics of Poverty in Canada. *Social Alternatives* 32:1 (2013): 19–23.

Mandle, Jay R. 2000. Viewpoint: What is Globalization? *Historically Speaking* 1:2 (2000): 9–11.

Merton, Robert K. Social Structure and Anomie. *American Sociological Review* 3:5 (1938): 672–682.

Minujin, Alberto, Enrique Delamonica, Alejandra Davidziuk, and Edward D. Gonzalez. The Definition of Child Poverty: A Discussion of Concepts And Measurements. *Environment and Urbanization* 18:2 (2006):481–500.

Mitchell, Ross E. Thorstein Veblen: Pioneer in Environmental Sociology. *Organization Environment* 14:4 (2001):389–408.

Mizruchi, Ephraim H. Aspiration and Poverty: A Neglected Aspect of Merton's Anomie. *Sociological Quarterly* 8:4 (1967): 439–446.

Mojtehedzadehwork, Sara, and Laurie Monsebraaten. Precarious Work Is Now the New Norm, United Way Report Says. *Toronto Star,* May 21, 2015.

Mosco, Vincent. Knowledge and Media Workers in the Global Economy: Antimonies of Outsourcing. *Social Identities* 12:6 (2006): 771–790.

Muller, Georg P. Explaining Poverty: On the Structural Constraints of Income Mobility. *Social Indicators Research* 59:3 (2002): 301–319.

Murphy, Daniel S. and Mathew B. Robinson. The Maximizer: Clarifying Merton's Theories of Anomie and Strain. *Theoretical Criminology* 12:4 (2008): 501–521.

Nelson, Kenneth. Social Assistance and EU Poverty Thresholds 1990–2008. Are European Welfare Systems Providing Just and Fair Protection Against Low Income? *European Sociological Review* 29:2 (2013): 386–401.

References

Osberg, Lars, and Kuan Xu. How Well Do Canadian Provinces Compare? *Canadian Public Policy* 25:2 (1999): 179–95.

Patsiaouras, Georgios, and James A. Fitchett. The Evolution of Conspicuous Consumption. *Journal of Historical Research in Marketing* 4:1 (2012): 154–176.

Peterson, Richard A. Understanding Audience Segmentation: From Elite and Mass to Omnivore and Univore. *Poetics* 21:4 (1992): 243–58.

Picot, Garnett, Feng Hou, and Simon Coulombe. Poverty Dynamics among Recent Immigrants to Canada. *International Migration Review* 42:2 (2008): 393–424.

Preston, Valerie et al. Seeking Affordable Homeownership in the Suburbs: A Case Study of Immigrants in the York Region. In J. David Hulchanski et al. (eds.), *Finding Home: Policy Options for Addressing Homelessness in Canada*. Toronto: The Canadian Homelessness Research Network, 2009.

Remennick, Larissa. Intergenerational Transfer in Russian–Israeli Immigrant Families.Parental Social Mobility and Children's Integration. *Journal of Ethnic and Migration Studies* 38:10 (2012): 1533–1550.

Rexe, Kate. A Nation in Distress: The Political Economy of Urban Aboriginal Poverty. Master's thesis, Carleton University, 2007.

Richter, Solina, et al. Homelessness Coverage in Major Canadian Newspapers, 1987–2007. *Canadian Journal of Communications* 36:4 (2011): 619–635.

Rivera, L. A. Hiring as Cultural Matching: The Case of Elite Professional Service Firms. *American Sociological Review* 77:6 (2012): 999–1022.

Roberson, Ian. Blaming the Victim: Does Education Change Where We Point the Finger? Master's thesis, California State University, 2012.

Robinson, Gail and Barbara Mullins Nelson. Pursuing Upward Mobility: African American Professional Women Reflect on Their Journey. *Journal of Black Studies* 40:6 (2010): 1168–1188.

Roos, Leslie E., et al. Relationship between Adverse Childhood Experiences and Homelessness and the Impact of Axis I and II Disorders. *American Journal of Public Health* 103, Supplement No. 2 (2013): 275–281.

Scherger, Simone and Mike Savage. Cultural Transmission, Educational Attainment and Social Mobility. *The Sociological Review* 58:3 (2010): 406–428.

Schumaker, Katherine. An Exploration of the Relationship between Poverty and Child Neglect in Canadian Child Welfare. PhD Thesis.

Sharma, R.N. Anomie of Economic Deprivation: Merton Re–Examined. *Sociological Bulletin* 29:1 (1980): 1–32.

Shillington, A. M., Bousman, C. A., and Clapp J. D. Characteristics of Homeless Youth Attending Two Different Youth Drop–In centers. *Youth and Society* 43:1 (2011):28–43.

Siepel, Michael M.O. Social Consequences of Malnutrition. *Social Work* 44:5 (1999): 416–425.

Smith, Michael R. and Heather Zhang. Globalization and Workplace Performance in Canada: Cross–Sectional and Dynamic Analyses of Productivity and Wage Outcomes. *Research in Social Stratification and Mobility* 30:3 (2012): 310–327.

Smith, Michael R. The Analysis of Labour Markets in Canadian Sociology. *The American Sociologist* 33:1 (2002): 105–125.

Smyth, Russell, Vinod Mishra, and Xiaolei Qian. Knowing a Person's Lot in Life Versus Climbing the Social Ladder: The Formation of Redistributive Preferences in Urban China. *Social Indicators Research* 96 (2010): 275–293.

Social Assistance Review. Tell Your Story. Retrieved from: http://sareview.ca/tell-your-story/.

Southwell, Psyche. The Measurement of Child Poverty in the United States. *Journal of Human Behavior in the Social Environment* 19 (2009): 317–329.

Swan, Samuel H., Sierd Hadley and Bernardette Cichon. Crisis behind Closed Doors: Global Food Crisis and Local Hunger. *Journal of Agrarian Change* 10:1 (2010):107–118.

Swidler, Ann. Culture in Action: Symbols and Strategies. *American Sociological Review* 51:2 (1986): 273.

Tansel, Aysit, and H. Mehmet Taşçı. Hazard Analysis of Unemployment Duration by Gender in a Developing Country: The Case of Turkey. *Labour* 24:4 (2009): 501–30.

Thio, Alex. A Critical Look at Merton's Anomie Theory. *The Pacific Sociological Review* 18:2 (1975): 139–158.

Tilman, Rick. Colin Campbell on Thorstein Veblen on Conspicuous Consumption. *Journal of Economic Issues* 40:1 (2006): 97.

Toronto Star. Readers' Letters: Outsourcing Our Jobs. April 27, 2013.

Tracy, Elizabeth and Randy Stoecker. Homelessness: The Service Providers' Perspective on Blaming the Victim. *Journal of Sociology and Social Welfare* 20:3 (1993): 43–59.

Trigg, Andrew B. Veblen, Bourdieu, and Conspicuous Consumption. *Journal of Economic Issues* 35:1 (2001): 99–115.

Van Berkel, Rik. Social Assistance Dynamics in the Netherlands: Exploring the Sustainability of Independence from Social Assistance via Labour Market Inclusion. *Social Policy and Society* 6:2 (2007): 127–139.

Veall, Michael R. Canadian Seniors and the Low Income Measure. *Canadian Public Policy* 34 (2008): 47–58.

Vernon, Raymond. *The Theory of the Leisure Class* by Thorstein Veblen. *Daedalus* 103:1 (1974): 53–57.

Vosko, L.F. *Precarious Employment: Understanding Labour Market Insecurity in Canada*. Montreal: McGill–Queen's University Press, 2006.

Williams, Sarah. Left–Right Ideological Differences in Blaming Victims. *Political Psychology* 5:4 (1984): 573–581.

Wright, James D. Poverty among the U.S. Elderly under Old and New Poverty Definitions. *Care Management Journals* 11:3 (2010): 200–203.

Wright, Susan E. Blaming the Victim, Blaming Society or Blaming the Discipline: Fixing Responsibility for Poverty and Homelessness. *Sociological Quarterly* 34:1 (1993): 1–16.

Yodanis, Carrie. A Place in Town: Doing Class in a Coffee Shop. *Journal of Contemporary Ethnography* 35:3 (2006): 341–366.

Zhang, Ye. The Sociological Analysis of Globalization and Labour Market Outcomes Reconsidered. Doctoral thesis, McGill University, 2010.

CHAPTER 3

Acquadro Maran, Daniela. Italian Nurses' Experience of Stalking: A Questionnaire Survey. *Violence and Victims* 29:1 (2014): 109–21.

Adefolalu, Adegoke O. Fear of the Perpetrator: A Major Reason Why Sexual Assault Victims Delayed Presenting at Hospital. *Tropical Medicine and International Health* 19:3 (2014): 342–347.

Al–Sahab, B., et al. Prevalence and Characteristics of Teen Motherhood in Canada. *Maternal and Child Health Journal* 16:1 (2012): 228–234.

Alves, Andre J. and Evan Roberts. Rosie the Riveter's Job Market: Advertising for Women Workers in World War II Los Angeles. *Labor* 9:3 (2012): 53–68.

Ambwani, Suman and Jaine Strauss. Love Thyself Before Loving Others? A Qualitative and Quantitative Analysis of Gender Differences in Body Image and Romantic Love. *Sex Roles* 56 (2007): 13–21.

Atwal, Sabrina, Gita Das, and Janki Shankar. Challenging Cultural Discourses and Beliefs That Perpetuate Domestic Violence in South Asian Communities: A Discourse Analysis. *Journal of International Women's Studies* 14:1 (2013): 248–62.

Bainbridge, Deidre, Giannetta Del Bove, and Lana Stermac. Comparisons of Sexual Assault among Older and Younger Women. *Journal of Elder Abuse and Neglect* 17:3 (2005): 1–18.

Balde, Thierno, Myrna Dawson, and Valerie Pottie Bunge. National Trends in Intimate Partner Homicides: Explaining Declines in Canada, 1976 to 2001. *Violence Against Women* 15:3 (2009): 276–306.

Barnet–Verzat, Christine and Francois–Charles Wolff. Gender Wage Gap and the Glass Ceiling Effect: A Firm-Level Investigation. *International Journal of Manpower* 29:6 (2008): 486–502.

Barrett, Betty Jo, and Melissa St. Pierre. Variations in Women's Help Seeking in Response to Intimate Partner Violence: Findings From a Canadian Population-Based Study. *Violence Against Women* 17:1 (2011): 47–70.

Bennett, L. *The Feminine Mistake*. New York: Voice/Hyperion, 2007.

Bergstrom, Rochelle L. and Clayton Neighbors. Body Image Disturbance and the Social Norms Approach: An Integrative Review of the Literature. *Journal of Social and Clinical Psychology* 25:9 (2006): 975–1000.

Blackstone, Amy, Heather McLaughlin, and Christopher Uggen. Sexual Harassment, Workplace Authority, and the Paradox of Power. *American Sociological Review* 77:4 (2012): 625–47.

Boisvert, Jennifer A. and W. Andrew Harrell. Ethnic and Age Differences in Eating Disorder Symptomatology among Albertan Women. *Canadian Journal of Behavioural Science* 41:3 (2009): 143–150.

Boroughs, Michael S., Ross Krawczyk and J. Kevin Thompson. Body Dysmorphic Disorder among Diverse Racial/Ethnic and Sexual Orientation Groups: Prevalence Estimates and Associated Factors. *Sex Roles* 63 (2010): 725–737.

Borstorff, Patricia C., Glenn Graham, and Michael B. Marker. E–Harassment: Employee Perceptions of E–Technology as a Source of Harassment. *Journal of Applied Management and Entrepreneurship* 12:2 (2007): 44–60.

Broadbridge, Adelina. Choice or Constraint? Tensions in Female Retail Executives' Career Narratives. *Gender in Management: An International Journal* 25:3 (2010): 244–260.

Brownlie, Robin J. Living the Same as the White People: Mohawk and Anishinabe Women's Labour in Southern Ontario, 1920–1940. *Labour/Le Travail* 61 (2008): 41–68.

Brownridge, Douglas A., et al. The Elevated Risk for Non–Lethal Post–Separation Violence in Canada: A Comparison of Separated, Divorced, and Married Women. *Journal of Interpersonal Violence* 23:1 (2008): 117–35.

Budig, Michelle J. Male Advantage and the Gender Composition of Jobs: Who Rides the Glass Escalator? *Social Problems* 49:2 (2002): 258–277.

Calado, Maria, et al. The Association between Exposure to Mass Media and Body Dissatisfaction among Spanish Adolescents. *Women's Health Issues* 21:5 (2011): 390–399.

Cannold, L. (2002). Understanding and Responding to Anti–Choice Women–Centred Strategies. *Reproductive Health Matters* 10:19 (2002): 171–179.

Cates, Steven V., and Lynn Machin. The State of Sexual Harassment in America: What Is the Status of Sexual Harassment in the US Workplace Today? *The Journal of Global Business Management* 8:1 (2012): 133–38.

Cech, Erin A. and Mary Blair–Loy. Perceiving Glass Ceilings? Meritocratic versus Structural Explanations of Gender Inequalityamong Women in Science and Technology. *Social Problems* 57:3 (2010): 371–397.

Charlesworth, Sara, Paula McDonald, and Somali Cerise. Naming and Saying: Workplace Sexual Harassment in Australia. *Austrialian Journal of Social Issues* 46:2 (2011): 141–61.

Chiappori, Pierre–Andre and Sonia Oreffice. Birth Control and Female Empowerment: An Equilibrium Analysis. *Journal of Political Economy* 116:1 (2008): 113–140.

Clay, Daniel, Vivian L. Vignoles, and Helga Dittmar. Body Image and Self–Esteem among Adolescent Girls: Testing the Influence of Sociocultural Factors. *Journal of Research on Adolescence* 15:4 (2005): 451–477.

Clements, B. Religion and the Sources of Public Opposition to Abortion in Britain: The Role of 'Belonging,' 'Behaving,' And 'Believing.' *Sociology* 48:2 (2014): 369–386.

Cognard-Black, Andrew J. Will They Stay, or Will They Go? Sex-Atypical Work Among Token Men Who Teach. *Sociological Quarterly* 45:1 (2004): 113–139.

Connelly, Patricia M. and Martha MacDonald. *Women and the Labour Force* Ottawa: Minister of Supply and Services Canada, 1990.

Cook, Alison and Christy Glass. Above the Glass Ceiling: When are Women and Racial/Ethnic Minorities Promoted to CEO? *Strategic Management Journal* 35 (2014): 1080–1089.

Corsun, David L. and Wanda M. Costen. Is the Glass Ceiling Unbreakable? Habitus, Fields, and the Stalling of Women and Minorities in Management. *Journal of Management Inquiry* 10:1 (2001): 16–25.

Cotter, David A., Joan M. Hermsen, Seth Ovadia and Reeve Vanneman. The Glass Ceiling Effect. *Social Forces* 80:2 (2001): 655–682.

Creese, Gillian, and Brenda Beagan. Gender at Work: Strategies for Equality in Neo–Liberal Times. In Edward G. Grabb and Neil Guppy (eds.), *Social Inequality in Canada: Patterns, Problems, and Policies* (5th ed.) (pp. 224–36). Toronto: Pearson/Prentice-Hall, 2009.

Crowley, Jocelyn E. Fathers' Rights Groups, Domestic Violence and Political Countermobilization. *Social Forces* 88:2 (2009): 723–756.

Dang, Rey, Duc Khuong Nguyen and Linh–Chi Vo. Does The Glass Ceiling Exist? A Longitudinal Study Of Women's Progress On French Corporate Boards. *The Journal of Applied Business Research* 30:3 (2014): 909–916.

Danis, Fran, et al. Barriers to Reporting Sexual Assault for Women and Men: Perspectives of College Students. *Journal of American College Health* 55:3 (2006): 157–62.

Darlow, Susan and Marci Lobel. Who is Beholding my Beauty? Thinness Ideals, Weight, and Women's Responses to Appearance Evaluation. *Sex Roles* 63 (2010): 833–843.

Datta, Kavita. A Coming of Age? Re–conceptualising Gender and Development in Urban Botswana. *Journal of Southern African Studies* 30:2 (2004): 251–268.

Davidson, Marilyn J., et al. A Model of Racialized Sexual Harassment of Women in the UK Workplace. *Sex Roles* 62:1–2 (2010): 20–34.

Dawson, Myrna, and Jordan Fairbairn. Canadian News Coverage of Intimate Partner Homicide: Analyzing Changes over Time. *Feminist Criminology* 8:3 (2013): 147–76.

DeKeseredy, Walter S., et al. TheMeanings and Motives for Women's Use of Violence in Canadian College Dating Relationships: Results from a National Survey. *Sociological Spectrum* (1997): 199–222.

Dennis, Cindy–Lee, and Simone Vigod. The Relationship between Postpartum Depression, Domestic Violence, Childhood Violence, and Substance Use: Epidemiologic Study of a Large Community Sample. *Violence Against Women* 19:4 (2013): 503–17.

Dickens, Pamela A., et al. Physical and Sexual Assault of Women with Disabilities. *Violence Against Women* 12:9 (2006): 823–37.

Digby, Tom. Male Trouble: Are Men Victims of Sexism? *Social Theory and Practice* 29:2 (2003): 247–273.

Dimovski, Vlado, Miha Skerlavaj and Mandy Mok Kim Man. Comparative Analysis of Mid–Level Women Managers' Perception of the Existence of 'Glass Ceiling' in Singaporean and Malaysian Organizations. *The International Business and Economics Research Journal* 9:8 (2010): 61–77.

Downs, Daniel M., Shaan James, and Gloria Cowan. Body Objectification, Self–Esteem, and Relationship Satisfaction: A Comparison of Exotic Dancers and College Women. *Sex Roles* 54 (2006): 745–752.

Dreher, George F. Breaking the Glass Ceiling: The Effects of Sex Ratios and Work–Life Programs on Female Leadership at the Top. *Human Relations* 56:5 (2003): 541–562.

Dumas, Tara M., Janet Chung–Hall, and Wendy E. Ellis. The Role of Peer Group Aggression in Predicting Adolescent Dating Violence and Relationship Quality. *Journal of Youth and Adolescence* 42:4 (2013): 487–99.

Durante, Kristina M., et al. Sex Ratio and Women's Career Choice: Does a Scarcity of Men Lead Women to Choose Briefcase over Baby? *Journal of Personality and Social Psychology* (2012): 1–14.

Edley, Nigel and Margaret Wetherell. Jekyll and Hyde: Men's Constructions of Feminism and Feminists. *Feminism and*

Psychology 11:4 (2001): 439–457.

Elliott, Susan J., Susan Keller-Olaman, and Michelle M. Vine. To Disrupt and Displace: Placing Domestic Violence on the Public Health Agenda. *Critical Public Health* 20:3 (2010): 339–55.

Eriksson, Mia. Wronged White Men: The Performativity of Hate in Feminist Narratives about Anti-Feminism in Sweden. *Nordic Journal of Feminist and Gender Research* 21:4 (2013): 249–263.

Farrell, Warren, with Steven Svoboda and James P. Sterba. *Does Feminism Discriminate against Men? A Debate.* Oxford: Oxford University Press, 2007.

Fennell, Julie L. Men Bring Condoms, Women Take Pills: Men's and Women's Roles in Contraceptive Decision Making. *Gender and Society* 25:4 (2011): 496–521.

Fergusson, D. M., Boden, J. M., and Horwood, J. L. Abortion among Young Women and Subsequent Outcomes. *Perspectives on Sexual and Reproductive Health* 39:1 (2007): 6–12.

Fernandez, Maria L., et al. Sexism, Vocational Goals, and Motivation as Predictors of Men's and Women's Career Choice. *Sex Roles* 55 (2006): 267–272.

Fitzsimmons–Craft, Ellen E. and Anna M. Bardone-Cone. Examining Prospective Mediation Models of Body Surveillance, Trait Anxiety, and Body Dissatisfaction in Afrimay American and Caucasian College Women. *Sex Roles* 67 (2012): 187–200.

Forste, Renata and Kiira Fox. Household Labor, Gender Roles, and Family Satisfaction: A Cross–National Comparison. *Journal of Comparative Family Studies* 43:5 (2012): 613–31.

Fox, John. How Men's Movement Participants View Each Other. *Journal of Men's Studies* 12:2 (2004).

Franzoi, Stephen L. and Jeffrey R. Klaiber. Body Use and Reference Group Impact: With Whom Do We Compare Our Bodies? *Sex Roles* 56 (2007): 205–214.

Goodwin P. and Ogden, J. (2007). Women's Reflections upon Their Past Abortions: An Exploration of How and Why Emotional Reactions Change over Time. *Psychology and Health* 22:2 (2007): 231–248.

Groves, Julian and Lake Lui. The 'Gift' of Help: Domestic Helpers and the Maintenance of Hierarchy in the Household Division of Labour. *Sociology* 46:1 (2012): 57–73.

Hague, Gill. Learning from Each Other: The Special Cell and Domestic Violence Activist Responses in Different Contexts Across the World. *Violence Against Women* 19:10 (2013): 1224–1245.

Håkansson, Carita, and Gunnar Ahlborg. Perceptions of Employment, Domestic Work, and Leisure as Predictors of Health among Women and Men. *Journal of Occupational Science* 17:3 (2010): 150–57.

Hamilton, Emily A., Laurie Mintz, and Susan Kashubeck–West. Predictors of Media Effects on Body Dissatisfaction in European American Women. *Sex Roles* 56 (2007): 397–402.

Hébert, Martine, et al. Risky Lifestyle as a Mediator of the Relationship between Deviant Peer Affiliation and Dating Violence Victimization among Adolescent Girls. *Journal of Youth and Adolescence* 40:7 (2011): 814–24.

Hedlin, Maria. How the Girl Choosing Technology Became the Symbol of the Non–Traditional Pupil's Choice in Sweden. *Gender and Education* 23:4 (2010): 447–459.

Herlitz, Claes A., and Jennifer L. Steel. The Association between Childhood and Adolescent Sexual Abuse and Proxies for Sexual Risk Behavior: A Random Sample of the General Population of Sweden. *Child Abuse and Neglect* 29:10 (2005): 1141–1153.

Hibino, Yuri, et al. Exploring Factors Associated with the Incidence of Sexual Harassment of Hospital Nurses by Patients. *Journal of Nursing Scholarship* 41:2 (2009): 124–31.

Hillis, S. D., et al. The Association between Adverse Childhood Experiences and Adolescent Pregnancy, Long–Term Psychosocial Consequences, and Fetal Death. *Pediatrics* 113 (2004): 320–327.

Hodson, Randy, Steven H. Lopez, and Vincent J. Roscigno. Power, Status, and Abuse at Work: General And Sexual Harassment Compared. *Sociological Quarterly* 50:1 (2009): 3–27.

Hultin, Mia. Some Take the Glass Escalator, Some Hit the Glass Ceiling? Career Consequences of Occupational Sex Segregation. *Work and Occupations* 30:1 (2003): 30–61.

Hunnicutt, G. Varieties of Patriarchy and Violence against Women: Resurrecting Patriarchy as a Theoretical Tool. *Violence Against Women* 15:5 (2009): 553–73.

Isaac, Carol A., Anna Kaatz and Molly Carnes. Deconstructing the Glass Ceiling. *Sociology Mind* 2:1 (2012): 80–86.

Jablonska, Beata, et al. Men's Experiences of Violence: Extent, Nature and Determinants. *International Journal of Social Welfare* 16:3 (2007): 269–77.

Jackson, Jerlando F.L. and Elizabeth M. O'Callaghan. What Do We Know About Glass Ceiling Effects? A Taxonomy and Critical Review to Inform Higher Education Research. *Research in Higher Education* 50 (2009): 460–482.

Jackson, Robert A., J. Mitchell Pickerill, and Meredith A. Newman. Changing Perceptions of Sexual Harassment in the Federal Workforce, 1987–94. *Law Policy* 28:3 (2006): 368–94.

Johnson, J. A., and M. S. Johnson. New City Domesticity and the Tenacious Second Shift. *Journal of Family Issues* 29:4 (2008): 487–515.

Jones, Kevin J., and Lisa A. Mainiero. Workplace Romance 2.0: Developing a Communication Ethics Model to Address

References

Potential Sexual Harassment from Inappropriate Social Media Contacts between Coworkers. *Journal of Business Ethics* 114:2 (2013): 367–79.

Jung, Jaehee and Seung-Hee Lee. Cross–Cultural Comparisons of Appearance Self-Schema, Body Image, Self-Esteem, and Dieting Behavior between Korean and U.S. Women. *Family and Consumer Sciences Research Journal* 34:4 (2006): 350–365.

Krantz, G., and P. Ostergren. Double Exposure: The Combined Impact of Domestic Responsibilities and Job Strain on Common Symptoms in Employed Swedish Women. *The European Journal of Public Health* 11:4 (2001): 413–19.

Krcmar, Marina, Steve Giles, and Donald Helme. Understanding the Process: How Mediated and Peer Norms Affect Young Women's Body Esteem. *Communication Quarterly* 56:2 (2008): 111–130.

Kullberg, Karin. From Glass Escalator to Glass Travelator: On the Proportion of Men in Managerial Positions in Social Work in Sweden. *British Journal of Social Work* 43 (2013): 1492–1509.

Kumar, A., Hessini, L., and Mitchell, E.M.H. Conceptualizing Abortion Stigma. *Culture, Health and Sexuality* 11:6 (2009): 625–639.

Kurtz, Don L. Roll Call and the Second Shift: The Influences of Gender and Family on Police Stress. *Police Practice and Research* 13:1 (2012): 71–86.

Legenbauer, Tanja, Ilka Ruhl and Silja Vocks. Influence of Appearance–Related TV Commercials on Body Image State. *Behaviour Modification* 32:3 (2008): 352–371.

Light, David, and Elizabeth Monk-Turner. Circumstances Surrounding Male Sexual Assault and Rape: Findings from the National Violence Against Women Survey. *Journal of Interpersonal Violence* 24:11 (2009): 1849–58.

Littlejohn, Krystale E. 'It is Those Pills that are Ruining Me': Gender and the Social Meanings of Hormonal Contraceptive Side Effects. *Gender and Society* 27:6 (2013): 843–863.

Lonsway, Kimberly A. Are We There Yet? *Women and Criminal Justice* 18:1–2 (2007): 1–48.

Luke, Nancy, Hongwei Xu, and Binitha V. Thampi. Husbands' Participation in Housework and Childcare in India. *Journal of Marriage and Family* 76:3 (2014): 620–637.

Lu–Ming, Tseng. Customer First and Customer Sexual Harassment: Some Evidence from the Taiwan Life Insurance Industry. *Gender, Work and Organization* (2013): 692–708.

Luxton, Meg and Leah F. Vosko. Where Women's Effort Counts: The 1996 Census Campaign and Family Politics in Canada. *Studies in Political Economy* 56 (1998): 49–81.

Man Yee Kan, Oriel Sullivan, and Jonathan Gershuny. Gender Convergence in DomesticWork: Discerning the Effects of Interactional and Institutional Barriers from Large–ScaleData. *Sociology* 45:2 (2011): 234–251.

Mastekaasa, Arne and Jens–Christian Smeby. Educational choice and persistence in male– and female–dominated fields. *Higher Education* 55 (2008): 189–202.

McDonald, Steve, Nan Lin and Dan Ao. Networks of Opportunity: Gender, Race, and Job Leads. *Social Problems* 56:3 (2009): 385–402.

McKay, Alexander. Trends in Canadian National and Provincial/Territorial Teen Pregnancy Rates: 2001–2010. *The Canadian Journal of Human Sexuality* 21:3–4 (2012): 161–175.

Milkie, M. A., S. B. Raley, and S. M. Bianchi. Taking on the Second Shift: Time Allocations and Time Pressures of U.S. Parents with Preschoolers. *Social Forces* 88:2 (2009): 487–517.

Mischner, Isabelle H.S., Hein T. van Schie, and Rutger C.M.E. Engels. Breaking the Circle: Challenging Western Sociocultural Norms for Appearance Influences Young Women's Attention to Appearance–Related Media. *Body Image* 10 (2013): 316–325.

Mitchell, L. M. *Baby's First Picture: Ultrasound and the Politics of Fetal Subjects*. Toronto: University of Toronto Press, 2001.

Moore, Maureen. Wives as Main Breadwinners. *Perspectives on Labour and Income* 2:1 (1990).

New Brunswick Advisory Council on the Status of Women. *The Pay Gap: Causes, Consequences and Actions: A Working Paper*. 1990.

Noonan, Mary C. The Impact of Domestic Work on Men's and Women's Wages. *Journal of Marriage and Family* 63:4 (2001): 1134–145.

Oaks, Laury. What Are Pro–Life Feminists Doing on Campus? *NWSA Journal* 21:1 (2009): 178–203.

Pankratow, Melanie, Tanya R. Berry and Tara–Leigh F. McHugh. Effects of Reading Health and Appearance Exercise Magazine Articles on Perceptions of Attractiveness and Reasons for Exercise. *PLOS One* 8:4 (2013).

Perez, Gloria et al. Social and Economic Inequalities in Induced Abortion in Spain as a Function of Individual and Contextual Factors. *European Journal of Public Health* 24:1 (2013): 162–169.

Perkins, H. W., and D. K. Demeis. Gender and Family Effects on the Second-Shift Domestic Activity of College-Educated Young Adults. *Gender and Society* 10:1 (1996): 78–93.

Pinho, Patricia de Santana and Elizabeth Bortolaia Silva. 2010. Domestic Relations in Brazil: Legacies and Horizons. *Latin American Research Review* 45:2 (2010): 90–113.

Piotrowski, Chris. From Workplace Bullying to Cyberbullying: The Enigma of E–Harassment in Modern Organizations.

Organization Development Journal 30:4 (2012): 44–53.

Pitt, Richard N. and Elizabeth Borland. Bachelorhood and Men's Attitudes about Gender Roles. *Journal of Men's Studies* 16:2 (2008): 140–158.

Presser, Harriet B. Employment Schedules among Dual–Earner Spouses and the Division of Household Labor by Gender. *American Sociological Review* 59:3 (1994): 348.

Price–Glynn, Kim and Carter Rakovski. Who Rides the Glass Escalator? Gender, Race and Nationality in the National Nursing Assistant Study. *Work, Employment and Society* 26:5 (2012): 699–715.

Purcell, David, Kelly R. MacArthur and Sarah Samblanet. Gender and the Glass Ceiling at Work. *Sociology Compass* 4:9 (2010): 705–717.

Richman, Judith A., Kathleen M. Rospenda, and Candice A. Shannon. Prevalence and Mental Health Correlates of Harassment and Discrimination in the Workplace: Results From a National Study. *Journal of Interpersonal Violence* 24:5 (2008): 819–43.

Ridolfi, Danielle R., et al. Do Appearance Focused Cognitive Distortions Moderate the Relationship between Social Comparisons to Peers and Media Images and Body Image Disturbance? *Sex Roles* 65 (2011): 491–505.

Russo, Giovanni and Wolter Hassink. Multiple Glass Ceilings. *Industrial Relations* 51:4 (2012): 892–915.

Salami, Samuel O. Influence of culture, family and individual differences on choice of gender–dominated occupations among female students in tertiary institutions. *Women in Management Review* 22:8 (2007): 650–665.

Samuels, Harriet. A Defining Moment: A Feminist Perspective on The Law of Sexual Harassment in the Workplace in the Light of the Equal Treatment Amendment Directive. *Feminist Legal Studies* 12:2 (2004): 181–211.

Sanderson, Catherine A., et al. Who Feels Discrepant and How Does Feeling Discrepant Matter? Examining the Presence and Consequences of Feeling Discrepant from Personal and Social Norms Related to Thinness in American and British High School Girls. *Journal of Social and Clinical Psychology* 27:9 (2008): 995–1020.

Sayer, Liana C., et al. How Long Is the Second (Plus First) Shift? Gender Differences in Paid, Unpaid, and Total Work Time in Australia and the United States. *Journal of Comparative Family Studies* 40:4 (2009): 523–45.

Sears, Heather A. The Co-occurrence of Adolescent Boys' and Girls' Use of Psychologically, Physically, and Sexually Abusive Behaviors in Their Dating Relationships. *Journal of Adolescence* 30 (2007): 487–504.

Simpson, Ruth and Yochanan Altman. The Time Bounded Glass Ceiling and Young Women Managers: Career Progress and Career Success: Evidence From The UK. *Journal of European Industrial Training* 24:2/3/4 (2000): 190–198.

Smith, Ryan A. Money, Benefits, and Power: A Test of the Glass Ceiling and Glass Escalator Hypotheses. *The Annals of the American Academy of Political and Social Science* 693 (2012): 149–172.

Snyder, Karrie Ann and Adam Isaiah Green. Revisiting the Glass Escalator: The Case of Gender Segregation in a Female Dominated Occupation. *Social Problems* 55:2 (2008): 271–299.

Stark–Wroblewski, Kim, Barbara J. Yanico and Steven Lupe. Acculturation, Internalization of Western Appearance Norms, and Eating Pathology among Japanese and Chinese International Student Women. *Psychology of Women Quarterly* 29 (2005): 38–46.

Statistics Canada. *Changes in The Occupational Profile Of Young Men And Women in Canada.* 2014. Catalogue no. 75-006-X.

Statistics Canada. *Generational Change in Paid and Unpaid Work.* 2011. Component of Statistics Canada Catalogue no. 11–008–X: Canadian Social Trends.

Steinberg, J. R. and Russo, N. F. Abortion and Anxiety: What's the Relationship? *Social Science and Medicine* 67 (2008): 238–175.

Stevens, Daphne, Gary Kiger, and Pamela J. Riley. Working Hard and Hardly Working: Domestic Labor and Marital Satisfaction among Dual–Earner Couples. *Journal of Marriage and Family* 63:2 (2001): 514–26.

Stockemer, Daniel and Maeve Bryne. Women's Representation around the World: The Importance of Women's Participation in the Workforce. *Parliamentary Affairs* 65 (2011): 802–821.

Strahan, Erin J., et al. Victoria's Dirty Secret: How Sociocultural Norms Influence Adolescent Girls and Women. *Personality and Social Psychology Bulletin* 34:2 (2008): 288–301.

Strahan, Erin J., et al. Comparing to Perfection: How Cultural Norms for Appearance Affect Social Comparisons and Self-Image. *Body Image* 3 (2006): 211–227.

Strahan, Erin J., Steven J. Spencer and Mark P. Zanna. Do Not Take Another Bite: How Sociocultural Norms for Appearance Affect Women's Eating Behavior. *Body Image* 4 (2007): 331–342.

Sullivan, Oriel. Changing Differences by Educational Attainment in Fathers' Domestic Labour and Childcare. *Sociology* 44:4 (2010): 716–733

Szabo, Michelle. Foodwork or Foodplay? Men's Domestic Cooking, Privilege and Leisure. *Sociology* 47:4 (2013): 623–638.

Taylor, John P. The Social Life of Rights: 'Gender Antagonism', Modernity and Rate in Vanuatu. *The Australian Journal of Anthropology* 19:2 (2008): 165–178.

Thomas, Jan E. and Ingegerd Hildingsson. Who's Bathing the Baby? The Division of Domestic Labour in Swe-

References

den. *Journal of Family Studies* 15:2 (2009): 139–152.

Tierney, Daniel, Patrizia Romito, and Karen Messing. She Ate Not the Bread of Idleness. *Women and Health* 16:1 (1990): 21–42.

Torr, Berna Miller, and Susan E. Short. Second Births and the Second Shift: A Research Note on Gender Equity and Fertility. *Population and Development Review* 30:1 (2004): 109–30.

Urquhart, Christie S. and Tanis V. Mihalynuk. Disordered Eating in Women: Implications for the Obesity Pandemic. *Canadian Journal of Dietetic Practice and Research* 72:1 (2011): 115–125.

Valor–Segura, Inmaculada, Francisca Exposito, and Miguel Moya. Victim Blaming and Exoneration of the Perpetrator in Domestic Violence: The Role of Beliefs in a World and Ambivalent Sexism. *The Spanish Journal of Psychology* 14:1 (2011): 195–206.

Vernet, Jean Pierre, Jorge Vala and Fabrizio Butera. May Men Promote Feminist Movements? Outgroup Influence Sources Reduce Attitude Change Toward Feminist Movements. *Group Processes and Intergroup Relations* 14:5 (2011): 723–733.

Vopni, Vicki. Young Women's Experiences with Reporting Sexual Assault to Police. *Canadian Woman Studies* 25 (2006): 107–14.

Wannell, Ted. Male–Female Earnings Gap among Recent University Graduates. *Perspectives on Labour and Income* 2:2 (1990).

Weyer, Birgit. Twenty Years Later: Explaining the Persistence of the Glass Ceiling for Women Leaders. *Women in Management Review* 2:6 (2007): 482–496.

Williams, Christine L. The Glass Escalator, Revisited: Gender Inequality in Neoliberal Times. *Gender and Society* 27:5 (2013): 609–629.

Williams, Christine L. The Glass Escalator: Hidden Advantages for Men in the Female Professions. *Social Problems* 39:3 (1992): 253–267.

Wingfield, Adia Harvey. Racializing the Glass Escalator: Reconsidering Men's Experiences with Women's Work. *Gender and Society* 23.1 (2009): 5–26.

Winterich, Julie A. Aging, Femininity, and the Body: What Appearance Changes Mean to Women with Age. *Gender Issues* 24 (2007): 51–69.

Yanowitz, Karen L. Influence of Gender and Experience on College Students' Stalking Schemas. *Violence and Victims* 21:1 (2006): 91–100.

Yap, Margaret and Alison M. Konrad. Gender and Racial Differentials in Promotions: Is There a Sticky Floor, a Mid–Level Bottleneck, or a Glass Ceiling? *Relations Industrielles* 64:4 (2009): 593–619.

Zeytinoglu, Isik U., Cooke Gordon B. et al. Employer Offered Family Support Programs, Gender and Voluntary and Involuntary Part-Time Work. *Relations Industrielles* 65:2 (2010): 177–195.

CHAPTER 4

Aboriginal Affairs and Northern Development Canada, 2010. Accessed at https://www.aadncaandc.gc.ca/eng/1100100 015397/1100100015404.

Aboriginal Offenders: A Critical Situation. Ottawa: Office of the Correctional Investigator, Canada, 2013. Accessed at http://www.oci–bec.gc.ca/cnt/rpt/oth–aut/oth–aut20121022info–eng.aspx.

Adams, Michael. *Unlikely Utopia: The Surprising Triumph of Canadian Pluralism.* Toronto: Viking, 2007.

Agocs, C. Canada's Employment Equity Legislation and Policy, 1987–2000. *International Journal of Manpower*, 23:3 (2002): 256–276.

Ahmed, Sara. A Phenomenology of Whiteness. *Feminist Theory* 8:2 (2007): 149–168.

Ata, Abe, Brock Bastian, and Dean Lusher. Intergroup Contact in Context: The Mediating Role of Social Norms and Group-based Perceptions on the Contact-Prejudice Link. *International Journal of Intercultural Relations* 33:6 (2009): 498–506.

Aujla, Angela. Others in Their Own Land: Second Generation South Asian Canadian Women, Racism, and the Persistence of Colonial Discourse. *Canadian Woman Studies* 20:2 (2000): 41–47.

Backhouse, C. What is Access to Justice? In J. Bass et al. (eds.), *Access To Justice For A New Century: The Way Forward.* Canada: Law Society of Upper Canada, 2005.

Bauder, Harald and Bob Sharpe. Residential Segregation of Visible Minorities in Canada's Gateway Cities. *Canadian Geographer* 46:3 (2002): 204–222.

Bennett–Abuayyash, Caroline, et al. Prejudice in the Workplace: The Role of Bias against Visible Minorities. *Canadian Issues* (2007): 114–18.

Boesveld, Sarah. What It's Actually Like to be a Muslim Girl in Canada. *Chatelaine*, December 17, 2015. Retrieved from http://www.chatelaine.com.

Bogardus, Emory Stephen. *Social Distance.* Los Angeles: University of Southern California Press, 1959.

Bonizzoni, Paola. Living Together Again: Families Surviving Italian Immigration Policies. *International Review of Soci-*

ology 19:1 (2009): 83–101.

Boyd, Monica, and Thomas Derrick. Match or Mismatch? The Employment of Immigrant Engineers in Canada's Labor Force. *Population Research and Policy Review* 20:1–2 (2001): 107–33.

Bracken, Denis C. Canada's Aboriginal People, Fetal Alcohol Syndrome and the Criminal Justice System. *British Journal of Community Justice*, 6:3 (2008): 21–33.

Brazeau, James, et al. Initial Therapeutic Alliance and Treatment Engagement of Aboriginal and Non–Aboriginal Youths in a Residential Treatment Center for Substance Abuse. *Journal of Ethnic and Cultural Diversity in Social Work* 22:2 (2013): 145–61.

Breton, Raymond. Institutional Completeness of Ethnic Communities and the Personal Relations of Immigrants. *American Journal of Sociology* 70 (1964): 193–205.

Brock, William A., et al. On the Observational Implications of Taste–based Discrimination in Racial Profiling. *Journal of Econometrics* 166 (2012): 66–78.

Buhr, Karen J. Do Immigrant Nurses in Canada See a Wage Penalty? An Empirical Study. *Business Economics* 45:3 (2010): 210–23.

Burch, Traci. The Old Jim Crow: Racial Residential Segregation and Neighborhood Imprisonment. *Law and Policy* 36:3 (2014): 233–255.

Busby, N. Affirmative Action in Women's Employment: Lessons from Canada. *Journal of Law and Society*, 33:1 (2006): 42–58.

Canadian Council for Refugees. *Canada's National Settlement Program: Moving Forward.* 2013. Retrieved from http://ccrweb.ca/files/submission_cic_dec2013.pdf.

Cao, Liqun. Aboriginal People and Confidence in the Police. *Canadian Journal of Criminology and Criminal Justice* 56:5 (2014): 1–34.

Carrington, Peter, and Robin Fitzgerald. Disproportionate Minority Contact in Canada: Police and Visible Minority Youth. *Canadian Journal of Criminology and Criminal Justice* 53:4 (2011): 449–86.

Charles, Camille Zubrinsky. The Dynamics of Racial Residential Segregation. *Annual Review of Sociology* 29 (2003): 167–207.

City-Data.com. Retrieved from http://www.city–data.com/forum/toronto/1283865-what-really-like-blacks-toronto-canada.html.

Corrado, Raymond R., Sarah Kuehn, and Irina Margaritescu. Policy Issues Regarding the Over–representation of Incarcerated Aboriginal Young Offenders in a Canadian Context. *Youth Justice* 14:1 (2014): 40–62.

Costigan, Catherine L., and Dokis, Daphne, P. Similarities and Differences in Acculturation among Mothers, Fathers, and Children in Immigrant Chinese Families. *Journal of Cross-Cultural Psychology* 37:6 (2006): 723–741.

Costigan, Catherine L., Su, Tina F., and Hua, Josephine M. Ethnic Identity among Chinese Canadian Youth: A Review of the Canadian Literature. *Canadian Psychology* 50:4 (2009): 261–272.

Currie, Cheryl L., et al. Racial Discrimination, Post Traumatic Stress, and Gambling Problems among Urban Aboriginal Adults in Canada. *Journal of Gambling Studies* 29:3 (2013): 393–415.

Curtis, Josh, Jennifer Elrick, and Jeffrey G. Reitz. Immigrant Skill Utilization: Trends and Policy Issues. *Journal of International Migration and Integration* 15:1 (2014): 1–26.

Darroch, A. Gordon. Another Look at Ethnicity, Stratification and Social Mobility in Canada. *Canadian Journal of Sociology* 4:1 (1979): 1–25.

Dechief, Diane and Oreopoulos, Philip. Why Do Some Employers Prefer to Interview Matthew But Not Samir? New Evidence from Toronto, Montreal and Vancouver. *Canadian Labour Market and Skills Researcher Network*, 2012.

Denis, Ann B. Adaptation to Multiple Subordination? Women in the Vertical Mosaic. *Ethnic Studies* 18:3 (1986): 61–74.

Deveau, J. Louis. Workplace Accommodation and Audit–Based Evaluation Process for Compliance with the Employment Equity Act: Inclusionary Practices that Exclude: An Institutional Ethnography. *Canadian Journal of Sociology* 36:3 (2011).

Driedger, Leo, and Richard A. Mezoff. Ethnic Prejudice and Discrimination in Winnipeg High Schools. *Canadian Journal of Sociology* 6:1 (1981): 1–17.

Driedger, Leo. (1973). Impelled Group Migration: Minority Struggle to Maintain Institutional Completeness. *International Migration Review* 7:3 (1973): 257–269.

Driedger, Leo. Multiculturalism: Bridging Ethnicity, Culture, Religion and Race. *Forum on Public Policy* (2008): 1–44.

Durand, Jorge and Massey, Douglas S. New World Order: Continuities and Changes in Latin American Migration. *Annals of the American Academy of Political and Social Science* 630: 20–52.

Dusenbery, V. Canadian Ideology and Public Policy: The Impact on Vancouver Sikh Ethnic and Religious Adaptation. *Canadian Ethnic Studies* 13:3 (1981): 101–119.

Employment and Social Development Canada, 2015. At http://www4.hrsdc.gc.ca/.3ndic.1t.4r@–eng.jsp?iid=36.

Farley, John E. Residential Interracial Exposure and Isolation Indices: Mean versus Median Indices, and the Difference It Makes. *Sociological Quarterly* 46:1 (2005): 19–45.

References

Fee, Margery and Lynette Russell. 'Whiteness' and 'Aboriginality' in Canada and Australia. *Feminist Theory* 8:2 (2007): 187–208.

Fennema, Meindert. The Concept and Measurement of Ethnic Community. *Journal of Ethnic and Migration Studies* 30:3 (2004): 429–447.

Fong, Eric and Kumiko Shibuya. The Spatial Separation of the Poor in Canadian Cities. *Demography* 37:4 (2000): 449–459.

Fong, Eric and Rima Wilkes. Racial and Ethnic Residential Patterns in Canada. *Sociological Forum* 18:4 (2003): 577–602.

Fong, Eric. A Comparative Perspective on Racial Residential Segregation: American and Canadian Experiences. *Sociological Quarterly* 37:2 (1996): 199–226.

Fossett, Mark. Ethnic Preferences, Social Distance Dynamics, and Residential Segregation: Theoretical Explorations Using Simulation Analysis. *Journal of Mathematical Sociology* 30:3–4 (2006): 185–273.

Friedman, S. Do Declines in Residential Segregation Mean Stable Neighborhood Racial Integration in Metropolitan American? A Research Note. *Social Science Research* 37:3 (2008): 920–933.

Fuller, Sylvia and Todd Martin. Predicting Immigrant Employment Sequences in the First Years of Settlement. *International Migration Review* 46:1 (2012): 138–190.

Garner, Steve. The Uses of Whiteness: What Sociologists Working on Europe Can Draw from US Research on Whiteness. *Sociology* 40:2 (2006): 257–275.

Gillborn, David. Rethinking White Supremacy: Who Counts in WhiteWorld. *Ethnicities* 6:3 (2006): 318–340.

Gosine, Kevn. Revisiting the Notion of a 'Recast' Vertical Mosaic in Canada: Does a Post Secondary Education Make a Difference? *Canadian Ethnic Studies* 32:3 (2000): 89–104.

Government of Canada. Employment Equity Act (S.C. 1995, C. 44).

Government of Canada. *Family Sponsorship*. 2014. Retrieved from http://www.cic.gc.ca /english/immigrate/sponsor/.

Grove, Natalie J. and Anthony B. Zwi. Our Health and Theirs: Forced Migration, Othering, And Public Health. *Social Science and Medicine* 62 (2006): 1931–1942.

Guo, Shibao. Difference, Deficiency, and Devaluation: Tracing the Roots of Non-Recognition of Foreign Credentials for Immigrant Professionals in Canada. *The Canadian Journal for the Study of Adult Education* 22:1 (2009): 37–52.

Guo, Shibao. Economic Integration of Recent Chinese Immigrants in Canada's Second–Tier Cities: The Triple Glass Effect and Immigrants' Downward Social Mobility. *Canadian Ethnic Studies* 45:3 (2013): 95–115.

Hanson, Erin. The Indian Act. Vancouver: UBC First Nations Studies Program, 2009.

Herberg, E. N. The Ethno–Racial Socioeconomic Hierarchy in Canada: Theory and Analysis of the New Vertical Mosaic. *International Journal of Comparative Sociology* 31:3–4 (1990): 206–21.

Hicks, Tessa. Humanizing the Other in Us and Them. *Peace Review: A Journal of Social Justice* 18 (2007): 499–506.

Hossain, Belayet and Laura Lamb. The Impact of Human and Social Capital on Aboriginal Employment Income in Canada. *Economic Papers* 31:4 (2015): 440–450.

Iceland, John and Rima Wilkes. Does Socioeconomic Status Matter? Race, Class, and Residential Segregation. *Social Problems* 53:2 (2006): 248–273.

Ilić, Dragan. Marginally Discriminated: The Role of Outcome Tests in European Jurisdiction. *European Journal of Law and Economics* 36:2 (2013): 271–94.

Isajiw, W. The Process of Maintenance of Ethnic Identity: The Canadian Context. In Paul M. Migus (ed.), *Sounds Canadian: Languages and Cultures in Multi–ethnic Society*. Toronto: Peter Martin Associates, 2003.

Ishaq, Zunera. Why I Intend To Wear a Niqab at My Citizenship Ceremony. *Toronto Star*, March 16, 2015.

Jacobson, Cardell K., and Tim B. Heaton. Comparative Patterns of Interracial Marriage: Structural Opportunities, Third–Party Factors, and Temporal Change in Immigrant Societies. *Journal of Comparative Family Studies* 39:2 (2008): 129–48.

Jaenen, Cornelius J. The Implantation of Belgian Iimmigrants in Western Canada. *Canadian Ethnic Studies* 43:1–2 (2011): 237–251.

Jain, H., et al. Effectiveness of Canada's Employment Equity Legislation for Women (1997–2004): Implications for Policy Makers. *Relations Industrielles* 65:2 (2010).

James, Carl E. African–Caribbean Canadians Working Harder to Attain Their Immigrant Dreams: Context, Strategies, and Consequences. *Wadabagei* 12:1 (2009): 92–108.

James, Lou. I Admit It: I Hold Racist Views about Native People In Canada. *Huffington Post*, August 22, 2013.

Jargowsky, Paul A. Immigrants and Neighbourhoods of Concentrated Poverty: Assimilation or Stagnation? *Journal of Ethnic and Migration Studies* 35:7 (2009): 1129–1151.

Jeffries, Samantha, and Philip Stenning. Sentencing Aboriginal Offenders: Law, Policy, and Practice in Three Countries. *Canadian Journal of Criminology and Criminal Justice* 56:4 (2014): 447–94.

Jobard, Fabien, et al. Measuring Appearance–Based Discrimination: An Analysis of Identity Checks in Paris. *Population* 67:3 (2012): 349.

Kasprzak, Gabriela Pawlus. (2011). A History Reawakened: Contemporary Approaches to the Study of Poles in Canada. *Polish American Studies* 68:2 (2011): 5–12.

Kearney, Melissa S. Intergenerational Mobility for Women and Minorities in the United States. *The Future of Children* 16:2 (2006): 37–53.

Kerkman, D. D., et al. Social Attitudes Predict Biases in Geographic Knowledge. *The Professional Geographer* 26 (2004): 258–269.

Khazzoom, Aziza. Orientalism at the Gates: Immigration, the East/West Divide, and Elite Iraqi Jewish Women in Israel in the 1950s. *Signs* 32:1 (2006): 197–220.

Lamb, Danielle. Earnings Inequality among Aboriginal Groups in Canada. *Journal of Labor Research* 34:2 (2015): 224–240.

Leck, J. and Saunders, D. Canada's Employment Equity Act: Effects on Employee Selection. *Population Research and Policy Review* 11:1 (1992): 21–49.

Lian, Jason Z., and David Ralph Matthews. Does the Vertical Mosaic Still Exist? Ethnicity and Income in Canada, 1991. *Canadian Review of Sociology* 35:4 (1998): 461–81.

Lieb, Christian. (2008). *Moving West: German-Speaking Immigration to British Colonies, 1945–1961.* 2008. Doctoral dissertation. Retrieved from ProQuest, UMI Dissertations Publishing (NR41195).

Light, R., Roscigno, V.J., and Kalev, A. Interpretation and Legitimation at Work. *The Annals of the American Academy* 634 (2011): 39–59.

MacDonald, John S., and MacDonald, Leatrice D. (1964). Chain Migration, Ethnic Neighbourhood Formation and Social Networks. *Millbank Memorial Fund Quarterly* 42:1 (1964): 82–97.

Manole, Diana. 2015. Veiled Prejudices: Muslim–Canadian Women Speak Out on Niqab Debate. *NowToronto.com*, 2015.

Marginalization of Aboriginal Women. Retrieved from indigenousfoundations.arts.ubc.ca.

Matthews, Justin L., and Teenie Matlock. Understanding the Link between Spatial Distance and Social Distance. *Social Psychology* 42:3 (2011): 185–92.

Maume, David. 2011. Minorities in Management: Effects on Income Inequality, Working Conditions, and Subordinate Career Prospects among Men. *The Annals of the American Academy of Political and Social Science* 639:1 (2011): 198–216.

McDonald, Lynn. Theorising about Ageing, Family and Immigration. *Ageing and Society* 31 (2011): 1180–1201.

McIntosh, Peggy. *White Privilege and Male Privilege: A Personal Account of Coming to See Correspondences through Work in Women's Studies.* Wellsley, MA: Center for Research on Women, 1988.

McLean, Sarah J., Andrew P. Wheeler, and Robert E. Worden. Testing for Racial Profiling With the Veil-of-Darkness Method. *Police Quarterly* 15:1 (2012): 92–111.

Melchers, Ronald, and Julian V. Roberts. The Incarceration of Aboriginal Offenders: Trends from 1978 to 2001. *Canadian Journal of Criminology and Criminal Justice* 45:2 (2003): 211–42.

Merritt, Shaun. Monument to Multiculturalism. *Spacing Toronto.* Spacing.ca.

Moore, Thomas S. (2010). The Locus of Racial Disadvantage in the Labor Market. *American Journal of Sociology* 116:3 (2010): 909–942.

Morgan, Anthony. 2015. The Suffocating Experience of Being Black In Canada. *Toronto Star*, July 31, 2015.

Moshman, David. Us and Them: Identity and Genocide. *Identity: An International Journal of Theory and Research* 7:2 (2007): 115–135.

Nakhaie, M. Reza and Abdolmohammad Kazemipur. Social Capital, Employment and Occupational Status of the New Immigrants in Canada. *Journal of International Migration and Integration* 14:3 (2013): 419–437.

Neborak, Jaclyn. Family Reunification? A Critical Analysis of Citizenship and Immigration Canada's 2013 Reforms to the Family Class. *Ryerson Centre for Immigration and Settlement* 8 (2013). At http://www.ryerson.ca/content/dam/rcis/documents/RCIS_WP_Neborak_No_2013_8.pdf.

Orellana, M.F., et al. Transnational Childhoods: The Participation of Children in Processes of Family Migration. *Social Problems* 48:4 (2001): 572–591.

Oreopoulos, Philip. (2011). Why Do Skilled Immigrants Struggle in the Labor Market? A Field Experiment with Thirteen Thousand Resumes. *American Economic Journal: Economic Policy* 3 (2011): 148–171.

Owen, David S. Towards a Critical Theory of Whiteness. *Philosophy and Social Criticism* 33:2 (2007): 203–222.

Pager, D., Western B., and Bonikowski, B. Discrimination in a Low-Wage Labor Market: A Field Experiment. *American Sociological Review* 74:5 (2009): 777–799.

Pager, Devah and Western, Bruce. Identifying Discrimination at Work: The Use of Field Experiments. *Journal of Social Issues* 68:2 (2012): 221–237.

Pasztor, A. Talking the Same Language. In Jaap Dronkers (ed.), *Quality and Inequality of Education: Cross–National Perspectives.* New York: Springer, 2010.

Pendakur, R. and K. Pendakur. Aboriginal Income Disparity in Canada. *Canadian Public Policy* 37:1 (2011): 61–83.

References

Perry, Pamela. White Means Never Having to Say You're Ethnic: White Youth and the Construction of Cultureless Identities. *Journal of Contemporary Ethnography* 30:1 (2001): 56–91.

Pfeffer, Daniel. The Integration of Groups. *Ethnicities* 14:3 (2014): 351–370.

Portes, Alejandro and Alejandro Rivas. The Adaptation of Migrant Children. *The Future of Children* 21:1 (2011): 219–246.

Quillian, L. and Devah Pager. Black Neighbors, Higher Crime? The Role of Racial Stereotypes in Evaluations of Neighborhood Crime. *American Journal of Sociology* 107:3 (2001): 717–767.

Rafferty, Anthony. Ethnic Penalties in Graduate Level Over–Education, Unemployment and Wages: Evidence from Britain. *Work, Employment and Society* 26:6 (2012): 987–1006.

Ryberg, Jesper. Racial Profiling and Criminal Justice. *The Journal of Ethics* 15:1–2 (2011): 79–88.

Skaggs, Sheryl and Jennifer Bridges. Race and Sex Discrimination in the Employment Process. *Sociology Compass* 7:5 (2013): 404–415.

Smith, Ryan A. Do the Determinants of Promotion Differ for White Men Versus Women and Minorities? An Exploration of Intersectionalism through Sponsored and Contest Mobility Processes. *American Behavioral Scientist* 48:9 (2005): 1157–1181.

Spinner–Halev, Jeff. Feminism, Multiculturalism, Oppression, and the State. *Ethics* 112:1 (2001): 84–113.

Thomsen, Frej Klem. The Art of the Unseen: Three Challenges for Racial Profiling. *The Journal of Ethics* 15:1–2 (2011): 89–117.

Tully, J. *Public Philosophy in a New Key*. Cambridge: Cambridge University Press, 2008.

Vesselinov, Elena. Members Only: Gated Communities and Residential Segregation in the Metropolitan United States. *Sociological Forum* 23:3 (2003): 536–555.

Wagmiller, Robert L. Race and the Spatial Segregation of Jobless Men in Urban America. *Demography* 44:3 (2007): 539–562.

Walks, Alan R. and Larry S. Bourne. Ghettos in Canada's Cities? Racial Segregation, Ethnic Enclaves and Poverty Concentration in Canadian Urban Areas. *The Canadian Geographer* 50:2 (2006): 273–297.

Walks, Alan. Gated Communities, Neighbourhood Selection and Segregation: The Residential Preferences and Demographics of Gated Community Residents in Canada. *Town Planning Review* 85:1 (2014): 39–66.

Walks, R. Alan, and Larry S. Bourne. Ghettos in Canada's Cities? Racial Segregation, Ethnic Enclaves and Poverty Concentration in Canadian Urban Areas. *The Canadian Geographer* 50:3 (2006): 273–97.

Wang, Shuguang and Lucia Lo. Chinese Immigrants in Canada: Their Changing Composition and Economic Perform. *International Migration* 43:3 (2005): 35–71.

Wark, Colin, and John F. Galliher. Emory Bogardus and the Origins of the Social Distance Scale. *The American Sociologist* 38:4 (2007): 383–95.

Widner, Daniel and Stephen Chicoine. It's All in the Name: Employment Discrimination Against Arab Americans. *Sociological Forum* 26:4 (2011): 806–823.

Wortley, Scot. Justice for All? Race and Perceptions of Bias in the Ontario Criminal Justice System: A Toronto Survey. *Canadian Journal of Criminology* (1996): 439–67.

Yu, Bin. *Chain Migration Explained: The Power of The Immigration Multiplier*. El Paso, TX: LFB Scholarly Publishing, 2007.

Zhou, Min and Lee, Rennie. Transnationalism and Community Building: Chinese Immigrant Organization in the United States. *The Annals of the American Academy* 647 (2013): 22–49.

Zhou, Min. How Neighbourhoods Matter for Immigrant Children: The Formation of Educational Resources in Chinatown, Koreatown and Pico Union, Los Angeles. *Journal of Ethnic and Migration Studies* 35:7 (2009): 1153–1179.

Zhou, Min. Revisiting Ethnic Entrepreneurship: Convergencies, Controversies, and Conceptual Advancements. *International Migration Review* 38:3 (2004): 1040–1074.

CHAPTER 5

Barak, Benny. Age Identity: A Cross–Cultural Global Approach. *International Journal of Behavioral Development* 33:1 (2009): 2–11.

Benson, Janel E., Glen H. Elder Jr. and Monica K. Johnson. The Implications of Adult Identity for Educational and Work Attainment in Young Adulthood. *American Psychological Association* 48:6 (2011): 1752–1758.

Benson, Janel E. and Glen H. Elder Jr. Young Adult Identities and Their Pathways: A Developmental and Life Course Model. *American Psychological Association* 47:6 (2011): 1646–1657.

Binstock, Robert H. From Compassionate Ageism to Intergenerational Conflict? *The Gerontologist* 50:5 (2010): 574–585.

Bosick, Stacey Jean. Crime and the Transition to Adulthood: A Person–Centered Analysis of At–Risk Boys Coming of Age in 1940s Boston, 1970s London, and 1990s Pittsburgh. Diss., Harvard University, 2009.

Brown, Tyson H. Divergent Pathways: Racial/Ethnic Inequalities in Wealth and Health Trajectories. Diss., University of

North Carolina at Chapel Hill, 2008.

Cain, Leonard D. Alternative Perspectives on the Phenomena of Human Aging: Age Stratification and Age Status. *The Journal of Applied Behavioural Science* 23:2 (1987): 277–294.

Canadian Museum of History. The History of Canada's Public Pensions. Accessed at http://www.historymuseum .ca/cmc/exhibitions/hist/pensions/cpp–timeline_e.shtml.

Chappell, Neena L., and Karen Kusch. The Gendered Nature of Filial Piety: A Study among Chinese Canadians. *Journal of Cross-Cultural Gerontology* 22:1 (2007): 29–45.

Chappell, Neena L., and Laura Funk. Filial Responsibility: Does It Matter for Care–Giving Behaviours? *Ageing and Society* 32:7 (2012): 1128–1146.

Cheung, Chau–Kiu, and Alex Yui–Huen Kwan. The Erosion of Filial Piety by Modernisation in Chinese Cities. *Ageing and Society* 29:2 (2009): 179–198.

CTV News. Parents Paying for Kids: 'Not My Fault! I Can't Find A Job!' Retrieved from: http://canadaam.ctvnews.ca /finance/parents–paying–for–kids–not–my–fault–i–can–t–find–a–job–1.2545990.

Dykstra, Pearl A., and Tineke Fokkema. Relationships between Parents and Their Adult Children: A West European Typology of Late–Life Families. *Ageing and Society* 31:4 (2011): 545–569.

Elder Jr., Glen H. Time, Human Agency, and Social Change: Perspectives on the Life Course. *Social Psychology Quarterly* 57:1 (1994): 4–15.

Elmelech, Yuval. Attitudes toward Familial Obligation in the United States and in Japan. *Sociological Inquiry* 75:4 (2005): 497–526.

Funk, Laura M., and Karen M. Kobayashi. Choice in Filial Care Work: Moving Beyond a Dichotomy. *Canadian Review of Sociology* 46:3 (2009): 235–252.

Giles, Howard and Scott A. Reid. Ageism across the Lifespan: Towards a Self–Categorization Model of Ageing. *Journal of Social Issues* 61:2 (2005): 389–404.

Government of Canada. Canada Pension Plan Overview. 2014. Accessed at http://www.service canada.gc.ca/eng/ser vices/pensions/cpp/retirement/index.shtml#ch.

Government of Canada. Old Age Security Pension. 2014. Accessed at http://www.service canada.gc.ca/eng/services /pensions/oas/pension/index.shtml.

Higgs, Paul and Chris Gilleard. Generational Conflict, Consumption and the Ageing Welfare State in the United Kingdom. *Ageing and Society* 30 (2010): 1439–1451.

Khalaila, Rabia, and Howard Litwin. Modernisation and Filial Piety among Traditional Family Care–Givers: A Study of Arab–Israelis in Cultural Transition. *Ageing and Society* 32:5 (2012): 769–789.

Koffman, Ofra, and Rosalind Gill. 'The Revolution Will Be Led by a 12–Year–Old Girl': Girl Power and Global Biopolitics. *Feminist Review* 105:1 (2013): 83–102.

Krekula, Clary. Age Coding: On Age-Based Practices Of Distinction. *International Journal of Ageing and Later Life* 4:2 (2009): 7–31.

Morrow, Virginia. What's in a Number? Unsettling the Boundaries of Age. *Childhood* 20:2 (2013): 151–155.

Oosterveld-Vlug et al. Dignity and the Factors that Influence It According to Nursing Home Residents: A Qualitative Interview Study. *Journal of Advanced Nursing* 70:1 (2013).

Panek, Paul E., Sara Staats and Amanda Hiles. College Students' Perceptions of Job Demands, Recommended Retirement Ages, and Age of Optimal Performance in Selected Occupations. *International Journal of Aging and Human Development* 62:2 (2006): 87–115.

Powell, Jason L. and Azrini Wahidin. Ageing in the 'Risk Society.' *International Journal of Sociology and Social Policy* 25:8 (2005): 70–83.

Pudrovska, Tetyana. Early-Life Socioeconomic Status and Mortality at Three Life Course Stages: An Increasing Within-Cohort Inequality. *Journal of Health and Social Behaviour* 55:2 (2014): 181–195.

Roth, Erin G. et al. Baby Boomers in an Active Adult Retirement Community: Comity Interrupted. *The Gerontologist* 52:2 (2012): 189–198.

Sandell, Neil. 2012. How Did We Create Such Bleak Job Prospects for Canada's Youth? *Toronto Star,* November 30, 2012.

Sennott, Christie and Stefanie Mollborn. College-Bound Teens' Decisions about the Transition to Sex: Negotiating Competing Norms. *Advances in Life Course Research* 16:2 (2011): 83–97.

Umberson, Debra, Tetyana Pudrovska and Corinne Reczek. Parenthood, Childlessness, and Well-Being: A Life Course Perspective. *Journal of Marriage and Family* 72:3 (2010): 612–629.

CHAPTER **6**

Adam, Barry. Theorizing Homophobia. *Sexualities* 1:4 (1998): 387–404.

Adamczyk, Amy, and Cassady Pitt. Shaping Attitudes about Homosexuality: The Role of Religion and Cultural Context. *Social Science Research* 38:2 (2009): 338–51.

References

Alden, Helena L. and Karen F. Parker. Gender Role Ideology, Homophobia and Hate Crime: Linking Attitudes to Macro-Level Anti-Gay and Lesbian Hate Crimes. *Deviant Behavior* 26 (2005): 321–343.

Andersen, Robert, and Tina Fetner. 2008. Cohort differences in tolerance of homosexuality. *Public Opinion Quarterly* 72 (2) (2008): 311–30.

Ault, Amber. Ambiguous Identity in an Unambiguous Sex/Gender Structure: The Case of Bisexual Women. *The Sociological Quarterly* 37:3 (1996): 449–463

Bartoszuk, Karin, and Joe Pittman. Does Family Structure Matter? A Domain–Specific Examination of Identity Exploration and Commitment. *Youth and Society* 42:2 (2010): 155–73.

Bean, Lydia, Marco Gonzalez, and Jason Kaufman. Why Doesn't Canada Have an American–Style Christian Right? A Comparative Framework for Analyzing the Political Effects of Evangelical Subcultural Identity. *Canadian Journal of Sociology* 33:4 (2008): 899.

Bell, James G. and Barbara Perry. Outside Looking In: The Community Impacts of Anti–Lesbian, Gay, and Bisexual Hate Crime. *Journal of Homosexuality* 62 (2015): 98–120.

Benshoff, Harry M. and Sean Griffin. *Queer Images: A History of Gay and Lesbian Film in America.* Lanham, MD: Rowman and Littlefield, 2006.

Bernstein, Mary, and Paul Swartwout. Gay Officers in Their Midst: Heterosexual Police Employees' Anticipation of the Consequences for Coworkers Who Come Out. *Journal of Homosexuality* 59 (2012): 1145–1166.

Bianchi, Suzanne. Family Change and Time Allocation in American Families. *The Annals of the American Academy of Political and Social Science* 638:1 (2011): 21–44.

Black Coffee Poet. Interview with Noami Sayers: Anishinaabe Academic, Activist, Blogger, and Former Sex Worker. BlackCoffeePoet.com, February 14, 2013.

Boesveld, Sara. Ontario's New Sex Ed Covers Homosexuality, Masturbation—and Consent. Not Everyone's Saying 'Yes.' *National Post*, February 25, 2015.

Bohnert, Nora, and Anne Milan. Fifty Years of Families in Canada: 1961 to 2011. Statistics Canada: Census in Brief. September 1, 2012. Accessed May 14, 2015 at: http://www12.statcan.gc.ca/census–recensement/2011/as–sa/98–312–x/98–312–x2011003_1–eng.pdf.

Boislard, Marie-Aude, and Melanie Zimmer-Gembeck. Sexual Subjectivity, Relationship Status and Quality, and Same-sex Sexual Experience among Emerging Adult Females. *Journal of Educational and Developmental Psychology* 1:1 (2011): 54–64.

Bonds-Raacke, Jennifer M., et al. Remembering Gay/Lesbian Media Characters: Can Ellen and Will Improve Attitudes Toward Homosexuals? *Journal of Homosexuality* 53:3 (2007): 19–34.

Boon, Stacey, and Kevin Alderson. A Phenomenological Study of Women in Same-sex Relationships Who Were Previously Married to Men. *The Canadian Journal of Human Sexuality* 18:4 (2009).

Bos, Henny, et al. Civic Competence of Dutch Children in Female Same-sex Parent Families: A Comparison with Children of Opposite-Sex Parents. *Youth and Society* 25:3 (2013).

Bostwick, Wendy. Assessing Bisexual Stigma and Mental Health Status: A Brief Report. *Journal of Bisexuality* 12: 2 (2012): 214–222.

Bowring, Michèle A., and Joanna Brewis. Truth and Consequences. *Equal Opportunities International* 28:5 (2009): 361–77.

Bramlett, Frank, and Jefferson, Stephen. The Moderating Roles of Gender and Anti–Gay Prejudice in Explaining Stigma by Association in Male Dyads. *Journal of Homosexuality* 57:3 (2010): 401–14.

Brammer, Robert. Spirituality, AIDS, and Sexuality. *Journal of GLBT Family Studies* 5:3 (2009): 203–14.

Brown, Travor. Sexual Orientation Provisions in Canadian Collective Agreements. *Relations Industrielles* 58:4 (2003): 644.

Bryan, A. Dear Straight People. *Technician* (2015). Retrieved from: http://www.technicianonline.com/opinion/article_15d5267e–d825–11e4–9ae1–b7d7bd07bad7.html.

Buddel, Neil. Queering the Workplace. *Journal of Gay and Lesbian Social Services* 23 (2011): 131–146.

Burdge, Barbara. Legal Discrimination against Lesbian, Gay, And Bisexual Employees: A Multi–Theoretical Model To Explain An Elusive Civil Rights Law. *Journal of Policy Practice* 8 (2009): 4–20.

Callis, April Scarlette. Bisexual, Pansexual, Queer: Non–Binary Identities and the Sexual Borderlands." *Sexualities* 17:1 (2014): 63–80.

Callis, April Scarlette. The Black Sheep of the Pink Flock: Labels, Stigma, and Bisexual Identity. *Journal of Bisexuality* 13:1 (2013): 82–105.

Campaign Life Coalition. Ontario's Radical Sex Ed Curriculum. May 12, 2015.

CBC News. Same-Sex Rights in Canada. Last modified January 12, 2012. Accessed at http://www.cbc.ca/news/canada/timeline–same–sex–rights–in–canada–1.1147516.

CBC News. What is a Hate Crime? Last modified June 17, 2011. Accessed at http://www.cbc.ca/news/canada/what–is–a–hate–crime–1.1011612.

Chevrette, Roberta. Outing Heteronormativity in Interpersonal and Family Communication: Feminist Applications of Queer Theory 'Beyond the Sexy Streets'. *Communication Theory* 23 (2013): 170–190.

Claes, Ellen, et al. Anti–Gay Sentiment among Adolescents in Belgium and Canada: A Comparative Investigation into the Role of Gender And Religion. *Journal of Homosexuality* 57:3 (2010): 384–400.

Clermont, Michel and Guy Sioui-Durand. Adapting Health and Social Services to Homosexuals. Quebec: Quebec Ministry of Health and Ministry of Social Services, 1997. Accessed at http://publications.msss.gouv.qc.ca/ acrobat/f/documentation/1997/97_762an.pdf.

Colgan, Fiona, et al. Equality and Diversity Policies and Practices at Work: Lesbian, Gay and Bisexual Workers. *Equal Opportunities International* 26:6 (2007): 590–609.

Coren, Michael. Why Critics of Ontario's New Sex Ed Curriculum are Wrong. *National Post*, February 26, 2015.

Croce, Mariano. Homonormative Dynamics and the Subversion of Culture. *European Journal of Social Theory* 18:1 (2014): 3–20.

Csanady, Ashley. Read Ontario's New Sex–Ed Curriculum for Yourself. *National Post*, February 23, 2015.

Davis, Kingsley. The Sociology of Prostitution. *American Sociological Review* 2 (1937): 744–755.

Denike, Margaret. Religion, Rights, and Relationships: The Dream of Relational Equality. *Hypatia* 22:1 (2007): 71–91.

Dixon, Jenny, and Debbie Dougherty. A Language Convergence/Meaning Divergence Analysis Exploring How LGBTQ and Single Employees Manage Traditional Family Expectations in the Workplace. *Journal of Applied Communication Research* 42:1 (2014): 1–19.

Dnes, Antony. Marriage, Cohabition and Same–Sex Marriage. *The Independent Review*, (2007): 85.

Dodge, Brian, et al. Community Involvement among Behaviourally Bisexual Men in the Midwestern USA: Experiences and Perceptions across Communities. *Culture, Health and Sexuality* 14:9 (2012): 1095–1110.

Dotson, Michael J., Eva M. Hyatt, and Lisa Petty Thompson. Sexual Orientation and Gender Effects of Exposure to Gay- and Lesbian-Themed Fashion Advertisements. *Sexual Orientation and Gender Effects* 13:3 (2009): 431–447.

Drucker, Peter. Changing Families and Communities: An LGBT Contribution to an Alternative Development Path. *Development in Practice* 19:7 (2009): 825–836.

Ehrenhofler, C. Being Asexual In A Heteronormative World. *Huffington Post* (2014, October 25).

Eliason, Mickey. Bi–Negativity: The Stigma Facing Bisexual Men. *Journal of Bisexuality* 1 (2001): 137–154.

Elling, Agnes, Paul De Knop, and Annelies Knoppers. Gay/Lesbian Sport Clubs and Events. *International Review for the Sociology of Sport* 38:4 (2003): 441–56.

Employment and Social Development Canada. Canadians in Context: Households and Families. Employment and Social Development Canada. 2007. Accessed May 14, 2015 at http://well–being.esdc.gc.ca/misme–iowb/.3ndic.1t.4r@.js p?iid=37.

Erdem–Akçay, Ebru. Expanding Women's Rights versus Conserving the Traditional Family in the Civil Code Amendment Debates in Turkey. *Middle Eastern Studies* 49:1 (2013): 76–91.

Fairclough, Norman. *Critical Discourse Analysis: The Critical Study of Language.* London: Longman, 1995.

Fingerhut, Adam, Ellen Riggle, and Sharon Rostosky. Same-Sex Marriage: The Social and Psychological Implications of Policy and Debates. *Journal of Social Issues* 67:2 (2011): 225–41.

Gamson, Joshua. *Freaks Talk Back: Tabloid Talk Shows and Sexual Nonconformity.* Chicago: University of Chicago Press, 1998.

Gates, Trevor G., and Christopher G. Mitchell. Workplace Stigma–Related Experiences among Lesbian, Gay, and Bisexual Workers: Implications for Social Policy and Practice. *Journal of Workplace Behavioral Health* 28 (2013): 159–71.

Gayoso, Mary Grace et al. Homosexuality in Films: Trends of Portrayal in Hollywood and Asia. *Media Asia* 36:1 (2009): 38–46.

Giuffre, Patti, Kirsten Dellinger, and Christine L. Williams. No Retribution For Being Gay? Inequality In Gay-Friendly Workplaces. *Sociological Spectrum* 28 (2008): 254–77.

Globerman, Jason and Sanjana Mitra. Facilitators and Barriers to Health Care for Lesbian, Gay and Bisexual (LGB) People. N.p.: Rapid Response Service, Ontario HIV Treatment Network, 2014. Accessed at http://www.ohtn.on.ca/Pages/Knowledge–Exchange/Rapid–Responses/Documents/RR79.pdf.

Gotell, Lise. Queering Law: Not by *Vriend*. *Canadian Journal of Law and Society* 17:1 (2002): 89–113.

Government of Canada. Department of Canadian Heritage. Sexual Orientation and Human Rights. August 22, 2013.

Government of Canada. Department of Justice Website. How to Apply for a Divorce. January 7, 2015.

Government of Canada. Public Health Agency of Canada. Federal Initiative to Address HIV/AIDS in Canada. 2012. Accessed at http://www.phac–aspc.gc.ca/aids–sida/fi–if/index–eng.php.

Grace, André P. Reparative Therapies: A Contemporary Clear and Present Danger Across Minority Sex, Sexual, and Gender Differences. *Canadian Woman Studies* 24:2–3 (2005): 145–151.

Green, Adam. Queer Unions: Same–Sex Spouses Marrying Tradition and Innovation. *Canadian Journal of Sociology* 35:3 (2010): 399–436.

References

Green, Donald P., Dara Z. Strolovitch, Janelle S. Wong, and Robert W. Bailey. Measuring Gay populations and Antigay Hate Crime. *Social Science Quarterly* 82:2 (2001): 281–296.

Hallgrímsdóttir, Helga Kristín, et al. Sporting Girls, Streetwalkers, and Inmates of Houses of Ill Repute: Media Narratives and the Historical Mutability of Prostitution Stigmas. *Sociological Perspectives* 51 (2008): 119–128.

Hammond, Natalie and Kingston, Sarah. Experiencing Stigma as Sex Work Researchers in Professional and Personal Lives. *Sexualities* 17 (2014): 329–347.

Hart, G., et al. AIDS Care: Psychological and Sociomedical Aspects of AIDS/HIV. London: Routledge, 1990.

Health Canada. Canada Health Act Annual Report 2014–2015. 2015. Retrieved from: http://www.hc–sc.gc.ca/hcs–sss/pubs/cha–lcs/2015–cha–lcs–ar–ra/index–eng.php.

Henrickson, Mark. Sexuality, Religion, and Authority: Toward Reframing Estrangement. *Journal of Religion and Spirituality in Social Work: Social Thought* 28:1–2 (2009): 48–62.

Herek, Gregory M., et al. Hate Crime Victimization among Lesbian, Gay, and Bisexual Adults: Prevalence, Psychological Correlates, and Methodological Issues. *Journal of Interpersonal Violence* 12:1 (1997): 195–215.

Hettinger, Vanessa and Joseph Vandello. Balance Without Equality: Just World Beliefs, the Gay Affluence Myth, and Support for Gay Rights. *Social Justice Research* 27:4 (2014): 444–463.

Hooghe, Marc, et al. Anti–Gay Sentiment among Adolescents in Belgium and Canada: A Comparative Investigation into the Role of Gender and Religion. *Journal of Homosexuality* 57:3 (2010): 384–400.

Htun, Mala, and S. Laurel Weldon. State Power, Religion, and Women's Rights: A Comparative Analysis of Family Law. *Indiana Journal of Global Legal Studies* 18:1 (2011): 145–65.

Hubbard, Phil. Sexuality, Immorality and the City: Red–Light Districts and the Marginalization of Female Street Prostitutes. *Gender, Place and Culture* 5 (1998): 55–76.

Hudspith, Maria. Caring for Lesbian Health: A Resource for Health Care Providers, Policy Makers and Planners. Victoria, BC: British Columbia Ministry of Health and Ministry for Seniors, 1999. Accessed at http://www.health.gov.bc.ca/library/publications/year/1999/caring.pdf.

Jackson, Vance, Kristen Perrone, and Stephen Wright. Traditional and Nontraditional Gender Roles and Work–Family Interface for Men and Women. *Journal of Career Development* 36:1 (2009): 8–24.

Jacobsen, Christine M, and Skilbrei, May–Len. Reproachable Victims? Representations and Self-Representations of Russian Women Involved in Transnational Prostitution. *Ethnos* 75:2 (2010): 190–212.

Jagose, Annamarie. Feminism's Queer Theory. *Feminism and Psychology* 19:2 (2009): 157–174.

Järvinen, Margaretha. Prostitution in Helsinki: A Disappearing Social Problem? *Journal of the History of Sexuality* 3 (1993): 608–630.

Jewel, Lisa M. and Melanie A. Morrison. Prevalence of and Reasons for Directing Negative Behaviors toward Gay Men in a Canadian University Campus. *Journal of Interpersonal Violence* 25:11 (2010): 2092–2112.

Jones, O. (2015). We Need to See Realistic LGBT People on Our Screens, Not Toxic Caricatures. *The Guardian*, April 16, 2015.

Kilgard, Amy K. Tossing and Turning: Queering Performances of Family Narrative. *Cultural Studies* 14:2 (2014): 95–101.

King, Melissa J. *Personal and Sociocultural Factors in Heterosexual Women's Friendships with Lesbian Women.* Thesis. Drake University, 2008.

Klie, Shannon. LGBT Employees Still Face Barriers. *Canadian HR Reporter*, July 13, 2009.

Kurth, James. A Tale of Two Collapses: The Twin Declines of the Christian Faith and the Traditional Family. *Harvard Theological Review* 106:4 (2013): 479–89.

LaSala, Michael. Extradyadic Sex and Gay Male Couples: Comparing Monogamous and Nonmonogamous Relationships. *Families in Society* 85:3 (2004): 405.

Lau, Charles. The Stability of Same–Sex Cohabitation, Different–Sex Cohabitation, and Marriage. *Journal of Marriage and Family* 74:5 (2011): 973–88.

Lazarus, Lisa, et al. Occupational Stigma as a Main Barrier to Health Care for Street–Based Sex Workers in Canada. *Culture, Health and Sexuality* 14 (2012): 139–150.

Leichtentritt, Ronit D, and Arad, Bilha Davidson. Young Male Street Workers: Life Histories and Current Experiences. *British Journal of Social Work* 35 (2005): 483–509.

Lesbian, Gay, Bisexual and Trans People and Mental Health. Toronto: Canadian Mental Health Association, 2015. Accessed at http://ontario.cmha.ca/mental–health/lesbian–gay–bisexual–trans–people–and–mental–health/.

Links of Interest to Rainbow Services Clients and Supporters. Toronto: Centre for Addiction and Mental Health, 2012. Accessed at http://www.camh.ca/en/hospital/care_program_and_services/addiction_programs/Pages/rainbow_links.aspx.

Logan, D. Trevon. Personal Characteristics, Sexual Behaviors, and Male Sex Work: A Quantitative Approach. *American Sociological Review* 75 (2010): 679–704.

MacIntosh, H., E. Reissing, and H. Andruff. Same-sex Marriage in Canada: The Impact of Legal Marriage on the First

Nicole Meredith and Lorne Tepperman

Cohort of Gay and Lesbian Canadians to Wed. *Canadian Journal of Human Sexuality* 19:3 (2010): 79–90.

Macklem, Timothy. Vriend v. Alberta: Making the Private Public. *McGill Law Journal* 44 (1999): 197–230.

Malloy, Jonathan. Between America and Europe: Religion, Politics and Evangelicals in Canada. *Politics, Religion and Ideology* 12:3 (2011): 317–33.

Masson, Scott. Why the Critics of the Ontario Sex–Ed Curriculum are Right. *National Post*, March 31, 2015.

Mazur, Paul. Gay and Lesbian Rights in Canada: A Comparative Study. *International Journal of Public Administration* 25:1 (2002): 45–62.

McGouran, Kathleen. 'One Week No School': Ontario Parents Threatening to Pull Their Kids From Classes to Protest Sex–Ed Changes. *National Post*, May 4, 2015.

McIntosh, Mary. The Homosexual Role. *Social Problems* 16:2 (1968): 182–192.

Meyer, Doug. Evaluating the Severity of Hate Motivated Violence: Intersectional Differences among LGBT Hate Crime Victims. *Sociology* 44:5 (2010): 980–995.

Mimeault, Isabelle. Silent No More: Making Health and Social Services Accessible to Lesbians. N.p.: Quebec Women's Health Action Network, 2003. Accessed at http://rqasf.qc.ca/files/resume_lesb_anglais.pdf.

Minichiello, Victor, Scott, John, and Callander, Denton. New Pleasures and Old Dangers: Reinventing Male Sex Work. *Journal of Sex Research* 50 (2013): 263–275.

Moore, Dawn and Angus MacLean Rennie. Hated Identities: Queers and Canadian Anti–hate legislation. *Canadian Journal of Criminology and Criminal Justice* 48:5 (2006): 823–836.

Moran, Leslie, Beverly Skeggs, Paul Tyrer, and Karen Corteen. The Formation of Fear in Space: The 'Straights' Story. *Capital and Class* 27:2 (2003): 173–98.

Moreau, Sophia. The Wrongs of Unequal Treatment. *The University of Toronto Law Journal* 54:3 (2004): 291–326.

Neitz, Mary Jo. Becoming Visible: Religion and Gender in Sociology. *Sociology of Religion* 75:4 (2014): 511–23.

Nierobisz, Annette, Mark Searl, and Charles Throux. Human Rights Commissions and Public Policy: The Role of the Canadian Human Rights Commission in Advancing Sexual Orientation Equality Rights in Canada. *Canadian Public Administration* (2008): 239–63.

Nolan, James J. III, et al. Learning to *See* Hate Crimes: A Framework for Understanding and Clarifying Ambiguities in Bias Crime Classification. *Criminal Justice Studies* 17:1 (2004): 91–105.

November, J. So Why Did You Get Into It? 14 Ways Sex Work Is Real Work. *Born Whore*, September 2, 2013. Retrieved from: https://bornwhore.com/2013/09/02/happy–labour–day/.

Oakenfull, Gillian K. and Timothy B. Greenlee. Queer Eye for a Gay Guy: Using Market–Specific Symbols in Advertising to Attract Gay Consumers without Alienating the Mainstream. *Psychology and Marketing* 22:5 (2005): 421–439.

Oakenfull, Gillian K. and Timothy B. Greenlee. The Three Rules of Crossing Over from Gay Media to Mainstream Media Advertising: Lesbians, Lesbians, Lesbians. *Journal of Business Research* 57 (2004): 1276–1285.

Ontario Human Rights Commission. The Changing Face of Canadian Families. Ontario Human Rights Commission. Accessed May 16, 2015 at http://www.ohrc.on.ca/en/human–rights–and–family–ontario/changing–face–cana dian–families#fn16.

Oswald, Ramona Faith, et al. Structural and Moral Commitment among Same–sex Couples: Relationship Duration, Religiosity, and Parental Status. *Journal of Family Psychology* 22:3 (2008): 411–419.

Padva, Gilad. Media and Popular Culture Representations of LGBT Bullying. *Journal of Gay and Lesbian Social Services* 19.3–4 (2008): 105–118.

Parliament of Canada. Bill C–250.

Peel, Elizabeth. Violence against Lesbians and Gay Men: Decision-making in Reporting and Not Reporting Crime. *Feminism and Psychology* 9:2 (1999): 161–167.

Perry, Barbara. Policing Hate Crime in a Multicultural Society: Observations from Canada. *International Journal of Law, Crime and Justice* 38 (2010): 120–140.

Phillips, Rachel, et al. Courtesy Stigma: A Hidden Health Concern among Front Line Service Providers to Sex Workers. *Sociology of Health and Illness* 84 (2012): 681–696.

Pickering, Michael. Racial Stereotypes. In Gary Taylor and Steve Spencer (eds.), *Social Identities: Multidisciplinary Approaches* (pp. 91–106). New York: Routledge, 2004.

Pierre, Teresa. Stop Graphic Revisions to Ontario's Sex Education Curriculum. *Parents as First Educators*, November 1, 2014.

Pilkington, Neil W. and Anthoni R. D'Augelli. Victimization of Lesbian, Gay, and Bisexual Youth in Community Settings. *Journal of Community Psychology* 23 (1995): 34–56.

Porche, Michelle, and Diane Purvin. Never in Our Lifetime: Legal Marriage for Same–Sex Couples in Long–Term Relationships. *Family Relations* 57 (2008): 144–59.

Pratesi, Alessandro. A Respectable Scandal: Same–Sex Parenthood, Emotional Dynamics, and Social Change. *Journal of GLBT Family Studies* 8 (2012): 305–33.

Ragins, Belle Rose, and John M. Cornwell. Pink Triangles: Antecedents and Consequences of Perceived Workplace Discrimination against Gay and Lesbian Employees. *Journal of Applied Psychology* 86:6 (2001): 1244–1261.

Ragins, Belle Rose, Romila Singh, and John M. Cornwell. Making the Invisible Visible: Fear and Disclosure of Sexual Orientation at Work. *Journal of Applied Psychology* 92:4 (2007): 1103–1118.

Rayburn, Nadine Recker, Mitchell Earleywine, and Gerald C. Davison. An Investigation of Base Rates of Anti-Gay Hate Crimes Using the Unmatched-Count Technique. *Journal of Aggression, Maltreatment and Trauma* 6:2 (2003): 137–150.

Raymond, Chase Wesley. Gender and Sexuality in Animated Television Sitcom Interaction. *Discourse and Communication* 7:2 (2013): 199–220.

Renzetti, Elizabeth. Why Improve Sex Education for Kids When They Can Easily Access Porn Sites? *Globe and Mail*, May 9, 2015.

Rich, Adrienne. Compulsory Heterosexuality and Lesbian Existence. *Signs* 5:4 (1980): 631–660.

Riggle, Ellen D. B., Alan L. Ellis, and Anne M. Crawford. The Impact of Media Contact on Attitudes towards Gay Men. *Journal of Homosexuality* 31:3 (1996): 55–69.

Roberts, Simon. Exploring How Gay Men Manage Their Social Identities in the Workplace: The Internal/External Dimensions of Identity. *Equality, Diversity and Inclusion: An International Journal* 30:8 (2011): 668–85.

Robinson, Cynthia Cole. Feminist Theory and Prostitution. *Counterpoints* 302 (2007): 21–36

Robinson, Margaret. LGBTQ Mental Health. N.p.: Rainbow Health Ontario, 2012. Accessed at http://www.rainbowhealthontario.ca.

Rose, Hilary. Canada's Same-Sex Marriage Law: Exception to or Exemplar of Canada's Family Policy? *Journal of Child and Family Studies* 21:1 (2012): 88–94.

Rosenfeld, Michael. Couple Longevity in the Era of Same-Sex Marriage in the United States. *Journal of Marriage and Family* 76 (2014): 905–18.

Rosik, Christopher H., Lois K. Griffith, and Zenaida Cruz. Homophobia and Conservative Religion: Toward a More Nuanced Understanding. *American Journal of Orthopsychiatry* 77:1 (2007): 10–19.

Ryder, Bruce. Equality Rights and Sexual Orientation: Confronting Heterosexual Family Privilege. *Canadian Journal of Family Law* 9:1 (1990): 39–97.

Sallmann, Jolanda. Living with Stigma: Women's Experiences of Prostitution and Substance Use. *Journal of Women and Work* 25 (2010): 146–159.

Sanders, Teela. 2008. *Paying for Pleasure: Men Who Buy Sex*. Devon, UK: Willan Publishing, 2008.

Schmitt, Irina. Gender Sexuality and Canadian Politics. *Zeitschrift für Kanada-Studien* 28:1 (2008): 46–69.

Schneiderman, David. Canada: Supreme Court Addresses Gay-Positive Readers in Public Schools. *International Journal of Constitutional Law* 3:1 (2005): 77–85.

Schumacher, Michele. A Plea for the Traditional Family: Situating Marriage within John Paul II's Realist, or Personalist, Perspective of Human Freedom. *The Linacre Quarterly* 81:4 (2014): 314–42.

Seckler, Valerie. Fashion's Steady Play for Gays. *Women's Wear Daily* (2006, August 23): 10.

Shallenberger, David. Reclaiming the Spirit: The Journeys of Gay Men and Lesbian Women toward Integration. *Qualitative Sociology* 19:2 (1996).

Shipley, Heather. 2014. Religious and Sexual Orientation Intersections in Education and Media: A Canadian Perspective. *Sexualities* 17:5–6 (2014): 512–28.

Short, Donn. 2008. Queers, Bullying and Schools: Am I Safe Here? *Journal of Gay and Lesbian Social Services* 19:3–4 (2008): 31–45.

Smith, B. Amber Rose, a Montreal–Based Sex Worker, Shares her Story. Flare.com, 2015. Retrieved from: http://www.flare.com/culture/amber–rose–a–montreal–based–sex–worker–shares–her–story/.

Smith, Miriam. Gender Politics and the Same-Sex Marriage Debate in the United States. *Social Politics: International Studies in Gender, State and Society* 17:1 (2010): 1–28.

Smith, Miriam. Social Movements and Judicial Empowerment: Courts, Public Policy, and Lesbian and Gay Organizing in Canada. *Politics and Society* 33:2 (2005): 327–353.

Statista. Global Views on Premarital Sex 2013. Retrieved from: http://www.statista.com/statistics/297288/global–views–on–premarital–sex/.

Statistics Canada. Same–Sex Couples and Sexual Orientation . . . By the Numbers. Accessed May 11, 2015.

Supreme Court of Canada. Vriend v. Alberta, [1998] 1 S.C.R. 493.

Thomas, N. (2016). MsNikki Thomas.com. 2016. Retrieved from: http://www.msnikkithomas.com.

Tjepkema, Michael. Health Care Use among Gay, Lesbian and Bisexual Canadians. Component of Statistics Canada Catalogue no. 82–003–XHealth Reports, 2008. Accessed at http://thebridgebrant.com/wp–content/uploads/2014/03/Health–care–among–LGBT–Canada–stats–Can.pdf.

Vanwesenbeeck, I. Prostitution Push and Pull: Male and Female Perspectives. *Journal of Sex Research* 50 (2013): 11–16.

Vogel, L. Abortion Access Grim in English Canada. *Canadian Medical Association Journal* 181:1 (2015): 17.

Ward, James, and Diana Winstanley. Coming Out at Work: Performativity and the Recognition and Renegotiation of

Identity. *Sociological Review* 53:3 (2005): 447–75.

Weitzer, Ronald. Moral Crusade against Prostitution. *Society* (2006): 33–38.

Weitzer, Ronald. Prostitution: Facts and Fictions. *Contexts* 6 (2007): 28–33

Weitzer, Ronald. Sex Trafficking and the Sex Industry: The Need for Evidence–Based Theory and Legislation. *The Journal of Criminal Law and Criminology* 101 (2011): 1337–1369.

Whitley, Bernard E., Jr. 2009. Religiosity and Attitudes toward Lesbians and Gay Men: A Meta–Analysis. *International Journal for the Psychology of Religion* 19:1 (2009): 21–38.

Wight, Richard, Allen LeBlanc, and Lee Badgett. Same–Sex Legal Marriage and Psychological Well–Being: Findings From the California Health Interview Survey. 2014.

Woermke, Meredith. Toward Reducing Health Inequality. Vancouver, BC: Population and Public Health, Provincial Health Services Authority, 2011. Accessed at http://www.phsa.ca.

Wolff, Kristina B. and Carrie L. Cokely. To Protect and to Serve: An Exploration of Police Conduct in Relation to the Gay, Lesbian, Bisexual, and Transgender Community. *Sex Cult* 11 (2007): 1–23.

Wong, William C.W, Holroyd, Eleanor, and Bingham, Amie. Stigma and Sex Work from the Perspective of Female Sex Workers in Hong Kong. *Sociology of Health and Illness* 33 (2011): 50–65.

Woodford, Michael R., et al. Social Work Faculty Support for Same-Sex Marriage: A Cross-National Study of U.S. and Anglophone Canadian MSW Teaching Faculty. *Social Work Research* 36:4 (2012): 301–12.

Woodford, Michael R., N. Eugene Walls, and Denise L. Levy. Religion and Endorsement of Same-Sex Marriage: The Role of Syncretism between Denominational Teachings about Homosexuality and Personal Religious Beliefs. *Interdisciplinary Journal of Research on Religion* 8 (2012).

Woodford, Michael, Eugene Walla, and Denise Levy. Religion and Endorsement of Same-Sex Marriage: The Role of Syncretism between Denominational Teachings about Homosexuality and Personal Religious Beliefs. *Interdisciplinary Journal of Research on Religion* 8:4 (2012): 2–29.

Wright, Nathan. Attendance Matters: Religion and Ethical Affirmation of Gay and Lesbian Sexuality. *Review of Religious Research* 56:2 (2014): 245–73.

Young, Pamela D. Taking Account of Religion in Canada: The Debates over Gay and Lesbian Marriage. *Studies in Religion/Sciences Religieusies* 39:3 (2010): 333–361.

CHAPTER 7

Abelson, Julia, et al. Trends: Canadians Confront Health Care Reform. *Health Affairs* 23:3 (2004): 186–193.

About BodyBreak. BodyBreak: Keep Fit and Have Fun. Accessed July 2, 2015, http://www.bodybreak.com.

Adjaye–Gbewonyo, Kafui, and Ichiro Kawachi. Use of the Yitzhaki Index as a Test of Relative Deprivation for Health Outcomes: A Review of Recent Literature. *Social Science and Medicine* 75 (2012): 129–37.

Allin, Sara, and Mark Stabile. Socioeconomic Status and Child Health: What Is the Role of Health Care, Health Conditions, Injuries and Maternal Health? *Health Economics, Policy and Law* 7 (2012): 227–42.

Alter, David A., et al. Lesson from Canada's Universal Care: Socially Disadvantaged Patients Use More Health Services, Still Have Poorer Health. *Health Affairs* 30 (2011): 274–283.

Ariss, R. (2009). Are the KI Six Outlaws or Prisoners of Conscience? *Globe and Mail*, May 20, 2008.

Arkes, Jeremy. How The Economy Affects Teenage Weight. *Social Science and Medicine* 68 (2009): 1943–1947.

Aronowitz, Robert. Framing Disease: An Underappreciated Mechanism for the Social Patterning of Health. *Social Science and Medicine* 67 (2008): 1–9.

Atler, David A., et al. Lesson from Canada's Universal Care: Socially Disadvantaged Patients Use More Health Services, Still Have Poorer Health. *Health Affairs* 30:2 (2011): 274–283.

Bach, Michael, and Lana Kerzner. *A New Paradigm for Protecting Autonomy and the Right to Legal Capacity.* Toronto: Law Commission of Ontario, 2010. Accessed at http://www.lco-cdo.org/disabilities/bach-kerzner.pdf.

Baliski, Christopher, et al. Influence of Nurse Navigation on Wait Times for Breast Cancer Care in a Canadian Regional Cancer Center. *The American Journal of Surgery* 207 (2014): 686–92.

Bambury, Brent. Pregnant in Limbo: How Vulnerable Women Pay for Canada's Universal Health Care. CBC Radio. Accessed at http://www.cbc.ca/radio/day6/episode-226-pilots-and-mental-illness-dot-sucks-and-pregnant-in-limbo-1.3009231.

Baral, Stefan D., et al. Worldwide Burden of HIV in Transgender Women: A Systematic Review and Meta–Analysis. *The Lancet* 13 (2013): 214–222.

Baranowski, Tom, et al. Are Current Health Behavioral Change Models Helpful in Guiding Prevention of Weight Gain Efforts? *Obesity Research* 11: S10 (2003): 23S–43S.

Barua, Bacchus and Nadeem Esmail. Drug Coverage for Low Income Families. (2015, April). Retrieved from http://www.fraserinstitute.org/uploadedFiles/fraser-ca/Content/research-news/research/publications/drug-coverage-for-low-income-families.pdf.

Bauer, Greta R., et al. I Don't Think This Is Theoretical; This Is Our Lives: How Erasure Impacts Health Care for

References

Transgender People. *Journal of the Association of Nurses in Aids Care* 20 (2009): 348–361.

Bauer, Greta R., et al. Suicidality among Trans People in Ontario: Implications for Social Work and Social Justice. *Service Social* 59 (2013): 35–62.

Bauer, Greta R., et al. Reported Emergency Department Avoidance, Use, and Experiences of Transgender Persons in Ontario, Canada: Results from a Respondent-Driven Sampling Survey. *Annals of Emergency Medicine* (2013): 1–8.

Beckfield, Jason, Sigrun Olafsdottir, and Elyas Bakhtiari. Health Inequalities in Global Context. *American Behavioral Scientist* 57:8 (2013): 1014–039.

Blanchflower, David G. and Andrew J. Oswald. Hypertension and Happiness across Nations. *Journal of Health Economics* 27:2 (2008): 218–233.

Blatt, Sidney J. and Kenneth N. Levy. Attachment Theory, Psychoanalysis, Personality Development, and Psychopathology. *Psychoanalytic Inquiry* 23 (2003): 102–150.

Block, Sheila. *Rising Inequality, Declining Health: Health Outcomes and the Working Poor*. Toronto: Wellesley Institute, 2013.

Bombay, Amy, Kim Matheson, and Hymie Anisman. Intergenerational Trauma: Convergence of Multiple Processes among First Nations peoples in Canada. *Journal of Aboriginal Health* 5:3 (2009): 6–47.

Boodoo, Umar, Rafael Gomez, and Morley Gunderson. Relative Income, Absolute Income and the Life Satisfaction of Older Adults: Do Retirees Differ from the Non–retired? *Industrial Relations Journal* 45:4 (2014): 281–99.

Booth, Christopher M., et al. The Impact of Socioeconomic Status on Stage of Cancer at Diagnosis and Survival. *Cancer* 116:17 (2010): 4160–4167.

Born, Karen and Andreas Laupacis. Public and Private Payment for Health Care in Canada. *Healthy Debate* (2011, July 20). Retrieved from http://healthydebate.ca/2011/07/topic/cost–of–care/publicprivate.

Born, Karen and Irfan Dhalla. (July 6, 2011). National Pharmacare: Who Are the Winners and Losers? *Healthy Debate* (2011, July). Retrieved from http://healthydebate.ca/2011/07/topic/cost–of–care/pharmacare.

Bosman, Maarten and Alwyn Mwinga. Tropical Diseases and the 10/90 Gap. *The Lancet* 356 (2000): S63.

Boudreau, Donald J., Eric J. Cassell, and Abraham Fuks. A Healing Curriculum. *Medical Education* 41 (2007): 1193–1201.

Brennan, Shannon. Self-Reported Spousal Violence, 2009. *Family Violence in Canada: A Statistical Profile*. Ottawa: Statistics Canada, 2011.

British Columbia Ministry of Health. *Summary of Input on the Conversation on Health*. Victoria, BC: Ministry of Health, 2007.

Brown, Judith E., et al. Television Viewing by School-Age Children: Associations with Physical Activity, Snack Food Consumption and Unhealthy Weight. *Social Indicators Research* 101:2 (2011): 221–225.

Burkhauser, Richard V. and John Cawley. Adding Biomeasures Relating to Fatness and Obesity to the Panel Study of Income Dynamics. *Biodemography and Social Biology* 55:2 (2009): 118–139.

Byles, Julie. Obesity: The New Global Threat to Healthy Ageing and Longevity. *Health Sociology Review* 18:4 (2009): 412–422.

Canadian Health Services Research Foundation. Myth: For-Profit Ownership of Facilities Would Lead to a More Efficient Health Care System. *Journal of Health Services Research and Policy* 10:4 (2005): 255–256.

Canadian Institute for Health Information. *National Health Expenditure Trends, 1975 to 2014*. Ottawa: Canadian Institute for Health Information, 2014.

Canadian Population Health Initiative. *Reducing Gaps in Health a Focus on Socio–economic Status in Urban Canada*. Ottawa: Canadian Population Health Initiative, 2008.

Carpenter, Christopher S. The Effects of Employment Protection for Obese People. *Industrial Relations* 45:3 (2006): 393–415.

Carriere, Gisele, and Claudia Sanmartin. Waiting Time for Medical Specialist Consultations in Canada, 2007. *Health Reports* 21:2 (2010, June): 7–14.

Casey, Rebecca. Disability and Unmet Health Care Needs in Canada: A Longitudinal Analysis. *Disability and Health Journal* 8:1 (2015): 173–81.

CBC News. Prospectors, Landholders Raise Concerns about Ontario Mining Act Meetings. 2008. Retrieved from: http://www.cbc.ca/news/canada/ottawa/prospectors-landholders-raise-concerns-about-ontario-mining-act-meetings-1.711080.

CBC News. Brad Badiuk, Winnipeg Teacher, On Leave after Controversial Facebook Posts on Aboriginals. 2014. Retrieved from: http://www.cbc.ca/news/canada/manitoba/brad-badiuk-winnipeg-teacher-on-leave-after-controversial-facebook-posts-on-aboriginals-1.2869065.

Centers for Disease Control and Prevention. Childhood Obesity Facts. Last modified April 24, 2015. Accessed at http://www.cdc.gov/healthyyouth/obesity/facts.htm.

Chen, Edith. Protective Factors for Health among Low-Socioeconomic-Status Individuals. *Current Directions in Psy-*

chological Science 21:3 (2012): 189–93.

Coburn, David. Beyond The Income Inequality Hypothesis: Class, Neo-liberalism, And Health Inequalities. *Social Science and Medicine* 58 (2004): 41–56.

Collin, Chantal, and Bonnie Campbell. *Measuring Poverty: A Challenge for Canada*. Ottawa: Library of Parliament, 2008. Accessed at http://www.parl.gc.ca/Content/LOP/ResearchPublications/prb0865-e.htm#a1.

Crimmins, Eileen M., Samuel H. Preston, and Barney Cohen. *Explaining Divergent Levels of Longevity in High-Income Countries*. Washington, D.C.: National Academies Press, 2011.

Crosnoe, Robert. Gender, Obesity, and Education. *Sociology of Education* 80:3 (2007): 241–260.

Dauvergne, M. Family Violence against Older Adults. In C. Trainor (ed.), *Family Violence in Canada: A Statistical Profile 2002* (pp. 26–33). Ottawa: Statistics Canada, 2002.

De Maio, Fernando. *Global Health Inequities: A Sociological Perspective*. Basingstoke, UK: Palgrave Macmillan, 2014.

Deber, Raisa. Profits and Health Care Delivery. *Inroads* 12 (2003):37–47.

DeKeseredy, Walter and Molly Dragiewicz. Woman Abuse in Canada: Sociological Reflections on the Past, Suggestions for the Future. *Violence Against Women* 20:2 (2014): 228–244.

Devaney, Julie, et al. Navigating Healthcare: Gateways to Cancer Screening. *Disability and Society* 24:6 (2009): 739–51.

Devaux, Marion and Franco Sassi. Social Inequalities in Obesity and Overweight in 11 OECD Countries. *European Journal of Public Health*, 23:3 (2013): 464–469.

Diener, Ed and Micaela Y. Chan. Happy People Live Longer: Subjective Well-Being Contributes to Health and Longevity. *Applied Psychology: Health and Wellbeing* 3:1, (2011): 1–43.

Dietz, William H. Health Consequences of Obesity in Youth: Childhood Predictors of Adult Disease. *Pediatrics* 101:3 (1998): 518–525.

Diez Roux, Ana V. Integrating Social and Biologic Factors in Health Research: A Systems View. *Annals of Epidemiology* 17:7 (2007): 569–574.

Doherty, Deborah and Dorothy Berglund. *Psychological Abuse: A Discussion Paper*. Ottawa: Public Health Agency of Canada, 2008.

Donnelly, C., et al. Utilization, Access and Satisfaction with Primary Care among People with Spinal Cord Injuries: A Comparison of Three Countries. *Spinal Cord* 45:1 (2007): 25–36.

Frank, Lawrence Douglas, et al. Stepping Towards Causation: Do Built Environments or Neighborhood and Travel Preferences Explain Physical Activity, Driving, and Obesity? *Social Science and Medicine* 65 (2007): 1898–1914.

Doyal, Lesley. Gender and the 10/90 Gap in Health Research. *Bulletin of the World Health Organization* 82:3 (2004): 162.

Egeland, Byron and Alan Sroufe. Developmental Sequelae of Maltreatment in Infancy. *New Directions for Child and Adolescent Development* 11 (1981): 77–92.

Ellison, George. Letting the Gini Out of the Bottle? Challenges Facing the Relative Income Hypothesis. *Social Science and Medicine* 54 (2002): 561–76.

Epstein, Steven. *Inclusion: The Politics of Difference in Medical Research*. Chicago: University of Chicago Press, 2007.

Erickson, M. F. and B. Egeland. Child Neglect. In J. E. B. Myers (ed.), *The APSAC Handbook on Child Maltreatment*, 3rd ed. (pp. 103–124). Thousand Oaks, CA: Sage, 2011.

Evans, Bethan and Rachel Colls. Measuring Fatness, Governing Bodies: The Spatialities of the Body Mass Index (BMI) in Anti-Obesity Politics. *Antipode* 41:5 (2009): 1051–1083.

Fay, Marianne, et al.. Achieving Child–Health–Related Millennium Development Goals: The Role of Infrastructure. *World Development* 33:8 (2005): 1267–1284.

Feldman, M. A., et al. Health Self-advocacy Training for Persons with Intellectual Disabilities. *Journal of Intellectual Disability Research* 56:2 (2012): 1110–1121.

Fiori, Katherine L., and Justin Jager. The Impact of Social Support Networks on Mental and Physical Health in the Transition to Older Adulthood: A Longitudinal, Pattern-Centered Approach. *International Journal of Behavioural Development* 36:2 (2011): 117–129

Firebaugh, Glenn, and Matthew B. Schroeder. Does Your Neighbor's Income Affect Your Happiness? *American Journal of Sociology* 115:3 (2009): 805–31.

Fitzpatrick, Kevin M. and Mark LaGory. 'Placing' Health in an Urban Sociology: Cities as Mosaics of Risk and Protection. *City and Community* 2:1 (2003): 33–46.

Fletcher, Isabel. Defining an Epidemic: The Body Mass Index in British and US Obesity Research 1960–2000. *Sociology of Health and Illness* 36:3 (2014): 338–353

Follingstad, Diane R. and Dana D. DeHart. Defining Psychological Abuse of Husbands Toward Wives: Contexts, Behaviors, and Typologies. *Journal of Interpersonal Violence* 15:9 (2000): 891–920.

Follingstad, Diane R., Dana D. DeHart, and E. P. Green. Psychologists' Judgments of Psychologically Aggressive Actions When Perpetrated by a Husband versus a Wife. *Violence and Victims* 19:4 (2004): 435–452.

Friedman, Howard S., Margaret L. Kern, and Chandra A. Reynolds. Personality and Health, Subjective Well-Being, and

References

Longevity. *Journal of Personality*, 78:1 (2010): 179–215.

Frohlich, Katherine, Nancy Ross, and Chantelle Richmond. Health Disparities in Canada Today: Some Evidence and a Theoretical Framework. *Health Policy* 79 (2006): 132–143.

Frumkin, Howard. Urban Sprawl and Public Health. *Public Health Reports* 117 (2002): 201–217.

Fyson, R., and J. Cromby. Human Rights and Intellectual Disabilities in an Era of 'Choice'. *Journal of Intellectual Disability Research* 57:12 (2013): 1164–172.

Galea, Sandro and David Vlahov. Urban Health: Populations, Methods, and Practice. In Sandro Galea and David Vlahov (eds.), *Handbook of Urban Health: Populations, Methods, and Practice 2005* (pp.1–15). New York: Springer, 2005.

Galea, Sandro, Nicholas Freudenberg, and David Vlahov. Cities and Population Health. *Social Science and Medicine* 60 (2005): 1017–1033.

Garasky, Steven, et al. Family Stressors and Child Obesity. *Social Science Research* 38 (2009): 755–766.

Gelinas, Sylvie, Shannon Wagner, and Henry Harder. Private Health Care Option: Disability Management in Canada. *Journal of Disability Policy Studies* 21:2 (2010): 116–25.

Gerdtham, Ulf-G., and Magnus Johannesson. Absolute Income, Relative Income, Income Inequality and Mortality. *Journal of Human Resources* 29:1 (2004): 205–18.

Gershon, Andrea, et al. Chronic Obstructive Pulmonary Disease and Socioeconomic Status: A Systematic Review. *Journal of Chronic Obstructive Pulmonary Disease* 9 (2012): 216–26.

Gibson, Barbara, and Roxanne Mykitiuk. Health Care Access and Support for Disabled Women In Canada: Falling Short of the UN Convention on the Rights of Persons with Disabilities: A Qualitative Study. *Women's Health Issues* 22:1 (2012): 111–18.

Glauser, Wendy. Private Clinics Continue Explosive Growth. *Canadian Medical Association Journal* 183:8 (2011).

Gordon, Jane, Lorraine Sheppard, and Sophie Anaf. The Patient Experience in the Emergency Department: A Systematic Synthesis of Qualitative Research. *International Emergency Nursing* 18 (2010).

Gore, Dana and Anita Kothari. Social Determinants of Health in Canada: Are Healthy Living Initiatives There Yet? A Policy Analysis. *International Journal for Equity in Health* 11:41 (2012): 1–14.

Gori-Maia, Alexandre. Relative Income, Inequality and Subjective Wellbeing: Evidence for Brazil. *Social Indicators Research* 113 (2013): 1193–204.

Gortmaker, Steven L., et al. Social and Economic Consequences of Overweight in Adolescence and Young Adulthood. *New England Journal of Medicine* 329:14 (1993): 1008–1012.

Government of Canada. Facts on Psychological and Emotional Abuse of Seniors. 2015a. Accessed at http://www.seniors.gc.ca/eng/pie/eaa/psychologicalandemotional.shtml.

Government of Canada. About Family Violence. 2015b. Accessed at http://www.justice.gc.ca/eng/cj–jp/fv-vf/about-apropos.html.

Government of Canada, Public Health Agency of Canada. Obesity in Canada: Prevalence among Aboriginal Populations. Last modified June 23, 2011. Accessed at http://www.phac-aspc.gc.ca/hp-ps/hl–mvs/oic-oac/abo-aut-eng.php.

Government of Canada. Childhood Obesity. 2016. Accessed at http://healthycanadians.gc.ca/healthy–living–vie–saine/obesity–obesite/risks–risques–eng.php#a2.

Gregory, Deborah, Julia Temple Newhook, and Laurie K. Twells. Patients' Perceptions of Waiting for Bariatric Surgery: A Qualitative Study. *International Journal for Equity in Health* 12:1 (2013): 86–106.

Griffith, Derek M., et al. Race, SES, and Obesity among Men. *Race and Social Problems* 3:4 (2011): 298–306.

Hajizadeh, Mohammad, M. Karen Campbell, and Sisira Sarma. Socioeconomic Inequalities in Adult Obesity Risk in Canada: Trends And Decomposition Analyses. *European Journal of Health Economics* 15 (2014): 203–221.

Harrold, Jessie, and Lois Jackson. Hurry up and Wait. The Experiences of Young Women in Rural Nova Scotia Accessing Specialized Care. *Canadian Journal of Rural Medicine* 16:3 (2011): 83–88.

Health Canada. Canadian Guidelines for Body Weight Classification in Adults. Last modified July 3, 2011. Accessed at http://www.hc–sc.gc.ca/fn–an/nutrition/weights–poids/guide–ld–adult/qa–qr–pub–eng.php#a4.

Health Canada. Emotional Abuse. National Clearinghouse on Family Violence. Cat. No. H 72–22/18–1996E (1996).

Hibbard, Roberta, Jane Barlow, and Harriet MacMillan. Psychological Maltreatment. *American Academy of Pediatrics* 130:2 (2012): 372–378.

Hildyard, Kathryn L. and David A. Wolfe. Child Neglect: Developmental Issues and Outcomes. *Child Abuse and Neglect* 26:6–7 (2002): 679–695.

Hill, Peter S., et al. From Millennium Development Goals to Post-2015 Sustainable Development: Sexual and Reproductive Health and Rights in an Evolving Aid Environment. *Reproductive Health Matters* 21:42 (2013): 113–124.

Hiscock, Rosemary, Linda Bauld, Amanda Amos, Jennifer A. Fidler, and Marcus Munafò. Socioeconomic Status and Smoking: A Review. *Annals of the New York Academy of Sciences* (2012): 107–23.

Hutchison, Brian, et al. Primary Health Care in Canada: Systems in Motion. *Milbank Quarterly* 89:2 (2011): 256–288.

Huurre, Taina, et al. Does Social Support Affect the Relationship between Socioeconomic Status and Depression? A Longitudinal Study from Adolescence to Adulthood. *Journal of Affective Disorders* 100 (2007): 55–64

Hyde, Martin, et al. The Effects of Pre-Retirement Factors and Retirement Route on Circumstances in Retirement: Findings from the Whitehall II Study. *Aging and Society* 24 (2004): 279–296

Iadicola, Peter and Anson Shupe. *Violence, Inequality, and Human Freedom.* Lanham, MD: Rowman & Littlefield, 2012.

Izquierdo, C. When 'Health' Is Not Enough: Societal, Individual And Biomedical Assessments of Well-Being among the Matsigenka of the Peruvian Amazon. *Social Science and Medicine*, 61:4 (2005): 767–783.

Johnson, Michael P. and Kathleen J. Ferraro. Research on Domestic Violence in the 1990s: Making Distinctions. *Journal of Marriage and the Family* 62:4 (2000): 948–963.

Joshi, Devin. Good Governance, State Capacity, and the Millennium Development Goals. *Perspectives on Global Development and Technology* 10:2 (2011): 339–360.

Joynt, Karen E., David J. Whellan, and Christopher M. O'Connor. Depression and Cardiovascular Disease: Mechanisms of Interaction. *Biological Psychiatry* 54:3 (2003): 248–261.

Kahneman, Daniel and Angus Deaton. High Income Improves Evaluation of Life But Not Emotional Well-Being. *PNAS* 107:38 (2010): 16489–16493.

Karlsdotter, Kristina, et al. Multilevel Analysis of Income, Income Inequalities and Health in Spain. *Social Science and Medicine* 74 (2012): 1099–106.

Karlsson, Martin, et al. Income Inequality and Health: Importance of a Cross–country Perspective. *Social Science and Medicine* 70 (2010): 875–85.

Kilama, Wen L. The 10/90 Gap in Sub–Saharan Africa: Resolving Inequities in Health Research. *Acta Tropica* 112 (2009): S8–S15.

Kramer, Michael. Socioeconomic Disparities in Preterm Birth. *Paediatric and Perinatal Epidemiology* 29 (2015): 169–71.

Kurzweil, Rachel C. Justice is What Love Looks Like in Public: How the Affordable Care Act Falls Short on Transgender Health Care Access. *Washington and Lee Journal of Civil Rights and Social Justice* 196 (2014): 195–269.

Labonte, Ronald, et al. *Healthy Populations: A Report of the Canadian Index of Wellbeing (CIW).* Waterloo, ON: University of Waterloo, 2010.

Lebel, Alexandre, et al. Geographic Variability in the Association between Socioeconomic Status and BMI in the USA and Canada. *Public Library of Science* 9:6 (2014): 1–11.

Lee, Chung Yul, et al. Development of a Community Health Promotion Center Based on the World Health Organization's Ottawa Charter Health Promotion Strategies. *Japan Journal of Nursing Science* 6 (2009): 83–90.

Lee, Hedwig, et al. Trends in Body Mass Index in Adolescence and Young Adulthood in the United States: 1959 –2002. *Journal of Adolescent Health* 49 (2011): 601– 608.

Lemke, Thomas. Foucault, Governmentality, and Critique. *Rethinking Marxism* 14:3 (2002): 49–64.

Lemstra, Mark. Socioeconomic Status of Natives Affects Health. *Star Phoenix* (2011, February 3).

Letourneau, N. L., L. Duffett-Leger, L. Levac, B. Watson, and C. Young–Morris. Socioeconomic Status and Child Development: A Meta–Analysis. *Journal of Emotional and Behavioral Disorders* 21:3 (2011): 211–24.

Lewis, Ricki. Fighting the 10/90 Gap. *The Scientist* (2002, May 13).

Longenberg, C., et al. Central and Total Obesity in Middle Aged Men and Women in Relation to Lifetime Socioeconomic Status: Evidence from a National Birth Cohort. *Journal of Epidemiology and Community Health* 57:10 (2003): 816–822.

Loriggio, Paola. Party Aims to Give People with Disabilities A Chance to Explore Sexuality. *Winnipeg Free Press*, August 9, 2015. Accessed at http://www.winnipegfreepress.com/breakingnews/party–aims–to–give–people–with–disabilities–a–chance–to–explore–sexuality–321170861.html.

Loring, Marti Tamm. *Emotional Abuse: The Trauma and the Treatment.* New York: Wiley, 1998.

Macdonnell, Judith A., and Grigorovich, Alisa. Gender, Work, and Health for Trans Health Providers: A Focus on Transmen. *ISRN Nursing* (2012): 1–11.

Madore, Odette and Marlisa Tiedemann. Private Health Care Funding and Delivery under the Canada Health Act. Ottawa: Parliamentary Information and Research Service, 2005.

Mandlis, Lane R. Human Rights, Transsexed Bodies, and Health Care in Canada: What Counts as Legal Protection? *Canadian Journal of Law and Society* 26 (2011): 509–529.

Marcellin, Roxanne Longman, Bauer, Greta R., and Scheim, Ayden I. Intersecting Impacts of Transphobia and Racism on HIV Risk among Trans Persons of Colour in Ontario, Canada. *Ethnicity and Inequalities in Health and Social Care* 6 (2013): 97–107.

Marmot, M.G, et al. Health Inequalities among British Civil Servants: The Whitehall II Study. *The Lancet* 337 (1991): 1387–1393

Marmot, Michael. Interview by Harry Kreisler. University of California at Berkeley, 2002.

Marmot, Michael. Social Determinants of Health Inequalities. *Lancet* 365 (2005): 1099–1104.

McColl, Mary, and Sam Shortt. Another Way to Look at High Service Utilization: The Contribution of Disability. *Journal of Health Services Research and Policy* 11:2 (2006): 74–80.

McColl, Mary, Anna Jarzynowska, and S.E.D. Shortt. Unmet Health Care Needs of People with Disabilities: Population Level Evidence. *Disability and Society* 25:2 (2010): 205–18.

McColl, Mary, et al. Physician Experiences Providing Primary Care to People with Disabilities. *Healthcare Policy* 4:1 (2008): 129–147.

McColl, Mary, et al. Disentangling the Effects of Disability and Age on Health Service Utilisation. *Disability and Rehabilitation* 33:13–14 (2011): 1253–261.

McColl, Mary. Disability Studies at the Population Level: Issues of Health Service Utilization. *The American Journal of Occupational Therapy* 59:5 (2005): 516–26.

McLaren, Lindsay. Socioeconomic Status and Obesity. *Epidemiologic Reviews* 29:1 (2007): 29–48.

McPhail, Deborah. Resisting Biopedagogies of Obesity in a Problem Population: Understandings of Healthy Eating and Healthy Weight in a Newfoundland and Labrador Community. *Critical Public Health*, 23:3, (2013): 289–303.

Mikkonen, Juha, and Dennis Raphael. *Social Determinants of Health: The Canadian Facts.* Toronto: York University, 2010.

Miller, Douglas L., and Christina Paxson. Relative Income, Race, and Mortality. *Journal of Health Economics* 25 (2006): 979–1003.

Miller, Grant. Waiting for an Operation: Parent's Perspective. *Canadian Journal of Surgery* 47:3 (2004): 179.

Molidor, Christian E. Gender Differences of Psychological Abuse in High School Dating Relationships. *Child and Adolescent Social Work Journal* 12:2 (1995): 119–134.

Morgan, Steven G., et al. Estimated Cost of Universal Public Coverage of Prescription Drugs in Canada. *Canadian Medical Association Journal* (2015, March 16). Accessed at http://www.cmaj.ca/content/early/2015/03/16/cmaj.141564.

Moss, William, et al. Research Priorities for the Reduction of Perinatal and Neonatal Morbidity and Mortality in Developing Country Communities. *Journal of Perinatology* 22 (2002): 484–495.

Namaste, Viviane K. *Invisible Lives: The Erasure of Transsexual and Transgendered People.* Chicago: University of Chicago Press, 2000.

Nuru–Jeter, Amani, et al. Socioeconomic Predictors of Health and Development in Middle Childhood: Variations by Socioeconomic Status Measure and Race. *Issues in Comprehensive Pediatric Nursing* 33 (2010): 59–81.

O'Donnell, Vivian, and Susan Wallace. *First Nations, Métis and Inuit Women.* Ottawa: Statistics Canada, 2011.

O'Neil, James M., et al. Psychological Abuse in Family Studies: A Psychoeducational and Preventive Approach. *Marriage and Family Review* 38:4 (2006): 41–58.

Obedin–Maliver, Juno. Time for OBGYNs to Care for People of All Genders. *Journal of Women's Health* 24 (2015): 109–111.

Odhayani, Abdulaziz Al, William J. Watson, and Lindsay Watson. Behavioural Consequences of Child Abuse. *Canadian Family Physician* 59:8 (2013): 831–836.

OECD [Organization for Economic Cooperation and Development]. *Health at a Glance 2013: OECD Indicators.* N.p.: OECD Publishing, 2013.

OECD [Organization for Economic Cooperation and Development]. OECD Health Statistics 2014. 2012. Accessed June 20, 2015.

OECD [Organization for Economic Cooperation and Development]. What Is the OECD? United States Mission to the Organization for Economic Cooperation and Development. Accessed at http://usoecd.us mission.gov/mission/overview.html.

Ogrodnik, L. Spousal Homicide or Attempts and Prior Police Contact for Spousal Abuse. In *Family Violence in Canada: A Statistical Profile 2007* (pp. 9–19). Ottawa: Statistics Canada, Canadian Centre for Justice Statistics, 2007.

Olah, Michelle E, Gregory Gaisano, and Stephen W. Hwang. The Effect of Socioeconomic Status on Access to Primary Care: An Audit Study. *Canadian Medical Association Journal* (2013): 263–269.

Orellana, Marcos A. Climate Change and the Millennium Development Goals: The Right to Development, International Cooperation and the Clean Development Mechanism. *Sur: International Journal of Human Rights* 7:12 (2010): 141–171.

Oshio, Takashi, Kayo Nozaki, and Miki Kobayashi. Relative Income And Happiness In Asia: Evidence From Nationwide Surveys In China, Japan, And Korea. *Social Indicators Research* 104 (2011): 351–67.

Ostir, Glenn V., et al. The Association between Emotional Well-Being and the Incidence of Stroke in Older Adults. *Psychosomatic Medicine* 63:2 (2001): 210–215.

Oswald, Andrew J. and Stephen Wu. Objective Confirmation of Subjective Measures of Human Well–Being: Evidence from the U.S.A. *Science* 327 (2010): 576–579.

Ottawa Charter for Health Promotion. *Canadian Journal for Public Health* 77:6 (1986): 425–430.

Owusu–Ampomah, K. Chasing Shadows? Policies and Actions that Undermine Efforts towards the Millennium Development Goals (MDGs). *Review of Human Factor Studies* 17 (2011): 1–39.

Padavic, Irene and Barbara F. Reskin. *Women and Men at Work*. 2nd ed. London: Sage Publications, 2002.

Padwal, Raj, et al. Health Status, Quality of Life, and Satisfaction of Patients Awaiting Multidisciplinary Bariatric Care. *BMC Health Services Research* 12 (2012).

Pampel, Fred C., Justin T. Denney, and Patrick M. Krueger. Obesity, SES, and Economic Development: A Test of the Reversal Hypothesis. *Social Science and Medicine* 74 (2012): 1073–1081.

Parish, Susan L., et al. State-level Income Inequality and Family Burden of US Families Raising Children with Special Health Care Needs. *Social Science and Medicine* 74 (2012): 399–407.

Petrelli, Alessio, et al. Socioeconomic Differences in Waiting Times for Elective Surgery: A Population–based Retrospective Study. *BMC Health Services Research*, 2012.

Pickett, Kate E., et al. Wider Income Gaps, Wider Waistbands? An Ecological Study of Obesity and Income Inequality. *Journal of Epidemiology and Community Health* 59 (2005): 670–674.

Pickett, Kate, and Richard Wilkinson. People like Us: Ethnic Group Density Effects on Health. *Ethnicity & Health* 13:4 (2008): 321–34.

Poku, Nana and Jim Whitman. The Millennium Development Goals: Challenges, Prospects and Opportunities. *Third World Quarterly* 32:1 (2011): 3–8.

Poku, Nana K. and Jim Whitman. The Millennium Development Goals and Development after 2015. *Third World Quarterly* 32:1 (2011): 181–198.

Prus, Steven G. Comparing Social Determinants of Self–Rated Health across the United States and Canada. *Social Science and Medicine* 73:1 (2011): 50–59.

Public Health Agency of Canada. Canadian Incidence Study of Reported Child Abuse and Neglect. Ottawa: Public Health Agency of Canada, 2008.

Rabiu, Taopheeq Bamidele and James Ayokunle Balogun. Repositioning Health Research in Developing Countries. *Archives of Medical Research* 40:3 (2009): 223.

Radnofsky, Louise. 5 Things about People Who Remain Uninsured despite Obamacare. *The Wall Street Journal* (2015, June 24).

Raphael, Dennis. Grasping at Straws: A Recent History of Health Promotion in Canada. *Critical Public Health* 18:4 (2008): 483–495.

Raphael, Dennis. Social Determinants of Health: Present Status, Unanswered Questions, and Future Directions. *International Journal of Health Services* 36:4 (2006): 651–677.

Raymond, Émilie, Amanda Grenier, and Jill Hanley. Community Participation of Older Adults with Disabilities. *Journal of Community and Applied Social Psychology* 24:1 (2014): 50–62.

Razzouk, D., et al. Challenges to Reduce the 10/90 Gap: Mental Health Research in Latin American and Caribbean Countries. *Acta Psychiatrica Scandinavica* 118:6 (2008): 490–498.

Reid, Collen and Carol Herbert. 'Welfare Moms and Welfare Bums': Revisiting Poverty as a Social Determinant of Health. *Health Sociology Review* 14:2 (2005): 161–173.

Reid, John. A Personal View: Sir John Reid. *Health Promotion International* 1:4 (1986): 405.

Reinier, K., et al. Socioeconomic Status and Incidence of Sudden Cardiac Arrest. *Canadian Medical Association Journal* 183:15 (2011): 1705–712.

Riggs, Shelley A. and Patricia Kaminsky. Childhood Emotional Abuse, Adult Attachment, and Depression as Predictors of Relational Adjustment and Psychological Aggression. *Journal of Aggression, Maltreatment and Trauma* 19:1 (2010):75–104.

Ritzema, A. M., et al. Improving Outcomes for Children with Developmental Disabilities through Enhanced Communication and Collaboration between School Psychologists and Physicians. *Canadian Journal of School Psychology* 29:4 (2014): 317–37.

Rotondi, Nooshin Khobzi, et al. Nonprescribed Hormone Use and Self–Performed Surgeries: Do-It-Yourself Transitions in Transgender Communities in Ontario, Canada. *Research and Practice* 103 (2013): 1830–1836.

Rutty, Christopher and Sue C. Sullivan. *This Is Public Health: A Canadian History*. Ottawa: Canadian Public Health Association, 2010.

Sackett, Leslie A. and Daniel G. Saunders. The Impact of Different Forms of Psychological Abuse on Battered Women. *Violence and Victims* 14:1 (1999): 1–13.

Sanders, Shane. A Model of the Relative Income Hypothesis. *Journal of Economic Education* 41:3 (2010): 292–305.

Sanmartin, Claudia, et al. Waiting for Medical Services in Canada: Lots of Heat, but Little Light. *Canadian Medical Association Journal* 162:9 (2000):1305–10.

Schafer, Markus H. and Kenneth F. Ferraro. Distal and Variably Proximal Causes: Education, Obesity, and Health. *Social Science and Medicine* 73 (2011): 1340–1348.

Shields, M., et al. The Bias in Self–reported Estimates of Obesity in Canadian Health Surveys: An Update on Establishing Correction Equations for Adults. *Health Reports* 22:3 (2011): 1–11.

References

Sit, Arthur. Socioeconomic Factors and Vision Health in Canada. *Canadian Journal of Ophthalmology* 45 (2010): 441–42.

Snelgrove, John W., et al. Complete Out-At-Sea with Two-Gender Medicine: A Qualitative Analysis of Physician-Side Barriers to Providing Healthcare for Transgender Patients. *BMC Health Services Research* 12 (2012): 1–13.

Sobal, Jeffery and Albert J. Stunkard. Socioeconomic Status and Obesity: A Review of the Literature. *Psychological Bulletin* 105:2 (1989): 260–275.

Srebrolow, Gary and Tracey Tremayne-Lloyd. 'Private' Health Care in Ontario: Current Status and Future Outlook. Paper originally presented at OBA Program entitled Critical Issues in Health Law: A National Summit in May 2007.

Stafford, Mai, et al. Characteristics of Individuals and Characteristics of Areas: Investigating Their Influence on Health in the Whitehall II Study. *Health and Place* 7 (2001): 117–129.

Stainton, Tim, and Isabel Clare. Human Rights and Intellectual Disabilities: An Emergent Theoretical Paradigm? *Journal of Intellectual Disability Research* 56:2 (2012): 1011–013.

Statistics Canada. Life Expectancy. 2012. Accessed June 20, 2015.

Steinberger, Julia and Stephen R. Daniels. Obesity, Insulin Resistance, Diabetes, and Cardiovascular Risk in Children. *Circulation* 107:10 (2003): 1448–1453.

Steptoe, A. and J. Wardle. Positive Affect and Biological Function in Everyday Life. *Neurobiology of Aging* 26:1 (2005): 108–112.

Stevens, Philip. *Diseases of Poverty and the 10/90 Gap*. London: International Policy Network, 2004. Accessed at http://www.who.int/intellectualproperty/submissions/InternationalPolicyNetwork.pdf.

Stratton, J., et al. Income Disparities in Life Expectancy in the City of Toronto and Region of Peel, Ontario. *Chronic Diseases and Injuries in Canada* 32:4 (2012).

Stromwall, Layne K., et al. Parents with Co-Occurring Mental Health and Substance Abuse Conditions Involved in Child Protection Services: Clinical Profile and Treatment Needs. *Child Welfare* 87:3 (2008): 95–113.

Strumberg, Joachim P. and Carmel M. Martin. Complexity and Health: Yesterday's Traditions, Tomorrow's Future. *Journal of Evaluation in Clinical Practice* 15, (2009): 543–548.

Sun, Yiguo, and Thanasis Stengos. The Absolute Health Income Hypothesis Revisited: A Semiparametric Quantile Regression Approach. *Empirical Economics* 35:1 (2008): 395–412.

Sutherland, Ross. The Effect of For-Profit Laboratories on the Accountability, Integration, and the Cost of Canadian Health Care Services. *Open Medicine* 6:4 (2012):166–170.

Terris, Milton. Newer Perspectives on the Health of Canadians: Beyond the Lalonde Report. *Journal of Public Health Policy* 5:3 (1984): 327–337.

Theobald, Sally, Bertha Nhlema Simwaka, and Barbara Klugman. Gender, Health and Development III: Engendering Health Research. *Progress in Development Studies* 6:4 (2006): 337–342.

Thibedeau, Wayne. Peakes Woman Loses Her Baby, Dignity While Awaiting Hospital Treatment. *The Guardian* (Charlottetown), July 29, 2010.

Tozer, April, Paul Belanger, Kieran Moore, and Jaelyn Caudle. Socioeconomic Status of Emergency Department Users in Ontario, 2003 to 2009. *Canadian Journal of Emergency Medicine* 16:3 (2014): 220–25.

Turcotte, Martin. Trends in Social Capital in Canada. Ottawa: Statistics Canada, 2015.

Turcotte, Pier-Luc, et al. Are Health Promotion and Prevention Interventions Integrated into Occupational Therapy Practice with Older Adults Having Disabilities? Insights from Six Community Health Settings in Québec, Canada. *Australian Occupational Therapy Journal* 62:1 (2015): 56–67.

Turshen, Meredeth. A Global Partnership for Development and Other Unfulfilled Promises of the Millennium Project. *Third World Quarterly* 35: 3 (2014): 345–357.

Tutty, Leslie. *Husband Abuse: An Overview of Research and Perspectives*. Ottawa: National Clearinghouse on Family Violence, 1999.

United Nations. The Millennium Development Goals Report 2015. New York: United Nations, 2015.

United Nations. We Can End Poverty: Millennium Development Goals and Beyond. New York: United Nations, 2015. Accessed at http://www.un.org/millenniumgoals/.

Vandemoortele, Jan. If Not the Millennium Development Goals, Then What? *Third World Quarterly* 32:1 (2011): 9–25.

Vertrees, Stephanie M. Medical Humanities, Ethics, and Disability. *Cambridge Quarterly of Healthcare Ethics* 21:1 (2012): 260–66.

Vidyasagar, D. Global Notes: The 10/90 Gap, Disparities in Global Health Research. *Journal of Perinatology* 26 (2006): 55–56.

Vonneilich, Nico, et al. Does Socioeconomic Status Affect the Association of Social Relationships and Health? A Moderator Analysis. *International Journal for Equity in Health* 10:43 (2011): 1–10

Wade, Derick T. and Peter W. Halligan. Do Biomedical Models of Illness Make for Good Healthcare Systems? *British Medical Journal* 329:7479 (2004): 1398–1401.

Wagstaff, Adam, and Eddy Van Doorslaer. Income Inequality and Health: What Does the Literature Tell Us? *Annual Re-*

view of Public Health 21 (2000): 543–67.

Walker, Lenore E. *The Battered Woman Syndrome*. New York: Springer Publishing Company, 1984.

Wallace, Barbara C., and Carter, Robert T. *Understanding and dealing with violence: a multicultural approach*. Thousand Oaks, CA: Sage Publications, 2003.

Wellstood, Katie, Kathi Wilson, and John Eyles. 'Unless You Went in with Your Head under Your Arm': Patient Perceptions of Emergency Room Visits. *Social Science and Medicine* 61 (2005).

Wilkinson, Richard. Politics and Health Inequalities. *The Lancet* 368 (2006): 1299–230.

Wilkinson, Richard. The Impact of Inequality. *Social Research: An International Quarterly* 73:2 (2006): 711–32.

Wind, Tiffany Weissmann and Louise Silvern. Parenting and Family Stress as Mediators of the Long–Term Effects of Child Abuse. *Child Abuse and Neglect* 18:5 (1994): 439–453.

Wolbring, Tobias, Marc Keuschnigg, and Eva Negele. Needs, Comparisons, and Adaptation: The Importance of Relative Income for Life Satisfaction. *European Sociological Review* 29:1 (2013): 86–104.

Woolhandler, Steffie and David U. Himmelstein. The High Costs of For–Profit Care. *Canadian Medical Association Journal* 170:12 (2004):1814–1815.

World Bank. Infant Mortality Rate (per 1,000 Live Births). 2015. Accessed June 30, 2015.

World Bank. Under–5 Mortality Rate (per 1,000 Live Births). 2015. Accessed June 30, 2015.

World Health Organization [WHO]. Country Statistics. 2015. Accessed June 20, 2015.

World Health Organization [WHO]. World Health Statistics 2014. Geneva: World Health Organization, 2014.

World Health Organization [WHO]. Child Maltreatment. Fact sheet no. 150 (2014). Accessed at http://www.who .int/mediacentre/factsheets/fs150/en/.

World Health Organization [WHO]. Research for Universal Health Coverage. *The World Health Report: Report of the Director-General* (2013): 27–52.

Wright, James, and Rena Menaker. Waiting for Children's Surgery in Canada: The Canadian Paediatric Surgical Wait Times Project. *Canadian Medical Association Journal* 183(9) (2011, June 14): E559–E564.

Yancey, Antronette K., Joanne Leslie, and Emily K. Abel. Obesity at the Crossroads: Feminist and Public Health Perspectives. *Signs* 31:2 (2006): 425–443.

Yip, Winnie, et al. Does Social Capital Enhance Health and Well-Being? Evidence from Rural China. *Social Science and Medicine* 64 (2007): 35–49.

Zelder, Martin. How Private Hospital Competition Can Improve Canadian Health Care. *The Fraser Institute: Public Policy Sources* 35 (2000):1–21.

Ziai, Aram. The Millennium Development Goals: Back to the Future? *Third World Quarterly* 32:1 (2011): 27–43.

CHAPTER **8**

Abracen, Jeffrey, et al. Mental Health Diagnoses and Recidivism in Paroled Offenders. *International Journal of Offender Therapy and Comparative Criminology* 58:7 (2014): 765–779.

Agnew, Robert. A Revised Strain Theory of Delinquency. *Social Forces* 64 (1985): 151–67.

Agnew, Robert. Foundation for a General Strain Theory of Crime and Delinquency. *Criminology* 30 (1992): 47–88.

Agnich, Laura, James Hawdon, and John Ryan. Crime as a Source of Solidarity: A Research Note Testing Durkheim's Assertion. *Deviant Behavior* 31:8 (2010): 679–703.

Alarid, Leanne Fiftal, and Ofelia Lisa Vega. Identity Construction, Self Perceptions, and Criminal Behavior of Incarcerated Women. *Deviant Behavior* 31 (2010): 704–28.

Alexandrescu, L. Mephedrone, Assassin of Youth: The Rhetoric of Fear in Contemporary Drug Scares. *Crime, Media, Culture* 10:1 (2013): 23–37.

Alicke, Mark D., and David Rose. Culpable Control and Causal Deviance. *Social and Personality Psychology Compass* 10 (2012): 723–35.

Allen, Mary. *Victim Services in Canada, 2011/2012*. Ottawa: Canadian Center for Justice Statistics, 2014.

Ananat, Elizabeth Oltmans. The Wrong Side(s) of the Tracks: The Causal Effects of Racial Segregation on Urban Poverty and Inequality. *American Economic Journal: Applied Economics* 3:2 (2011): 34–66.

Anomaly, Jonathan, and Geoffrey Brennan. Social Norms, the Invisible Hand, and the Law. *University of Queensland Law Journal* 33:2 (2014): 263–83.

Another Blow for RCMP White Collar Crime Effort. *Yorkton This Week*, January 16, 2013.

Asencio, Emily K., and Peter J. Burke. Does Incarceration Change the Criminal Identity? A Synthesis of Labeling and Identity Theory Perspectives on Identity Change. *Sociological Perspectives* 54:2 (2011): 163–82.

Aubuchon-Rubin, Ashley T. Rehabilitating Durkheim: Social Solidarity and Rehabilitation in Eastern State Penitentiary, 1829–1850. *International Journal of Punishment and Sentencing* 5:1 (2009):12 – 38.

Bauder, Harald. Brain Abuse, or the Devaluation of Immigrant Labour in Canada. *Antipode* 34:4 (2003): 688–717.

Baumer, Eric P. Untangling Research Puzzles in Merton's Multilevel Theory. *Theoretical Criminology* 11:1 (2007): 66–93.

References

Becker, G. Crime and Punishment: An Economic Approach. *Economic Analysis of the Law* (1974): 1–54.

Bell, B., A. Bindler, and S. Machin. Crime Scars: Recessions and the Making of Career Criminals. London School of Economics and Political Science, 2014.

Blais, Etienne, Marie-Pier Gagne, and Isabelle Linteau. The Effect of Gun Control Laws on Homicide in Canada, 1974–2004. *Canadian Journal of Criminology and Criminal Justice* 53:1 (2011): 27–62.

Blau, J. R., and Blau, P. M. The Cost of Inequality: Metropolitan Structure and Violent Crime. *American Sociological Review* 47 (1982): 45–62.

Boda, Z., and G. Szabo. The Media and Attitudes towards Crime and the Justice System: A Qualitative Approach. *European Journal of Criminology* 8:4 (2011): 329–42.

Boggess, Lyndsay N., and John R. Hipp. The Spatial Dimensions of Gentrification and the Consequences for Neighborhood Crime. *Justice Quarterly* (2014): 1–30.

Bonn, Scott A. Greedy Elite Criminals Get Away with Murder: White-Collar Crime Does Far More Damage Than Street Crime. *Psychology Today* (2014, March 10).

Boyce, Jillian. *Adult Criminal Court Statistics in Canada, 2011/2012.* Ottawa: Canadian Center for Justice Statistics, 2013.

Braithwaite, John. Poverty, Power, White-Collar Crime and the Paradoxes of Criminological Theory. *Australian and New Zealand Journal of Criminology* 24:1 (1991): 40–58.

Brennan, P. K., & Spohn, C. The Joint Effects of Offender Race/Ethnicity and Sex on Sentence Length Decisions in Federal Courts. *Race and Social Problems* 1:4 (2009): 200–217.

Browning, Sarah and Patricia Erickson. Neighbourhood Variation in the Link between Alcohol Use and Violence among Canadian Adolescents. *Canadian Journal of Criminology and Criminal Justice* 54:2 (2012): 169–202.

Brush, Jesse. Does Income Inequality Lead to More Crime? A Comparison of Cross-sectional and Time-series Analyses of United States Counties. *Economics Letters* 96:2 (2007): 264–68.

Bryant, M., and V. Higgins. Self-confessed Troublemakers: An Interactionist View of Deviance during Organizational Change. *Human Relations* 63:2 (2010): 249–77.

Carver, Alison, Anna Timperio, and David Crawford. Playing It Safe: The Influence of Neighbourhood Safety on Children's Physical Activity: A Review. *Health and Place* 14:2 (2008): 217–27.

Cid, José and Joel Martí. Turning Points and Returning Points: Understanding the Role of Family Ties in the Process of Desistance. *European Journal of Criminology* 9:6 (2012): 603–620.

Cloward, Richard A. and Lloyd E. Ohlin. *Delinquency and Opportunity: A Theory of Delinquent Gangs.* New York: Free Press, 1961.

Cohen, Albert Kircidel. *Delinquent Boys: The Culture of the Gang.* Glencoe, IL: Free Press, 1955.

Cohen, Mark A. *The Costs of Crime and Justice.* New York: Routledge, 2005.

Cohen, Stanley. *Folk Devils and Moral Panics: The Creation of the Mods and Rockers.* London: MacGibbon and Kee, 1972.

Coid, Jeremy W., et al. Gang Membership, Violence, and Psychiatric Morbidity. *American Journal of Psychiatry* 170:9 (2013): 985–93.

Coleman, James William. Toward an Integrated Theory of White–Collar Crime. *American Journal of Sociology* 93:2 (1987): 406–439.

Collins, R. E. The Construction of Race and Crime in Canadian Print Media: A 30–Year Analysis. *Criminology and Criminal Justice* 14:1 (2013): 77–99.

Cooney, Mark and Callie Harbin Burt. Less Crime, More Punishment. *American Journal of Sociology* 114:2 (2008): 491–527.

Corrado, R. R., S. Kuehn, and I. Margaritescu. Policy Issues Regarding the Overrepresentation of Incarcerated Aboriginal Young Offenders in a Canadian Context. *Youth Justice* 14:1 (2014): 40–62.

Crosby, Faye. A Model of Egoistic Relative Deprivation. *Psychological Review* 83:2 (1976): 85–113.

Dahlberg, Matz, and Magnus Gustavsson. Inequality and Crime: Separating the Effects of Permanent and Transitory Income. *Oxford Bulletin of Economics and Statistics* 70 (2008): 129–53.

Daly, Martin, Margo Wilson, and Shawn Vasdev. Income Inequality and Homicide Rates in Canada and the United States. *Canadian Journal of Criminology* 43:2 (2001): 219–236

Dauvergne, Mia. *Adult Correctional Statistics in Canada, 2010/2011.* Ottawa: Statistics Canada, 2013.

Demuth, Stephen and Darrell Steffensmeier. Ethnicity Effects on Sentence Outcomes in Large Urban Courts: Comparisons among White, Black, and Hispanic Defendants. *Social Science Quarterly* 85:4 (2004): 994–1011.

Detotto, Claudio and Edoardo Otranto. Does Crime Affect Economic Growth? *Kyklos* 63 (2010): 330–345.

Devine, P. G., and A. J. Elliot. Are Racial Stereotypes Really Fading? The Princeton Trilogy Revisited. *Personality and Social Psychology Bulletin* 21:11 (1995): 1139–50.

Dolan, Paul and Tessa Peasgood. Estimating the Economic and Social Costs of the Fear of Crime. *The British Journal of Criminology* 47 (2007): 121–132.

Dolan, Paul, Graham Loomes, Tessa Peasgood, and Aki Tsuchiya. Estimating the Intangible Victim Costs of Violent Crime. *The British Journal of Criminology* 45 (2005): 958–976.

Dollar, Cindy Brooks. Conceptual Remixing in Criminology: Tracing Durkheim and Marx's Influence on Etiological Theories of Crime. *Sociology Compass* 8:10 (2014): 1157–1166.

Dowler, Ken, Thomas Fleming, and Stephen L Muzzatti. Constructing Crime: Media, Crime, and Popular Culture. *Canadian Journal of Criminology and Criminal Justice* 48:6 (2006): 837–850.

Dowler, Kenneth. Comparing American and Canadian Local Television Crime Stories: A Content Analysis. *Canadian Journal of Criminology and Criminal Justice* 46:5 (2004): 573–596.

Dunn, Jennifer. Vocabularies of Victimization: Toward Explaining the Deviant Victim. *Deviant Behavior* 31 (2010): 159–83.

Durkheim, Emile. *Suicide.* New York: Free Press, 1951.

Durkheim, Emile. *The Division of Labor in Society.* New York: Free Press, 1984.

Dutton, Donald G. and Stephen D. Hart. Evidence for Long–Term, Specific Effects of Childhood Abuse and Neglect on Criminal Behavior in Men. *International Journal of Offender Therapy and Comparative Criminology* 36:2 (1992): 129–137.

Ehrlich, Isaac. Participation in Illegitimate Activities: A Theoretical and Empirical Investigation. *Journal of Political Economy* 81:3 (1973): 521.

Estébanez, P., et al. The Role of Prisons in the HIV Epidemic among Female Injecting Drug Users. *AIDS Care* 14:1 (2002): 95–104.

Ezeonu, Ifeanyi. Gun Violence in Toronto: Perspectives from the Police. *The Howard Journal of Criminal Justice* 49:2 (2010): 147–165.

Faucher, Chantal. Fear and Loathing in the News: A Qualitative Analysis of Canadian Print News Coverage of Youthful Offending in the Twentieth Century. *Journal of Youth Studies* 12:4 (2009): 439–456.

Fougere, D., Kramarz K., and Pouget J. Youth Unemployment and Crime. *Journal of the European Economic Association* 7 (2009): 909–38.

Fowler, Roger. *Language in the News: Discourse and Ideology in the Press.* London: Routledge, 1996.

Gabor, Thomas and Fernando Mata. Victimization and Repeat Victimization over the Life Span: A Predictive Study and Implications for Policy. *International Review of Victimology* 10:3 (2004): 193–221.

Garland, D. On the Concept of Moral Panic. *Crime, Media, Culture* 4:1 (2008): 9–30.

Garrett, Linda. Sexual Assault in the Workplace. *American Association of Occupational Health Nurses* 59:1 (2011): 15–22.

Goode, Erich, and Nachman Yehuda. *Moral Panics: The Social Construction of Deviance.* 2nd ed. Oxford: Blackwell, 2002.

Gosine, Andil and Cheryl Teelucksingh. *Environmental Justice and Racism in Canada: An Introduction.* Toronto: Emond Montgomery, 2008.

Goulas, Eleftherios and Athina Zervoyianni. Economic Growth and Crime: Is there an Asymmetric Relationship? *Economic Modelling* 49 (2015): 286–295.

Government of Canada. Annual Report of the Office of the Correctional Investigator 2013–2014. Ottawa: Office of the Correctional Investigator, 2014.

Graham, Kathryn, Sharon Bernards, Sharon C. Wilsnack, and Gerhard Gmel. Alcohol May Not Cause Partner Violence But It Seems to Make It Worse: A Cross National Comparison of the Relationship Between Alcohol and Severity of Partner Violence. *Journal of Interpersonal Violence* 26:8 (2011): 1503–1523.

Greenberg, Joshua. Opinion Discourse and the Canadian Newspapers: The Case of the Chinese 'Boat People'. *Canadian Journal of Communication* 25:4, (2000): 517–537.

Gronqvist, H. Youth Unemployment and Crime: Lessons from Longitudinal Population Records. Unpublished Manuscript, Swedish Institute for Social Research, 2013.

Gutierrez, Leticia, et al. The Prediction of Recidivism with Aboriginal Offenders: A Theoretically Informed Meta-Analysis. *Canadian Journal of Criminology and Criminal Justice* 55:1 (2013): 55–99.

Haapasalo, Jaana and Elina Pokela. Child-Rearing and Child Abuse Antecedents of Criminality. *Aggression and Violent Behavior* 4:1 (1999): 107–127.

Haapasalo, Jaana and Juha Moilanen. Official and Self-Reported Childhood Abuse and Adult Crime of Young Offenders. *Criminal Justice and Behavior* 31:2 (2004): 127–149.

Hall, Stuart, et al. *Policing the Crisis: Mugging, the State, and Law and Order.* London: Macmillan, 1978.

Harper, C. A., and T. E. Hogue. The Emotional Representation of Sexual Crime in the National British Press. *Journal of Language and Social Psychology* 34:1 (2015): 3–24.

Harrison, Lana D., et al. The Drugs–Violence Nexus among American and Canadian Youth. *Substance Use and Misuse* 36:14 (2001): 2065–2086.

Hawdon, James E. The Role of Presidential Rhetoric in the Creation of a Moral Panic: Reagan, Bush, and the War on

Drugs. *Deviant Behavior* 22:5 (2001): 419–45.

Hill, James K. Common Reactions to Crime. In *Working with Victims of Crime: A Manual Applying Research to Clinical Practice* (2nd ed.). Ottawa: Department of Justice, 2009.

Hipp, John R. Income Inequality, Race, and Place: Does the Distribution of Race and Class Within Neighborhoods Affect Crime Rates. *Criminology* 45:3 (2007): 665–697.

Hsieh, C., and M. D. Pugh. Poverty, Income Inequality, and Violent Crime: A Meta-Analysis of Recent Aggregate Data Studies. *Criminal Justice Review* 18:2 (1993): 182–202.

Hubert, R.E. and Charles W. Wright. Durkheim and Quinney on the Inevitability of Crime: A Comparative Theoretical Analysis. *Deviant Behavior* 4:1 (1982): 67–87.

Human Rights Watch World Report. New York: Human Rights Watch, 2008.

Hutchins, Hope. Police Resources in Canada, 2014. Ottawa: Canadian Center for Justice Statistics, 2015.

Jackson, J., and E. Gray. Functional Fear and Public Insecurities about Crime. *British Journal of Criminology* 50 (2010): 1–22.

Jackson, J., and M. Stafford. Public Health and Fear of Crime: A Prospective Cohort Study. *British Journal of Criminology* 49 (2009): 832–47.

Jankoa, Zuzana and Gurleen Poplib. Examining the Link between Crime and Unemployment: A Time-Series Analysis for Canada. *Applied Economics* 47:37 (2015): 4007–4019.

Jargowsky, Paul and Yoonhwan Park. Cause or Consequence? Suburbanization and Crime in U.S. Metropolitan Areas. *Crime and Delinquency* 55 (2009): 28–50.

Jargowsky, Paul. Sprawl, Concentration of Poverty, and Urban Inequality. In G. Squires (ed.), *Urban Sprawl: Causes, Consequences and Policy Response* (pp. 39–72). Washington, DC: Urban Institute Press, 2002.

Jeffries, Samantha, and Philip Stenning. Sentencing, Aboriginal Offenders: Law, Policy, and Practice in Three Countries. *Canadian Journal of Criminology and Criminal Justice* (2014): 447–94.

Johnson, Holly. Contrasting Views of the Role of Alcohol in Cases of Wife Assault. *Journal of Interpersonal Violence* 16:1 (2001): 54–72.

Kelly, M. Inequality and Crime. *Review of Economics and Statistics* 82:4 (2000): 530–539.

Kempa, Michael. Combating White–Collar Crime in Canada: Serving Victim Needs and Market Integrity. *Journal of Financial Crime* 17:2 (2010): 251–264.

Kennedy, B.P., et al. Social Capital, Income Inequality, and Firearm Violent Crime. *Social Science and Medicine* 47 (1998): 7–17.

Kilpatrick, Dean G., and Ron Acierno. Mental Health Needs of Crime Victims: Epidemiology and Outcomes. *Journal of Traumatic Stress* 16:2 (2003): 119–132.

Kim, Andrew Tae–Hyun. Culture Matters: Cultural Differences in the Reporting of Employment Discrimination Claims. *William and Mary Bill of Rights Journal* 20 (2011): 405–55.

Klocke, Brian V., and Glenn W. Muschert. A Hybrid Model of Moral Panics: Synthesizing the Theory and Practice of Moral Panic Research. *Sociology Compass* 4:5 (2010): 295–309.

Krahn, H., Hartnagel, T., and Gartrell, J. Income Inequality and Homicide Rates: Cross-National Data and Criminological Theories. *Criminology* 24 (1986): 269–294.

Krinsky, Charles, ed. *The Ashgate Research Companion to Moral Panics.* Farnham, UK: Ashgate, 2013.

Krug, Etienne G., and Linda Dalhberg. Violence: A Global Public Health Problem. In *World Report on Violence and Health.* Geneva: World Health Organization, 2002.

Langevin, Ron and Suzanne Curnoe. Are Dangerous Offenders Different From Other Offenders? A Clinical Profile. *International Journal of Offender Therapy and Comparative Criminology* 58:7 (2014): 780–801.

Lappi–Seppala, Tapio and Michael Tonry. Crime, Criminal Justice, and Criminology in the Nordic Countries. *Crime and Justice* 40:1 (2011): 1–32.

Leenaars, Antoon A. and David Lester. Gender, Gun Control, Suicide and Homicide: A Reply. *Archives of Suicide Research* 5:1 (1999): 77–79.

Linteau, Isabelle and Etienne Blais. The Effect of Bill C–68 on Homicides in Quebec: an Analysis of the Extreme Limitations. *Criminologie* 45:2 (2012): 219–248.

Lorenc, Theo, et al. Crime, Fear of Crime and Mental Health: Synthesis of Theory and Systematic Reviews of Interventions and Qualitative Evidence. *Public Health Research* 2:2 (2014): 1–398.

Lorenc, Theo, et al. Crime, Fear of Crime, Environment, and Mental Health and Wellbeing: Mapping Review of Theories and Causal Pathways. *Health and Place* 18:4 (2012): 757–65.

Loukaitou-Sideris, Anastasia, and John E. Eck. Crime Prevention and Active Living. *American Journal of Health Promotion* 21:4 (2007): 380–89.

Machin, S., and G. Meghir. Crime and Economic Incentives. *J Hum Res* 39 (2004): 958–979.

Malloch, Margaret S. Caring for Drug Users? The Experiences of Women Prisoners. *The Howard Journal of Criminal Justice* 39:4 (2000): 354–68.

Manzoni, Patrik, Benedikt Fischer, and Jurgen Rehm. Local Drug–Crime Dynamics in a Canadian Multi–Site Sample of Untreated Opioid Users. *Canadian Journal of Criminology and Criminal Justice* 49:3 (2007): 341–373.

Manzoni, Patrik, et al. Determinants of Property Crime among Illicit Opiate Users Outside of Treatment across Canada. *Deviant Behavior* 27:3 (2006): 351–376.

Matsueda, Ross L., and Maria S. Grigoryeva. Social Inequality, Crime, and Deviance. In Jane McLeod, Edward Lawler, and Michael Schwalbe (eds.), *Handbook of the Social Psychology of Inequality*. New York: Springer, 2014.

McMullan, John L. News, Truth, and the Recognition of Corporate Crime. *Canadian Journal of Criminology and Criminal Justice* 48:6 (2006): 905–939.

Merton, Robert K. Social Structure and Anomie. *American Sociological Review* 3(1938): 672–682.

Merton, Robert K. *Social Theory and Social Structure*. New York: Simon and Schuster, 1968.

Messner, S.F. and R. Rosenfeld. *Crime and the American Dream*. Belmont, CA: Wadsworth, 1994, 1997.

Millar, Paul, and Akwasi Owusu–Bempah. Whitewashing Criminal Justice in Canada: Preventing Research through Data Suppression. *Canadian Journal of Law and Society* 26:3 (2011): 653–61.

Millar, Paul. Punishing Our Way Out of Poverty: The Prosecution of Child–Support Debt in Alberta, Canada. *Canadian Journal of Law and Society* 25:2 (2010): 149–65.

Minelle Mahtani. Representing Minorities: Canadian Media and Minority Identities. *Canadian Ethnic Studies* (2001): 1–42.

Minister of Industry. *Adult Correctional Statistics in Canada, 2013/2014*. Ottawa: Correctional Services, 2015.

Monchalin, Lisa. Canadian Aboriginal Peoples Victimization, Offending and Its Prevention: Gathering the Evidence. *Crime Prevention and Community Safety* 12:2 (2010): 119–32.

Morrall, P., P. Marshall, S. Pattison, and G. Macdonald. Crime and Health: A Preliminary Study into the Effects of Crime on the Mental Health of UK University Students. *Journal of Psychiatric and Mental Health Nursing* 17:9 (2010): 821–28.

Neeganagwedgin, Erica. 'They Can't Take Our Ancestors Out of Us': A Brief Historical Account of Canada's Residential School System, Incarceration, Institutionalized Policies and Legislations against Indigenous Peoples. *Canadian Issues* (2014): 31–36.

Neil, Roland, and Jason T. Carmichael. The Use of Incarceration in Canada: A Test of Political and Social Threat Explanations on the Variation in Prison Admissions across Canadian Provinces, 2001–2010. *Sociological Inquiry* 85:2 (2015): 309–32.

Neville, Fergus G., Christine A. Goodall, Anna J. Gavine, Damien J. Williams, and Peter D. Donnelly. Public Health, Youth Violence, and Perpetrator Well-being. *Peace and Conflict: Journal of Peace Psychology* 21:3 (2015): 322–33.

Nilsson, A. Income Inequality and Crime: The Case of Sweden. Institute for Labour Market Policy Evaluation (IFAU) Working Paper (2004):6.

O'Grady, William, Patrick F. Parnaby, and Justin Schikschneit. Guns, Gangs, and the Underclass: A Constructionist Analysis of Gun Violence in a Toronto High School. *Canadian Journal of Criminology and Criminal Justice* 52:1 (2010): 55–78.

Opsal, Tara. 'Livin' on the Straights': Identity, Desistance, and Work among Women Post–Incarceration. *Sociological Inquiry* 82:3 (2012): 378–403.

Owusu-Bempah, Akwasi and Scott Wortley. Race, Crime, and Criminal Justice in Canada. In Sandra M. Bucerius and Michael Tonry (eds.), *The Oxford Handbook of Ethnicity, Crime, and Immigration 2014* (pp. 281–320). Oxford: Oxford University Press.

Owusu-Bempah, Akwasi, et al. Years of Life Lost to Incarceration: Inequities between Aboriginal and Non-Aboriginal Canadians. *BMC Public Health* 14 (2014): 585.

Palmater, Pamela. Stretched Beyond Human Limits: Death By Poverty in First Nations. *Canadian Review of Social Policy* 65 (2011).

Pare, Paul-Philippe and Richard Felson. Income Inequality, Poverty, and Crime across Nations. *British Journal of Sociology* 65:3 (2014): 434–458.

Pellerin, Bruno, Michel St–Yves, and Jean–Pierre Guay. The Theory of Abuse–Abuser in Sexual Deviance: Is It True? *Canadian Journal of Criminology and Criminal Justice* 45:1 (2003): 81–98.

Pratt, Travis C. and Francis T. Cullen. Assessing Macro-Level Predictors and Theories of Crime: A Meta-Analysis. *Crime and Justice* 32 (2005): 373–450.

PricewaterhouseCoopers. *Economic Crime in a Downturn: The 2009 Global Economic Crime Survey: The Canadian Perspective*. Toronto: Pricewaterhousecoopers, 2009.

Purdy, Sean. Framing Regent Park: The National Film Board of Canada and the Construction of 'Outcast Spaces' in the Inner City, 1953 and 1994. *Media, Culture and Society* 27:4 (2005): 523–549.

Rankin, Jim and Patty Winsa. Unequal Justice: Aboriginal and Black Inmates Disproportionately Fill Ontario Jails. *Toronto Star*, March 1, 2013.

Reed, J. L. Inpatient Care of Mentally Ill People in Prison: Results of a Year's Programme of Semistructured Inspections. *British Medical Journal* 320:7421 (2000): 1031–1034.

Reily, B., and A. Rattner. Domestic Burglaries and the Real Price of Audio Visual Goods: Some Time Series Evidence for Britain. *Economic Letters* 100 (2008): 96–100.

Rich, Karen, and Patrick Seffrin. Police Interviews of Sexual Assault Reporters: Do Attitudes Matter? *Violence and Victims* 27:2 (2012): 263–79.

Robinson, Fred, and Jane Keithley. The Impacts of Crime on Health and Health Services: A Literature Review. *Health, Risk and Society* 2:3 (2000): 253–66.

Royal Canada Mounted Police. History of Firearms Control in Canada: Up to and Including the Firearms Act. Last modified June 19, 2012.

Rufrancos, H.G, M. Power, K.E Pickett, and R. Wilkinson. Income Inequality and Crime: A Review and Explanation of the Time-Series Evidence. *Social Criminology* 1:1 (2013).

Saunders, Doug. Residential Schools, Reserves and Canada's Crime against Humanity. *Globe and Mail*, June 5, 2015.

Savage, Joanne and Christina Yancey. The Effects of Media Violence Exposure on Criminal Aggression: A Meta-Analysis. *Criminal Justice and Behavior* 35:6 (2008): 772–791.

Savage, Joanne. Does Viewing Violent Media Really Cause Criminal Violence? A Methodological Review. *Aggression and Violent Behavior* 10:1 (2004): 99–128.

Sciandra, M., et al. Long-term Effects of the Moving to Opportunity Residential Mobility Experiment on Crime and Delinquency. *Journal of Experimental Criminology* 9 (2013): 451–89.

Shankar, Janki, Gita Das, and Sabrina Atwal. Challenging Cultural Discourses and Beliefs That Perpetuate Domestic Violence in South Asian Communities: A Discourse Analysis. *Journal of International Women's Studies* 14:1 (2013): 248–62.

Shaw, Clifford and Henry McKay. *Juvenile Delinquency and Urban Areas*. Chicago: University of Chicago Press, 1942.

Sheptycki, James. Guns, Crime and Social Order. *Criminology and Criminal Justice* 9:3, (2009): 307–336.

Sinha, Maire. Section 1: Prevalence and Severity of Violence against Women. Statistics Canada, February 25, 2015.

Smith, Philip. Durkheim and Criminology: Reconstructing the Legacy. *The Australian and New Zealand Journal of Criminology* 41:3 (2008): 333–344.

Statistics Canada. Aboriginal Peoples in Canada: First Nations People, Métis and Inuit. 2011. Accessed at https://www12.statcan.gc.ca/nhs-enm/2011/as-sa/99-011-x/99-011-x2011001-eng.cfm.

Statistics Canada. Adult Correctional Statistics in Canada, 2010/2011. Statistics Canada, May 31, 2013.

Statistics Canada. An Overview of Challenges in Collecting the Aboriginal Identity of People in the Criminal Justice System. Statistics Canada, May 10, 2005.

Statistics Canada. The Incarceration of Aboriginal People in Adult Correctional Services. Statistics Canada, October 28, 2009.

Stewart, Lynn A, and Geoff Wilton. Correctional Outcomes of Offenders with Mental Disorders. *Criminal Justice Studies: A Critical Journal of Crime, Law and Society*, 27:1 (2014): 63–81.

Stotzer, Rebecca L. Sexual Orientation–Based Hate Crimes on Campus: The Impact of Policy on Reporting Rates. *Sexuality Research and Social Policy* 7 (2010): 147–54.

Strohschein, Lisa and Matthew Alvinelle. Adolescent Problem Behavior in Toronto, Canada. *Sociological Inquiry* 85:1 (2015): 129–147.

Stucky, T., S. Payton and J. Ottensmann. Intra- and Inter-Neighborhood Income Inequality and Crime. *Journal of Crime and Justice* (2015): 1–18.

Stys, Yvonne and Rick Ruddell. Organized Crime Offenders in Canada: Risk, Reform, and Recidivism. *Journal of Offender Rehabilitation* 52:2 (2013): 75–97.

Tamang, Ritendra. Portrayal of Crime in Televised News in Canada: Distortion And Privileges. *Journal of the Institute of Justice and International Studies* 9 (2009): 193–199.

Tomm, Matthew. Public Reason and the Disempowerment of Aboriginal People in Canada. *Canadian Journal of Law and Society* 28:3 (2013): 293–314.

Tremonti, Anna Maria. History of Residential Schools Ignored in Canadian Curriculum. CBC, June 10, 2015.

Tuberculosis Control in Prisons: A Manual for Programme Managers. Geneva: WHO/ICRC, 2001.

Ungerleider, Charles S. Media, Minorities, and Misconceptions: The Portrayal by and Representation of Minorities in Canadian News Media. *Canadian Ethnic Studies/Etudes Ethniques au Canada* 23:3 (1991): 158–164.

Van Dijk, Jan, John Van Kesteren and Paul Smit, Paul. *Criminal Victimisation in International Perspective: Key Findings from the 2004–2005 ICVS and EU ICS*. 2007.

Viggiani, Nick De. Unhealthy Prisons: Exploring Structural Determinants of Prison Health. *Sociology of Health and Illness* 29:1 (2007): 115–35.

Walby, S. *The Costs of Domestic Violence*. London: Women and Equity Statistics, 2004.

Watson, Roger, Anne Stimpson, and Tony Hostick. Prison Health Care: A Review of the Literature. *International Jour-*

nal of Nursing Studies 41 (2004): 119–28.

Weatherburn, Don, and Kevin T. Schnepel. Economic Adversity and Crime: Old Theories and New Evidence. *Australian Journal of Social Issues* 50:1 (2015): 89–108.

Weisburd, David, S. Wheeler, E. Waring, and N. Bode. *Crimes of the Middle Classes: White-Collar Offenders in the Federal Courts.* New Haven, CT: Yale University Press, 1991.

White-Collar Crime In Canada: Too Trusting: Why Does Justice Move So Much More Slowly North Of The 49th Parallel? *The Economist*, April 2, 2009.

Whitley, Rob, and Martin Prince. Fear of Crime, Mobility and Mental Health in Inner-city London, UK. *Social Science and Medicine* 61 (2005): 1678–688.

Wijck, Peter. The Economics of Pre-Crime Interventions. *European Journal of Law and Economics* 35 (2013): 441–458.

Williams, James W. The Lessons of Enron: Media Accounts, Corporate Crimes, and Financial Markets. *Theoretical Criminology* 12:4 (2008): 471–499.

Wood, Jane and Emma Alleyne. Street Gang Theory and Research: Where Are We Now and Where Do We Go from Here? *Aggression and Violent Behavior* 15:2 (2010): 100–111.

Wortley, Scot. Introduction. The Immigration-Crime Connection: Competing Theoretical Perspectives. *Journal of International Migration and Integration* 10:4 (2009): 349–58.

Wortley, Scott and Akwasi Owusu-Bempah. Race, Ethnicity, Crime and Criminal Justice in Canada. In Anita Kalunta–Crumpton (ed.), *Race, Ethnicity, Crime and Criminal Justice in the Americas* (pp. 11–40). London: Palgrave Macmillan, 2012.

Wu, Dongxu and Zhongmin Wu. Crime, Inequality and Unemployment in England and Wales. *Applied Economics* 44:29 (2012): 3765–3775.

Young, J. Moral Panic: Its Origins in Resistance, Ressentiment and the Translation of Fantasy into Reality. *British Journal of Criminology* 49:1 (2009): 4–16.

Young, Jacob T. N., Cesar J. Rebellon, J. C. Barnes, and Frank M. Weerman. Unpacking the Black Box of Peer Similarity in Deviance: Understanding the Mechanisms Linking Personal Behavior, Peer Behavior, and Perceptions. *Criminology* 52:1 (2014): 60–86.

Ziyanak, Sebahattin and James L. Williams. Functionalist Perspective on Deviance. *International Journal of Human Sciences* 11:2 (2014): 1–9.

CHAPTER **9**

Alesina, Alberto, et al. Fractionalization. *Journal of Economic Growth* 8:2 (2003): 155–194.

Annan, Kofi. Peace and Development: One Struggle, Two Fronts. Address to the World Bank Staff, Washington, D.C., October 19, 1999.

Auger, Martin. *Canadian International Military Operations in the 21st Century.* Ottawa: Library of Parliament, 2011.

Baines, Erin and Emily Paddon. 'This Is How We Survived': Civilian Agency and Humanitarian Protection. *Security Dialogue* 43:3 (2012): 231–247.

Barnard, Anne. Beirut, Also the Site of Deadly Attacks, Feels Forgotten. *New York Times*, November 16, 2015, p. A6.

Besançon, Marie. Relative Resources: Inequality in Ethnic Wars, Revolutions, and Genocides. *Journal of Peace Research* 42:4 (2005): 393–415.

Bhavnani, Ravi and Dan Miodownik. Ethnic Polarization, Ethnic Salience, and Civil War. *Journal of Conflict Resolution* 53:1 (2009): 30–49.

Bird, Graham, S. Brock Blomberg, and Gregory D. Hess. International Terrorism: Causes, Consequences and Cures. *World Economy* 31:2 (2008): 255–274.

Blomberg, S. Brock, and Gregory D. Hess. From (No) Butter to Guns? Understanding the Economic Role in Transnational Terrorism. In *Terrorism, Economic Development, and Political Openness* (pp. 83–115) Cambridge: Cambridge University Press, 2008.

Boutton, Andrew. US Foreign Aid, Interstate Rivalry, and Incentives for Counterterrorism Cooperation. *Journal of Peace Research* 51:6 (2014): 741–754.

Brauman, Rony, Philippe Petit, and Sarah Clift. From Philanthropy to Humanitarianism: Remarks and an Interview. *The South Atlantic Quarterly* 103:2 (2004): 397–417.

Bricker, Noah Q. and Mark C. Foley. 2013. The Effect of Youth Demographics on Violence: The Importance of the Labor Market. *International Journal of Conflict and Violence* 7:1 (2013): 180–194.

Cederman, Lars–Erik, Nils B. Weidmann and Kristian Skrede Gleditsch. Horizontal Inequalities and Ethnonationalist Civil War: A Global Comparison. *American Political Science Review* 105:3 (2011): 478–495.

Chang, Lei, et al. The Face that Launched a Thousand Ships: The Mating-Warring Association in Men. *Personality and Social Psychology Bulletin* 37:7 (2011): 976–984.

Cohen, Darla Kay. Female Combatants and the Perpetration of Violence: Wartime Rape in the Sierra Leone Civil War. *World Politics* 65:3 (2013): 383–415.

References

Dafoe, Allan, Jonathan Renshon, and Paul Huth. Reputation and Status as Motives for War. *Annual Review of Political Science* 17:1 (2014): 371–393.

Denov, Myriam S. Wartime Sexual Violence: Assessing a Human Security Response to War-Affected Girls in Sierra Leone. *Security Dialogue* 37:3 (2006): 319–342.

Denov, Myriam. 2012. Child Soldiers and Iconography: Portrayals and (Mis)Representations. *Children and Society* 26 (2012): 280–292.

Dragotesc, Andra–Mirona. Imagined(?) Identities: The Victim and the Villain in Awareness Raising Re-Presentations of Wartime Violence against Women. *Studia Universitatis Babes-Bolyai, Europaea* (2011, Issue 2): 125–144.

Erjavec, Karmen, and Zala Volcic. Living with the Sins of Their Fathers: An Analysis of Self–Representation of Adolescents Born of War Rape. *Journal of Adolescent Research* 25:3 (2010): 359–86.

Esteban, Joan and Debraj Ray. Polarization, Fractionalization and Conflict. *Journal of Peace Research* 45:2 (2008): 163–182.

Esteban, Joan-María, and Debraj Ray. On the Measurement of Polarization. *Econometrica* 62 (4) (1994): 819–851.

Flores, Thomas Edward. Vertical Inequality, Land Reform, and Insurgency in Colombia. *Peace Economics, Peace Science and Public Policy* 20:1 (2014): 5–31.

Ghobarah, Hazem Adam, Paul Huth, and Bruce Russett. The Post-war Public Health Effects of Civil Conflict. *Social Science and Medicine* 59 (2004): 869–884.

Gretry, Lucille. Child Soldiers: Our Representation Challenged by Their Reality. *International Journey of Sociology and Social Policy* 31:9 (2011): 583–593.

Gubler, Joshua and Joel Selway. Horizontal Inequality, Crosscutting Cleavages, and Civil War. *Journal of Conflict Resolution* 56:2 (2012): 206–232.

Gurr, Ted Robert. *Peoples Versus States: Minorities at Risk in the New Century.* Washington, D.C.: United States Institute of Peace Press, 2000.

Habbick, Brian. Casualties in a Nuclear War. *Canadian Journal of Public Health* 74:1 (1983).

Heit, Shannon. Waging Sexual Warfare: Case Studies of Rape Warfare Used by the Japanese Imperial Army During World War II. *Women's Studies International Forum* 32 (2009): 363–370.

Henry, Nicola. The Fixation on Wartime Rape: Feminist Critique and International Criminal Law. *Social and Legal Studies* 23:1 (2014): 93–111.

Hermenau, K., et al. Growing Up in Armed Groups: Trauma and Aggression among Child Soldiers in DR Congo. *European Journal of Psychotraumatology* 4:10 (2013).

Hill, Leonidas E. 1981. Towards a New History of German Resistance to Hitler. *Central European History* 14:4 (1981): 369–399.

Hintjens, Helen M. When Identity Becomes a Knife: Reflecting on the Genocide in Rwanda. *Ethnicities* 1:1 (2001): 25–55.

Hudson, John. Introduction: Aid and Development. *The Economic Journal* 114:496 (2004): F185–F190.

Hultman, Lisa, Jacob Kathman, and Megan Shannon. United Nations Peacekeeping and Civilian Protection in Civil War. *American Journal of Political Science* 57:4 (2013): 875–891.

Humphreys, Macartan. Natural Resources, Conflict, and Conflict Resolution: Uncovering the Mechanisms. *Journal of Conflict Resolution* 49:4 (2005): 508–537.

International Committee of the Red Cross. Rape and Other Forms of Sexual Violence. Customary IHL–Rule 93. Rape and Other Forms of Sexual Violence. 2015. Accessed at https://www.icrc.org/customary–ihl/eng/docs/v1_rul_rule 93.

International Committee of the Red Cross. The Geneva Conventions of 12 August 1949.

Irwin, Kara C., Candace Konnert, May Wong, and Thomas A. O'Neill. PTSD Symptoms and Pain in Canadian Military Veterans: The Mediating Roles of Anxiety, Depression, and Alcohol Use. *Journal of Traumatic Stress* (2014): 175–81.

Isgandarova, Nazila. Rape as a Tool against Women in War. *CrossCurrents* 63 (2013): 174–84.

Jansen, Golie G. Gender and War: The Effects Of Armed Conflict On Women's Health And Mental Health. *Affilia: Journal Of Women and Social Work* 21:2 (2006): 134–145.

Jebbin Maclean Felix and Tubo Pearce Okumoko. Combating Insecurity in Nigeria: An Integrated Conflict Management Approach. *Journal of Empirical Economics* 3:4 (2014): 232–238.

Joly, M.-P., and B. Wheaton. The Impact of Armed Conflict in the Country of Origin on Mental Health after Migration to Canada. *Society and Mental Health* 5:2 (2015): 86–105.

Keating, Joshua E. Please, Don't Send Food. *Foreign Policy* 194 (2012):26–27.

Keenan, Thomas. Introduction to *Humanism without Borders: A Dossier on Human, Humanitarianism, and Human Rights. Alphabet City* no. 7 (Fall 2000): 41.

Kirby, Paul. How Is Rape a Weapon of War? Feminist International Relations, Modes of Critical Explanation and the Study of Wartime Sexual Violence. *European Journal of International Relations* 19:4 (2012): 797–821.

Koubi, Vally, et al. Do Natural Resources Matter for Interstate and Intrastate Armed Conflict? *Journal of Peace Research* 51:2 (2014): 227–243.

Lafreniere, Ginette, and Lamine Diallo. In the Interest of Working with Survivors of War, Torture And Organized Violence: Lessons From a University/Community Research Collaborative in Southwestern Ontario. *Canadian Issues* (2010): 84–87.

Le Billon, Philippe. The Political Ecology of War: Natural Resources and Armed Conflicts. *Political Geography* 20:5 (2001): 561–584.

Lee, Sabine. A Forgotten Legacy of the Second World War: GI Children in Post-war Britain and Germany. *Contemporary European History* 20:2 (2011): 157–181.

Legal Information Institute. Geneva Conventions. Cornell University Law School. Accessed at https://www.law.cornell.edu/wex/geneva_conventions.

LeRiche, Matthew. Unintended Alliance: The Co–option of Humanitarian Aid in Conflicts. *Parameters* 34.1 (2004): 104–120.

Levy, Guillermo. Considerations on the Connections between Race, Politics, Economics, and genocide1. *Journal of Genocide Research* 8:2 (2006): 137–148.

Liddle, James R., Todd K. Shackelford, and Viviana A. Weekes–Shackelford. Why Can't We All Just Get Along? Evolutionary Perspectives on Violence, Homicide, and War. *Review of General Psychology* 16:1 (2012): 24–36.

Llussá, Fernanda, and José Tavares. Economics and Terrorism: What We Know, What We Should Know, and the Data We Need. In *Terrorism, Economic Development, and Political Openness* (pp. 233–254). Cambridge: Cambridge University Press, 2008.

Marks, Zoe. Sexual Violence in Sierra Leone's Civil War: 'Virgination', Rape, and Marriage. *African Affairs* 113:450 (2013): 67–87.

Mathias, Christopher. A Running List of Shameful Islamophobic Acts Since the Paris Attacks. *Huffington Post*, November 20, 2015.

McDonald, Melissa M., Carlos David Navarrete, and Mark Van Vugt. Evolution and the Psychology of Intergroup Conflict: The Male Warrior Hypothesis. *Philosophical Transactions of the Royal Society B: Biological Sciences*, 367:1589 (2012): 670–679.

McDoom, Omar Shahabudin. 2012. The Psychology of Threat in Intergroup Conflict: Emotions, Rationality, and Opportunity in the Rwandan Genocide. *International Security* 37:2 (2012): 119–155.

Mokhtanzadeh, Leila. Ending War Rape: A Matter of Cumulative Convictions. *Fordham International Law Journal* 36 (2013): 1021–061.

Mousseau, Michael. Market Civilization and Its Clash with Terror. *International Security* 27:3 (2002): 5–29.

Narang, Neil. Assisting Uncertainty: How Humanitarian Aid Can Inadvertently Prolong Civil War. *International Studies Quarterly* 59 (2015): 184–195.

Nunn, Nathan and Nancy Qian. US Food Aid and Civil Conflict. *American Economic Review* 104:6 (2014): 1630–1666.

Østby, Gudrun. Polarization, Horizontal Inequalities and Violent Civil Conflict. *Journal of Peace Research* 45:2 (2008): 143–162.

Parens, Henri. War Is Not Inevitable. *Peace Review* 25:2 (2013): 187–194.

Park-Sonen, Michele. Healing Multidimensional Wounds of Injustice Intersectionality and the Korean Comfort Women. *Berkeley La Raza Law Journal* 22:1 (2012): 269–300.

Pedersen, Duncan. Political Violence, Ethnic Conflict, And Contemporary Wars: Broad Implications For Health And Social Well-being. *Social Science and Medicine* 55 (2002): 175–190.

Peter Hulm. WHO Increases Estimates of Casualties following Nuclear War. *Ambio* 15:2 (1986): 70–71.

Pilzer, Joshua. Music and Dance in the Japanese Military Comfort Women System. *Women and Music: A Journal of Gender and Culture* 18 (2014): 1–23.

Pittman, James O. E., et al. Post-traumatic Stress Disorder, Depression, and Health-related Quality of Life in OEF/OIF Veterans. *Quality of Life Research* 21:1 (2012): 99–103.

Rafael Reuveny and Katherine Barbieri. On the Effect of Natural Resources on Interstate War. *Progress in Physical Geography* 38:6 (2014): 786–806.

Ragnhild Nordås and Christian Davenport. Fight the Youth: Youth Bulges and State Repression. *American Journal of Political Science* 57:4 (2013): 926–940.

Sachs, Jeffrey D. Ending Africa's Poverty Trap. *Brookings Papers on Economic Activity* 1 (2004): 117–216.

Sachs, Jeffrey D. *The End of Poverty: Economic Possibilities for Our Time*. London: Penguin, 2006.

Salvage, Jane. Casualties of War. Nursing Standard, 2007.

Schabas, William A. Jurisdiction: Genocide: *An Introduction to the International Criminal Court*. Cambridge: Cambridge University Press, 2011.

Schneider, Gerald, Lilli Banholzer and Laura Albarracin. Ordered Rape: A Principal-Agent Analysis of Wartime Sexual Violence in the DR Congo. *Violence Against Women* 21:11 (2015), 1341–1363.

References

Schott, Robin May. War Rape, Natality and Genocide. *Journal of Genocide Research* 13:1 (2011): 5–21.

Schwabe, Klaus. 2014. World War I and the Rise of Hitler. *Diplomatic History* 38(4) (2014): 864–879.

Selway, Joel Sawat. Cross-Cuttingness, Cleavage Structures and Civil War Onset. *British Journal of Political Science* 41:1 (2011): 111–138.

Shay, Jonathan. Casualties. *Daedalus* (2011): 179–188.

Simi, Demi, and Jonathan Matusitz. War Rape Survivors of the Second Congo War: A Perspective from Symbolic Convergence Theory. *Africa Review* 6:2 (2014): 81–93.

Simo-Algado, S., et al. Occupational Therapy Intervention with Children Survivors of War. *Canadian Journal of Occupational Therapy* 69:4 (2002): 205–217.

Stermac, Lana, Paulette Brazeau, and Theresa C. Kelly. Traumatic Stress and Mental Health among War-zone Immigrants in Toronto. *International Journal of Health Promotion and Education* 46:2 (2008): 57–64.

Stewart, Frances. Crisis Prevention: Tackling Horizontal Inequalities. *Oxford Development Studies* 28:3 (2000): 245–262.

Stewart, Frances. Horizontal Inequality: Two Types of Trap. *Journal of Human Development and Capabilities* 10:3 (2009): 315–340.

Stewart, Frances. Why Horizontal Inequalities are Important for a Shared Society. *Development* 57:1 (2014): 46–54.

The Future of World Religions: Population Growth Projections, 2010–2050. Pew Research Centers Religion Public Life Project RSS. April 2, 2015.

Trelles, Miguel, Lynette Dominguez, and Barclay T. Stewart. Surgery in Low–income Countries during Crisis: Experience at Médecins Sans Frontières Facilities in 20 Countries between 2008 and 2014. *Tropical Medicine and International Health* (2015): 968–71.

United Nations. Sexual Violence and Armed Conflict: United Nations Response. *Women 2000*, 1998, 1–25.

United Nations. United Nations Millennium Development Goals. Accessed at http://www.un.org/millenniumgoals/.

Uvin, Peter. Development Aid and Structural Violence. *Development* 42:3 (1999): 49–56.

Uvin, Peter. Prejudice, Crisis and Genocide in Rwanda. *African Studies Review* 40:2 (1997): 91–115.

Vindevogel, Sofie, Eric Broekaert, and Ilse Derluyn. It Helps Me Transform in My Life From the Past to the New: The Meaning of Resources for Former Child Soldiers. *Journal of Interpersonal Violence* 28:12 (2013): 2413–2436.

Wachala, Kas. The Tools to Combat the War on Women's Bodies: Rape and Sexual Violence Against Women in Armed Conflict. *The International Journal of Human Rights* 16:3 (2012): 533–53.

Watson, Alison M.S. Children Born of Wartime Rape. *International Feminist Journal of Politics* 9:1 (2007): 20–34.

Wimmer, Andreas, Lars–Erik Cederman, and Brian Min. Ethnic Politics and Armed Conflict: A Configurational Analysis of a New Global Data Set. *American Sociological Review* 74:2 (2009): 316–337.

Yakeley, Jessica and J. Reid Meloy. Understanding Violence: Does Psychoanalytic Thinking Matter? *Aggression and Violent Behavior* 17 (2012): 229–239.

Yourish, Karen, Derek Watkins, and Tom Giratikanon. ISIS Is Likely Responsible for Nearly 1,000 Civilian Deaths Outside Iraq and Syria. *The New York Times*, November 17, 2015.

CHAPTER 10

Adams, A. A Sex Worker Explains How to Talk to Sex Workers. *Vice*, May 20, 2015.

âpihtawikosisân. 2012. Building Relationships Requires Education. Blog post, December 2011. Retrieved from: http://apihtawikosisan.com/2011/12/building–relationships–requires–education/.

âpihtawikosisân. Canada, It's Time. We Need to Fix This in Our Generation. Blog post, December 2012. Retrieved from: http://apihtawikosisan.com/2012/12/canada–its–time–we–need–to–fix–this–in–our–generation/.

âpihtawikosisân. Idle No More: Where Do We Go From Here? Blog post, December 2012. Retrieved from: http://apihtawikosisan.com/2012/12/idle–no–more–where–do–we–go–from–here/.

Beltrame, Julian. IMF Debunks Myth: Taxing Rich Not Bad for Economy. CTV News, February 26, 2014.

CBC News. Muslim Women Sound Off On 'Stupid' Niqab Debate. Retrieved from: http://www.cbc.ca/news/canada/toronto/muslim–women–sound–off–on–stupid–niqab–debate–1.3256417.

CBC News. Vote Compass: Canadians Say Rich Should Pay More Tax, Divided on How to Spur Growth. CBC News, September 15, 2015.

Chalmers, B., and K. Omer-Hashi. What Somali Women Say About Giving Birth in Canada. *Journal of Reproductive and Infant Psychology*, 20:4 (2002).

Deschamps, Tara. Toronto Students Organize 'Crop Top Day' to Protest Dress Codes. *Toronto Star*, May 26, 2015.

Easton, Tre. The Gay Best Friend Must Die. *Huffington Post*, February 27, 2015. Retrieved from: http://www.huffingtonpost.com/tre–easton/the–gay–best–friend–must–die_b_6764376.html.

Frisk, Adam. Moncton teen disciplined for wearing full–length halter dress to school. *Global News*, May 13, 2015.

George, Pamela, Jenepher Lennox Terrion and Rukhsana Ahmed. Reproductive Health Behaviour of Muslim Immigrant Women in Canada. *International Journal of Migration, Health and Social Care* 10:2 (2014): 88–101.

Gerstein, Julie. This Woman Had The Perfect Response To People Body-Shaming An 8-Year-Old Girl. Buzzfeed, 2015. Retrieved from http://www.buzzfeed.com/juliegerstein/this–woman–had–the–perfect–response–to–people–bod y-shaming-a#.xayQzR41.

Hollet, Kevin. Sex workers speak out against new prostitution legislation. *Pivot*, November 6, 2014. Retrieved from: http://www.pivotlegal.org/sex_workers_speak_out_against_new_prostitution_legislation.

Income Security Advocacy Centre. Tell Your Story: The Online Stories of OW and ODSP Recipients: A Submission to the Commission for the Review of Social Assistance in Ontario. Retrieved from: http://www.mcss.gov.on.ca /documents/en/mcss/social/commission/F–J/Income%20Security%20Advocacy%20Centre%20– %20Tell%20Your%20Story.pdf.

Irwin, Nigel. 2013. Canada's First Nations Reserves Have a Faulty System of Government. *Vice*, July 30, 2013.

Jackson, Ed. How Gay Relationships Are Blown Apart by the Misuse of 'Heteronormative'. *Huffington Post*, October 25, 2011.

Kazia, Alexandra. Seniors Who Help Older Seniors a 'Tremendous Skilled Resource'. CBC News, May 4, 2013. Retrieved from www.cbc.ca/news/canada/seniors–who–help–older–seniors–a–tremendous-skilled-resource-1.1330825.

Mlotek, Haley. Put Out the Red Light: Are Sex Workers Being Heard in the Legal Dialogue over Prostitution? *The Globe and Mail*, May 14, 2014.

Rankin, Jim. 2010. Race Matters: Blacks Documented by Police at High Rate. *Toronto Star*, February 6, 2010.

Salvation Army. *Canada Speaks: Exposing Persistent Myths About the 150,000 Canadians Living on the Streets.* Toronto: Salvation Army, 2011. http://salvationarmy.ca/DPresources/CanadaSpeaks_report_May2011.pdf.

Slaughter, Anne-Marie. 2012. Why Women Still Can't Have it All. *The Atlantic* (2012, July/August).

Smith, B. (2015). 3 Canadian Sex Workers on What Their Jobs Are Really Like. *Flare*, August 11, 2015. Retrieved from: http://www.flare.com/sex-and-relationships/3-canadian-sex-workers-on-what-their-jobs-are-really-like/.

Spurr, Ben. Five Homeless Youth Share Their Stories. *Toronto Star*, October 19, 2015.

Tatum, Erin. 'Who's the Man?': Heteronormativity and Queer Relationships. *Everyday Feminism*, April 2, 2014. Retrieved from: http://everydayfeminism.com/2014/04/whos-the-man/.

Thomson, Janet, Manmeet Ahluwalia and Kathryn Weatherley. For Seniors, Losing Driver's Licence Like Having 'Arm Cut Off'. CBC News, 2013. Retrieved from: www.cbc.ca/news/canada/for-seniors-losing-driver-s-licence-like-hav ing-arm-cut-off-1.1346585.

Tutty, Leslie M. Addressing the Safety and Trauma Issues of Abused Women: A Cross-Canada Study of YWCA Shelters. *Journal of International Women's Studies* 16:3 (2015): 101-116.

Wear, Delese et al. Retheorizing Sexual Harassment in Medical Education: Women Students' Perceptions at Five U.S. Medical Schools. *Teaching and Learning in Medicine*, 19:1 (2007): 20–29.

Wood, Sarah. This Is My Life Now: An Interview with a Nursing Home Resident. Retrieved from: http://www. caregiver.com/channels/ltc/articles/nursing_home_interview3.htm.

Zaman, Habiba. Pakistani Skilled/Educated Immigrant Women in Canada: An Exploratory Study. *Pakistan Journal of Women's Studies* 17.2 (2010): 1–23.

Index